The BIG Book of
GARDEN
SOLUTIONS

TIME®
LIFE
BOOKS

Alexandria, Virginia

5

GROWING A HEALTHY LAWN

126

6

CONTROLLING WEEDS

140

7

COPING WITH GARDEN PESTS

156

8

PREVENTING PLANT DISEASE

192

REFERENCE

CHAPTER ONE

Garden Solutions

Every gardener faces challenges of one sort or another, from extreme temperatures, dense shade, or persistent weeds to steep slopes, unsightly views, or seasonal gaps in color. Fortunately, for every gardening problem there is a solution—or sometimes even several. It may be as simple as planting hardy bulbs or adding compost to the soil. Or it may be as complex as identifying a specific garden pest, then trying several different methods to control or eradicate it. No matter which problems you encounter and how you ultimately solve them, however, you're sure to find tips and information in this book that will help you.

The gardens presented on the following pages are just a few examples of solutions gardeners have found to particular problems. The northern California garden at left, for instance, was designed so that it would still look lush after the owner collected her bouquets. By densely planting colonies of annuals that thrive in the area's climate, she is guaranteed blooms from summer until fall. For a planting guide to this enchanting cutting garden, as well as to other gardens shown in this chapter, see pages 28-37.

The dependable annuals dominating this Portland, Oregon, front yard ensure continuous bloom from midsummer to first frost. Snowy white sweet alyssum edges a bed that includes lemon yellow signet marigolds, pink zonal geraniums, multi-hued zinnias, and tall, bright yellow African marigolds. Sculpted pines and evergreen shrubbery provide the framework for the garden.

An artful blend of plants makes this small Virginia garden appear larger than it is. For a bold look and continuous color, the owners turned to such annuals as the two massive castor bean plants near the corner of the walkway. The maroon foliage of hybrid polka-dot plants creates a pool of deep color amid the greenery. Rose-pink verbena (foreground) and yellow lantana add textural contrast and continuous bloom.

Contrasting textures and harmonious greens combine to form a foliage border in Pennsylvania that is anything but dull. Fan-leafed hyacinth bean, which covers the rustic fence, and the feathery foliage of daphne and cleome provide a beautiful textural backdrop for the dramatically veined, broad leaves of 'Striata' canna and its bold orange blossoms. Silvery mounds of dusty-miller and tall white orbs of cleome add a luminous glow. Touches of yellow marigolds and purple Brazilian verbena pull the planting together and spark color interest.

The owners of this timber-and-mortar cottage in Virginia wanted to add interest without obscuring the architecture. The 6-foot-tall plume poppies framing the doorway make a dramatic vertical statement, while their huge, deeply lobed, blue-green leaves act as a light foliage screen along the walls. The plume poppy's invasive growth habit is held in check by equally aggressive purple coneflower and pink wild sweet William.

This verdant Pennsylvania shade garden offers color and interest throughout the year, yet requires little maintenance. A river of fern moss (*Thuidium delicatulum*), interrupted by mounded deep green islands of haircap moss (*Polytrichum communa*), provides year-round cushiony green paths through this north-facing, gently sloped site. Located under a canopy of deciduous trees, borders of easy-care dwarf evergreen shrubs, evergreen ground covers, and ferns are highlighted throughout the growing season by pockets of seasonal flowers such as dwarf Japanese iris, *Phlox stolonifera* (creeping phlox), and *Lobelia cardinalis* (cardinal flower), providing color from March through October.

Plants that can withstand harsh waterside conditions are the key to the success of this lush Bridgehampton, New York, garden located on a pond near the Atlantic Ocean. Proclaiming the start of the summer season, a red Oriental poppy adds drama to the scene. Deep pink and bright white, salt-tolerant rugosa roses are just beginning to produce blossoms that will continue through late summer, when the clumps of daylilies flanking the poppy will commence their own spectacular show of color. The thin, willowy stems of phragmites at the rear of the 4-foot-wide border will last into winter. Although the garden is a full 80 feet long, it requires only an hour a week of care—namely, weed pulling. Once a year, in spring, the garden is top-dressed with rotted manure. Should the need arise, an underground watering system augments the local rainfall, which usually measures a generous 45 inches a year.

Overlooking Long Island Sound and Manhattan, this large New York coastal garden blends evergreens, grasses, and perennials that tolerate wind and salt spray. A wide stand of rudbeckia just beginning to show its golden flowers is the backdrop for a low juniper spilling gracefully over a boulder; at the boulder's base, several clumps of annual 'Daybreak Mix' gazania have burst into bloom. Farther back, tall, arching maiden grass mixes with pastel clumps of 'Blue Lacecap' hydrangea and 'Betty Prior' shrub roses, here in their July splendor. For added protection from the elements, the garden receives a thick layer of cedar-bark mulch that is refreshed every 18 to 24 months. The plot is watered by an automatic irrigation system, so the gardener's most demanding chore is deadheading.

A surprising variety of textures, shapes, and colors abound in this sun-scorched Arizona garden, where a scant 7 inches of rain fall in a year. Many of the plants are imports that are well adapted to the American desert: The Cape marigold, with its white daisylike flowers, and the bright yellow bulbine (foreground) are from South Africa, and the medicinal aloe, bearing tall stalks topped by bright orange blossoms, is native to North Africa. American desert natives include ocotillo, a shrub with tall, unbranched stems (upper left); rounded bunny-ears cactus; and pinkish purple desert penstemon and moss verbena. Along the fence at the rear of the garden is a mass of tall, yellow-blooming brittlebush.

The plants in this informal Maryland garden were selected to withstand steamy summer temperatures, erratic periods of drought, and winter lows that regularly approach zero. Shrubs ranging in hue from the blue-green of the blue spruce at the center of the border to the deep green of the San Jose holly at the back give the scene a cool feel. The owners spend just 2 hours each week maintaining the garden.

A rainbow of color, this Richmond, Virginia, garden was designed to stand up to the area's high heat and humidity. 'Pink Gumpo' azaleas, reddish orange gaillardias, and feathery rose-pink astilbes blooming among hostas and other foliage plants add bright color in spring. Later, annuals and daylilies keep the garden in bloom through October. After spring planting, only an hour's worth of cleanup is required each week to maintain the quiet elegance.

17

A night garden such as this one in Alabama is the perfect solution for gardeners who are often away from home during the daylight hours. Cool and inviting, the white, green, and silver tones cast a pale glow in the evening or on a moonlit night. The luminous effect is created by a variety of perennials, including summer-blooming daisylike Japanese asters (far right foreground) and airy stalks of rose campion (right, center of border), which flower among dense silver and green foliage for up to 9 months of the year. Although the lines of the borders are formal, they are softened by an overhanging edging of velvety gray-leaved lamb's ears, mingled with white pansies and snow-in-summer.

Designed in the tradition of a romantic English border, this striking California garden provides color throughout the year. Spiky purple Mexican bush sage, purple Peruvian verbena, and pink gloxinia penstemon contribute to the cascade of color. Roses and herbs are planted among the perennials to create interesting textures while maintaining color harmony and progression. For all of its showy good looks, this garden requires relatively little attention: Dead flower heads are removed once a week, and the entire garden is fertilized once a month. The plants are also mulched with redwood shavings to which nitrogen has been added.

Late-season color abounds in this Washington State garden, where flowers bloom from mid-July to late October. The large bronze-purple leaves of canna make a regal backdrop for the simple beauty of low-growing, daisylike dahlias. Towering sunflowers and a carpet of pink geraniums complete the arresting combination.

To extend the life of this Pennsylvania border, the owners chose cultivated dahlias with an array of flower forms, including cactus, water lily, anemone, and decorative. Blooming from summer to late fall, the dahlias offer a colorful display when many other bedding plants are waning or have stopped flowering for the season.

This problematic slope in Washington State was transformed into a lovely hillside border punctuated by summer bloomers. Dense umbels of showy, deep blue Agapanthus 'Bressingham Blue' (African lily) stand out in bold contrast to golden mounds of orange coneflower, slender trumpets of Cape fuchsia, and lemon yellow daylilies. Vigorous summer-flowering tubers, the African lilies bloom throughout the season, preferring full sun but tolerating partial shade. Their large clumps of fleshy, straplike leaves provide handsome fill-in foliage even when the plants are not in flower.

Designed to thrive under the hot Virginia sun, this terraced bed is highlighted with clusters of dazzling lilies. These Asiatic hybrids—orange 'Milano' and creamy white 'Roma'—are hardy and easy to grow. Best planted in groups of three or more, they have an erect growth habit and flower heads that add an exotic touch to the garden.

Wet feet aren't a problem for swamp roses (Rosa palustris), which arch gracefully over a quiet pool in this Texas garden; unlike other roses, they can thrive right at the water's edge. Here, the pool not only reflects the plant's graceful shape but also serves to display its delicate fallen petals. R. palustris blooms for 6 weeks or longer in this garden, emitting a sweet scent when the buds first open. The rose's pink color is intensified by the yellow-and-green foliage of the variegated canna. With its dark, smooth bark, flowing lines, and oval hips that appear after flowering, the swamp rose provides four-season interest in the garden.

A(5) K(1)
J(1) I(1)
L(1) H(3) D(1)
B(1) G(3) G(3)
C(1) B(1)
B(1)
D(1)
E(2)
F(1)
F(1)

pages 4-5

A. *Cleome hasslerana
'Lavender Queen', 'Pink Queen',
'Rose Queen'* (5)
B. *Zinnia elegans cv.* (3)
C. *Salvia guaranitica* (1)

D. *Celosia argentea* (2)
E. *Lobularia maritima* (2)
F. *Chrysanthemum x
morifolium* (2)
G. *Cosmos bipinnatus
'Sensation Mix'* (6)
H. *Euphorbia marginata* (3)

I. *Tithonia rotundifolia* (1)
J. *Dahlia cv.* (1)
K. *Rosa 'Meidiland Red'* (1)
L. *Salvia uliginosa* (1)

NOTE: *The key lists each plant type and the total quantity needed to replicate the garden shown.
The diagram's letters and numbers refer to the type of plant and the number sited in an area.*

page 6

A. *Acer palmatum* (1)
B. *Rhododendron 'Vulcan'* (1)
C. *Tagetes erecta cv.* (many)
D. *Photinia x fraseri* (many)
E. *Zinnia elegans cv.* (many)
F. *Tagetes erecta 'Lulu'* (many)
G. *Pelargonium x hortorum 'Blues'* (8)
H. *Lobularia maritima* (many)
I. *Pinus mugo var. mugo* (1)
J. *Pseudotsuga menziesii* (1)
K. *Hydrangea macrophylla* (1)
L. *Pinus densiflora 'Umbraculifera'* (2)

pages 6-7

A. *Ricinus communis* (1)
B. *R. communis 'Carmencita'* (1)
C. *Berberis thunbergii 'Aurea'* (1)
D. *Yucca filamentosa 'Golden Eagle'* (1)
E. *Sedum x 'Autumn Joy'* (4)
F. *Hosta 'Gold Standard'* (1)
G. *Nicotiana alata 'Nikki'* (3)
H. *Tradescantia pallida 'Purple Heart'* (3)
I. *Lantana camara 'Flava'* (2)
J. *Digitalis purpurea 'Shirley Hybrids'* (14)
K. *Iris sibirica 'Flight of Butterflies'* (1)
L. *Verbena 'Sissinghurst'* (2)
M. *Coreopsis verticillata 'Moonbeam'* (6)
N. *Berberis thunbergii 'Crimson Pygmy'* (1)
O. *Ceratostigma plumbaginoides* (3)
P. *Spiraea japonica 'Limemound'* (1)
Q. *Centranthus ruber* (3)
R. *Achillea x 'Moonshine'* (4)
S. *Spiraea japonica 'Little Princess'* (1)
T. *Hemerocallis 'Stella d'Oro'* (3)
U. *Hypoestes phyllostachya* (3)
V. *Rosa 'The Fairy'* (1)
W. *Miscanthus sinensis 'Variegatus'* (1)
X. *Rosa 'Betty Prior'* (1)

pages 8-9

A. *Verbena bonariensis* (many)
B. *Senecio vira-vira* (10)
C. *Daphne x 'Carol Mackie'* (2)
D. *Cleome 'Helen Campbell'* (many)

E. *Dolichos lablab* (3)
F. *Elymus glaucus* (2)
G. *Calendula officinalis*
(volunteer seedlings)

H. *Dahlia 'David Howard'* (2)
I. *Canna x generalis 'Striata'* (3)
J. *Dahlia 'My Love'* (3)
K. *Pyrus* (1)

page 9

A. *Macleaya cordata* (9)
B. *Echinacea purpurea*
'Bright Star' (5)

C. *Liatris spicata* (2)
D. *Phlox maculata*
'Alpha' (6)

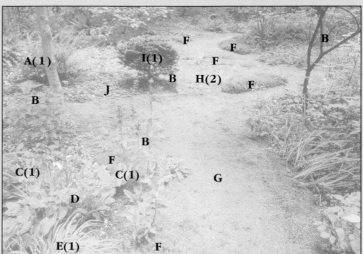

pages 10-11

A. *Polystichum acrostichoides* (1)
B. *Lobelia cardinalis* (many)
C. *Scutellaria integrifolia* (2)
D. *Hosta sp.* (many)

E. *Iris gracilipes* (1)
F. *Polytrichum communa* (many)
G. *Thuidium delicatulum* (many)

H. *Gentiana scabra* (2)
I. *Chamaecyparis obtusa 'Nana'* (1)
J. *Phlox stolonifera* (many)

page 12

A. *Rosa rugosa* (2)
B. *Papaver orientale* (1)
C. *Hemerocallis fulva 'Europa'* (7)

D. *Hibiscus moscheutos* (1)
E. *Phragmites communis* (6)

NOTE: The key lists each plant type and the total quantity needed to replicate the garden shown. The diagram's letters and numbers refer to the type of plant and the number sited in an area.

pages 12-13

A. *Gazania 'Daybreak Mix'* (3)
B. *Juniperus chinensis 'Nana'* (5)
C. *Pinus mugo* (1)
D. *Rudbeckia fulgida 'Goldsturm'* (8)

E. *Ilex glabra 'Compacta'* (2)
F. *Hibiscus 'Lord Baltimore'* (1)
G. *Miscanthus sinensis 'Gracillimus'* (3)

H. *Amelanchier x 'Cumulus'* (1)
I. *Hydrangea 'Blue Lacecap'* (3)
J. *Rosa 'Betty Prior'* (4)
K. *Alyssum 'Carpet of Snow'* (7)

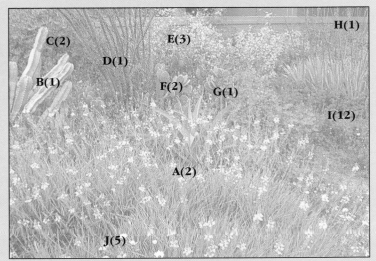

pages 14-15

A. *Bulbine caulescens* (2)
B. *Cereus hildmannianus* (1)
C. *Simmondsia chinensis* (2)
D. *Fouquieria splendens* (1)
E. *Encelia farinosa* (3)

F. *Opuntia microdasys* (2)
G. *Penstemon parryi* (1)
H. *Aloe barbadensis* (1)
I. *Verbena tenuisecta* (12)
J. *Dimorphotheca sinuata* (5)

pages 16-17

A. *Liriope 'Silver Dragon'* (36)
B. *Picea pungens 'Hoopsii'* (1)
C. *Rhododendron
'Koromu Shikibu'* (5)

D. *Ilex x attenuata
'Foster #2'* (2)
E. *Ilex 'San Jose'* (1)
F. *Zelkova serrata* (1)

G. *Ligularia dentata* (3)
H. *Impatiens wallerana* (6)
I. *Hosta undulata
'Albo-marginata'* (6)

page 17

A. *Cornus florida* (1)
B. *Astilbe simplicifolia
'Bronze Elegans'* (3)
C. *Buxus sempervirens* (1)
D. *Paeonia lactiflora
'Sarah Bernhardt'* (3)
E. *Coreopsis verticillata
'Moonbeam'* (1)
F. *Salvia farinacea 'Victoria'* (7)
G. *Rhododendron
'Pink Gumpo'* (3)
H. *Rosa 'Blaze'* (1)
I. *Hibiscus syriacus* (1)
J. *Hemerocallis 'Hyperion'* (3)
K. *Tagetes erecta
'Primrose Lady'* (10)
L. *Lilium regale* (7)
M. *Rhododendron
'Spring Dawn'* (2)
N. *Impatiens
'New Guinea hybrid'* (3)
O. *Gaillardia sp.* (1)

NOTE: *The key lists each plant type and the total quantity needed to replicate the garden shown.
The diagram's letters and numbers refer to the type of plant and the number sited in an area.*

pages 18-19

A. *Lychnis coronaria 'Alba'* (12)
B. *Campanula latiloba (C. persicifolia) 'Alba'* (3)
C. *Salvia greggii 'Alba'* (1)

D. *Viola 'Crystal Bowl'* (18)
E. *Asteromoea mongolica* (18)
F. *Stachys byzantina* (24)
G. *Senecio 'New Look'* (2)

H. *Cerastium tomentosum* (4)
I. *Veronica spicata 'Icicle'* (3)
J. *Phlox maculata 'Miss Lingard'* (6)

pages 20-21

A. *Penstemon gloxinioides 'Firebird'* (7)
B. *Salvia leucantha* (2)
C. *Iris 'Babbling Brook'* (2)
D. *Erigeron karvinskianus* (6)
E. *Convolvulus cneorum* (3)
F. *Verbena peruviana* (3)
G. *Dianthus caryophyllus* (2)
H. *Oenothera berlandieri* (4)

I. *Lobelia erinus* (1)
J. *Stachys byzantina* (2)
K. *Penstemon gloxinioides 'Midnight'* (2)
L. *Chrysanthemum maximum* (3)
M. *Penstemon gloxinioides 'Apple Blossom'* (1)
N. *Rosa sp. 'Cl. First Class Prize'* (1)

O. *Aquilegia x hybrida ('McKana Hybrids')* (12)
P. *Rosa sp. 'The Reeve'* (2)
Q. *Rosa sp. 'Fair Bianca'* (1)
R. *Rosa sp. 'Mary Austin'* (1)
S. *Rosa sp. 'Graham Thomas'* (1)
T. *Rosmarinus officinalis* (1)
U. *Limonium perezii* (3)

A. *Helianthus annuus
'Autumn Beauty'* (5)
B. *Canna x generalis
'Red King Humbert'* (4)
C. *Dahlia hybrid* (5)
D. *Geranium x riversleaianum
'Mavis Simpson'* (1)
E. *Sedum x 'Autumn Joy'* (4)

pages 22-23

A. *Pyrus cv.* (1)
B. *Cleome spinosa
'Helen Campbell'* (12)
C. *Dahlia cv.* (5)
D. *Salvia uliginosa* (4)
E. *Dahlia 'Snow Country'* (3)

F. *Dahlia 'David Howard'* (4)
G. *Daphne x burkwoodii
'Carol Mackie'* (2)
H. *Senecio vira-vira* (6)
I. *Bidens ferulifolia
'Golden Goddess'* (10)

J. *Dahlia 'Gerry Hoek'* (9)
K. *Verbena bonariensis* (4)
L. *Agastache mexicana
'Toronjil Mirado'* (2)
M. *Dolichos lablab* (3)
N. *Canna x generalis 'Striata'* (3)

*NOTE: The key lists each plant type and the total quantity needed to replicate the garden shown.
The diagram's letters and numbers refer to the type of plant and the number sited in an area.*

pages 24-25

A. *Helianthus decapetalus* (1)
B. *Artemisia*
'Huntington Garden' (2)
C. *Agapanthus*
'Bressingham Blue' (10)

D. *Hemerocallis cv.* (3)
E. *Achillea ageratum*
'W. B. Child' (3)
F. *Phygelius capensis* (1)

G. *Rudbeckia fulgida*
'Goldsturm' (6)
H. *Hemerocallis 'Corky'* (4)

page 25

A. *Lilium 'Roma'* (3)
B. *Lilium 'Milano'* (9)
C. *Veronica austriaca*
'Crater Lake Blue' (2)

D. *Tagetes erecta 'Inca Gold'* (9)
E. *Achillea*
'Coronation Gold' (3)

F. *Antirrhinum majus*
Wedding Bells Series (6)
G. *Cosmos bipinnatus*
'Seashells' (4)

36

pages 26-27

A. *Pontederia cordata* (1)
B. *Canna sp.* (3)
C. *Iris Louisiana Hybrids* (6)
D. *Salvia farinacea* (12)
E. *Rosa palustris* (1)
F. *Lonicera sempervirens* (1)
G. *Myriophyllum aquaticum* (1)

NOTE: The key lists each plant type and the total quantity needed to replicate the garden shown. The diagram's letters and numbers refer to the type of plant and the number sited in an area.

CHAPTER TWO

Design Strategies

Designing a garden involves both aesthetic and practical considerations: Ideally, how would you like the garden to look? How do you intend to use it? How much space do you have to use? What are the contours of your property? Does the site get a lot of sun, shade, or wind? Are there any unattractive views you'd like to screen out? The challenge is to fulfill your vision of the garden while also taking the practical realities into account.

In the Maryland garden at left, for example, the owners started with a problematic slope and transformed it into a lovely patio garden for entertaining and relaxing. By using ornamental grasses and other plants with relaxed habits, they were also able to solve another problem: how to link the house with a meadow in the background.

On the following pages, you'll learn various design strategies for solving common problems encountered by gardeners, from container gardening for small spaces and terracing for steep slopes to using plants as fillers and screens. For additional design solutions, see Garden Plans for Difficult Areas on pages 208-217.

Annuals to the Rescue

No other group of plants can so dramatically change the look of your garden in so short a time as annuals. Whether you need to fill in gaps between perennials and shrubs that are still maturing, to provide color and interest after bulbs or short-blooming perennials have faded, or to simply create a display of dependable bloomers from spring to frost, annuals are the way to go.

Annuals—which in gardening parlance include their short-season cousins, biennials and tender perennials—are unbeatable when it comes to sheer variety, too. They span the color rainbow, from the bluest blues to the hottest scarlets. They grow in bushy mounds, creep along the ground, cascade down a wall, climb a fence, or tower from the back of a border. And the size and shape of their flowers and foliage vary enormously. Indeed, the different cultivated varieties that are available number in the thousands, and each year hybridizers produce still more.

Augmenting their remarkable résumé is the fact that annuals are exceedingly easy to care for.

With uncomplicated, shallow root systems, they are dependable performers that require little in the way of nutrients, space, and maintenance. And they grow at a rambunctious rate, racing to maturity and flowering in a matter of weeks—and gratifying the most impatient gardener with a prolific and long-lasting display.

Annuals as Fillers

If you've just planted a mixed border, annuals can supply eye-catching contrasts and harmonies during the time it takes for perennials and shrubs to fill out and mature. For example, soft pink *Diascia barberae* and a pale blue cultivar of *Lobelia erinus* contrast soothingly with the large, lustrous dark green leaves of Oregon grape or the simple blue-green to gray-green foliage of *Daphne mezereum*. Tall pink *Cleome hasslerana* can supply height at the back of the border and pull the composition together by repeating tints of pink.

Blazing red Salvia splendens 'Hot Shot' sizzles around 'Ultra White Madness' petunias, deep purple Salvia farinacea 'Rhea', and the coarse foliage of rose daphne (right), igniting this Pacific Northwest garden with hot color.

'Raspberry Rose' and 'Jolly Joker' pansies and pink and peach 'Oregon Rainbow' Iceland poppies (below) brighten the front of this mixed border in Oregon. Pink and creamy white spires of Digitalis purpurea 'Excelsior' and ruby blooms of 'Red Charm' peonies are shaded by a backdrop of white, yellow, and salmon azaleas.

If it's bold color you like, try yellow and crimson 'Double Madame Butterfly' snapdragons with
a smattering of 'Giant Double Mixed' zinnias in
red, scarlet, orange, and yellow. Low-growing clusters of white *Iberis umbellata* nestled among the
fiery hues will help temper them.

Other annuals combine marvelous color with a
flower shape so distinctive that they are worthy of
a spot in the most prominent border. Perfectly at
home among showy perennials are the jewel-like
red-orange blooms of *Emilia javanica,* which
look like miniature paintbrushes atop wiry 2-foot
stems; the quill-petaled, urn-shaped, rose-red
flowers of *Cirsium japonicum,* which hover 2 feet
above dark green spiny leaves; and the enormous
sunburst-shaped pink, lavender, or white flower
clusters of cleome, which float on 3- to 4-foot
stems. When designing with such striking flowers,
plant each species together in large groups, weaving in drifts of gray-leaved plants such as *Stachys
byzantina* (lamb's ears), *Artemisia, Senecio,* and
Santolina to soften the color scheme.

Some annuals with distinctive blooms have
forms that are equally elegant. Consider *Lavatera
trimestris* (rose mallow), which grows 3 feet tall
and wide. Its densely branching stems, large, cup-
shaped pink or white flowers, and lower leaves
that resemble those of a maple blend in effortless-
ly with border regulars such as iris, lady's-mantle,
bergenia, and old-fashioned shrub roses. In a border with big, downy, early-summer-blooming peonies, rose mallow can carry the flower show from
midsummer to early fall.

Annuals that have sparse foliage are at their best
when mated with plants that have abundant leaves.
Stiff stands of easy-to-grow *Verbena bonariensis,*
with its pale lilac-colored flat-topped blooms, pair
well with lemon yellow daylilies, whose slender,
arching leaves mask the strong but spindly stems
of the verbena. The verbena offers summer color
long after the perennial's petals have dropped.
Simply pull up the stalks of the daylilies once they
turn dry and brown, and leave the foliage intact to
provide a green backdrop for the verbena.

Annual flowering and foliage plants are perfect
for hiding the decline of spring-flowering bulbs
such as tulips and daffodils, whose foliage must be
allowed to go through an unsightly withering if
they are to bloom again the following year. Sow
the seeds of hardy annuals among the bulbs in autumn or late winter. After the bulb flowers bloom
and fade, the burgeoning annuals will conceal the

flat splotches of yellowing leaves. Shallow-rooted ground huggers such as *Iberis umbellata* (globe candytuft), *Brachycome iberidifolia* (Swan River daisy), pansies, and forget-me-nots can neatly carpet the garden without disturbing the bulbs, as deeper-rooted perennials might.

Yet another way that annuals come to the rescue is when drought or a long hot spell sends established perennials into summer dormancy. Indeed, many annuals—including *Rudbeckia hirta* (black-eyed Susan) and *Papaver rhoeas* (corn poppy)—flourish in dry weather. Use these to fill in while your garden regulars recover.

Annuals as Eye-Catchers

Simple borders composed of only a few judiciously chosen flowering plants often have the greatest impact. *Cuphea ignea,* an eye-catcher whose abundant scarlet cigar-shaped flowers have black-and-white tips resembling cigar ash, forms a compact foot-high mat of color; place it before soaring red-blooming cannas with their curled, wide-bladed leaves to create a pleasing contrast in form and a harmony of color. An ideal backdrop for this marriage would be a yellow-green hedge of *Philadelphus coronarius* 'Aureus' (mock orange) or tall, woody layers of fast-growing green-leaved *Spiraea prunifolia* (bridal wreath).

For a tall border with a tropical effect, try combining gold, yellow, and apricot cannas with the 5-foot stems of *Abelmoschus manihot* (sunset hibiscus), a Brazilian native whose large, fragile-looking flowers come in shades of pale to buttery yellow with maroon centers. To create a striking border in limited space, pair the red-plumed form of *Celosia cristata* (feather amaranth) with deep yellow marigolds and golden-hued calendulas. In back of the combination, plant a fountain of *Miscanthus sinensis* 'Zebrinus', a perennial ornamental grass whose 5- to 6-foot-tall, arching, straplike leaves display horizontal bands of creamy yellow and green.

Probably the easiest way to make the most of annual color is to plant a solid mass of a single variety that has especially striking blossoms. Choose an area of your yard that you want to highlight, and plant enough of the annual variety to make a bold statement. Because dramatic shocks of color dominate the area in which they're placed, resist the temptation to repeat the bold planting all around your property—or else the sheer numbers of the one color will overwhelm the viewer and lose its impact.

No matter how stunning the hue of an individual bloom, however, a stretch of unbroken color

How to Keep Annuals Blooming All Season

Once an annual has formed seeds, its life cycle is over and the plant stops producing flowers. For this reason, you'll need to prune off spent flowers before they go to seed if you want your annuals to bloom continuously through the season. In addition, cutting back plants that have become tall and scraggly encourages new, leafy growth. Pruned stems usually form new flower buds within 2 to 3 weeks.

Cut main stems just above a leaf or pair of leaves *(below, left)*. The joint where the leaf or leaves emerge from the stem is the place from which side shoots will grow. Make a clean cut with pruning shears, removing about one-third or more of the stem. This will stimulate branching and the production of new flowers throughout the summer *(below, right)*.

Salvia, zinnias, and most annuals with daisylike blooms take readily to this method of pruning. Trailing and soft-stemmed annuals—such as nasturtiums, petunias, portulaca, and sweet alyssum—that have grown shabby-looking benefit from a more drastic treatment that removes all but a few inches of leafy stem. For annuals with decorative seedpods, such as love-in-a-mist, and those whose seed you plan to collect, stop cutting back at least 2 months before the first fall frost to give them time to mature.

tends to tire the eye. Masses of color look best in out-of-the-way settings seen briefly and from a distance. The far corner of your backyard or the side wall of your garage is ideal; a mass of color in such removed, even remote, locations comes as a pleasant surprise when the viewer's eye discovers it. And you can extend the pleasure for months by changing the planting as the growing season progresses—replacing an expanse of fading summer-blooming purple petunias, for instance, with the fall flowers of lemon yellow chrysanthemums.

Versatile Vines

As darkness descends on a September evening in this Virginia garden, the scented white blooms of Ipomoea alba (moonflower) begin to unfurl. Cords attached to the walls of the house support the fast-growing vine, whose bright green heart-shaped leaves give it daytime interest as well.

Vines contribute a lot more than just good looks to your garden. They can camouflage unsightly fences or walls, accent pleasing architecture, or frame a view, for example, all the while adding color, texture, and height to your garden design. You can also press them into service to provide shade or to form a windbreak or privacy screen, and if planted on sloping terrain as a ground cover, they'll help prevent erosion.

For gardeners who would like to attract a variety of wildlife to their property, vines create a hospitable habitat for all sorts of creatures. Birds appreciate the sheltered perches that vines offer, as well as the banquet of insects that live among the stems. Hummingbirds, bees, and butterflies are drawn to the nectar and pollen of flowering vines. And dense vines such as hyacinth bean and clematis make good aerial highways and jungle gyms for squirrels and chipmunks.

Vines as Screens

Many species of vines grow 20 feet long, leaf out, and come into bud in a matter of weeks. This makes them ideal to plant as screens against sun, wind, or unattractive views. Left to their own devices, vines tend to flower mostly among top growth, leaving several feet of leggy stem exposed at their base. To force better distribution of the blooms, fasten young vine shoots horizontally along supports such as trellises and fences when they begin to grow; this encourages them to form low, lateral shoots that will flower. See page 47 for illustrated instructions on training vines.

Vines can easily transform a small townhouse garden or a narrow side yard by capitalizing on vertical space. Train them up a simple rot-resistant wood post or a freestanding arch or pergola to add overhead interest to your garden. Vines grown on a wood-framed arbor can provide summer shade over a deck or patio; those that die back after frost will let the winter sunshine in. To clothe an exterior wall in summer blooms, install a trellis of wood or metal tubing about 3 inches away from the wall and plant the climbers along its base.

If you're placing a screen across open space, you will need to provide adequate support for the vines. Start with a sturdy, well-built frame of wood or metal and sink the legs of the structure at least 2 feet into the ground—deeper in regions with cold weather so that it won't be heaved up by the freezing and thawing of the ground. Indulge in diagonal or free-form trellis designs, square latticework, or a wide range of other shapes you can find or build. (For more on vertical garden structures, see pages 58-59.) For a swag effect, suspend sturdy chains between posts and train vines up the posts and then along the chains, tying them loosely at 4-inch intervals. Always set your supports in place before you plant the vines; otherwise, you may damage the roots or any new growth.

Vines with dense foliage, such as hyacinth bean, are the best choice for totally concealing an unat-

tractive wall or view. *Phaseolus coccineus* (scarlet runner bean) also makes a tough yet beautiful screen, as do common pole or runner beans, which develop thick, attractive foliage and white flowers—as well as a tasty crop. Species with sparser leaf growth, such as canary creeper, soften a wall or veil a view without covering it completely.

Other Uses for Vines

Just as you use annuals in mixed beds and borders to maintain color and interest all through the season, you can interplant annual vines among your perennial climbers. Morning glories or moonflower vines make good companions for wall-climbing ivy and Virginia creeper. In most zones, annual vines bloom from midsummer to frost; pair them with early-flowering clematis, tall or climbing roses, or spring-flowering bushes and specimen trees so the vines can take over when the other blossoms fade.

To mingle annual climbers with a shrub or tree,

Annual Vines

Cardiospermum halicacabum
(balloon vine)
Cobaea scandens
(cup-and-saucer vine)
Cucumis melo
(pomegranate melon)
Cucurbita ficifolia
(Malabar gourd)
Cucurbita maxima 'Turbaniformis'
(Turk's-cap squash)
Cucurbita pepo var. ovifera
(pumpkin gourd)
Dolichos lablab
(hyacinth bean)
Humulus japonicus
(Japanese hopvine)
Ipomoea alba
(moonflower)
Ipomoea purpurea
(common morning glory)

Lagenaria siceraria
(calabash gourd)
Mina lobata
(crimson starglory)
Phaseolus coccineus
(scarlet runner bean)
Rhodochiton atrosanguineum
(purple bell vine)
Thunbergia alata
(black-eyed Susan vine)
***Tropaeolum* spp.**
(nasturtium)

Note: The abbreviation "spp." stands for the plural of "species"; where used in lists it means that many, but not all, of the species in a genus meet the criterion of the list.

The owner of this Oregon garden planted Tropaeolum majus (common nasturtium) across the front of the border for several purposes: The plants not only provide cheerful red and orange blooms and bold round leaves, they also hide spent bulb foliage and even camouflage an unsightly tree stump.

sow seeds or transplant seedlings beside the specimen plant and train the vine stems to climb up the plant as the season progresses. Pull the vines off again at summer's end to display the shrub's autumn color or winter fruits. You can use the same tactic to add color accents to a natural (not clipped) evergreen hedge. Plant scarlet runner beans, cup-and-saucer vines, or *Mina lobata* (crimson starglory) beside forsythia or holly, for example, to cover the dull green summer bushes with flowers.

When planting a vine next to mature perennials, shrubs, or trees, prepare an ample hole for the vine's roots, but take care not to disturb those of the other plant. The vine will have to compete with the established plant's root system for nutrients, so fertilize it with a commercial slow-release formula, taking care not to overfertilize and burn the tender tissue. When choosing a vine for this purpose, be sure to match the scale of the vine to its host plant: A fine-foliaged companion like *Genista hispanica* (broom) makes a good partner for delicate *Thunbergia alata* (black-eyed Susan vine), but it will take a vine with a more commanding presence, such as hyacinth bean, to show up nicely against bold-foliaged witch hazel.

A number of annual vines make splendid ground covers, particularly trailing types such as *Tropaeolum majus* (common nasturtium), *Cucurbita* species (gourds), and *Pelargonium peltatum* (ivy-leaved geranium). Planted in a dry, sunny spot, nasturtium spreads and sprawls rapidly. Ivy-leaved geranium is noted for its reliable, constant bloom and its vigorous colonizing habit. You can also set annual vines among established perennial ground covers to increase the area's visual interest.

The Beauty of Annual Vines

The glory of many annual vines is their spectacular or unusual flowers. The impact of fully open 'Heavenly Blue' morning glories massed on a fence is hard to beat for drama, but there are other vines with intricate and subtle blooms that have a beauty all their own. For example, *Cobaea scandens* produces white or purplish red, cup-shaped blossoms with contrasting green calyxes, giving rise to its common name, cup-and-saucer vine.

There is more beauty to annual vines than their flowers, however. Certain climbers are distinguished by exceptional foliage: The leaves of *Ipomoea quamoclit* (cypress vine) split into thin, frondlike segments that flutter in the breeze; the dark purple stems of *Dolichos lablab* (hyacinth bean) boast purple-tinted heart-shaped leaves; and *Tropaeolum peregrinum* (canary creeper) produces elegant five-lobed leaves reminiscent of the fig plant.

Some annual vines also offer pretty fruits or

Growing and Using Gourds

Gourd species, including the *Cucurbita pepo* shown here, are renowned for their useful or decorative fruits. Thanks to their bold foliage, they also make good screening plants when trained up a sturdy trellis—and even do well on overhead arbors.

Because gourds need a long season for their fruit to mature, you should start seeds indoors a month before your garden soil is warm enough for tender annuals. Plant the seedlings outdoors in full sun, allowing plenty of room for vigorous growth, and fertilize lightly with low-nitrogen compounds. Trimming the main stem to 10 feet will encourage the growth of fruiting lateral stems. When the tendrils beside the stems are brown, cut the fruits off, leaving a short stem on the fruit.

Cure gourds on screens or slats in any dry place, turning them weekly until they feel light and their skins are hard; this may take up to 4 months. Dried gourds can be varnished, painted, or even carved for decoration.

Training Vines

Vines use various strategies for climbing, but the planting and maintenance needs for the different types are much the same. First, sow seeds or plant seedlings as close as possible to their support. If you're training them up a solid fence or wall, attach a lath trellis, wires, or other plants such as wisteria or roses that the vines can twine around. Tie the stems loosely to the support to hold them in place (*below, far right*), and pinch back the most vigorous stems by several inches to encourage full, bushy growth. For best results with all flowering vines, water deeply and feed them with a low-nitrogen fertilizer.

Many vines, including Ipomoea species (morning glory) (left), climb by twining around another object. If this object has a slippery surface, wind a strip of cloth or string around it to give the vine a place to grip. Guide growing stems to the support, and poke them gently around it in the direction they tend to move until they begin to wrap on their own. To cover a trellis, arrange growing tips along the framework, and tie the stems to it as they lengthen.

Special plant features called tendrils hold vines such as Cobaea scandens (cup-and-saucer vine) (above) to their supports. Give these grabbers something slender to climb, since the coiling tendrils can't get around thick poles or slats. Tie the young stems to their supports; as soon as tendrils form, the vine will hold itself on. To control the shape of the vine, arrange the stem along the path you want it to follow, and tie it in place until the tendrils secure it.

Sprawling vines such as Tropaeolum species (nasturtium) (above) don't grip their supports as they climb but simply grow long, flexible stems that scramble over nearby objects. These sprawlers can be woven through the lattice of a trellis or the spaces in a chain-link fence, or spread out to ramble across the ground, a low bush, or a rock. When using such vines as ground cover, plant them thickly and trim rampant growth as necessary to keep them in bounds.

Fasten vine stems to their supports with cloth strips, twist ties from the grocery store, or special plant twine from garden centers. Begin tying the stems when they are still short so that the plant will be held from the bottom up as it grows and will not sag; tie each stem loosely to allow room for it to thicken as the plant matures. Check the ties occasionally during the season; they should be firm enough to hold the vine in place without cutting into the stems.

useful produce. Varieties of the genus *Cucurbita,* for example, yield edible squash and interestingly shaped ornamental gourds that can be dried for decoration *(page 46)*. Though they aren't typically grown as vines, other squashes, melons, and gourds can be coaxed to climb if the support is strong enough to bear their weight.

Selecting and Starting Vines

When you're choosing a vining plant, you'll want to consider not only its flowers, foliage, and fruit but also its ultimate height. Depending on the species, for instance, annual vines grow from about 6 feet to upwards of 30 feet per season. Make sure the species you select has the growth potential to fill the space you have in mind. If you're trying to blanket an old shed, for example,

consider 15-foot morning glories or Japanese hopvines; 6-foot nasturtium vines would be more suitable for covering a chain-link fence.

Follow seed-packet guidelines on spacing, and plant a sufficient number to ensure that your plants will be close enough to form a uniform cover yet have enough root room to flourish. Always plant on the windward side of any support so that prevailing breezes will blow the vines toward the support, not away from it.

For a long season of bloom, most annual vines should be started from seed in late winter and then transplanted outdoors in spring. Some varieties, however, including morning glories, nasturtiums, and sweet peas, should be sown in the ground outdoors after the last frost. Nearly all annual vines do best where they receive at least half a day's sun; less than this, and the plants grow grudgingly and may not flower at all.

Leafy Vines for the Shade

Nothing adds atmosphere to a shade garden like a leafy vine, as evidenced by the ivy festoons and pillars on the wooden fence in the Richmond, Virginia, garden above. Twining up a tree or trellis, vines such as *Akebia quinata* (five-leaf akebia) or *Euonymus fortunei* (winter creeper) can give your garden the cool, lush look of a jungle retreat. If you have a patio with a trellis overhead, you can grow *Parthenocissus quinquefolia* (Virginia creeper) or, in Zone 10, *Tetrastigma voinieranum* (chestnut vine) in large

containers and train them to roof your shady retreat.

For a shady wall or fence, consider clinging vines such as *Ficus pumila* (creeping fig), winter creeper, *Hydrangea anomala* ssp. *petiolaris* (climbing hydrangea), or *Parthenocissus tricuspidata* (Boston ivy). Ivy is a fast grower that thrives in deep shade as well as in full sun, and is ideal for cloaking walls or chain-link fences. Bear in mind, however, that it spreads like wildfire and can damage mortar, so use it with care.

Container Gardening for Small Spaces

Gardening in containers is the ideal solution when growing space is limited. Container plants can go almost anywhere to extend your growing area on patios, decks, balconies, sidewalks, and even walls. Since they aren't planted in the ground, you don't have to worry about poor or compacted soil, a common problem in small urban gardens. And perhaps best of all, potted plants can be moved around or replanted to suit your immediate needs.

Choosing Containers

Your plants will thrive in almost any type of container as long as it has a hole at the bottom for drainage. Experienced container gardeners prefer large, deep containers because they allow for a more diverse planting and because they don't need to be watered as often as small or shallow pots.

When choosing your containers, take into consideration where they'll be spending most of their time. Plastic pots hold moisture better than clay ones and, if placed in shadier spots, should be monitored to make sure the soil doesn't stay too wet. Pots and boxes made of clay, which is porous, provide good air circulation and drainage—and for this very reason need to be watered frequently so that the soil doesn't dry out. Use them anywhere, but check the soil daily if they receive full sun. Wooden tubs provide superior protection from both heat and cold and will do well anywhere; they'll need to be replaced eventually, though, because they rot. And if you want to use a copper pot, put your plants in another container placed inside the copper one, since most plants find the metal poisonous.

A large clay pot of pink Swan River daisies anchors the many fragrant container plants lining these porch steps in Washington State. The casual yet artful display includes an intriguing array of geraniums, such as the cultivars 'Persian Queen', with chartreuse foliage and magenta flowers; 'Wilhelm Langguth', with variegated leaves; and 'Lady Plymouth', a scented variety. The grouping is accented by the white-throated blue flowers of Nolana and the tiny purple blossoms of heliotrope.

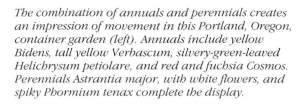

Single containers can add sparkle to any number of spots around your property. A large, elegant pot on your front step or a rustic one on a deck or balcony will both brighten and distinguish your home. Even a container placed among your bed or border plantings will add interest and dimension.

A container that isn't itself impressive can be brought to life with trailing plants, whose flowers and leaves will cover the sides. Sweet alyssum, baby-blue-eyes, or portulaca, with their draping foliage, will hide an unattractive concrete block, for instance. On the other hand, a pretty pot might be filled exclusively with an upright variety to highlight the container as well as its occupants.

Choosing Plants

Thanks to their shallow roots, vigorous growth, and prolific blooms, annuals are perfect for planting in containers. Colorful and versatile, annuals seem to take on a new character when they're planted in an attractive pot and given a place where their beauty can be enjoyed up close.

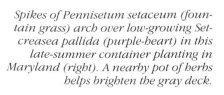

Spikes of Pennisetum setaceum (fountain grass) arch over low-growing Setcreasea pallida (purple-heart) in this late-summer container planting in Maryland (right). A nearby pot of herbs helps brighten the gray deck.

Some of the most beautiful arrangements combine different annuals with a variety of habits, colors, and foliage interest. Mix various flowering plants—some trailing and some tall and spiked—with light- and dark-colored foliage, such as pale dusty-miller and purple-toned basil, in sunny spots, or pair them with multihued coleus and polka-dot plants in partial shade. Annual grasses, including red or purple *Pennisetum* (fountaingrass), provide a nice change from flowers and are especially suitable in contemporary settings. Even a vegetable or two, like a purple eggplant or a red pepper, can add drama near summer's end.

When choosing your plants, match their size at maturity with the scale of the pot. An upright plant shouldn't rise more than about one and a half to two times the height of

Tuberous Begonias

Tuberous begonias *(Begonia* x *tuberhybrida)* have an upright or trailing habit and simple or compound blooms, and come in every color but blue. Although many gardeners treat them as potted annuals, these summer favorites are actually tender bulbs.

Start the tubers indoors in flats several weeks before the last frost date. When the shoots are 3 inches tall, move them to containers filled with a commercial potting-soil mix. Space three or four tubers concave side up in the container, 2 to 3 inches apart, with the top of the tuber at the soil line. For a hanging basket, choose a cascading form. Upright begonias, like the bright red varieties at left, are better suited to pots on the ground.

Tuberous begonias prefer partial to full shade. They thrive in cool and moist, but not soggy, soil. Keep them well fertilized and provide plenty of water throughout the season for maximum bloom.

the container, or the overall look will be top-heavy. Also, consider your plants' growth habits: Those that are especially dense and bushy, such as wax begonias and impatiens, are best grown by themselves rather than with other species if your container is small.

For visual impact, arrange several containers together. Try combining contrasting flower colors, for example, by placing a tub of golden *Calendula officinalis* (pot marigold) next to deep blue *Centaurea cyanus* (bachelor's-button). Or simply cluster pots blooming with assorted varieties of marigolds or geraniums. Usually, three or four medium-size containers look better than a large tub surrounded by small pots.

Hanging Baskets

Your container plants need not be confined to ground level. In fact, nothing shows off a trailing or spreading plant like a basket suspended from above. Hanging plants do need a little more care than those in other containers, however. Because they are meant to be seen from the bottom as well as the top, they require more grooming to stay attractive. And because hanging plants are exposed

to air on all sides, they dry out faster than other plants. In particular, moss-lined wire baskets *(pages 52-53),* which have no solid sides to hold moisture, need a great deal of water and should be placed out of the harsh sun.

Planting and Caring for Container Plants

Before you plant your container, decide on the arrangement if you're using different varieties. The tallest plants should go in the center or the back, the trailers around the rim, and the medium-sized bushy and upright plants in between. Be sure the plants you've chosen all prefer similar light and soil conditions.

Your pot should be at least 8 inches deep. Place a layer of rocks, gravel, or pottery shards in the bottom to keep the drainage holes clear of soil. Then fill the container to within 2 inches of the top with a potting-soil mix from a garden center or nursery, or with a homemade version. A soil composed of equal parts topsoil, compost, and vermiculite will do nicely.

Use healthy young plants that you've purchased or grown from seed. Remove the plants

Making a Moss-Lined Basket

A moss-lined hanging basket is typically fashioned from a simple wire frame and lined with sphagnum moss, both purchased from a garden center. This simple container is perfect for displaying lush foliage and colorful blossoms from all sides. Water the basket every day to maintain a fresh and vibrant show of blooms.

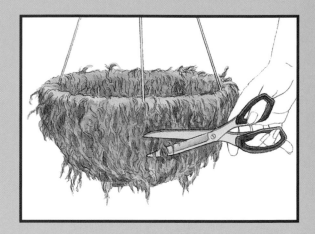

1. Soak the moss in water to make it pliable; squeeze out the excess moisture. Place it in a basket frame (left) and press it into an even 1-inch layer, adding or removing moss as necessary.

2. Cover up any wire showing on the outside of the basket by pressing additional moss around it. Next, attach the wire hanger, hang the basket, and trim any dangling moss with scissors to achieve a neat but natural appearance (above). In a separate bucket, mix enough commercial potting-soil mix to fill the basket, adding a few handfuls of peat moss to help retain moisture. Then cover the bottom of the basket with some of the soil mixture.

Hanging under a leafy arbor, a moss-lined wire basket overflows with hot pink Impatiens wallerana and dangling blooms of tender perennial fuchsia. Both plants prefer the partial shade and humid atmosphere of their Seattle home.

from their cell packs or pots, and gently spread apart the bottom of the rootball. Using a small trowel, dig a hole slightly bigger than the roots and position the plant, distributing its roots evenly in the space. Fill the hole with soil, pressing it firmly in place. Group plants closer together than you would in an outdoor garden. Water the container, and cover the soil with a bark mulch or sphagnum moss to help hold in moisture.

Sun, wind, and drought can be the mortal enemies of container plants because they dry them out quickly. Infrequent watering can kill your potted plants, and irregular watering will stress them, leaving them vulnerable to pests and diseases. To protect outdoor container plants that dry out quickly, water them daily—more often during the height of summer—and move them to sheltered locations during very hot weather. When watering, wet the soil thoroughly and avoid wetting the leaves, which can invite disease.

Although frequent watering is essential, it tends to leach nutrients out of the soil. Keep your plants supplied with vital minerals by feeding them regularly with a commercial liquid fertilizer that contains an equal balance of potassium, phosphorus, and nitrogen; too much nitrogen will encourage leafy growth at the expense of blooms. If you water several times a week, use the fertilizer at half strength and apply it every 2 weeks or so.

Rosy pink petunias flank this container garden, which hangs from a fence in a seaside Delaware town. Planted in a commercially available "hay basket," the garden also features white African daisies, trailing yellow Bidens, and blue Salvia farinacea 'Victoria'.

3. Use a pencil to poke a hole through the moss near the bottom of the basket. *Remove a seedling from its cell pack and insert it through the hole (above), firming the moss around it on the outside. Repeat to make a row around the basket, then cover the roots with soil. Continue planting in rows to within 2 inches of the top of the basket. Then plant a few seedlings at the top of the basket (right), and water.*

Planting in Window Boxes

A window box of annuals pleases the eye from both inside and outside the house. Geraniums are a favorite for window boxes, but you may want to experiment with combinations of unusual varieties of flowers and foliage to enliven a scene that may be growing too familiar.

When attaching boxes to your windows, keep in mind that they are heavy. Mount them securely with bolts or brackets, and check them yearly to make sure the hardware hasn't weakened from rusting. Also remember that if your boxes hang inside the drip line of the house, they may not get much rainfall. This—along with drying winds and the warmth from the house—means they will need diligent watering, although a mulch of shredded bark will help retain some moisture. On the plus side, the extra heat allows early planting in spring and extends the fall blooming season.

Terracing for Hard-to-Work Slopes

Working a garden situated on a hill can be a discouraging prospect. However, by building a few steps, or terraces, that cut across the slope, a resourceful gardener can transform a troublesome landscape into a multilevel spectacle of imagination and beauty. Terraces are essentially miniature retaining walls, and installing them on a slope will not only enhance your property's appearance but also solve any problems with erosion and water runoff caused by the natural terrain.

Bluestone granite rocks support terraces bisected by a brick walkway. The tiered slope displays begonias, catharanthus, and red geraniums amid a background of hostas, ferns, and other perennial foliage.

When to Terrace

Deciding whether to terrace a hillside depends on several factors. First, how steep is your incline?

You don't need to take formal measurements; just consider how difficult it is to perform your gardening chores. Does standing on the hill require some extra effort? If the slope is covered with grass, is mowing it unduly tiring? Does the mower slip out of your control? If you cannot work easily on the hill, then terracing may be the perfect solution for you.

If your slope is excessively steep, you may want to consult a professional landscape architect, who can quickly determine whether terracing is advisable. Your property may require sturdy retaining walls or banks instead, especially if you live in an area that experiences severe rains and mud slides. Other options for steep inclines include holding the slope back with ground covers *(box, page 57),*

and planting shrubs and trees into the side of your slope *(box, page 57)*.

Making a Terracing Plan

Terraces can be built of stone, railroad ties, landscaping timbers, or bricks. Choose a buttressing material that suits your garden design; for instance, you might select bricks for a formal effect, or railroad ties if you want a more rustic look.

The number of terrace steps you should install will depend on the slope's length, or run. The dimensions of your terraces—how high they will stand and how deep you make them—will vary with the run and the height, or rise, of the slope. How wide you make the terraces depends on the site and the amount of planting you'd like to do. In any case, all the terraces should be uniform in size. As a rule, terraces should be at least 1 foot deep, that is, 1 foot from the terrace's front edge to the rise where the next terrace begins. For visual definition and stability, each terrace should be

at least 5 inches but no more than 12 inches high. Because they drain so well, terraces may dry out too fast if they are higher than 12 inches. Also, you don't want to be climbing and working on steps more than a foot tall. Terraces with 8-inch rises and 2-foot depths work well on most slopes. To calculate the rise and run, see the box below.

As you develop your terracing plan, take into account any features such as trees and shrubs that presently exist on the slope. Can they be included

How to Size Your Terraces

Calculating the number of terraces your slope can accommodate and their dimensions is a matter of simple arithmetic. First you need to measure the rise (height) and the run (horizontal length) of your slope. For the rise, have a helper hold a 2-by-4 board horizontally, with one end resting on the top of the slope, as shown below. Check to see if the board is level. Then measure the vertical distance from the ground at the foot of the slope to the board. Measuring from one end of the board, mark off that distance. To calculate the run, reverse the position of the board so that it stands upright at the foot of the slope, and measure the horizontal distance from the top of the slope straight across to the point on the board that corresponds to the slope's rise. For a slope with a more gradual rise, measure the slope in increments and add the resulting figures together.

Next, divide the rise measurement by the height you want each terrace to be. For example, if the rise is 32 inches and you want terraces 8 inches high, divide 32 by 8, for a result of 4 steps. To find the depth of each terrace, divide the run measurement by the number of steps you want to build. If the run is 96 inches, divide 96 by 4; your terraces will be 24 inches, or 2 feet, deep. The numbers rarely work out this neatly, but you can adjust the measurements an inch or two to come up with some usable dimensions.

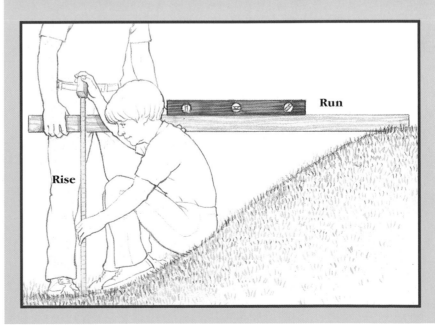

Building a Stone Terrace

One of the easiest ways to build terraces is to construct the tiers with large stones, which are available at local quarries and are relatively inexpensive. Select stones with at least one flat side; you'll place this side up so that the top edges of all the terraces look uniform.

Before starting your first tier, clear the slope of existing plants, including any sod. If there are any trees, it's best to build the terraces around them. Deep-rooted trees pose less of a problem than shallow-rooted ones, whose roots extend just below the ground surface and interfere with construction. If you have shallow-rooted trees, you may want to consider alternatives, such as building raised beds around the trunks or planting some kind of ground cover.

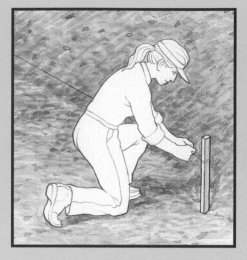

1. At the foot of the slope, measure off the width of the first terrace and drive a stake into the ground at either end. *Mark the height of the terrace on each stake. Stretch a string between the two stakes at the marked points. Use a line level or lay a carpenter's level lightly across the string to make sure that the guideline is exactly horizontal.*

2. Start laying the stones for the first terrace. *If necessary, scoop out some soil with a trowel to fit large or irregularly shaped stones neatly and solidly into the earth. Build up the rows of stones until the terrace wall lines up with the string. To ensure drainage, pour coarse gravel behind the stones until it reaches about three-quarters of the height of the terrace.*

3. Fill in the first terrace by scraping soil from farther up the slope *and shoveling it behind the stones until the entire terrace is at the right height. Make sure the terrace is flat by laying a carpenter's level across it, as shown above. Use a measuring tape to check that the terrace is as deep as you planned.*

4. Move the stakes and string to mark the position and height of the next terrace. *Lay stones as described in Step 2, then pour in gravel and level off the terrace with shovelfuls of earth. Repeat the process until you have terraced the entire slope. Amend the soil and let it settle for a few days before planting.*

in the terrace structure, or do they need to be removed? Large trees and shrubs are best left in place, since removing them could exacerbate erosion or runoff problems. Also, if the incline descends toward your house, plan on leaving a flat area at the bottom. This will keep water that is running off the terraced hill away from your foundation. An added benefit of this open space is that it may allow more daylight to enter your home. Planting ground covers or shrubs along the outer embankments of your terraces will also decrease runoff and erosion.

Preparations for Planting

When selecting plants for the terraces, look for low-growing types that creep or form mounds. Plants that cascade create a lovely display and also help unite the levels of the terraced area. Good choices are creeping phlox *(Phlox stolonifera)* or moss phlox *(P. subulata),* creeping juniper, sedums with trailing stems, small-leaved ivies, and herbs such as thyme. Mounded plants such as winter jasmine, prostrate abelia, and dwarf cutleaf stephanandra (lace shrub) help soften the edges of the terraces without obscuring them.

As is true for any new garden bed, you will need to work the soil in each of your terraces before planting. Amend it as necessary, keeping the soil level 1 to 2 inches below the top edge of the border. This prevents soil from being washed over the front of the terrace during heavy rains.

Planting Trees

A slope provides the opportunity to nurture a lovely tree or shrub in a spot you may not otherwise be inclined to plant. Too often trees and shrubs tilt aimlessly off the sides of steep slopes, but you can avoid this problem with proper planting. First, dig a hole deep enough so that the top of the rootball is flush with the uphill side of the slope. Fill in the hole and mound soil on the downhill side of the rootball until the entire rootball is well covered. Make a water basin for the trunk by building up a rim of earth around the top of the mound. Then cover the area with mulch and water slowly but thoroughly. If you plant a tree on a very steep incline, you may want to stake it from the uphill side.

Planting Ground Covers

Planting an erosion-controlling ground cover on a slope is sometimes the best option, especially on a short, steep drop. If you choose creeping juniper or another low-lying woody shrub whose 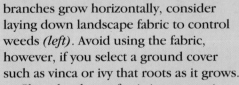 branches grow horizontally, consider laying down landscape fabric to control weeds *(left)*. Avoid using the fabric, however, if you select a ground cover such as vinca or ivy that roots as it grows.

Clear the slope of existing vegetation, and if grass abuts the edges, install mowing strips. Then lay panels of landscape fabric across the slope; overlap the lengths by 4 to 6 inches. To hold the fabric in place, stake it with bent wire. Measure and mark the correct spacing for your plants and cut Xs into the fabric at the marks. Dig holes large enough to accommodate the rootballs, then plant. Do not cover the fabric with chunky mulch; heavy rains may cause it to slide down the incline.

Vertical Structures for Shade and Privacy

Vertical structures—trellises, arbors, pergolas, lath houses, and gazebos—are extremely useful garden elements. Besides creating design interest or serving as focal points, they can provide shade for both plants and people. They can also be used to create privacy—sheltered spots for seating or a garden retreat, for example. And they can provide niches for container plants or act as supports on which to train climbing flowers and vines.

Vertical structures should be aesthetically pleasing, blending with your overall garden design and the architectural style of your house. A garden structure should also match the scale of the garden and home so that it doesn't overwhelm the landscape. Keep in mind, too, that unless the structure supports an evergreen climber, the framework of your arbor or pergola will be clearly visible during winter.

Construction materials used for vertical elements include wood, stone, brick, metal, and wrought iron. You can also fashion appealing rustic structures from willow twigs or grapevines gathered from your own garden or a nearby field (box, opposite).

An arched trellis laden with pink clematis beckons visitors to pass beneath it and into the Salem, Oregon, garden beyond. Along with the fence, the trellis acts as both a focal point and a garden divider. A border hedge of boxwood lines the walkway, and white hawthorn blooms in front of the fence.

Freestanding Structures

Pergolas, arbors, trellises, and gazebos are usually ornamental—even fanciful—elements within the garden. An arch or a pergola can resemble a piece of sculpture, beautiful in its own right and enhanced even further by the adornment you choose for it. Beyond their aesthetic appeal, freestanding garden structures provide shade along with privacy and protection—all without sacrificing light or air. They make wonderful supports for all kinds of plantings, too. A trellised archway draped with wisteria or fragrant roses, for instance, makes a lovely frame for a garden pathway. Keep in mind that your plantings should be in proportion to the size of your structures. Small, wispy climbers may look skimpy, or even sickly, when grown on a large, bold frame such as a pergola. On the other hand, heavy vines such as Japanese wisteria will overwhelm a more delicate trellis. In either case, be sure to prune your plantings regularly to control their growth.

Pergolas and Arbors

Pergolas—elongated structures of columns supporting a sturdy, overhead gridwork of wood rafters—are bold, linear affairs. Traditionally, they function as covered walkways and should therefore lead somewhere, connecting one area to another or perhaps just ending a garden path at a seat or ornament. A pergola takes up considerable room, so plan its location with care. You might build one over a patio as an extension of your house, or locate it as a freestanding unit at a distance from the house, creating a garden retreat.

Pergolas originated as frameworks for such climbing plants as grapevines. *Vitis vinifera* 'Purpurea' and the hybrid 'Brant' provide wonderful color on a pergola in the fall. Other climbing vines also do well on pergolas.

Arbors, with their graceful arches and enclosed seats, are generally less imposing than pergolas. An arbor can be used to create a private nook off the beaten path or a quiet spot for resting, reading, or just enjoying your garden in solitude. If you design it so that it faces a lovely view in the garden or occupies a particularly warm and sunny spot, you'll be sure to enjoy it to the fullest. Arbors are usually associated with climbing plants—traditionally, grapes and roses; train them to climb up the sides of the structure and cascade over the top.

Trellises

A trellis acts like a screen, creating a partial barrier that provides a measure of shade, shelter, and privacy but never completely blocks out air and light. A traditional trellis has panels of wood latticework that can either stand freely or abut a wall, a fence, or the side of a house. If you incorporate a seating area into your trellis, it can provide a wonderful spot for just relaxing.

Trellis panels are usually made from a grid of perpendicular wood slats attached to a frame. The design of the trellis can be simple or intricate, incorporating a variety of arches and posts. You can build a trellis from decay-resistant woods—such as redwood, cypress, or cedar—that weather naturally into a handsome hue over the years. If you use pine, however, it should be pressure-treated; otherwise, you will have to treat it with a preservative and either stain or paint it to prevent rotting.

Although a trellis primarily serves as a plant support, don't mask the underlying wood pattern with too much vegetation. Try to balance the style and intricacy of your trellis design with the habit and vigor of your climbing and twining plants. If your trellis has a tightly woven crisscross pattern, for example, it's better to use a light, airy climber like clematis than a larger-leaved climber, which would look too heavy.

Gazebos and Lath Houses

A gazebo is a roofed and often elevated pavilion that serves as a kind of ornate freestanding deck and gives a whimsical focus to the garden. It is usually circular, square, or octagonal, with low latticework sides that often support pretty flowering vines. A lath house is similar to a pergola in form but much more lightly constructed. Its main purpose is to create dappled shade rather than to support climbing plants, though it may bear light herbaceous vines.

Making a Rustic Trellis

Fashioning your own trellis from flexible grapevines or willow twigs is not difficult and can lend a pleasant rustic touch to an informal garden design. To make a trellis like the one shown at right, first construct a rectangular frame of sturdy branches—cedar, maple, walnut, or sycamore—by nailing the pieces of wood together to form posts and crosspieces. Then bend flexible grapevines or willow shoots so that they arch over the frame, and attach them to the supporting pieces with twine or plastic ties.

Wind additional grapevines around the crosspieces for a decorative touch. Then prop your finished trellis against a wall or fence and use it to support roses, vines, or even vegetables.

Solving Wind-Related Problems

One factor that is easy to overlook when you're designing a planting is the impact of wind. Moving air can be highly beneficial to your plants, cooling them in hot weather and reducing the incidence of insects and diseases that sultry, stagnant air encourages. However, in a garden that is excessively windy, the cooling and drying effects may become so intensified that plants are harmed. Such damage is most severe when wind is combined with either freezing winter weather or summer drought.

Some broadleaf evergreens, including rhododendrons and camellias, are especially vulnerable to winter winds because they retain their foliage year round. (Deciduous plants are nearly impervious to winter winds, since they shed their leaves.) When sunshine warms a broadleaf evergreen, moisture is drawn out of its foliage. As long as the ground isn't frozen, the roots can replace the lost moisture. When the ground freezes, however, sun and wind together can remove so much moisture

A slope rimmed with a windbreak of Pfitzer junipers and smothered by Algerian ivy protects this California terrace. Dwarf strawberry trees and pastel pansies ring the terrace.

that the plant suffers damage. The leaves turn brown and, if the desiccation is really severe, the plant dies.

A microclimate well suited to broadleaf evergreens is a bed against the north wall of a house or on the shady side of a tall hedge, either of which serves as shelter from the drying effect of the winter sun. You can create a microclimate in which a substantial portion of a garden will be shielded from cold winds by planting a windbreak. A windbreak is also in order if persistent winds in summer exacerbate drought. In either case, determine the prevailing direction of the wind and, as nearly as possible, plant the windbreak at a right angle to it *(opposite, top)*.

If large shade trees on your property prevent air from circulating around nearby plants, you may want to consider creating a wind channel. This involves removing the lower branches of the trees so that the wind can reach the plants, thus keeping them cool and well ventilated *(opposite, below)*.

Planting a Windbreak

A wall of evergreens—eastern red cedars in this illustration—protects an area equal to at least double the height of the trees from damaging winds *(below, right)*. The long arrows trace the path of the wind that is deflected up and over the windbreak. Wind also blows through the trees, whose branches and foliage dissipate its force and slow it down, as indicated by the short arrows on either side of the trees. A solid wall of stone or brick makes a poor barrier against wind, producing strong eddies on the sheltered side that are harmful to plants. For an effective windbreak, plant two or three staggered rows of closely spaced trees *(inset);* the junipers shown here are set 5 to 6 feet apart.

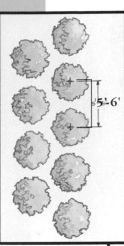

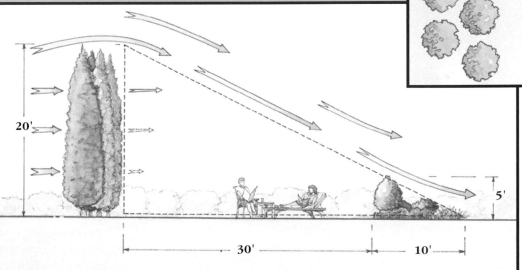

Clearing a Wind Channel

Removing the lower branches of large trees that impede air circulation—a process known as limbing up—allows a cooling breeze to flow into a garden. In the diagram at right, a pair of scarlet oaks has been limbed up to the level of the roof line. The dotted line indicates the extent of the growth that was pruned away. Good ventilation is particularly desirable in hot, humid climates, making the garden more livable and creating better growing conditions for plants.

Shade Trees to Limb Up

Acer rubrum
(red maple)
Cladrastis kentukea
(yellowwood)
Nyssa sylvatica
(black gum)
Quercus coccinea
(scarlet oak)

Quercus phellos
(willow oak)
Quercus rubra
(red oak)
Sophora japonica
(Japanese pagoda tree)
Tilia cordata
(littleleaf linden)

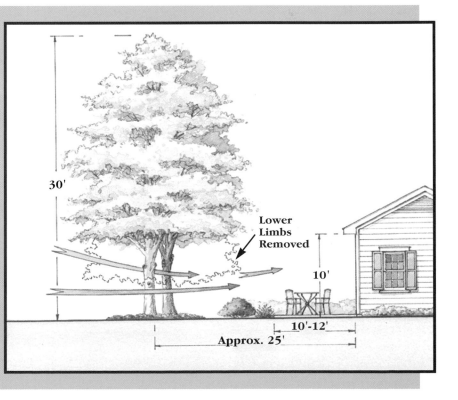

Lower Limbs Removed

Color for Shady Gardens

Red- and white-flowering trillium, blooming amid native bleeding heart in this Portland, Oregon, garden, is a wide-ranging native. Over 30 Trillium species grow wild in woodlands throughout the United States.

A shady garden doesn't have to be dark and dull. In fact, by adding shade-tolerant flowering plants, you can create brilliant color that will rival that of your sunniest beds.

Shade plants were among the first flowering vegetation to appear on earth. Cousins of those primordial flowers flourish in shady gardens today in the form of *Rhododendron* and *Magnolia* species. Many other shade plants have since evolved in the shadows of taller neighbors, and nurseries now offer a steady stream of new shade-tolerant varieties.

Trees, Shrubs, and Vines

Ornamental trees are the most prominent plants to display brilliant color in the shade. Many produce not only flowers but also colorful fruit. Dogwood *(Cornus)* trees, for example, bear flowerlike bracts in the spring and may display bright berries or tinted bark in the winter. *Stewartia* produces white flowers in summer and exhibits handsome mottled bark throughout the winter.

Like ornamental trees, shrubs can bring sparkling color to the shade garden not only with flowers but also with berries in many hues. *Rhododendron* species—which include azaleas—are mainstays for shady areas throughout much of North America. Their bloom times range from early spring into the summer, and flower colors run from white to deep purple. While most azaleas are deciduous shrubs, almost all other rhododendrons are evergreen, helping to maintain the garden's structure year round.

Hydrangea is another reliable shade shrub, with long-lasting summer blooms in white, pink, or blue. Soil chemistry governs color in some cultivars: Acid soil produces blue flowers, and alkaline soil, pink. A climbing form, *H. anomala* ssp. *petiolaris,* winds along walls or around trees.

Other handsome, though less common shrubs for the shade garden include the evergreen *Mahonia* (Oregon grape), with cascades of yellow flowers in early spring, then edible berries. In late spring, *Gaultheria shallon* (salal) yields spikes of tiny white or pink flowers, followed by purple to black berries.

Strong performers for partial shade include *Chionanthus virginicus* (old-man's-beard), which produces fragrant white flowers in late spring, and mountain laurel *(Kalmia latifolia)*, which fares well in full shade but flowers best with some sun.

Most flowering vines are considered sun lovers. However, a few, such as *Gelsemium sempervirens* 'Pride of Augusta', *Akebia quinata* (five-leaf akebia), and some species of *Clematis* and *Lonicera* (honeysuckle), will bloom in partial shade, and some, such as x *Fatshedera lizei* (miracle plant) and *Aristolochia macrophylla* (Dutchman's-pipe), don't care for direct sun at all.

Herbaceous Bloomers

Shade-loving herbaceous perennials make up a long and colorful list. Some are also very adaptable. For example, gardeners in the South can use partially shaded sites to grow a large number of perennials that require full sun in northern zones. Indeed, no matter where you live, you may be able to grow perennial species and cultivars you never thought you could simply by understanding their origins and getting tips from other gardeners who have grown them.

Annuals, like flowering vines, are generally considered sun-loving plants, but many can bloom in dappled or partial shade. The beautiful, easy-care impatiens—a dependable favorite of shade gardeners—flowers freely in whites, pinks, reds, oranges, and a few blue-violets. Ageratum, a tidy little plant with blue, pink, or white flowers, tolerates partial shade and blooms for a long time without deadheading. Begonias flower dependably from spring to the first frost—or year round, in frost-free zones. Similarly, fuchsia blooms as an annual in the shade, and hardy varieties survive the year in mild climates.

Wildflowers hold a special place in shade gardens: Shade-tolerant native plants can provide color and interest from earliest spring through late summer. Some, like jack-in-the-pulpit or dogtooth violet, grow, bloom, and disappear quickly. But others, including the dainty Solomon's-seal, can last for weeks.

Bulbs are another good source of herbaceous flowers for the shade garden. About half of all bulbs tolerate, prefer, or require a degree of shade. A few are comfortable even in full shade—for example, *Achimenes* (orchid pansy), *Arisaema* (dragonroot), *Begonia* x *tuberhybrida* (tuberous begonia), *Hyacinthoides,* and *Ornithogalum nutans* (nodding star-of-Bethlehem).

Ground Covers

Carpeting the shade-garden floor with blossoms are some of the most popular evergreen and deciduous ground covers, with flowers ranging from white to yellow to blue-purple. *Vinca* (periwinkle) sends evergreen strands across almost any type of soil and produces blossoms in white or violet, depending on the cultivar. *Heuchera* displays beau-

The sprightly pale lavender blooms of the perennial Anemone nemorosa (wood anemone) spread a frothy carpet from which the compact forms of the evergreen Rhododendron yakusimanum emerge, bursting with bell-shaped pink flowers. Forming a backdrop to this cheerful Oregon garden is another, larger rhododendron and the pendulous, brilliant yellow blossoms of a small Laburnum (bean tree).

tifully veined foliage and red, pink, or greenish white flowers. And several types of *Epimedium* (bishop's hat), such as *E. perralderanum* and *E. x versicolor* 'Sulphureum', blanket the ground even in dry shade and produce lovely yellow blossoms.

Virtues of Shade Plants

Most shade-loving plants have shallow roots, which makes planting them easy; even large rhododendrons have manageable rootballs. Shade lovers are also highly sensitive to moisture levels in the soil. Many require a natural layer of leaf litter or an application of mulch to keep them from drying out. This makes the shady flower garden relatively easy to maintain: In the fall, you'll need to remove only the heaviest drifts of fallen leaves from areas planted with flowering species.

Shade-flowering plants have other virtues as well. Many of them self-sow, so if you don't tidy up too much, you'll get more seedlings to increase your stock of plants. In addition, those plants pollinated by insects are often extremely fragrant or colorful. For example, shrubs such as *Chionanthus* (fringe tree), which blooms in spring, or those that flower in late winter, such as *Hamamelis* (witch hazel) and *Chimonanthus* (wintersweet), use rich fragrance to entice pollinators. Foraging bees respond to blue and yellow more than any other colors, and bright yellow is among the most common flower colors of shade-blooming species. The vivid red of cardinal flower (*Lobelia cardinalis*), one of only a few shade-blooming plants pollinated by birds, attracts hummingbirds to the garden.

In the partial shade of this Pennsylvania cottage garden, a gold-tipped Chamaecyparis obtusa 'Crippsii' (Hinoki false cypress) and a white-blossomed viburnum anchor drifts of pale lavender-blue forget-me-not and snowy candytuft. Hybrid tulips provide splashes of pink.

Color in the Shade

Besides attracting pollinators, the color offered by shade-flowering plants contributes a great deal to the mood of a garden. The glowing yellow of spring flowers warms us and draws us in; the heat of summer seems moderated by pastel flowers under trees, adding to the shade's cooling effect.

Shadows tend to make colors look deeper and to heighten blue tones. White flowers appear brighter in shade. In fact, the same blossom on a given plant may take on a color in shade that is markedly different from the one it wears in sun. And because shade softens contrasting flower colors, you can use bolder combinations than you might otherwise. Bear in mind, too, that a given flower color can look different on different types of plants. For instance, a sprinkling of pink lily blooms is gentle and soothing, while the massed blossoms of one pink azalea can inflame an entire area.

Flowering dogwood glows in the dappled shade of spring in this St. Louis garden. The tree's fall foliage and bright berries will shine long after the bluebells and bleeding heart below it have retired, providing interest throughout the year.

Fall and Winter Color

As summer's soft days fade into autumn, your flower borders may look somewhat woebegone. The once-lush foliage is now worn, the old blooms spent. Yet with care and planning, your garden can continue to reward you with bouquets of color. For example, some late-summer varieties can be encouraged to keep blooming into fall. You can also add plants that put on a floral display until the first hard frost.

As the coldest months descend, the garden can still offer interest. A number of perennials and shrubs flower in late winter and earliest spring. The hues tend to be paler than those of their brilliant summer counterparts, but they are no less welcome for providing splashes of color against the winter gray and snow.

Frost has traced a delicate silver margin on the finely serrated leaves of Filipendula ulmaria (queen-of-the-meadow). The crystals mirror the white edges of Chrysanthemum pacificum, which bears button-shaped gold flowers in the fall and can withstand mild frosts.

Perennials to Take the Garden into Fall

A kind of rampant abundance characterizes a garden of robust fall perennials. Warm colors—hot pinks, plums, and purples, burnt orange, and every tint of yellow—dominate the ornamental border. Summer-flowering acanthus, coreopsis, dianthus, and salvia keep on blooming valiantly, while Japanese anemones, sunflowers, goldenrod, sedum, and chrysanthemums are just coming into flower.

In northern zones, where forests and wooded lots are fiery with color, the best approach to planning a fall garden is to seek out flowers that blend well with the surrounding trees and shrubs. Look for yellow, gold, bronze, pink, and wine red chrysanthemums. Add the yellow of sneezeweed and goldenrod and the contrasting blue and lavender of Michaelmas daisies for a long-lasting autumn display.

A Glory of Grasses

Ornamental grasses are a splendid complement to fall-blooming perennials. Prized in the summer garden for their blade-shaped leaves and sweeps of subtle color, many grasses are in full flowering

Fall-Blooming Perennials

Aconitum carmichaelii (azure monkshood)	(Joe-Pye weed)
Anemone hupehensis **'September Charm'** (Japanese anemone)	***Helenium autumnale*** (sneezeweed)
Anemone vitifolia (grapeleaf anemone)	***Helianthus angustifolius*** (sunflower)
Aster novae-angliae (New England aster)	***Hosta tardiflora*** (late-flowering hosta)
Chrysanthemum* x *morifolium (garden chrysanthemum)	***Liriope muscari*** (big blue lilyturf)
Chrysanthemum pacificum (gold-and-silver chrysanthemum)	***Perovskia atriplicifolia*** (Russian sage)
Chrysanthemum parthenium (feverfew)	***Rudbeckia fulgida*** **'Goldsturm'** (coneflower)
Eupatorium coelestinum (hardy ageratum)	***Salvia azurea*** **'Grandiflora'** (sage)
Eupatorium fistulosum	***Sedum* x 'Autumn Joy'** (stonecrop)
	Sedum sieboldii (stonecrop)

glory by September. Texturally, the blooms make an interesting contrast to the grass itself. Soft and feathery—in the form of foxtails, bottle brushes, open fans, or upright sheaves—the flowers and the seed heads that follow them glow in the autumn sunlight.

The majestic maiden grass grows to 5 feet and taller, and its many cultivars take on different hues, from silver to taupe to rusty brown, with fan-shaped plumes that range from silver-white to brown. On the smaller side, *Helictotrichon sempervirens* (blue oat grass) forms compact 2-foot mounds with erect, straw-colored panicles. Cultivars of fountain grass bloom in black, purple, or rose-pink.

When the grasses are finished blooming, you can let them dry in place over the winter. They keep their shape handsomely, the feathery seed heads nodding gently in the wind.

Fall Fanfares of Shrubs and Trees

Many deciduous shrubs and small trees also bloom as the season cools, offering virtually every color but blue. The delicately flowered *Camellia sasanqua* bears blooms ranging from white to dark pink, beginning in early autumn and continuing until hard frost. *Hamamelis virginiana* (common witch hazel) has threadlike lemon yellow flowers that burst forth as its foliage turns deep gold. *Buddleia davidii* (butterfly bush) bears clusters of honey-scented, violet-purple tubular flowers from summer into fall. And the vigorous summer- and fall-blooming vine *Clematis maximowicziana* produces a thick blanket of tiny, fragrant white blooms.

Among the trees offering flowers late in the season is *Franklinia alatamaha* (franklinia), which grows to a height of 15 feet or more and bears 3-inch, camellia-like white blossoms, in striking contrast to its bright red fall foliage; the flower petals unfurl from knobby buds resembling large pearls. Late-blooming crape myrtles have intricate crinkled flowers that range from hot pink through lavender to white. The branches of Higan cherry

In a cluster of contrasting, star-shaped autumn flowers, the brightest is the pure white hardy chrysanthemum 'White Gloss', set off by the purple of 'King George' Italian aster, the deep rose of Japanese anemone 'Prinz Heinrich', and the pink of 'September Glow' sedum.

are covered with masses of lavender-pink buds that open on warm days in both autumn and winter.

Planning for Winter Blooms

Compared with the fall landscape, the winter garden is somewhat austere, but it need not be barren. Late-winter-blooming perennials, though less showy than their warm-weather relatives, can lift the spirits on a cold, bleak afternoon.

Among the first and most welcome are the helle-bores, whose colorful roselike flowers offer as much style and substance as any summer beauty *(below)*. Slightly later comes yellow or satin white Amur adonis; *Doronicum* (leopard's-bane), with its daisylike yellow flowers; *Primula denticulata* (drumstick primrose), bearing flowers in lilac, purple, or pink; and the exotic-looking *Pulmonaria* (lungwort), its white-speckled green foliage setting off small pink

flowers that eventually turn blue. These hardy plants tolerate shade and look natural clumped beneath shrubs and trees.

Hamamelis vernalis (vernal witch hazel) is the earliest of a long list of winter-blooming shrubs; it bursts into flower in February in Zone 4. Golden yellow to slightly reddish on bare branches, the blossoms glow against the dark green of sur-rounding rhododendrons, and the sweet fra-grance is a delight to the senses on a cold, crisp morning. Higan cherry continues its show, bloom-ing lavender-pink on sunny days through the cold-est months. And in earliest spring, *Rhododendron mucronulatum* produces flowers that range from rosy purple to white.

If your garden has moist conditions and acid soil, try planting a bed of assorted *Erica* (heath) and *Calluna* (heather). Their pink, lavender, and white flowers are set against fine, needlelike fo-liage that turns red or gold in winter.

Most of these winter-blooming shrubs have a pleasing fragrance as well. Sprigs of daphne, win-ter jasmine, or witch hazel—brought indoors and placed in water—will perfume a room nicely.

Mimicking Early Spring

Many plants can be stimulated to bloom early if you mimic the warmth of early spring. Situate your shrubs and perennials against south-facing walls or rocks that absorb the sun's heat and offer

Frost-Defying Hellebores

Members of the buttercup family, hellebores develop buds in late autumn and produce waxy, long-lasting flowers that enliven the garden from midwinter until early spring. The downward-facing blossoms sit on stems 15 to 20 inches tall, nodding over mounds of glossy gray-green leaves that remain evergreen to 10°F.

Named for the scent of its root—not its flower—*Helleborus foetidus* (stinking hellebore), shown at left set against spiky bram-ble canes, is but one of several attractive species: *H. niger* (Christ-mas rose), with shell pink cups and yellow stamens; *H. orientalis* (Lenten rose), which ranges from greenish white to green-stained purple; and *H. argutifolius* (Corsican hellebore), whose lime green flowers become canary yellow at their centers.

Hardy to Zones 3 and 4, hellebores need a moist, humus-rich soil and do best in partial shade with some protection. When divid-ing the plants in late summer, take care not to damage the brittle roots. In the fall, mulch with leaves and cover with evergreen boughs or an overturned fruit basket to keep off the worst of the ice and snow.

shelter from winter winds. Warmth and protection are crucial, because frost will damage blooms that arrive prematurely. This is a recurrent problem with the lovely star magnolia, whose delicately petaled blossoms will not survive even a moderate freeze, although the tree itself is hardy.

Autumn and Winter Bulbs

Bulbs can be wonderful transitional plants, taking the garden into fall and winter with brief but delightful bursts of color. Bulbs fall into two categories—tender and hardy. Tender bulbs cannot withstand hard frost and must be moved inside before temperatures turn frigid. Hardy bulbs are impervious to frost. Properly planted and then left to fend for themselves, they reappear year after year as if by magic, offering vivid hues against the warm tones of autumn and the browns and grays of the dormant season.

Fall-blooming bulbs begin to emerge when many perennials are still in flower and the colors that signal the changing season are just beginning. Because autumn bulbs come in a wide range of colors, it is easy to find a niche for them in the late-season garden.

Hardy fall bulbs are standards in beds and borders and also naturalize well. Lavender colchicums dotting a green lawn appear to glow from within. White *Crocus speciosus* 'Albus' poking out of a bed of variegated *Catharanthus* (periwinkle) will pick up the stripes in the surrounding foliage. And hardy cyclamen, with its pink, red, or white upswept flowers and mottled foliage, looks best nestled among fallen leaves at the base of a tree.

The foliage of these hardy bulbs emerges at unusual times. The tall, coarse leaves of fall crocuses and colchicums appear in spring and slowly die off before the blooms appear. Hardy cyclamen foliage begins to grow in the summer and remains even after the flowers have come and gone in the fall.

Of the tender bulbs, cannas are the most spectacular, with their greenish maroon leaves and huge flower trusses in shades of yellow, pink, orange, and red. Dahlias, in hues of yellow, apricot, orange, maroon, and scarlet, expand the palette, providing an enormous range from which to make pleasing combinations.

For a tropical note, try matching cannas with ornamental grasses. The 'Japanese Bishop' dahlia, with its scarlet flowers and rich black-green leaves, pairs beautifully with red-wine-colored *Berberis* 'Rosy Glow' (barberry) or purple-leaved *Cotinus coggygria* 'Purpurea' (smoke tree). Cannas, dahlias, and other tender fall bulbs, such as wavy-

petaled pink or red nerine and scented white-trumpeted *Amaryllis belladonna* (belladonna lily), must be brought inside to survive the winter. However, the tender *Lycoris radiata* (spider lily), with its feathery red blossoms, does not like to be moved and thus should be grown only in the South and on the West Coast.

Winter bulbs are available in a wide spectrum of colors, except brilliant red. The earliest to appear is *Galanthus* (snowdrop). It is followed closely by bright yellow winter aconites; blue, lavender, or yellow dwarf irises; crocuses in white, lavender, cream, yellow, burgundy, and purple; and *Chionodoxa* (glory-of-the-snow), with bright blue star-shaped flowers. Then, on the cusp of spring, come squills, with small bell-shaped flowers in blue,

Fragile species crocuses push through the protective ground cover of Juniperus x media 'Daub's Frosted' in the February sun. The chalice-shaped blooms are easily knocked over by snow and wind, but more buds and flowers emerge from each corm.

lavender, pink, and white, and early daffodils in varying tints of yellow.

In the colder zones, you can create contrasting combinations of brilliant yellow winter aconites with lavender crocuses or blue glory-of-the-snow, tempered by creamy snowdrops. Or you could combine early-blooming species of bulbous iris, such as the bright yellow *Iris danfordiae* or the blue or purple *Iris bakerana*, with snowdrops or cream to yellow *Narcissus cyclamineus*. In warmer climates (Zones 9 and 10), try interplanting snowdrops among *Cyclamen coum,* notable for its crimson-rose flowers and mottled, gray-green, heart-shaped leaves. In Zones 7 to 9, the giant snowdrop, a 10-inch version, makes a good match with cyclamen.

Daffodils generally bloom in early spring, but several miniature types can be counted on to appear in late winter. The hoop-petticoat narcissus *(Narcissus bulbocodium)* is a wild species with an oddly shaped, corolla-less gold flower. It is among several small varieties of daffodils that grow vigorously in moist conditions and full sun. They do well accompanied by winter heath or in a complementary blue-yellow color scheme with scillas and bluish white striped squills.

Designing for Impact

You can plant for a blaze of simultaneous bloom or choose species and varieties with staggered flowering times for a continuous show of color. Many gardeners plant large numbers of crocuses and snowdrops; both will naturalize easily in soil rich in humus, as will glory-of-the-snow.

Some people like a sprinkling of crocuses in a lawn; however, lawns often need their first cut before the crocus leaves have had time to absorb enough energy for the next season's growth. You

On the verge of opening their petals, bright yellow winter aconites pair with lavender species crocuses in this massed drift of miniature blossoms. Contrasting colors and shapes— the upright form of the crocuses against the frilled collars of the aconites—accentuate the pairing.

BULBS FOR FALL AND WINTER FLOWERS

		Amaryllis belladonna	Anemone blanda	Begonia grandis	Canna x generalis	Chionodoxa luciliae	Colchicum autumnale	Crocus goulimyi	Crocus tomasinianus	Cyclamen coum	Eranthis hyemalis	Galanthus nivalis	Ipheion uniflorum	Iris reticulata	Leucojum vernum	Lycoris squamigera	Narcissus bulbocodium	N. cyclamineus	Puschkinia scilloides	Ranunculus asiaticus	Scilla tubergeniana
SEASON	Fall	✔		✔	✔		✔	✔		✔											
	Winter		✔			✔			✔		✔	✔	✔	✔	✔		✔	✔	✔	✔	✔
COLOR	Purple						✔	✔	✔					✔							
	Blue		✔			✔			✔					✔					✔		✔
	White		✔		✔	✔	✔		✔			✔	✔		✔				✔		
	Yellow				✔						✔						✔	✔	✔		
	Pink/Red	✔	✔	✔	✔	✔	✔			✔						✔			✔		
HEIGHT	4" and Under								✔	✔	✔	✔		✔							✔
	5"-8"		✔			✔	✔	✔		✔			✔		✔		✔		✔		
	9" and Over	✔		✔	✔											✔		✔		✔	
LOCATION	Sun	✔	✔		✔	✔	✔	✔	✔		✔	✔	✔	✔	✔	✔	✔	✔	✔	✔	✔
	Part Shade		✔	✔			✔			✔	✔	✔	✔		✔	✔			✔		✔

may prefer to plant these bulbs amid perennials or ground covers that will conceal the foliage as it fades. Bugleweed, periwinkle, and English ivy are all good evergreen ground covers for this purpose. Their foliage also provides a good canvas for the bright flowers.

Treating Bulbs with Care

To encourage your bulbs to return year after year, give them a good start. Put them in the ground as soon as they arrive, so the roots will have time to develop before the ground freezes. The exceptions are the dahlias and cannas of autumn, which you should delay planting until mid-June to prevent them from blooming too early. Work in a little bone meal or 10-10-10 fertilizer, and add lime if your soil is acid; bulbs like alkaline conditions.

Dig individual holes for each bulb and place the growing end up; look for the remains of roots, then for the beginnings of growing points. If you are unsure about which end should go up, plant the bulb sideways; the growing tip will find its way. A rule of thumb is to bury a bulb three times as deep as its diameter: 6 to 12 inches for large bulbs such as daffodils, 2 to 3 inches for tiny crocuses. Space the bulbs according to size and how close together you want the blooms.

Once your colchicums, crocuses, and hardy cyclamens are in the ground, you can sit back and watch them expand their colonies year after year. Cannas, dahlias, and other tender bulbs are another matter, however. Immediately after the first frost, cut back the blackened foliage to 6 inches. Then, before a hard frost, carefully loosen the soil around the dahlia tubers or the canna rhizomes, and lift them out of the ground with a garden fork. Gently brush away the surplus soil and dry the plants for about 2 weeks, placing them upside down in a box of sand or peat moss to preserve the new growth around the old stems. Then store them in a cool, dry place away from drafts. Check through the winter for disease and shriveling. Shriveled tubers can be revived overnight in a bucket of water, then dried before being stored again.

Solutions for Clashing or Dominant Colors

Clashing combinations in the garden can result from the juxtaposition either of contrasting colors or of colors that, although they are closely related on the color wheel, are too strong and too saturated to work together comfortably. Such clashes can be tempered in many ways by the use of both flowers and foliage.

Moderating with Bicolored Flowers

The simplest and most direct way to moderate color clashes is to interplant a bicolored flower composed of the hues of the two competing groups. This repetition of color integrates the plantings so that they are seen as a unit rather than as individual drifts. Repeating such echoes throughout the border or bed strongly unifies the garden design.

A surprising number of bicolored flowers are available. Many have centers of contrasting or re-

lated hues; others have petals that are splashed, streaked, or rimmed with a second and even a third color. The daisylike flowers of *Gaillardia* x *grandiflora* (blanket-flower), for example, are red with yellow tips surrounding a dark brown eye. This combination makes them an ideal plant for bridging solid yellow and red flowers such as *Coreopsis lanceolata* and *Salvia splendens*.

To tone down a garden that is planted with an abundance of splashy primary colors such as yellow *Anthemis tinctoria* 'Beauty of Grallagh' (golden marguerite) and red *Pelargonium* x *hortorum* (common geranium), bridge them with *Potentilla* 'Red Robin' or *Paeonia* 'America'. Both of these selections produce red flowers with yellow centers.

Bicolored white flowers can not only bridge plants with combating hues but also temper an oversaturated color scheme. Examples include *Hemerocallis* 'Pandora's Box', a white daylily with a deep red-and-yellow center, and 'Golden Elegance', a white Oriental lily with yellow stripes and dark red flecks.

To bridge primary blues, plant yellow-centered Blackmore and Langdon Hybrids delphiniums or 'Russell Hybrids' lupines, which have a color range of blue, red, yellow, and apricot and are sometimes bicolored. Dependable low-growing annuals, such as pansy, *Nierembergia* (cupflower), and woodland forget-me-not, also offer pale and deep blues with yellow centers.

Sometimes the second color of a bicolored plant occurs in the stamen—as in certain daylilies, for example—or in the veins of its leaves, as in canna. Flowers such as *Penstemon digitalis* 'Huskers Red' (beardtongue) have stems of a contrasting color. In some plants, the second color does not appear until the seed heads or clusters of berries have ripened.

Linking Intense Colors

When strong colors predominate in the garden, you can link two potentially clashing hues with a middle color that has ingredients of both. This will help create a feeling of unity within groupings of sharply contrasting hues. Masses of such vivid flowers benefit when they are interplanted with masses of linking colors.

TIPS FROM THE PROS

An Outdoor Color Lab

A nursery bed, ordinarily used for raising young perennials until they are mature enough to flower and to set out in the garden, can also serve as a color laboratory. It is a wonderful place to translate color theory into practice through empirical observation.

The temporary nature of nursery-bed plantings makes it easy to combine and recombine all sorts of color matchups. You can obtain information, for example, about what colors can successfully moderate or bridge otherwise uncomfortable pairings.

Once you have created winning color combinations, the nursery bed gives you another

edge: By keeping a record of the bloom times of the perennials in the bed, you can make strategic decisions about which varieties to interplant with annuals and flowering shrubs to maintain your successful color arrangements throughout the growing season.

To create a nursery bed, prepare the soil of a sunny, out-of-the-way plot measuring about 10 feet by 10 feet. You can plant large numbers of flowers fairly close together in neat, geometric rows; since they are temporary plantings, they won't need room to expand, and you won't have to worry about placing them in aesthetically pleasing arrangements.

For example, when you plan a grouping of the strong primary colors, you can achieve greater harmony by separating each planting with a color midway between one strong hue and the other. Link yellow *Achillea* x 'Moonshine' and red *Monarda didyma* 'Gardenview Scarlet' (bee balm) with an orange *Calendula officinalis* (pot marigold), which contains both yellow and red. In turn, try linking bee balm and vivid *Agapanthus* 'Bressingham Blue' with violet *Salvia* x *superba* 'East Friesland', whose purple flowers contain both red and blue.

To add interest to small flowering trees that bear their blooms in long, pendulous clusters, such as *Wisteria sinensis* or *Laburnum* x *watereri* (golden-chain tree), underplant the trees with colors that hint at the hues of the overhanging flow-ers. A red-violet or lilac-blue wisteria, for example, could be underplanted with a progression of the more intense hues of blue-violet, violet, and red-violet found in ornamental onion, pansy, columbine, iris, and mountain pink. To enhance the deep yellow clusters of laburnum, choose under-plantings of orange, scarlet, and crimson, such as those found in gaillardia, *Potentilla* 'Gibson's Scarlet', daylily, pansy, and columbine.

When there is no obvious middle color, or when you do not desire one, you can use a neutral tone such as gray or light green. Pastels and creamy white can also mute the combativeness of strong colors. If you use pure white flowers, how-ever, you should plant them in small numbers so that they serve as accents; otherwise, they may create a sharp contrast.

Orange daylilies and scarlet Crocosmia 'Lucifer' are united by orange-yellow Kniphofia and the yellow throats of the daylilies in this Belle-vue, Washington, garden. Blue-violet salvia adds contrast.

In this garden near San Francisco, yellow-tipped threadleaf cypress and silver echeveria bridge the clashing red roses, bronze Cymbidium pumilum orchids, and fuchsia Spanish shawl.

Linking with Foliage

Foliage can provide another subtle bridge between clashing colors. When the blossoms of your perennials have faded, the surviving greenery can work as a link between strongly contrasting flower colors. Explore the possibility of planting perennials that leave a legacy of beautiful variegated leaves. Look for those that combine cooling tones of green with lemon, cream, or white, such as sweet iris, hosta, or *Polygonatum* (Solomon's-seal).

You can also grow *Perovskia atriplicifolia* (Russian sage), *Gypsophila* (baby's-breath), or *Stachys byzantina* (lamb's ears) to bridge plantings of stronger colors. Their clouds of pale blue or mauve flowers and their silvery gray foliage share the same pale intensities. After the flowers are gone, the foliage will act as a mediator.

Contrasting Foliage Textures

Foliage in the flower garden plays the important role of adding texture—in this case, variations in leaf surfaces—as well as color. Sometimes foliage textures, like flower colors, can clash. When this happens, the contrasting textures can be bridged with flowering plants whose foliage texture takes the middle ground between the two.

For example, matte purple and shiny purple foliage might not work well together when sharing one area of your garden. Although both *Perilla frutescens* and *Iresine herbstii* 'Brilliantissima' (beefsteak plant) have purplish foliage, the perilla's leaves are furrowed and deeply veined, while those of the beefsteak plant are shiny. To bridge the contrasting textures, you may want to introduce *Sedum maximum* 'Atropurpureum', which has compact clusters of starry flowers and fleshy

leaves in muted rose-purple tones. Other similar plantings of purple-red could also benefit from an accent of bright linked color—perhaps *Potentilla atrosanguinea* 'Gibson's Scarlet' or vibrant pink *Phlox paniculata* 'Starfire'.

When a cushion of the velvety soft, silvery gray-green leaves of *Stachys byzantina* 'Helene Von Stein' is growing near the crinkly, green-edged silver foliage of *Lamium maculatum* 'White Nancy' (dead nettle), the contrasting surface textures can be effectively bridged with a planting of *Achillea tomentosa*. Commonly known as woolly yarrow, *A. tomentosa* has fuzzy silver-gray foliage topped with small yellow flowers. To inject a dash of color into this planting arrangement, try including a vibrant pink *Dianthus* x *allwoodii,* a plant that forms dense mats of spiky gray foliage, or a deep blue flower on gray-silver foliage, such as *Lavandula angustifolia* 'Dwarf Blue'.

Tempering Colors with Foliage

Sometimes the relationship between the color of a plant's foliage and the color of its flowers works beautifully to cool a vibrant color. For instance, the soft silvery gray foliage of *Lychnis coronaria* (rose campion) is a perfect foil for its own intense magenta flowers. Silvery gray or silvery green

Deep lavender Clematis 'Will Goodwin' (above) coexists happily with yellow-and-scarlet trumpet honeysuckle, their differences eased by the surrounding leaves. At right, violet-colored Clematis texensis 'Ville de Lyon' intertwines with apricot-yellow 'Abraham Darby' roses against a foliage background.

leaves also work well with strong pinks, crimsons, blues, and violets. The velvety silver-gray foliage of *Stachys byzantina* blends effectively with pinks, blues, and violets.

Other plants with silver-green leaves and blue-violet flowers include common sage, catmint, and lavender, all of which provide a soothing background for flowers that have bright hues. When brilliant reds are teamed as accent plantings with subdued blue-greens and blue-grays, the reds appear more fiery and the bluish leaves more tranquil.

Yellow-green foliage is a better choice when separating a sequence of the warmer shades of the color wheel, such as intense yellows, oranges, and scarlets. A vivid yellow-green can also set off a

Spires of yellow-orange foxtail lily create a dramatic effect against deeply saturated blue delphinium (right). The potential clash of the strong hues is diffused by the surrounding white Shasta daisies.

Bright ribbons of white Chrysanthemum x superbum (Shasta daisy) prevent the muddying of dramatic color contrasts in this New Mexico garden of red bee balm, pink Polemonium caeruleum (Jacob's-ladder), lavender-blue delphinium, and brilliant yellow columbine.

planting of strong magenta beautifully. Good examples are yellow-green leaves of some of the hostas, such as *H.* 'Kabitan' and *H.* 'Sum and Substance', with their blooms of lavender and violet.

If you want a peaceful setting composed of flowers rather than background foliage, creamy whites are an excellent choice; when planted with vibrant colors, they integrate the bed rather than create separate pockets. For the front of the border, plant *Iberis sempervirens* 'Snowflake' (candytuft), mountain pink, *Geranium sanguineum* 'Album', *Geranium* x *cantabrigiense* 'Biokovo' (a white cranesbill that is washed with palest pink), and *Arabis sturii* (rock cress).

For midsize to taller plantings, consider peonies, daylilies, lilies, garden phlox, the hybrid shrub rose 'Sea Foam', and *Gardenia jasminoides* 'August Beauty'. For a combination of creamy white blooms and yellow-green leaves, *Yucca filamentosa* 'Goldsword' is hard to beat for the back of the border.

An exceptional perennial that blooms nonstop and adds height and long, drooping flower heads that mingle with midheight plantings is the shrub *Buddleia davidii* 'White Profusion', with its sil-

very green leaves. Other small shrubs that have cream or white flowers include *Spiraea japonica* 'Albiflora' (Japanese white spirea) and *Weigela florida* 'Bristol Snowflake', which also offer light green foliage.

Gray Leaves and Pastel Flowers

Corals and oranges planted together will benefit from the tempering values of soft silver or gray-green leaves. They can also be linked with tints of orange, such as salmon or pastel apricot. When stands of the striking 3- to 5-foot-tall *Kniphofia* (torch lily)—with its long, dense spikes of tubular, deep yellow and red-orange flowers—are paired with deep orange daylilies or brilliant yellow *Asclepias tuberosa* (butterfly weed), salmon and apricot yarrows add a harmonious pastel component. An underplanting of silver foaming baby's-

breath and fluffy gray wormwood is a fine counterpoint of foliage texture and color.

From late summer into late fall, some gardens are drenched in lipstick shades of rose-pink, deep pink, red-violet, and violet. For example, there are the thick spires of violet-pink *Physostegia virginiana* (false dragonhead), profuse deep pink blooms of 'Carefree Wonder' roses, and 4- to 6-foot-tall New York aster cultivars in varying tones of violet. These rose-purples blend well with a backdrop of the tall green leaves and silvery white plumes of flowering ornamental grasses, such as the 5- to 6-foot-tall *Cortaderia selloana* 'Pumila' (pampas grass), and an underplanting of the silver-gray velvety mounds of lamb's ears.

Using Form to Marry Colors

A flower's form can also help alleviate the clash of warring colors. This is evident when you scatter a

Brightly colored pink and carmine-rose dianthus in a Baton Rouge yard (above) combine nicely with purple, yellow, and lavender varieties of Viola x wittrockiana (pansy) because they all share similarly round-shaped flower heads.

Mellowing Out with Magenta

Gardeners either love magenta or they hate it. True magenta—like the 'James Walker' bougainvillea, below—is fairly rare among flowers, but many tints and shades are available, and their misuse in gardens has perhaps contributed to giving the color a bad name.

Magenta is not the least bit unruly when teamed with its own tones or with lavender, blue-violet, or blue tones. Planted in small drifts with gray or silver foliage, or surrounded with pearly white flowers, it brightens without blinding. Placed in front of a dark green hedge, it stands out; combined with gold, gold-and-green, or yellow-green leaves, it is striking.

If you would like magenta in your garden for several months, choose annuals such as petunia, *Portulaca* (moss rose), *Celosia* (cockscomb), or common geranium. Few perennial magentas can be found, and these bloom only briefly. Look instead for flowering shrubs such as azalea, bougainvillea, and *Rosa rugosa* 'Rubra'.

packet of zinnia seeds for annual display: They bloom in a riot of colors that don't look garish because the flowers all have the same shape. The daisylike blossoms of the Compositae family—*Echinacea purpurea* (purple coneflower), rudbeckia, chrysanthemum, helianthus, aster, and coreopsis—are other examples of contrasting colors mediated by their similarly shaped blooms.

The same principle applies to mass plantings of impatiens, where pale pink comfortably rubs elbows with salmon, and mauve with scarlet. You can get even greater variation with a planting of *Petunia* 'Celebrity Mixed', whose blooms come in almost every color of the rainbow.

When different plant types share both form and color, combining them sometimes creates a breathtaking display. A stunning example of such a pairing is *Magnolia* x *soulangiana* 'Ann Rosse' underplanted with plum-red 'First Lady' tulips. The flowers of both are upright and cup shaped, and the magnolia's rose-pink glows in concert with the plum color of the tulips.

Taming Dominant Colors

Although some of the loveliest flowers in the world have strong, rich color, many gardeners are wary of them, and for good reason. Brilliantly colored flowers can create a strident note in a bed or border. Hot, brassy hues of yellow, scarlet, and orange shout for attention; violet and magenta can be powerfully contentious and difficult to fit in. Yet a planting can be truly spectacular when such eye-catching colors are skillfully introduced. They stimulate the senses and invite the eye to focus and linger.

One way to handle dominant colors is to isolate them in a separate bed where their brilliance will not overshadow more subdued colors. But if you lack the space to do this, try planting them in partial shade (if they can prosper under these conditions), which will help reduce their impact. When bathed by shadows, these colors are often transformed from strong and garish to luminous and lovely.

You might also place your bold hues in a plot that is sited mainly for viewing either early or late in the day. The flowers will not be as overwhelming when seen in early-morning light or in the setting sun. The same principle holds true for the light of early spring or the waning light of fall. Flowers that might clash terribly in the unforgiving light of the summer sun will appear more subdued in pale spring light or in the soft glow cast by the sun as it travels lower on the horizon in the fall. A bed of tulips dressed in flaming orange, carmine, scarlet, and bright yellow, for example, will be a welcome—and well-behaved—burst of warmth in the cool light of spring.

Fighting Fire with Fire

A surprisingly effective way to tone down a bed of brilliant hues is to add a splash of a clashing color. For example, when intense magenta and purple or blue-violet are growing in jangling proximity to each other, a dash of orange will have the paradoxical effect of subduing them. The accent of orange flowers catches the eye first and helps to soften the impact of the larger and more powerful color combination.

Orange is the warmest hue on the color wheel. When used with other warm colors such as flame red, bronze, and deep red, it makes a harmonious, if bold, combination. You can achieve a less obtrusive effect by pairing it with its opposite on the wheel, true blue, or with a split complementary such as blue-green or blue-violet. For a striking combination, team orange lilies or daylilies with the vibrantly rich blue-violet spikes of *Salvia farinacea* 'Victoria'.

Bold colors can also be successfully joined in triads. For example, you may want to consider combining yellow-orange *Kniphofia* 'Ada' with lime-colored *Euphorbia characias* ssp. *wulfenii* (Mediterranean euphorbia) and magenta *Callirhoe involucrata* (poppy mallow) or *Liatris pycnostachya* (Kansas gay-feather).

If a pairing like orange and scarlet seems too gaudy, consider yellow and scarlet. You can produce this rich combination with Oriental poppy or crocosmia planted next to bright yellow coreopsis or *Rudbeckia hirta* 'Marmalade'. Add a backdrop of dark blue delphinium and throw in a few velvet heads of purple bearded iris, and you have a winning arrangement of strongly contrasting but compatible colors.

Of course, an uncomplicated, low-key way to tame vividly colored plants is to simply plant fewer of them. Used merely as an accent in the bed, they will not overwhelm the eye.

Scarlet Indian paintbrush, pink fireweed, and blue lupine, interplanted as accents in a Colorado garden (right), add excitement without the discord such colors can create when they are grown together in sweeping drifts.

CHAPTER THREE

Tough Plants for Tough Places

Selecting the right plants for your garden's conditions makes good sense, but it's especially important if the site is problematic. Hardscapes that reflect heat and light, low-lying spots with poor drainage, or narrow, densely shaded lots, for instance, all require plants that can withstand less-than-ideal conditions. Climatic extremes, such as intense heat or scant rainfall, also call for tough plants.

For the arid Phoenix garden at left, for example, the owners chose wildflowers that flourish in light clay soil. Purple-blooming Lupinus sparsiflorus (Coulter's lupine) mingles happily in this dry site with its native plant partners—pink-spired penstemon, Mexican gold poppy, and brittlebush.

In this chapter you will learn about some of the plants that can survive—and even thrive—in difficult sites and under difficult conditions. In addition, you'll learn how to use these stalwarts so that their natural beauty can be enjoyed to the fullest.

Planting Near Hardscapes

Paved driveways, brick paths, stone terraces, concrete walls, and other hard or rocky surfaces, known collectively as hardscapes, pose special challenges for plants growing close to them. For one thing, they absorb and radiate heat: On a sunny summer day a blacktopped driveway or stuccoed wall can significantly raise the temperature in the immediate area, so anything planted nearby must be reliably heat tolerant. Also, soil that is close to buildings or pavement may contain high levels of minerals deposited by water that has washed over these surfaces. And driveways are sources of chemical pollution in the form of oily runoff and vehicle exhaust fumes.

Fortunately, there are many heat-loving, poor-soil-tolerant plants that flourish unfazed in these locales. In addition, the microclimates created by hardscapes often enable you to grow more kinds of plants than would otherwise be possible under the normal conditions of your property. The warm environment created by a stone patio with a southern exposure, for example, might allow tender annuals to do well in a region where summers are short and cool.

Choosing the Right Plants

When planning any garden, you'll get the best results if you consider the conditions of the site and choose plants that are best suited to them. This is especially true of hardscape locations, which may be dramatically affected by patterns of light and shade, heat, and traffic. Start by noting how many hours of sunlight the site receives. Be aware that the amount may vary widely from one spot to the next; vertical hardscapes such as walls and buildings can block light, forming pools of shade in the midst of sun. Bear in mind, too, that the heat given off by pavement or other hardscape surfaces will cause the surrounding soil to dry out faster than normal. In addition, walls can keep rainfall from reaching the ground adjacent to

Sweet alyssum, purple pansies, silver dusty-miller, and white geraniums fill the beds of this California garden in the spring. The alyssum guards the pansies from contact with heat-retaining gravel and also softens the straight lines and sharp corners created by the bricks. Pink geraniums make a grand focal point in the stone planter.

Plants for
Hardscapes

UPRIGHT

Abelmoschus spp.
(abelmoschus)
Ageratum houstonianum
(flossflower)
Antirrhinum majus
(snapdragon)
Arctotis stoechadifolia
(African daisy)
***Begonia* x *semperflorens-
cultorum*** (wax begonia)
Calendula officinalis
(pot marigold)
Canna* x *generalis
(canna lily)
Catharanthus roseus
(Madagascar periwinkle)
Cosmos spp.
(cosmos)
Dimorphotheca spp.
(Cape marigold)
Foeniculum vulgare
(fennel)
Gazania spp.
(gazania)
Kochia scoparia
(burning bush)
Ocimum basilicum
(basil)
Salvia spp.
(sage)
Senecio cineraria
(dusty-miller)
Tagetes spp.
(marigold)
Zinnia spp.
(zinnia)

SPRAWLING

Brachycome iberidifolia
(Swan River daisy)
Browallia speciosa
(browallia)
Celosia cristata
(celosia)
Dyssodia tenuiloba
(Dahlberg daisy)
Gaillardia pulchella
(Indian blanket)
Gypsophila elegans
(baby's-breath)
Impatiens spp.
(impatiens)
Lobelia erinus
(lobelia)
Lobularia maritima
(sweet alyssum)
Pelargonium peltatum
(ivy-leaved geranium)
Petunia* x *hybrida
(petunia)
Portulaca grandiflora
(moss rose)
Tropaeolum spp.
(nasturtium)
Verbena spp.
(verbena)

*Note: The abbreviation "spp."
stands for the plural of "species";
where used in lists it means that
many, but not all, of the species
in a genus meet the criterion of
the list.*

them. Plan on watering plants in these areas more often, and for added insurance, use plants that are especially drought resistant. A thick layer of mulch will also help keep the soil cool and moist.

Finally, consider the size of walkways and driveways and how they are used. Broad paths and lightly used hardscapes can accommodate plants that sprawl over their borders. On the other hand, narrow, heavily traveled hardscapes—the paths to back or side doors, for instance—are best edged with upright plants that won't spill onto the walkway and get trampled. Varieties of *Tagetes* (marigold), *Begonia* (wax begonia), and *Senecio* (dusty-miller) are just a few candidates for tight situations. The list at right features both upright and sprawling plants that do well under the hot, dry conditions often found in hardscape locations.

Dressing Up Hardscapes with Annuals

Bare hardscapes seem to cry out for the beauty and vitality annuals can bring. Grow the plants in beds and borders along patios, terraces, and decks. If space is narrow, try planting a mixed-color variety of a bushy annual that will grow 8 to 12 inches tall, such as *Salvia splendens* (sage) or *Zinnia elegans*

Undaunted by a sultry Virginia summer, the purple blooms of verbena overflow their raised planter. The dry heat produced by the bricks enclosing the bed is increased by a brick sidewalk beneath. But with regular watering, the verbena—descended from plants native to the Americas—is thriving.

(common zinnia). If you have room for a wide swath of color, place low-growing, compact plants, such as *Gazania* species and *Ageratum houstonianum* (flossflower), along the edges of the hardscape and larger accent plants—*Zinnia angustifolia* (narrowleaf zinnia) or *Kochia scoparia* (burning bush), for example—behind them.

You need not restrict the beauty to the perimeter of your hardscape. For a weed-inhibiting carpet of blossoms in the midst of a sunny patio where foot traffic is light, plant *Portulaca grandiflora* (moss rose) and *Lobularia maritima* (sweet alyssum) between the pavers. Just remove any grass or weeds, then fill the spaces with a fast-draining soil that contains 1 part builder's sand for every 2 parts topsoil. Sow seeds in the soil or set out seedlings, and water lightly.

On sloping terrain alongside a flight of stone or concrete steps, plant annuals that are naturally sprawling; they will drape gracefully on the incline, unlike upright species, which tend to lean uphill or downhill in their efforts to resist gravity. Raised flower beds with sides of brick or other stonework are also pretty when dressed with these trailing plants to soften their edges.

If a wall runs beside your driveway, patio, or walkway, with a narrow strip of land separating the two hard surfaces, try planting *Cobaea scandens* (cup-and-saucer vine) or *Ipomoea* species (morning glory) along the wall's base. These robust climbers should form lush upper growth in a short period of time. (See pages 44-48 for information on planting and using vines.)

In your search for hardscape plants, don't overlook herbs. Many, such as basil and sweet marjoram, like the hot, dry microclimate furnished by sunny hardscapes.

Rock Gardens

Like other hardscapes, a rock garden creates a special microclimate, since its stones absorb heat and block precipitation and wind. Rocks also help maintain moisture in the soil by shading it from the sun—and by returning water to the soil at night as humidity condenses on their cool surfaces and seeps into the ground. For these reasons, rock gardens often require little maintenance if the plants are well chosen.

In general, the most appealing rock gardens include a combination of small, mounded plants and sprawlers that can be trained over the edges of the rocks, brightening the surfaces with their flowers and foliage. Petite flowering annuals are well suited to the task because their small roots adapt to the confined spaces between stones and to the shallow soil on rocky outcrops. Also, they are ideal for providing color and interest in the hot season, when many perennials fade.

Spreading *Phlox drummondii* (annual phlox), brightly colored *Brachycome iberidifolia* (Swan River daisy), and dwarf varieties of *Cheiranthus cheiri* (English wallflower) are just a few annuals that thrive in sunny rock gardens. If your site is partially shaded, try snapdragon-like *Collinsia heterophylla* (Chinese houses) or delicate *Exacum*

Nestled between pavers on a southern Pennsylvania patio, Portulaca grandiflora (moss rose) self-sows from year to year. Blooms stay open through the day, providing maximum beauty in a cheerful mix of bright colors. Hugging the ground at heights of about 6 inches, the flowers tend to attract bees, so barefooted visitors should beware.

affine (German violet). The lee side of a partially shaded rock may be moist and chilly enough to let cool-loving *Iberis* species (candytuft) and *Nemophila menziesii* (baby-blue-eyes) bloom all summer long.

If you have a naturally rocky area on your property, try planting it with annual wildflowers that are native to your locale or to regions with comparable climates. Natives often self-sow, and they also blend well with other aspects of the landscape where they evolved. Talk to your local Cooperative Extension Service or check catalogs that sell seeds and young plants specifically for your region to find the right annual wildflowers for your rock garden.

To plant rock-garden annuals, create pockets of well-drained soil, using 2 parts topsoil to 1 part builder's sand. If the site is partially shaded and you're installing plants that prefer fertile soil, add 1 part compost or leaf mold and 1 part peat moss to the mix as well. Either sow seeds or transplant seedlings into the spaces. Once the seedlings are a few inches high, spread a mulch of shredded bark around them to keep the soil cool and moist.

Heat-loving annuals add a soft touch to the stone surfaces in a walled garden niche in Connecticut (above). Red-violet Petunia integrifolia surrounds the base of the center sculpture, while tall white Nicotiana alata, which self-sows from year to year, brightens the entire space.

Petite yellow Dahlberg daisies, open-faced Gaillardia aristata 'Burgundy', spiky Salvia coccinea 'Lady in Red', and orange California poppies flourish through the summer in the rocky Missouri garden at left. The limestone chunks bordering the raised bed prevent rainwater from draining through the soil too quickly.

Naturalized Bulb Plantings for Difficult Areas

A planting of Spanish bluebells in a grove of rhododendrons makes a spectacular display in early spring. The dappled light filtering through the trees adds to the charm of this simple, naturalized woodland garden.

Naturalized bulb plantings are well suited to spots that are difficult to cultivate, such as areas of dry shade under trees, hard-to-mow banks, or spots that are rocky or wet. Most woodland bulbs that naturalize well don't require full sun, flourishing instead in the pale sunlight of early spring and the dappled shade of the summer woods. Many other bulbs can be naturalized in a meadow or grassy area. But, of course, because it is necessary to leave the bulb foliage in place after flowering, plantings in meadows and lawns must be left unmowed for a time.

One of the charms of naturalized bulb plantings is the reward they bring you in return for very little effort. You need only make sure the ground is well fertilized at the time of planting, especially for woodland bulbs, which must compete with shrubs and trees for water and nutrients. After the initial work is done, these bulbs can be left alone.

Species bulbs are the best candidates for naturalizing because they spread by seed or underground by natural division, forming new plants year after year. However, some hybrid bulbs—daffodils, for example—do not self-seed. Though technically perennial, hybrid bulbs generally do not grow beyond the original clump and can only be spread by lifting and division.

To be effective, a naturalized bulb planting should be compatible with the existing environment. When making plans for such a planting, study the landscape to determine its natural contours. Imagine water flowing across the area: This

is how seeds might naturally be carried. Think of the way seeds tend to collect in pockets, such as among roots at the base of a tree. If you are planting on an embankment, consider what the undersides of various plants look like, since these will be visible from the foot of the slope. In a meadow, imagine how the natural undulation of the ground will cause plants to spread or bunch.

Bulbs in a Woodland Setting

Woodland plantings must be carried out on a fairly grand scale, or the result will look skimpy. Use trees and shrubs as the backbone of the landscape, then put in enough of a given bulb to make a visible impact. Small woodland bulbs such as scilla, glory-of-the-snow, or snowdrops, for example, must be laid down in quantities of around 100 or more bulbs per planting in order to make an effective display.

Naturalized plantings look better if different bulb varieties are not mixed. If you are planting two different species of daffodils, for example, keep them in separate clumps and blend them gently, feathering the two into each other where the edges of the plantings touch. In a meadow, create broad swaths of single types of bulbs in simple curved or spiral shapes. Remember that there are few straight lines in nature.

Naturalizing in Early Spring

Among the first spring bloomers—appearing in late winter—are snowdrops and winter aconites. Spring snowflakes, similar to snowdrops but with smaller bell-shaped flowers, bloom a few weeks later and spread freely.

Many varieties of hardy cyclamen bloom in springtime. Cyclamen is one of the few bulbs that grow well beneath evergreen trees, and its delicate appearance belies its vigorous self-seeding habit. Spring-blooming *Cyclamen hederifolium* is the most free-flowering species. It does well in woodlands, preferring moist, well-drained soil.

Crocuses are good candidates for naturalizing on a lawn. If you postpone the first spring mowing for a short while, they will be able to store enough nutrients and moisture to meet their needs for the next year's growth before their foliage is cut down. *Crocus tomasinianus*, which spreads by seed and by cormels, multiplies easily in a naturalized setting. And unlike other *Crocus* species, it is unappealing as a food for animal pests such as squirrels and voles.

Another spring bloomer is *Scilla siberica*, whose drooping, bright blue flowers look good under shrubs and with other bulbs, such as early daffodil cultivars. *Chionodoxa* (glory-of-the-snow) is another early blue-flowered bulb. It needs to be planted in quantity in order to make a good show initially, but it soon spreads readily. *Anemone nemorosa*, an early bloomer with pretty, fernlike foliage, produces 1-inch white flowers faintly tinged with pink.

Midspring Naturalizers

Among the next wave of spring bloomers is *Hyacinthoides non-scripta*. This blue-flowered bulb

Protecting Endangered Wild Bulbs

The destruction of habitats around the world, combined with the removal of bulbs from the wild by unscrupulous plant collectors, now threatens bulbs that were once abundant in nature—such as the trout lily above—with extinction. In an effort to reduce such depredations, an international trade convention limits the export of galanthus, cyclamen, and sternbergia bulbs from their countries of origin. You can help prevent the loss of wild bulbs by purchasing only those labeled "nursery propagated." And remember: Never dig up plants from the wild.

prefers light shade during bloom time and makes a beautiful display in wooded areas. It grows 18 to 20 inches tall and spreads rapidly by seed and bulb division. Summer snowflake, another midspring bloomer, naturalizes easily in moist areas. This bulb resembles spring snowflake but has larger flowers and grows to 18 inches tall.

Daffodils, which usually require full sun, nevertheless have a long tradition of being naturalized in woodland settings. Where the trees are deciduous, enough sun filters through bare branches to reach the foliage in the spring. By the time the trees have leafed out, blocking sun and moisture, the bulbs have become dormant.

Good candidates for wooded sites include the small cyclamineus daffodils—for example, early-blooming 'February Gold' and 'Jetfire', which blooms later in spring. South of Zone 9, paperwhites multiply in shady woodland. In Zones 3 to 6, most trumpet, large-cupped, and double daffodils do well in a naturalized setting.

Another traditional use for daffodils is to plant them in orchards or unmowed meadows, where the foliage can remain undisturbed. As with other bulbs of the amaryllis family, the foliage is toxic, so animals such as deer, voles, and squirrels who might be attracted by fruit trees or other plants will avoid the daffodils.

Tulips tend to be thought of as bulbs for beds and borders. However, some growers are developing hybrid tulips that perennialize successfully in areas similar to the tulip's native habitat in Asia and the eastern Mediterranean. In the United States, this means roughly Zones 6 to 8, where the summers are dry and the soil drains well. Try the Darwin hybrids 'Golden Apeldorn' or 'Jewel of Spring', or the lily-flowering tulip 'West Point'. In American prairie lands of the Dakotas and eastern Colorado, species tulips such as *Tulipa tarda, T.*

Interplanting Bulbs with Ground Covers

Mingling your bulbs with ground covers produces year-round benefits. First, when the bulbs are in flower, a ground cover offers contrasting color, texture, and form. An example is *Crocus vernus* above, emerging through *Cyclamen hederifolium*. Later, the ground cover hides the ripening bulb foliage. Finally, during the bulbs' dormancy, it serves as a living mulch, protecting the soil from erosion and temperature changes that can heave bulbs out of the soil.

Ground Covers

SHADE OR WOODLAND

Alchemilla
(lady's-mantle)
Ceratostigma plumbaginoides
(leadwort)
Galium odoratum
(sweet woodruff)
Hedera
(ivy)
Lamium
(dead nettle)

Pachysandra
(pachysandra)
Phlox divaricata
(wild sweet William)
Primula x polyantha
(polyanthus primrose)
Vinca minor
(periwinkle)

SUNNY SPOTS

Arabis
(rock cress)
Cerastium

(snow-in-summer)
Euonymus
(winter creeper)
Helianthemum
(sun rose)
Iberis
(candytuft)
Mazus
(mazus)
Phlox subulata
(moss pink)
Sedum
(stonecrop)

humilis, and *T. linifolia* can be planted in meadows and left to spread.

Summer and Fall Bloomers

A good summertime naturalizer is *Allium cernuum*, a member of the ornamental onion family that is native to the Allegheny Mountains and other parts of the eastern United States. It has light pink flowers and grows from 8 to 18 inches tall. This bulb also does well in rock gardens.

Two members of the lily family—*Lilium canadense* and *L. superbum*—are native to North America and naturalize well here. *L. canadense* grows wild, usually in shady areas, from Nova Scotia to Alabama, and produces yellow flowers dotted with red. It can reach a height of 6 feet. *L. superbum* has orange flowers with deep maroon centers. It, too, can tolerate some shade; plants may grow to 5 feet. Both *L. canadense* and *L. superbum* can be naturalized in a wet meadow or along the edge of a woodland.

Autumn-flowering bulbs such as crocuses and *Cyclamen hederifolium* tend to be small, modest bloomers that need to be planted in large groups to make a good show. Of the several species cro-cuses that bloom in autumn, the blue-flowered *C. speciosus* is one of the easiest to grow. This crocus blooms in early fall and spreads rapidly by seed and natural division. It can be naturalized in lawns and grassy areas, where it soon runs rampant.

Colchicum autumnale is so eager to bloom that it will flower without even being planted, so put these bulbs in the ground as soon as possible. The pink, lilac, or white blooms appear on leafless stems; the foliage that grows in early spring begins to die down in summer and must be left undisturbed over the winter. *Colchicum* seeds are spread by ants, which are attracted to the seeds' sweet coating. The plants prefer sun and will form good-size clumps.

Native North American Bulbs

Native North American bulbs are well suited to the home garden, where they thrive in conditions that approximate those of their natural environment. The Pacific Northwest native *Camassia quamash,* shown here blooming alongside red sorrel in an Oregon meadow, bears blue or white flowers and thrives in wet meadows and near streams. This plant was once used as a food source by native Americans, who cooked the bulbs.

Although not as large or showy as their hybridized foreign cousins, many North American woodland bulbs make charming contributions to naturalized plantings. Bulbs such as *Arisaema triphyllum* (jack-in-the-pulpit), *Dicentra cucullaria* (Dutchman's-breeches), *Erythronium americanum* (trout lily), and *Sanguinaria canadensis* (bloodroot) have an intrinsic beauty that, paradoxically, can seem exotic when compared with the more familiar tulips, daffodils, and hyacinths.

Claytonia virginica (spring-beauty), with its narrow, spoon-shaped leaves and small pink flowers, seems delicate, but it has a robust habit and spreads quickly in woodlands and open thickets. *Uvularia* (great merrybells) and *Polygonatum* (Solomon's-seal) are also easy to grow in the home garden.

Annuals are ideal for growing in climates of all sorts. Whether you live in an area where summers are hot, winters are harsh, or rainfall is scarce, there are annuals that fill the bill. If you choose those species that are well suited to your geographic region, you'll be well on your way to cultivating a top-performing garden of flowers.

Warm- and Cool-Season Annuals

In regions where summer afternoons are hot and the temperature never dips below 65° F at night, choose tender annuals and tender perennials for your garden. While other plants may languish and even die under such difficult conditions, these warm-season flowers—impatiens, Madagascar peri-

winkles, Dahlberg daisies, and creeping zinnias, to name a few—will flourish.

In addition to atmospheric temperatures, soil temperatures also affect the vigor of warm-season annuals. Rarely will these plants mature in soils that are cooler than 70° F. Some annuals, such as impatiens, will be stunted if planted too early. Keep in mind, though, that it is warm temperatures rather than direct sun that prompts these plants to do their best. Impatiens, for example, are happiest in partial shade.

Before installing warm-season annuals, check your soil to make sure it has warmed sufficiently. You can do this with an inexpensive thermometer such as the kind used in fishtanks. Simply insert the thermometer gently into damp—but not wet—soil about 6 inches deep and read the results a minute or so later. You may want to take read-

White-eyed purple lobelia and a frothy swath of pink-tinted Lobularia maritima (sweet alyssum) border this rock-garden path in Montana. Most at home in cool climates and full sun, these annuals make excellent edging plants.

Purple and scarlet salvia blooms, yellow-orange marigolds, and white Cleome hasslerana endure Georgia's heat and humidity with flair in a shaded enclave between a house and a vine-covered trellis. Around the corner, other annuals, including red cosmos, bloom unfazed by the sun's full force.

ings from different parts of your site to be sure the entire area is ready for planting.

If the area where you live experiences comfortable daytime temperatures that stay between 60° and 80° F, cool-season annuals will do well in your garden. These plants, many of which are listed at right, need moderate temperatures if they are to grow and flower to their full potential; they will quickly lose their vitality if subjected to the full force of summer heat and humidity.

Pot marigolds, fragrant *Reseda odorata* (mignonette), and *Nemesia strumosa* (pouch nemesia), with its funnel-shaped blooms, all thrive in regions that experience a long, cool growing season like that of the coastal Northwest. Alternatively, in areas with a fairly traditional change of seasons—including the mid-Atlantic and lower midwestern

regions—tough and hardy cool-season plants such as pansies and ornamental cabbage can provide attractive displays that extend into winter and may even last until spring. Biennials such as *Myosotis sylvatica* (forget-me-not) and *Lunaria annua* (honesty) are cool-season plants that do beautifully when planted in the garden in fall. You can enjoy their leafy rosettes at the end of the season and, in late spring of the following year, their pretty blooms.

Regional Considerations

In northern and high-elevation areas where winters are long and cold—Nova Scotia and Maine, the northern plains, the Adirondacks, the Rockies, and the Yukon, for example—the growing season is short. To compensate for this shortened growing period, you can get a step up by starting most of your flowers indoors at least 6 to 8 weeks before the last frost date. In addition, consider choosing flower varieties that take less than 90 days to reach maturity and bloom, such as snapdragons, Swan

Cool-Season Annuals

Adonis aestivalis
(pheasant's-eye)
Agrostemma githago
(corn cockle)
Ammi majus
(bishop's flower)
Brachycome iberidifolia
(Swan River daisy)
Brassica oleracea
(ornamental cabbage)
Calendula officinalis
(pot marigold)
Callistephus chinensis
(China aster)
Campanula medium
(Canterbury bells)
Carthamus tinctorius
(safflower)
Centaurea cyanus
(bachelor's-button)
Cheiranthus cheiri
(English wallflower)
***Chrysanthemum* spp.**
(chrysanthemum)
Cirsium japonicum
(rose thistle)
***Clarkia* spp.**
(clarkia, godetia)
Consolida ambigua
(larkspur)
Crepis rubra
(hawksbeard)
Cynoglossum amabile
(hound's-tongue,
Chinese forget-me-not)
Dyssodia tenuiloba
(Dahlberg daisy)
Lathyrus odoratus
(sweet pea)
Linaria maroccana
(Moroccan toadflax)
Nemophila menziesii
(baby-blue-eyes)
Nigella damascena
(love-in-a-mist)
Papaver rhoeas
(corn poppy)
Papaver somniferum
(opium poppy)
Reseda odorata
(mignonette)
Salpiglossis sinuata
(painted tongue)
Schizanthus pinnatus
(butterfly flower)
Silybum marianum
(blessed thistle)
Tropaeolum peregrinum
(canary creeper)
Viola* x *wittrockiana
(common pansy)
Xeranthemum annuum
(everlasting)

Note: The abbreviation "spp." stands for the plural of "species"; where used in lists it means that many, but not all, of the species in a genus meet the criterion of the list.

The hot days and cool nights of Phoenix, Arizona, are easily tolerated by true blue Phacelia campanularia (California bluebell) and contrasting Lesquerella gordonii (yellow blanket), both Southwest natives.

River daisies, and *Lupinus texensis* (Texas blue-bonnet). To be safe, you might want to use devices such as cold frames or row covers to keep late frosts from killing your new seedlings and transplants. Although the season begins late in the North, your flowers will make up the time by taking advantage of the long hours of daylight during summer. Transplant and direct-seed as soon as conditions will allow.

Another way to jump-start the season is by gardening in raised beds, which warm up faster and maintain their heat more efficiently than in-ground beds. Raised beds for annuals only need to be 8 inches deep to accommodate the plants' roots. The easiest are simply unframed mounds of soil in a well-chosen sunny site. Or you can construct a frame with bricks, landscaping timbers, or rocks, which can absorb sunlight and radiate even more heat to your plants. Combine 3 parts topsoil with 1 part compost or other organic matter and 1 part builder's sand to fill the bed, and allow it to settle for 2 to 3 weeks before planting.

At the other extreme, along the Gulf Coast and in southern California, freezing temperatures are rare, allowing gardeners to enjoy a full range of annuals all year long. In these semitropical areas, you can plant in cycles so that you get several new crops of blooms throughout the year. Just be sure to plant any cool-season annuals during periods of mild winter temperatures and use warm-season flowers at all other times.

In semitropical regions such as these, certain plants, including fuchsia and New Guinea impatiens, can be treated as perennials. These are tender perennials, which are often short-lived even in mild climates because of their uncomplicated root systems. Nevertheless, they may perform for 2 or 3 years; cut them back to within 2 to 3 inches of the base of the plant at the end of the growing season to keep them looking full and healthy.

Hot summers come in two extremes: the humid type of the Deep South and the Atlantic seaboard, and the dry kind experienced by the Southwest and the central regions—Nebraska and

Idaho, for example. In very hot, humid areas, your flower beds are likely to perform at their best if you site them where they receive only morning sun, since many hours of direct rays can wither even the most ardent sun lovers. If the area you have in mind gets sun all day, consider building a fence or trellis to provide shade during the afternoon hours. Finally, and most important, choose annuals that can tolerate heat *(list, right)*.

Because even humid regions sometimes experience periods of drought that can last several weeks, you'll want to protect your soil with an organic mulch. Spread a 2- to 4-inch layer over the bed, keeping the material a couple of inches away from the stems of your seedlings or transplants, since mulch on the plant tissue encourages fungal and root diseases. If you plant seeds directly into the ground, wait until your seedlings are at least 3 to 4 inches high before mulching.

To grow annuals successfully in hot, dry climates, you'll need to prepare the soil carefully. Add extra organic matter to help the soil retain moisture and provide nutrients, incorporating at least 3 inches of compost, leaf mold, or other ma-

terial into 8 to 10 inches of unamended topsoil. Then space your annuals closer together than you would in other climates so that the plants' foliage can shade the soil. If you're direct-seeding, do it as early in the season as possible so that your plants will be well established before the stressful hot temperatures arrive.

An organic mulch is extremely important in helping to keep the soil cool and moist. Because annuals have small root systems that can't burrow deep down for water, they'll need careful monitoring—especially when they are newly emerging seedlings or recent transplants. Annuals, particularly those grown in containers, quickly show signs of heat and water stress. However, you can minimize your watering tasks by selecting annuals that are both heat and drought tolerant *(list, right)*.

Rudbeckia hirta 'Gloriosa Daisy' blazes in shades of gold and crimson, adding fire to a border planted with cool spikes of Salvia farinacea 'Blue Bedder'. Both are top performers during the occasional summer droughts that visit this Missouri garden.

Heat-Tolerant Annuals

Asclepias fruticosa
(bloodflower)
Catharanthus roseus
(Madagascar periwinkle)
Cleome basslerana
(spider flower)
Cuphea ignea
(Mexican cigar plant)
Dolichos lablab
(hyacinth bean)
Exacum affine
(German violet)
Gomphrena globosa
(globe amaranth)
Helichrysum bracteatum
(everlasting, strawflower)
Ipomoea spp.
(morning glory)
Mirabilis jalapa
(four-o'clock)
Oenothera spp.
(evening primrose)
Orthocarpus purpurascens
(owl's clover)
Rhodochiton atrosanguineum
(purple bell vine)
Ricinus communis
(castor bean)
Tagetes spp. (marigold)

HEAT- AND DROUGHT-TOLERANT ANNUALS

Celosia cristata (celosia)
Convolvulus tricolor
(dwarf morning glory)
Coreopsis tinctoria
(tickseed, calliopsis)
Cosmos bipinnatus
(cosmos)
Dimorphotheca spp.
(Cape marigold)
Dyssodia tenuiloba
(Dahlberg daisy)
Eschscholzia californica
(California poppy)
Eustoma grandiflorum
(prairie gentian)
Gaillardia pulchella
(blanket-flower)
Helianthus annuus
(sunflower)
Mentzelia lindleyi
(mentzelia)
Onopordum acanthium
(Scotch thistle)
Portulaca grandiflora
(portulaca, moss rose)
Sanvitalia procumbens
(sanvitalia, creeping zinnia)
Tithonia rotundifolia
(Mexican sunflower)
Zinnia angustifolia (zinnia)

Note: The abbreviation "spp." stands for the plural of "species"; where used in lists it means that many, but not all, of the species in a genus meet the criterion of the list.

Low-Maintenance Roses

Wild roses—about 200 distinct species of the genus *Rosa*—make wonderful easy-care additions to the landscape. Their vigorous habit and surprising stamina make them useful for hiding a chain-link fence or for standing sentinel at the far reaches of the yard where a hose won't reach. Most grow so large that they require more room than a bed or border has to offer. *R. rugosa*, which reaches a height of at least 8 feet and tolerates temperatures as low as -40° F, can serve as a thick hedge where space allows, spreading quickly into wide colonies by putting out new shoots from its roots. The super-long canes of *R. banksiae*, extending more than 25 feet, can be used to drape a shed or other structure you want to dress up with little fuss. And dense, 8-foot-high thickets of pink *R. palustris* do especially well in wet areas where other roses fail—a trait that earned it the nickname swamp rose.

Traits of Wild Species Roses

All species roses share an indefinable air of wildness: They simply look as though they can take care of themselves—and they can. In the process of adapting over millennia to their environments, these roses became completely self-reliant, needing no chemicals to ward off diseases and pests, no protection from winter cold, no fertilizer or watering or soil amendments—in short, no help from gardeners.

Rosa rugosa, grown as a hedge, separates a trim lawn from the wooded area behind it on this Washington State property. Flowers with deep pink petals surrounding a creamy center bloom repeatedly throughout the season, offering months of pleasing contrast to the bright green foliage.

Wild roses evolved throughout the Northern Hemisphere, and over thousands of years each has become as unique as its place of origin. Many grow rampantly, while others stay small and neat. Some are at home in extreme cold; others thrive in hot climates, sandy soil, or swamps. Even their fragrances are individually sweet, spicy, or earthy. The one defining feature of all species roses is their ability to reproduce true versions of themselves from self-pollinated seed that ripens in fruits known as hips. Hybrids, by contrast, don't breed true from self-pollinated seed.

Besides their reproductive ability, perhaps the only other feature shared by most wild roses is the single form of the flowers. These cheerfully open-faced blooms usually range from pale pink to deep purplish red. *R. rugosa*, which is exceptionally hardy and nearly impervious to most diseases, and *R. eglanteria*, known as the sweetbrier or eglantine rose, are two of the most popular. Some wild roses are white or yellow, and a handful are semi-double or double-bloomed forms. *R. banksiae banksiae* and *R. banksiae lutea*, for example, are beautiful white and yellow double-bloom forms of *R. banksiae*. Rugosa roses include the original dark pink species and its sports: *R. rugosa alba*, whose blooms are white, and *R. rugosa rubra*, which offers mauve flowers that are larger than those of its relatives.

Rugosas begin blooming in spring and produce their blossoms continuously into fall. But most species roses, like most other flowering shrubs, bloom just once during the season, putting on a display that can last up to several weeks. Species from warmer climates tend to bloom earlier than those native to regions where frequent spring frosts can damage a plant in flower. *R. banksiae*, from the temperate regions of China, blooms in early spring, for example; the eglantine rose, from Europe, flowers before midsummer; and North American *R. carolina* generally blooms anywhere between early and late summer.

Known as the eglantine or sweetbrier rose, Rosa eglanteria produces charming five-petaled blooms amid glossy apple-scented foliage (below). An ideal hedge rose, it grows to 8 feet or more, has a bushy habit, and has thorny canes to discourage intruders.

The Troubled Legacy of Rosa foetida

Species roses are generally the most resilient plants in the genus, and the wild Iranian rose *R. foetida* is no exception. Well adapted to the hot, dry climate of its native land, this rose is unfazed by the challenges such conditions pose. However, because *R. foetida* was never forced to defend itself against the most common rose disease—the fungus black spot, which thrives in moist conditions—it is very susceptible to it.

The solution is not as simple as banning *R. foetida* from your garden, though. Its blooms are a rich golden color—a trait that was rare and highly coveted during the 19th century, when rose breeders were crossing species and hybrids at a frenzied pace in a quest for new colors as well as other qualities in the offspring. In 1893 a French breeder named Joseph Pernet-Ducher produced a brilliant yellow rose using *R. foetida persiana*, a double-flowered form of the species. He named his prize 'Soleil d'Or'—sun of gold. 'Soleil d'Or' was then used to breed 'Rayon d'Or', the first yellow hybrid tea.

As might be expected, other hybridizers seized upon Pernet-Ducher's creations. The result was a revolution in the spectrum of modern roses: Most of today's yellow, orange, salmon, apricot, and flaming red-orange roses owe their brilliance to *R. foetida.* Unfortunately, along with their beautiful color, most of them—especially hybrid teas—inherited *R. foetida*'s vulnerability to black spot. If your climate isn't extremely dry and you want healthy roses without the help of chemical fungicides, your best bet is to choose a rose without *R. foetida* in its ancestry. But if your heart is set on a yellow rose, try an unusually resistant hybrid tea called 'Elina', the miniature 'Rise 'n' Shine', a medium yellow climber named 'Golden Showers', or the shrubby 'Sunsprite'.

Rosa foetida persiana

Although wild roses typically don't produce blossoms throughout the entire growing season, they often make up for the lack of blooms with interesting foliage. *R. rugosa*'s rounded foliage is a lustrous medium green with the appearance of textured leather, while the soft green leaves of *R. spinosissima*—a small, hardy bush known as the Scotch rose—are daintily edged, giving them a lacelike quality. The foliage of many species also turns attractive colors in the fall. *R. virginiana* takes on shades of scarlet, orange, and yellow, whereas *R. woodsii*, also called the mountain rose, and *R. gymnocarpa,* from the American West, turn red-orange and bright yellow. European *R. glauca* doesn't wait until fall to produce colorful foliage; the red tint of its leaves deepens during the growing season, becoming a smoky purple by autumn.

Native Roses

A number of species grow freely in North America because they originated here. If you'd like to grow roses in a wildflower garden, large natives such as *R. palustris* and the Virginia rose, *R. virginiana,* are perfectly suited. And although most species are a good size, a few natives are so compact and refined you can put them in a formal border. One of the loveliest of these is dark pink *R. carolina* (the pasture rose), which usually grows to a height of only 3 feet. *R. carolina* looks fragile and sounds as if it might be a tender plant from the South, but its native range stretches all the way from Nova Scotia west to Minnesota and south to Texas and Florida.

At home as far north as southern Ontario, pink-flowered *R. setigera* is the only North American native climber, with canes growing more than 16 feet. You can train it up a support or let it grow horizontally as a low-maintenance ground cover. Another native that has spread widely throughout the United States and Canada is *R. nitida,* a short, dainty shrub that produces deep pink blooms and, in the fall, crimson foliage. The state flower of Georgia, *R. laevigata*—also called the Cherokee rose—is actually from China but has established itself so thoroughly in the southern United States that most people think of its charming, floppy white spring flowers as native wildflowers.

New Roses from Wild Blood

Nonnative species like the Cherokee rose that thrive and spread without assistance have "naturalized," in horticultural parlance. Species roses sometimes come from such tough environments

The 2-inch-wide pink blooms of native Rosa carolina—the pasture rose—can be seen in clusters as well as one to a stem on this bush in New York. The hardy plant waits until late spring or early summer, long after the danger of frost is past, to put on its floral show. In fall, the foliage glows a warm orange and yellow.

that when they take root in more hospitable conditions, they don't simply naturalize but run rampant. Notorious among these is *R. multiflora,* from the poor mountain soils of Japan and Korea. This species can take over your landscape and should be avoided, but its boundless vigor has been an asset to rose hybridizers, who have used the species to breed most ramblers and a number of other modern varieties.

R. multiflora is also used as a rootstock. Rose growers often graft the buds of one rose onto the roots of another, combining the beauty of the former with the vigor or stamina of the latter. *R. multiflora* is one of the most popular rootstocks, supporting plants that are less aggressive but are quick to grow and reach maturity.

This species is not the only one with qualities that appeal to hybridizers. In the early 20th century, Dr. William Van Fleet produced climbers using the vigorous, disease-resistant Asian *R. wichuraiana.* The most famous of his cultivated varieties bears his own name: 'Dr. W. Van Fleet'. And in 1952, German hybridizer Wilhelm Kordes created a new species by crossing *R. wichuraiana* with resilient *R. rugosa.* The resulting *R. kordesii* has been used by a number of breeders to parent a group of exceptionally healthy and hardy modern hybrids called kordesii shrubs. The cold-hardy Explorer series from Canada, for example, includes some indomitable kordesiis bearing the names of famous explorers, such as 'Champlain' and 'John Cabot'.

At Iowa State University, plant scientist Griffith Buck has used diminutive, bristly *R. arkansana* and a Siberian species to breed a series of Dr. Buck roses, which can take extreme temperature changes. The Arkansas rose has also been used to breed Parkland (Morden) roses, which are prized for their hardiness, resistance to disease, and long bloom periods.

Additional Resilient Roses

Even if your garden seems altogether inhospitable to roses, there are solutions. For example, if a spot receives morning sun but is partly shaded during the afternoon, or if you live where summer heat and humidity are intense, roses exist that will tolerate these conditions (*list, below*). If your soil is slightly alkaline, it is best to amend it with sulfur and compost to bring the pH down to 6.5. But if these efforts prove futile, the list below also names a handful of ungrafted roses that will tolerate slightly alkaline soil. When you purchase these roses, check to make sure that they have indeed been grown on their own roots rather than on some less tolerant rootstock.

Roses for Difficult Conditions

SLIGHTLY ALKALINE SOIL

'Archduke Charles'
'Carefree Beauty'
'Duchesse de Brabant'
'Monsieur Tillier'
'Mutabilis'
'Mrs. B. R. Cant'
'Mrs. Dudley Cross'
'Nearly Wild'
'Old Blush'

PARTIAL SHADE

'Ballerina'
'Belinda'
'Buff Beauty'
'Golden Showers'
'Lavender Lassie'
'Madame Alfred Carrière'
'Nastarana'
'Penelope'
'Cl. Pinkie'
'Prosperity'
R. palustris
'Will Scarlet'

SUMMER HEAT AND HUMIDITY

'Archduke Charles'
'Camaieux'
'Cardinal de Richelieu'
'Catherine Mermet'
'Céline Forestier'
'Complicata'
'Duchesse de Brabant'
'Lamarque'
'Louis Phillipe'
'Madame Alfred Carrière'
'Maman Cochet'
'Monsieur Tillier'
'Mrs. B. R. Cant'
'Mrs. Dudley Cross'
'Mutabilis'
'Nastarana'
'Old Blush'
'Rêve d'Or'
'Rosa Mundi'
R. palustris
'Sombreuil'
'The Fairy'
'Tuscany'

Planting in Problem Shade

While some gardeners enjoy the wonderful growing conditions that prevail in bright shade, many others have to deal with truly daunting situations: for example, areas choked with tree roots; dry, deep shade where the soil is poor and thin; soggy patches where the soil is poorly drained; or a strip of dense, all-day shade in a city lot. Proper plant selection is the key to converting problem shade into beautiful garden vistas. In addition, there are a few tricks of the trade that can be useful in solving shade problems.

Shady Sites with Tree Roots

If your garden is shaded by trees with large, shallow roots, your choice of plants will be limited; most flowering shrubs and perennials languish in such conditions. Instead, try planting shallow-rooted ground covers. Among the best are *Epimedium alpinum,* which creates a blanket of gray-and-yellow blossoms with red spots; white-blooming *E. grandiflorum;* and yellow *E. pinnatum* var. *colchicum.* (For more on planting amid tree roots, see page 111.) But the most prudent solution may be to surround the trees with container plants.

While containers can be planted with everything from the tiniest flowers to shrubs and small trees, the most versatile are those you can move about—allowing you to vary the plants' effect or to give them more or less shade as the season progresses. Whatever their size, container plants usually need more watering, feeding, and general care than the same plants set in the ground, so use them judiciously.

This New Jersey garden displays a clever use of containers in the arid soil beneath a shallow-rooted maple (center) and a dogwood (far right, not seen). Impatiens are planted in boxes, some angled around the tree trunks, others concealed in the ground covers and sunk into the mulch.

Match your containers to the size and type of each plant. A shrub may need a half whiskey barrel, while a planting of impatiens will do fine in a 10-inch terra-cotta pot. Consider, too, your plants' growth habits. A sprawling fuchsia might look too casual in a formal stone urn but just right in a hanging rattan basket. Trailing species look best in hanging planters; tuberous begonias, with their large flowers in a wide range of colors, do particularly well in them. Hang the planters from the branches of shady trees or from walls, fences, or the sides of buildings. For a rugged, natural look, plant small woodland plants like *Viola* (violet) or shallow-rooted ones like *Ajuga* (bugleweed) in hollowed logs scavenged from the woods. Or consider hiding pots in soil or mulch, or among ground-cover plants.

Plants are more directly exposed to cold in containers than in the earth, so choose hardy species or move those that are borderline frost-tender onto a sheltered porch or into a greenhouse during cold weather. Shade-flowering plants that do well in containers include *Acanthus mollis* (common bear's-breech), anemone, *Bergenia,* camel-lia, *Convallaria* (lily of the valley), fatsia, fuchsia, hosta, impatiens, holly, mahonia, daffodil, *Nicotiana* (flowering tobacco), rhododendron, *Saxifraga* (saxifrage), *Pieris,* thunbergia, *Myosotis* (forget-me-not), skimmia, *Thalictrum* (meadow rue), *Viola,* and periwinkle.

Dry, Deep Shade or Hot Shade

Dry shade can occur under a tree whose canopy of leaf cover is so dense that it acts like an umbrella, diverting most rainfall to the soil outside its drip line. Few flowering shade plants thrive in dry, poor-soil areas. Your best bet is to turn dry shade into moister shade.

Digging organic matter—such as leaves, compost, or rotted manure—into the soil will help. If amending the soil directly is too difficult, spread a 2- to 4-inch layer of organic mulch on the ground and under shrubs to begin the process. Renewed over several seasons, the mulch will enrich the soil and help hold what little water soaks in. You can

Moisture-loving Ligularia 'Othello' sends up golden flowers between tall spears of iris and white-flowered bush honeysuckle in this tranquil poolside planting. During rainless spells, water is added to the garden to keep it from drying out, and enthusiastic colonizers that spread too fast and crowd their neighbors are trimmed back occasionally.

Making spectacular use of dappled vertical shade, this 30-year-old climbing hydrangea vine grows into the canopy of a large tulip poplar (Liriodendron tulipifera) in Delaware. The deciduous hydrangea blooms in midsummer; later on, its elegant shape and exfoliating bark make a fine winter display.

do well include begonia, *Enkianthus,* epimedium, *Gaultheria,* hellebore, heuchera, *Hosta lancifolia* (narrow-leaved plantain lily), hydrangea, saxifrage, skimmia, and yucca.

Boggy Shade and Poorly Drained Soil

At the other end of the soil spectrum is wet ground. Muddy patches that persist even in dry weather or areas where rainwater regularly pools are characterized by poor drainage and boglike conditions that are deadly to many plant species. Planting bog-tolerant species is an easy-care solution, one that is far simpler than trying to change soil drainage patterns.

Some of the many flowering shade dwellers that flourish in boggy soil are *Calycanthus floridus* (Carolina allspice), *Clethra alnifolia* (sweet pepperbush), *Hemerocallis* (daylily), forget-me-not, hosta, winterberry, impatiens, lobelia, sweet bay magnolia, bayberry, *Primula* (primrose), species irises, and *Rhododendron viscosum* (swamp azalea).

In moist but well-drained soil at the edge of a bog, try *Astilbe, Dicentra* (bleeding heart), *Ligularia* (leopard plant), or *Fothergilla;* just be sure their crowns are above the wet soil.

City-Lot Shade

City gardens often pose environmental challenges. Many lots are narrow, squeezed between buildings or fences that produce dense shade where few plants can grow. Painting walls, fences, and even paving stones a light color, so that they reflect available light, helps considerably. Even a 1-percent increase in ambient light can greatly increase plant growth and blooming.

Flowering vines such as climbing hydrangea *(Hydrangea anomala* ssp. *petiolaris)* or shade-tolerant varieties of clematis can turn those same walls and fences from liabilities into assets. You might train a shrub or small tree as an espalier against a wall, or let clematis climb along a fence. Use small, open-structured trees to showcase climbing plants as well, letting their flowers peek out among the branches.

Flowering shrubs, trees, and herbaceous plants can do much for a narrow lot; use them, in combination with foliage plants, as focal points and accents to lead the eye through the garden. And if your lot is very narrow and suffers from a wind-tunnel effect, a well-placed row of shrubs such as

also loop soaker hoses through the areas you want to plant; cover them with a leaf-litter mulch and water slowly on a regular basis.

Flowering herbaceous plants for dry shade include ajuga, *Aquilegia canadensis* (wild columbine), epimedium, heuchera, Japanese anemone, *Pulmonaria* (lungwort), *Scilla, Tradescantia,* and *Vinca.* Shrubs that bloom in these conditions include *Sarcococca,* kalmia, *Myrica cerifera* (wax myrtle), and some viburnum cultivars.

In parts of the West where dry shade is accompanied by high heat and low humidity, plants that

Chinese witch hazel, *Kerria japonica* (Japanese rose), *Ligustrum obtusifolium* (border privet), or *Osmanthus heterophyllus* 'Variegatus' (holly olive) can dissipate the wind's force and help create a calmer environment for plants.

City gardeners may also face compacted soil, as well as pollution in both soil and air. To improve the soil and make it more hospitable for your plants, double dig the beds and add compost, well-rotted manure, or peat moss. In some areas, park departments or similar public agencies give away composted leaf humus; check with your local government.

As a last resort for badly polluted soil, you may want to consider planting in containers filled with potting mix. Container plants recommended for city conditions include dogwood, holly, *Andromeda* (bog rosemary), hydrangea, laurel, rhododendron, witch hazel, dicentra, corydalis, daylily, epimedium, hosta, begonia, and impatiens. For tips on container gardening for small spaces, see pages 49-53.

Artful design expands the visual size of a tiny urban shade garden nestled amid buildings. An oakleaf hydrangea, hostas, and ground covers flower copiously in the scant summer sun; vines and espaliers soften the enclosing walls; and a small pond and waterfall highlight the island plantings.

Wildflowers for Difficult Areas

If you're faced with a difficult site—where the drainage is poor or the light is too intense, for instance—wildflowers are the perfect solution. These robust plants are notorious for flourishing under less-than-ideal conditions in the garden. That's because they've adapted beautifully to the same difficult conditions in the wild.

Almost every garden has a hot spot—frequently next to a sidewalk or driveway—with little or no relief from the sun all day; the soil dries out so quickly that drought-sensitive plants such as turf grasses are doomed to struggle. At the other extreme, trying to maintain grass in the shade of closely spaced trees is just as unrewarding. In the first case, gaillardias and other dry-prairie natives are well suited to the site; in the second, drifts of woodland natives are the solution.

For wildflowers from rocky, sandy soil or from the mountains, excellent drainage is imperative to keep them from succumbing to diseases like root rot. A fast-draining, steep or rocky slope is the perfect place to try plants such as the creamy-flowered *Eriogonum compositum* (wild buckwheat) from California's Coastal Range.

A low place that holds water after a rain makes a good home for perennials from meadows that are wet for a good portion of the year, such as Joe-Pye weed. If space allows, add a moisture-tolerant native tree or shrub such as *Magnolia virginiana* (sweet bay magnolia), which has fragrant white flowers, or *Ilex verticillata* (winterberry), which bears lovely red fruit.

Plants for Dry, Sunny Places

Agave spp. (agave)
Balsamorhiza sagittata (balsamroot)
Baptisia spp. (wild indigo)
Bouteloua curtipendula (sideoats grama)
Erigeron spp. (fleabane)
Gaillardia spp. (Indian blanket)
Melampodium leucanthum (blackfoot daisy)
Oenothera spp. (evening primrose)
Verbena spp. (verbena)
Yucca filamentosa (Adam's-needle)
Zauschneria californica (California fuchsia)

Note: The abbreviation "spp." stands for the plural of "species"; where used in lists it means that many, but not all, of the species in a genus meet the criterion of the list.

Kept comfortably hot and dry by the adjacent concrete sidewalk, Oenothera speciosa (evening primrose), from the shortgrass prairies of southern Kansas and Texas, grows luxuriously even in the moist climate of Bethesda, Maryland (below). Two evening primroses with showy lemon yellow flowers, O. missourensis and O. brachycarpa, can also be counted on to flourish in full sun and dry soil. Deadheading prolongs their season of bloom.

Plants for a Fast-Draining Slope

Aquilegia caerulea
(Rocky Mtn. columbine)
Campanula rotundifolia
(bellflower)
Eriogonum spp.
(wild buckwheat)
Eschscholzia californica
(California poppy)
Iris douglasiana
(Douglas iris)
Lewisia rediviva
(bitterroot)
Penstemon spp.

(beardtongue)
Sedum ternatum
(stonecrop)
Silene laciniata
(Mexican campion)

Note: The abbreviation
"spp." stands for the plural
of "species"; where used in
lists it means that many,
but not all, of the species
in a genus meet the criterion of the list.

*Glowing orange California pop-
pies, whose petals close on overcast days and at night, flourish
on a rocky incline in the Berke-
ley, California, garden at far
left. Also native to the area are
the creeping blue California
lilac in the foreground and the
manzanita trees, whose arching
branches echo the contour of
the slope. Beyond the manzani-
tas is a drift of pale blue Douglas irises, a species ideal for
West Coast gardens.*

*A few square yards of
sparse lawn under old
shade trees in a Con-
necticut garden were
transformed into the
inviting miniature
woodland shown at
left. The path of rough
stones allows for close-
up enjoyment of a wild
bleeding heart's pink
spring flowers and,
nodding above it, the
bicolored flowers
of wild columbine.*

Plants for Eastern Shade Gardens

Arisaema dracontium
(green dragon)
Asarum spp.
(wild ginger)
Aster divaricatus
(wood aster)
Dicentra eximia
(wild bleeding heart)
Eupatorium coelestinum
(hardy ageratum)
Geranium maculatum
(wild geranium)
Mitchella repens
(partridgeberry)
Podophyllum peltatum
(May apple)
Polygonatum biflorum
(Solomon's-seal)
Smilacina spp.
(false Solomon's-seal)
Tiarella cordifolia
(foamflower)
Viola spp. (violet)

Note: The abbreviation "spp."
stands for the plural of
"species"; where used in lists
it means that many, but not
all, of the species in a genus
meet the criterion of the list.

*The graceful foliage and nodding,
pale green seed heads of river oats
give a lush look to a garden where
water stands after a rain, then evapo-
rates in dry weather (above). Found
growing in the wild in the rich, moist
soils of lightly shaded stream banks,
this adaptable grass tolerates occasional flooding and also does well in
average garden soil.*

Plants for Damp Spots

**Andropogon
glomeratus**
(bushy bluestem)
Anemone canadensis
(Canada anemone)
Asclepias incarnata
(swamp milkweed)
Camassia quamash
(camass)
**Chasmanthium
latifolium**
(river oats)
Iris brevicaulis

(Lamance iris)
Monarda didyma
(bee balm)
Physostegia virginiana
(obedient plant)
**Thalictrum
dasycarpum**
(meadow rue)
**Veronicastrum
virginicum**
(Culver's root)
Zephyranthes atamasco
(atamasco lily)

CHAPTER FOUR

Problem-Solving Garden Techniques

Besides design and plant solutions, there are a host of techniques that can help you solve common problems in the garden. Even if you've selected suitable plants for your site, you may find that the drainage problem is too severe or the soil too poor for the plants to thrive. Or perhaps your plants are constantly flattened by the wind. Or maybe your flowers aren't blooming as profusely as they should.

The Charlottesville, Virginia, garden at left is a good example of a difficult site transformed by a problem-solving technique. By building a raised bed to support a variety of shade-loving plants, the owners overcame problems with drainage as well as with compacted soil around tree roots.

On the following pages are descriptions of various garden techniques, ranging from controlling invasive plants to using compost to improve your soil. Armed with this information, you can change a bare or dull site into a garden you'll be proud of.

Improving Your Soil with Compost

Compost is almost a panacea for imperfect soil. If a soil is loose and sandy, generous additions of compost will help pull it together and make it crumbly, so that water, nutrients, and plant roots can get a good foothold. If the soil is heavily compacted clay, compost will help loosen and lighten it. As a fertilizer, finished compost provides a good balance of 2 parts nitrogen to 1 part each of phosphorus and potassium. And if it is made from a large variety of materials, compost contains a healthy balance of trace elements as well. Even the best soil can benefit from periodic additions of compost to help maintain its structure and replenish its supply of nutrients.

Building a Compost Pile

A well-made compost pile is an ideal habitat for microorganisms, providing the food, water, air, and warmth they need to grow and reproduce at top speed. A thriving population quickly converts ordinary kitchen and garden waste into an invaluable fertilizer and soil conditioner.

The microorganisms need a balanced diet of carbon and nitrogen. Fibrous materials such as dry leaves, straw, and sawdust provide plenty of carbon, while nitrogen is furnished by green materials such as grass clippings, waste

from the vegetable garden or flower bed, and kitchen scraps (vegetables and fruits only).

To start a compost pile, spread a layer of brown fibrous material several inches deep and at least 3 feet wide and 3 feet across on bare soil. Add a layer of green material and sprinkle it with soil or a commercial compost activator to introduce microorganisms. Water until the materials are damp like a sponge. Continue in this fashion until the layered pile is at least 3 feet high—the size necessary to generate sufficient

heat. Turn the pile once or twice a week with a garden fork to aerate it and rid the center of excess moisture. Water as needed to keep the pile slightly moist. The compost is ready to use when it is dark and crumbly.

The three-bin composter shown below can produce a large, steady supply of compost. The decomposing pile in the center bin is flanked by a newly assembled pile *(right)* and a bin containing finished compost *(left)*. The slats on the front of the bin are removable, making it easy to turn the pile.

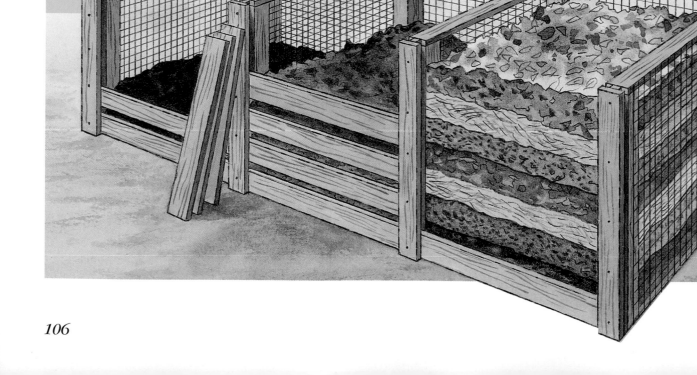

Decomposing waste occupies one of the two cinder-block bins at left; the other stores finished compost. The spaces between the blocks allow air to circulate. You can mortar the blocks at the back and the sides of the bins, but leave the front blocks free so you can remove the compost.

A Compost Bin to Suit Your Needs

Even the simplest compost bin keeps decomposing wastes tidy and compact. And as long as you have the right mix of ingredients and enough of them, it will generate the heat needed to ensure speedy decomposition. For free-standing compost piles or those in open bins, you should start with a pile measuring 3 feet wide, deep, and high. For the ready-made bins available at home and garden centers, simply fill them according to the manufacturer's instructions.

Each of the composters shown here can be easily constructed or purchased for less than a hundred dollars. Some require that the debris pile be turned manually, while others need little or no attention from the gardener.

To create the bin at right, wrap a length of hardware cloth 4 feet wide and 12 feet long around two stakes hammered into the ground. Secure the ends of the hardware cloth with wires. To aerate the compost pile, unfasten the cylinder, reposition the stakes adjacent to the loose pile, reassemble the cylinder, and turn the pile with a fork.

The plastic barrel composter at left is designed to produce finished compost in a month or less. The barrel rests on rollers; turning a handle rotates the barrel and aerates the contents thoroughly. Finished compost is removed through a hinged door on the barrel; a finished batch must be removed before starting a new one.

A compact plastic compost bin like the one at left is an excellent choice where space is limited. Fresh waste material can be added continually to the top of the bin while older material is decaying. Compost is retrieved from the pull-out drawer at the bottom of the bin. Enough air enters the bin through the large slots to make turning the pile unnecessary.

Solving a Drainage Problem

If the site you've chosen for a new garden is generally suitable but suffers from poor drainage, you can consider several remedies. One is to diligently double dig the selected plot, thoroughly loosening the heavy subsoil and then amending it until it drains nicely.

If the drainage problem persists, perhaps because the site is underlaid with a layer of impervious soil (hardpan), you might want to create a simple drainage system (*below*). This approach works well when the soggy ground lies fairly close to a potential runoff area, such as a gutter, a roadside ditch, or a low-lying spot on your property where you can dig a catchment basin.

However, the drainage may be so poor that you have no hope of improving it except at great expense. One indication that you have such a problem is if water pools in an area after a rain and

takes more than an hour or two to drain; another is if the soil is still soggy 12 to 24 hours after a rain. In either case, you can still have your garden where you want it, in the form of a raised bed. By creating your own soil for the bed, with perfect texture, structure, pH, and fertility, you can avoid not only a drainage problem but other site problems as well.

A raised bed can be any size or shape you wish, although its widest point should be no more than about two arm's lengths; otherwise, you might have difficulty reaching into the center of the bed from either side. The bed can be a simple, neat raised island of topsoil dug and mounded up from the surrounding ground. Or it can be bordered by a frame made of landscaping timbers, redwood or cedar planks, logs, bricks, cinder blocks, or stones.

Drying Out a Wet Patch

1. Working from the wet area toward a nearby street, *dig a trench 12 to 18 inches wide and 1 foot deep at the start. As you dig, gradually increase the depth to about 18 inches at the outlet end so that water drains in the right direction.*

2. If you lack an outlet to a street, *dig a dry well to serve as a basin for your drainage ditch: Dig a pit about 3 feet deep at a low spot. Fill it with water three times and monitor it; all water should be gone 1 hour after the last fill. Then fill the basin with gravel up to the point where the ditch joins it.*

Set off simply but handsomely with weathered planks, this raised bed of spiky larkspur, yarrow, daisies, and lamb's ears scintillates with color and robust growth. The plants flourish in an environment unaffected by problems with drainage, soil structure, or pH.

3. Lay a bed of gravel in the ditch and install a perforated drainpipe over it. *If your system empties into a dry well, extend the pipe a few inches into the well (above). Cover the pipe inlet with a piece of woven landscape fabric to screen out silt, sand, and stones.*

4. Cover the drainpipe with a layer of gravel, *and bring the level of gravel in the dry well up even with it. Cut out strips of landscape fabric as wide as the ditch and lay them over the gravel to keep overlying soil from sifting down and clogging the openings in the pipe.*

5. Fill in the ditch and the dry well with topsoil, *mounding the soil over them to allow for settling. Finally, go back to the original zone of poor drainage and build up the area with topsoil, contouring the surface to slope gently in the direction of the drainpipe.*

Containing Invasive Plants

Hemming In Fast Spreaders

Cut the bottom out of a 10-gallon or larger plastic pot (right). Other containers, such as old buckets with the bottoms cut out or holes punched in them for drainage, will also do. Then dig a hole large enough to hold all but the top inch or so of the container. Place the empty container in the hole and pour in just enough soil to bring the top of the plant's rootball level with the ground. Place the plant in the container, fill in around it with soil, and tamp the soil down (below). Water thoroughly, then mulch to hide the exposed rim of the pot.

Some plants spread so quickly, it's difficult—if not impossible—to keep them in bounds. If you're having trouble controlling invasive plants, try placing them in containers, which can then be buried in the soil, as shown at left, below.

Keep in mind that there are times when invasive plants can work to your advantage in difficult spots. For instance, plant them on a slope that is bordered by a lawn at the top and a sidewalk at the bottom to control the plants' growth, and you will have a low-maintenance ground cover that requires very little weeding.

Perennials That Need Controlling

Achillea millefolium
(common yarrow)
Ajuga
(bugleweed)
Artemisia pontica
(Roman wormwood)
Campanula glomerata
(clustered bellflower)
Coreopsis rosea
(pink coreopsis)
Coreopsis verticillata
(threadleaf coreopsis)
Eupatorium coelestinum
(hardy ageratum)

Lysimachia spp.
(loosestrife)
Macleaya cordata
(plume poppy)
Monarda didyma
(bee balm)
Physostegia virginiana
(false dragonhead)
Polygonatum multiflorum
(European Solomon's-seal)
Polygonatum odoratum thunbergii 'Variegatum'
(fragrant Solomon's-seal)
Verbascum
(mullein)

Note: The abbreviation "spp." stands for the plural of "species"; where used in lists it means that many, but not all, of the species in a genus meet the criterion of the list.

Physostegia virginiana (false dragonhead)

Planting Under Trees

It is possible to install flower beds under large shade trees without building a raised bed, but you'll have to take several factors into consideration: How much light and rain can penetrate the tree's canopy of leaves? How thick and shallow are the tree roots? Even if enough light and rain reach the soil, shallow tree roots can be an almost prohibitive problem. Tree roots do not grow straight down into the earth, as is commonly believed; they grow in the top 18 inches of soil, spreading out far beyond the drip line. Roots can quickly invade flower beds and sap all the water and nutrients from them. Maples, sycamores, and beeches are among the worst offenders, and planting beneath them almost always ends in disappointment. Some trees, however, such as oaks and conifers, have deeper-growing roots and can coexist well with other plantings. And beds planted beneath small trees—with a mature height of under 20 feet—typically do well, since such trees have smaller, less invasive root systems.

If you find relatively root-free areas under trees where you can place plants, you are in luck; some of the most beautiful landscape scenes are made up of lush plants that thrive and look their best in the shade of handsome trees.

Planting Amid Tree Roots

To grow herbaceous plants at the foot of a mature tree, the soil must be relatively free of roots—unless you are willing to cut away some roots, a method of last resort. To find out how dense the roots are, push a shovel into the ground. If the blade is stopped by a mesh of roots, move to a new spot and try again until the shovel penetrates at least as deep as the length of the blade.

If you must chop through a major root, take care not to overstress the tree. Don't cut away more than about 10 percent of the total root network, and have the crown pruned back a proportionate amount. After you finish digging, place landscape mesh around the perimeter of the hole to slow down encroachment by new root growth from the tree.

Always check the drainage of the soil in such a site. Dig a hole twice as wide and deep as the rootball you are planting and fill it with water. If the water doesn't drain away after 15 minutes, either improve the drainage (below) or put in plants that tolerate boggy conditions.

To speed drainage, dig the hole 4 inches deeper than twice the depth of the rootball and line the bottom with 4 inches of pebbles. Cover the pebble layer with 4 inches of soil mix made up of 1 part original soil, 4 parts compost or humus, and 1 part pebbles. Set the crown of the plant slightly above the soil level and fill with soil mix. Tamp down firmly, water and tamp down again, then cover with mulch.

Staking Unruly Plants

Most stems are strong enough to keep plants upright when their blossoms open. Nevertheless, you may find that in some cases—with perennials in particular and with some bulbs—you will need to devise simple supports to prevent your plants from falling over and to keep the garden looking neat and attractive.

Why Plants Fall Over

In general, plants over 2 feet tall are more likely to need staking for support, especially those with large, heavy blossoms; bulbs such as dahlias, tuberous begonias, and some gladiolus and lilies fall into this category. A severe thunderstorm can easily snap off the blooms and flatten such top-heavy plants to the ground. In addition, recently planted perennials that haven't had time to develop sturdy stems may need temporary support until they become established.

Sometimes, however, an apparent need for staking may actually indicate a separate problem. Weak stems, for example, may be a sign that the plants need better care. In the case of an old, overgrown clump of perennials, dividing the plants may be the best solution. Other common sources of trouble include improper watering and fertilizing *(box, page 114, top)*.

Location plays a role as well. Plants exposed to wind are more susceptible to toppling than those in a sheltered spot, and a sun-loving plant set in the shade may grow lanky and lean toward the light. In either case, transplanting when the plants are dormant should solve the problem.

Staking Methods

When staking is necessary, choose a method that is appropriate to the plant's growth habit. Use single stakes to brace the unbranched stems of tall

Three Ways to Stake

For a single-stemmed plant, use a stake about three-fourths the mature plant's height. Loop twine around the stem halfway up and tie it to the stake (left). When the plant is about two-thirds grown, add another loop of twine above the first one. Add a third tie at the base of the flower head when it is about to bloom (far left).

When a bushy plant is several inches tall, cut four or five stakes to the height of the mature plant's foliage and drive them into the ground (below). Loop twine from stake to stake 6 to 8 inches above the ground. When blooms appear, add a tier of twine just below the flowers.

The foliage and blossoms of blue bellflowers and white feverfew hide the bamboo stakes that keep them from sprawling (left). In the photograph below, a framework of twiggy branches is barely visible beneath a stand of yellow yarrow.

To stake a fine-textured plant such as baby's-breath (above), *choose several twiggy branches about 6 inches shorter than the plant's mature height and sharpen their ends. Push the branches into the ground around the plant, angling them toward its center.*

perennials such as pompon, cushion, and decorative chrysanthemums and the delphinium shown on the following page. Single staking is also appropriate for gladiolus, dahlias, and other heavy-bloomed bulbs. Bamboo canes, a half-inch in diameter and painted green, are perfect for blending in with the foliage of a fully grown plant. Steel stakes, sometimes coated with dark green plastic, are also available.

Push the support gently into the ground beside the plant's stem; if the stem's natural inclination is to bend a little, angle the stake to follow it. For bulbs, place the stake in the planting hole next to the bulb when you are planting it. Use twine, which may be green or tan colored, to tie the plant's stem to its support—or you may use raffia fiber, paper- or plastic-coated thin wire, or green-tinted plastic gardening tape, which is slightly elastic. Knot the twine around the stake, securing it tightly, then loop the twine loosely around the plant so that it does not constrict the stem.

For dense, bushy perennials such as heliopsis, Shasta daisies, and peonies, you can buy wire hoops or frames at garden centers. These supports are circular, square, or rectangular in shape,

How to Avoid Staking

André Viette, an internationally known horticulturist and past president of the Perennial Plant Association, grows more than 3,000 varieties of perennials at his nursery in Fishersville, Virginia. He doesn't stake any of them. Weak stems, he says, are often the product of improper watering and fertilizing. Viette recommends watering deeply, rather than lightly and more frequently, and favors organic fertilizer that is high in phosphorus and low in nitrogen.

Other ways expert gardeners avoid staking their plants include:
• Cutting back tall-growing perennials such as asters when they are about half grown to limit their ultimate height.
• Planting strong-stemmed annuals such as larkspur among newly planted perennials with still-floppy, immature stems.
• Designing a perennial border to have a cottage-garden look, suitable for plants with sprawling, informal growth habits.
• Choosing tall perennials with sturdy stems that don't need staking. This group includes:

Aconitum napellus
(monkshood)
Artemisia lactiflora
(white mugwort)
Aruncus dioicus
(goatsbeard)
Astilbe x *arendsii*
'Professor Weilen'
(astilbe)
Dictamnus albus

(gas plant)
Echinacea purpurea
(purple coneflower)
Hemerocallis cultivars
(daylily)
Iris sibirica cultivars
(Siberian iris)
Liatris pycnostachya
(gay-feather,
blazing star)

Ligularia stenocephala
'The Rocket'
(narrow-spiked ligularia)
Macleaya cordata
(plume poppy)
Miscanthus sinensis
cultivars
(eulalia)
Perovskia atriplicifolia
(Russian sage)

with three or four long legs. When the clump of growing foliage is about a foot tall, place the support over the plant and push its legs several inches into the ground until the frame is at the height of the plant growth.

A homemade frame of twine and stakes *(page 112)* is just as effective and much less expensive than wire hoops. For groups of spiky plants such as delphiniums, you may choose to stake them on a frame rather than tie each stem individually. Simply use four or five canes that are about three-fourths as tall as you expect the plant to grow, and push them into the ground around each cluster. As the flowers begin to bloom, tie twine to the stakes at height intervals of 12 inches and weave it among the stems.

To stake bushy plants as well as fine-textured plants like baby's-breath, try using twiggy branches *(page 113)*. Birch, oak, buddleia, and vitex are all good choices for branches.

When to Stake

The key to successful, unobtrusive staking is planning ahead. Put the stakes in place early in the season, while the plant is still growing upright and before flower buds appear. As the plant fills out, its foliage will hide the stakes *(page 113, top)*.

Perennials That Need Staking

TALL FLOWER STEMS
(Single Stakes)

Chrysanthemum
(pompon, cushion, decorative)
Delphinium
(elatum hybrids)
Digitalis
(foxglove)

BUSHY PLANTS
(Stakes and Twine or Twiggy Branches)

Anchusa azurea
'Dropmore'
(bugloss)
Aster novae-angliae
(New England aster)

Campanula
lactiflora
(milky bellflower)
Centaurea montana
(cornflower)
Chrysanthemum
maximum
(Shasta daisy)
Chrysanthemum x
morifolium
(florist's chrysanthemum)
Chrysanthemum
nipponicum
(Nippon daisy)
Chrysanthemum
parthenium
(feverfew)
Clematis heracleifolia
'Davidiana'
(clematis)
Gaillardia x *grandiflora*
(blanket-flower)

Helenium autumnale
'Bruno', 'Riverton
Beauty'
(sneezeweed)
Helianthus x *multiflorus*
(sunflower)
Heliopsis
(false sunflower)
Paeonia lactiflora
(peony)
Salvia azurea ssp.
pitcheri
(sage)
Solidago
(goldenrod)
Thalictrum delavayi
(Yunnan meadow rue)
Thalictrum
rochebrunianum
(lavender mist
meadow rue)
Thalictrum
speciosissimum
(dusty meadow rue)

FINE-TEXTURED
PLANTS
(Twiggy Branches)

Achillea millefolium
(yarrow)
Clematis integrifolia
'Caerulea'
(clematis)
Coreopsis grandiflora
'Badengold', 'Mayfield
Giant'
(tickseed)
Gypsophila paniculata
'Bristol Fairy',
'Perfecta'
(baby's-breath)
Limonium
(sea lavender, statice)
Linum
(flax)
Physostegia
(false dragonhead)
Veronica latifolia
'Crater Lake Blue'
(speedwell)

'Fanfare' Delphinium

Enhancing the Bloom

Applying special pruning methods at the right time and to the right plant will increase the number of flowers or the size of the blooms your perennials produce. Such techniques—including pinching, thinning, disbudding, deadheading, and cutting back—help to keep a plant looking its best and to direct energy that would otherwise be spent on seed production into creating more flowers and larger blooms.

Many perennials benefit from a combination of pruning methods. When delphiniums are in bloom, for example, deadheading, or removing faded blossoms, prolongs the display. When flowering stops, cutting back the stalks to the rosette of leaves at the base of each plant makes the plants look tidy and often stimulates a second flowering.

Annuals, like perennials, benefit from pruning to enhance the bloom. For information on keeping annuals blooming all season long, see page 43.

Why Deadhead?

Removing flowers as they begin to fade is an important garden chore, and not for appearance alone. Some perennials, such as pincushion flower and Stokes' aster, may stop blooming if they aren't attended to promptly, and a hybrid perennial allowed to go to seed may in time be crowded out by its less desirable offspring. Deadheading also stimulates some roses—hybrid teas,

Pinching Stem Tips

Using your fingers, pinch off emergent stem tips just above the topmost unfurled leaves. The net result will be three or four new branches, smaller but more plentiful flowers, and a stockier plant. This technique works well with plants that can develop numerous stems and buds, and that look attractive when bushy. Chrysanthemums can be pinched two or three times, up until the flower buds develop.

Perennials to Pinch

Anaphalis
(pearly everlasting)
Anthemis
(golden marguerite)
Artemisia (wormwood)
Aster (aster)
Boltonia (boltonia)
Centaurea (cornflower)
Chrysanthemum maximum (Shasta daisy)
Chrysanthemum x morifolium
(florist's chrysanthemum)
Chrysanthemum nipponicum (Nippon daisy)
Echinacea
(purple coneflower)
Erigeron (fleabane)
Eupatorium (boneset)
Gaillardia
(blanket-flower)
Gillenia
(bowman's root)
Heliopsis
(false sunflower)
Nepeta (catmint)
Perovskia
(Russian sage)
Phlox paniculata
(summer phlox)
Physostegia
(false dragonhead)

Deadheading Spent Flowers

For perennials with flowers at the tips of leafy stems, cut just below the fading flowers (right) to stimulate new buds. For plants with leafy flower stems and a rosette of leaves at the base of the plant, cut back to just above the topmost unopened bud. If there are no buds, cut the stem off just above the foliage rosette. For perennials with bare stems, cut off close to the ground to encourage new growth.

Perennials to Deadhead

Achillea (yarrow)	*Gaillardia*
Anthemis	(blanket-flower)
(golden marguerite)	*Heuchera* (alumroot)
Armeria	*Lobelia* (cardinal flower)
(thrift, sea pink)	*Nepeta* (catmint)
Campanula (bellflower)	*Penstemon*
Centaurea (cornflower)	(beardtongue)
Chrysanthemum maximum	*Phlox paniculata*
(Shasta daisy)	(summer phlox)
Chrysanthemum x morifolium	*Platycodon*
(florist's chrysanthemum)	(balloon flower)
Delphinium	*Salvia* (sage)
(delphinium)	*Scabiosa*
Digitalis (foxglove)	(pincushion flower)
Echinops (globe thistle)	*Sidalcea* (false mallow)
Eupatorium (boneset)	*Stokesia* (Stokes' aster)
	Verbena (verbena)
	Veronica (speedwell)

Deadheading Rhododendrons

Pinching off spent rhododendron flowers *can double or triple the number of blossoms the next year as well as make the bush more compact. Remove dead blossoms and developing seed pods by bending the woody stem, just above where new buds are forming, and pulling gently until it snaps (right, top). With the seed pods gone, growth will be concentrated in the new buds. After a few weeks, when the buds have grown out about 4 inches, pinch off the last inch or so of that growth to encourage more shoots to sprout (right, bottom).*

Rhododendron 'Centennial Celebration'

grandifloras, floribundas, and repeat-blooming climbers—to produce another round of flowers. Cut away the old blooms throughout the growing season, stopping several weeks before the first frost; you don't want to promote any new growth that would be vulnerable to the cold.

Not all plants require deadheading. Species, antique, and shrub roses, as well as climbers that bloom once per season, don't need this treatment. And neither do the blossoms of flax, geraniums, and penstemons, which fall off by themselves. Other plants, such as rudbeckia and 'Autumn Joy' sedum, have ornamental seed heads that enliven a garden through the fall and provide interest into the cold months of winter.

Pinching Plants to Stimulate Blooming

Perennials that bloom in midsummer or later, as well as annuals such as coleus and most vines, benefit from having their stem tips pinched back early in the growing season. In response to pinching, a stem produces several new branches that together may yield double or even triple the number of blooms on an unpinched stem. The technique makes plants shorter and more compact—and, in the case of perennials, less likely to need staking.

Pinching done early in the growing season has little or no effect on a plant's blooming schedule. If you want to delay a plant's flowering, pinch stem tips back in midsummer. This technique is not appropriate for spring perennials, however, because these plants don't have enough time to form new flower buds before their blooming season comes to an end.

Thinning for Larger Flowers

If you prefer fewer but larger flowers to an abundance of smaller ones, you can prune up to a third of a plant's stems, cutting them off at the base. Perennials that bloom in midsummer should be thinned in early spring, and fall bloomers in midsummer. As with pinching, this method isn't suitable for spring bloomers; it merely reduces the number of flowers, with no payoff in size.

Thinning is particularly useful for restoring a display of phlox, rudbeckia, or sunflower plants that are several seasons old and that, if left unattended, would likely produce a dense mass of stems with small blooms. In addition to rejuvenating a plant's blooming, thinning improves its form, opens its center up to more light, and reduces the risk of disease by improving air circulation. When a plant is heavily thinned, it sends up more vigorous growth from its roots.

Disbudding for Showy Blooms

For peonies, chrysanthemums, and other perennials whose flower buds appear in groups, removing all but the central bud yields a single blue-ribbon blossom. However, this showy flower is likely to make the stem so top-heavy that staking is required *(pages 112-114)*. For a different effect, pinch off the central bud but leave the side buds, which will develop into a spray of flowers.

For exhibition-size blooms on hybrid tea roses and grandifloras, pinch off any buds that sprout below the top, or terminal, bud *(box, right)*. Do this when the buds are tiny, because later disbudding will leave black scars on the stem.

On floribundas and miniature roses, which produce clusters of blossoms, pinch off the terminal, or central, bud in a cluster. Ordinarily, the terminal bud blooms first, then fades and leaves a hole in the cluster just as the adjacent buds are opening up. For prettier sprays that bloom together, remove the terminal bud as early as possible; the other blooms will fill in the space and be more uniform in size. Disbudding is not necessary for antique (old garden) roses, shrub roses, species roses, climbers, and polyanthas.

Cutting Back for Better Shape and Bloom

Cutting back simply means shortening a stem or branch to stimulate new growth, usually from the vegetative bud located just below the point where the branch or stem was pruned. You can steer the new growth in a particular direction—from the center of the plant outward, for example—by choosing where to make your cuts.

This pruning technique may be done at two different times in a perennial's growing cycle, and for different reasons. In both cases, all of the plant's stems should be reduced in height by one-third to one-half. Performed early in the growing season, cutting back results in shorter plants that bloom later than usual. Carried out later in the season, as soon as a plant stops flowering, the shearing stimulates the growth of new foliage and, in the case of catmint, bellflowers, and many other perennials, a second wave of blooms. Refer to the chart on pages 118-119 for more information on when and how to prune specific plants.

Encouraging Beautiful Rose Blooms

By disbudding, deadheading, and fertilizing your roses, you can spur them to produce abundant blooms that are even more gorgeous than usual. Removing certain buds affects the size or proportion of remaining buds and the flowers that follow; deadheading stimulates the plant to bloom again sooner than it normally would. A good diet ensures that the plant has the nutrients it needs to put on a spectacular show.

DISBUDDING *Grasp the cane securely and, with your fingers, gently pinch off all buds that sprout on the sides of the cane (right). Do this as soon as these lateral buds appear. If the rose is a type that produces clusters of blooms, pinch off the terminal, or central, bud to encourage blooms of equal size in the spray.*

DEADHEADING *After a bloom has passed its peak, use a clean pair of pruning shears to cut the stem and remove the flower. Make the cut at a 45° angle on the cane, ¼ inch above the highest outward-facing leaf bearing five leaflets (left). The dormant bud seated on the cane at the base of the leaf will grow into a new shoot and produce a bloom within 6 weeks.*

FEEDING *Water the soil thoroughly around the plant. The next day, measure an appropriate fertilizer according to the package directions, pull the mulch away from the plant to expose the soil, and sprinkle the fertilizer around the drip line—the area beneath the outermost leaves. Use a trowel to dig the food into the top 2 inches of soil (right). Finally, sprinkle the soil with water to dissolve the nutrients so they will seep into the soil.*

The perennials, shrubs, and vines listed below can be trimmed or pruned at strategic times during the year to encourage more blooms and produce shapelier plants. Perennials are deadheaded, pinched back, or cut back at intervals during the growing season to discourage seed production and encourage reblooming. Shrubs and vines can be thinned, which involves cutting an old branch or stem back to where it started as a bud or to the ground. Or you can give them a heading cut, which involves removing part of a branch back to a bud or leaf node. Some shrubs and vines benefit from deadheading; you can encourage them to produce new, flower-bearing branches by cutting them back hard in early spring. In all cases, timing is crucial: Prune shrubs that flower in early spring after they finish blooming; shrubs that flower later—which bloom on new spring growth—should be pruned in late winter or early spring.

	Bloom Season	When to Prune	Thin Out	Pinch Back	Dead-head	Comments
Achillea (yarrow)	summer				✔	cut back for second flowering
Anaphalis (pearly everlasting)	late summer to fall			✔		
Anthemis (golden marguerite)	midsummer to early fall			✔	✔	cut back for second flowering
Armeria (thrift)	spring to summer				✔	
Aster x *frikartii* (Frikart's aster)	early summer to fall				✔	
Boltonia (boltonia)	late summer to frost	early summer		✔		pinch back for compact growth
Campanula (bellflower)	early to midsummer				✔	
Centaurea (cornflower)	spring to summer			✔	✔	
Centranthus (red valerian)	summer					cut back for second flowering
Chrysanthemum x *morifolium* (florist's chrysanthemum)	late summer to frost	spring to midsummer		✔	✔	pinch back every 3 weeks until midsummer
Chrysanthemum x *superbum* (Shasta daisy)	spring to fall			✔	✔	
Delphinium (delphinium)	summer				✔	cut back for second flowering
Dianthus (pink, carnation)	spring to summer				✔	shear mat-forming types to promote compact growth
Digitalis (foxglove)	spring to summer				✔	
Echinacea (coneflower)	summer			✔		
Echinops (globe thistle)	summer				✔	cut back for second flowering
Erigeron (fleabane)	summer			✔		
Eupatorium (boneset)	summer			✔	✔	
Gaillardia (blanket-flower)	summer to fall			✔	✔	
Gillenia (bowman's root)	spring to summer					

PERENNIALS

118

	Bloom Season	When to Prune	Thin Out	Pinch Back	Dead-head	Comments
PERENNIALS						
Heliopsis (false sunflower)	midsummer to fall			✔		
Nepeta (catmint)	summer			✔	✔	cut back for second flowering
Penstemon (beardtongue)	spring to fall			✔	✔	cut back for second flowering
Perovskia (Russian sage)	summer			✔		
Phlox paniculata (summer phlox)	spring to fall			✔	✔	cut back for second flowering
Platycodon (balloon flower)	summer			✔	✔	
Scabiosa (pincushion flower)	summer				✔	
Stokesia (Stokes' aster)	summer				✔	cut back for second flowering
Veronica (speedwell)	spring to summer				✔	cut back for second flowering
SHRUBS						
Buddleia (butterfly bush)	summer	early spring			✔	cut to 12 inches to rejuvenate
Caryopteris (bluebeard)	summer to fall	early spring				cut to 12 inches to rejuvenate
Forsythia (forsythia)	early spring	after flowering	✔			cut branches in winter for indoor forcing
Halesia (silver bell)	midspring	after flowering				
Hibiscus (rose of Sharon)	summer to fall	early spring				head back to 2 or 3 buds in spring for larger flowers
Hydrangea (hydrangea)	summer	early spring	✔			head back in midsummer for second flowering
Philadelphus (mock orange)	early summer	after flowering	✔			cut to 12 inches to rejuvenate
Potentilla (bush cinquefoil)	summer to frost	late winter	✔			
Rhododendron (rhododendron)	spring	after flowering		✔	✔	snap off spent blooms; pinch back new growth a few weeks later
Spiraea (spirea)	spring to summer	after flowering	✔			cut to 8 inches to rejuvenate
Syringa (lilac)	spring	after flowering	✔		✔	cut to 3 feet to rejuvenate
Weigela (weigela)	spring	after flowering	✔			
VINES						
Campsis (trumpet creeper)	late summer	spring				head back summer growth to 3 or 4 buds
Clematis (spring-blooming clematis)	spring	after flowering				cut back old vines
Clematis (fall-blooming clematis)	summer to fall	early spring				head back to 3 or 4 buds
Lonicera japonica (Japanese honeysuckle)	summer	early spring				head back to 3 or 4 buds
Wisteria (wisteria)	midspring	late summer/ early spring				cut summer growth to 2 inches; cut end tips in spring

Renovating a Garden with Native Plants

Bright red bougainvillea crests a wall in this garden in Rancho Santa Fe, California, which features a profusion of native plantings, including aconitum, agave, euphorbia, and sedum.

If you have a bed or border with old plants you'd like to get rid of, or with plants that have become too crowded, try renovating it with wildflowers. Renovation allows you to sort through existing plants and clear them out or divide them. It's also a good way to improve drainage and add nutrients to the soil, since you'll be adding organic matter in the process.

The best time to tackle this project is in mid-spring, when you can see where your plants are coming up. A springtime renovation also gives your new and newly divided plants almost a full season to establish or reestablish themselves. There's another good reason to make these changes in the spring: If you redo the bed later, you'll have to live with a sparse appearance all season, whereas a spring makeover allows you to fill in the bare spots with colorful annuals.

After you've planted the bed, be sure to water it thoroughly, then cover it with a 2-inch layer of organic mulch such as shredded hardwood. Remember to keep the bed well watered during the first few weeks to make sure all the transplants become established.

Rejuvenating a Border with Wildflowers

1. Lay a tarp adjacent to the bed. *With a spading fork or spade, dig out all the existing plantings. As much as possible, keep the plants' root systems intact by digging at least 2 to 3 inches outside of their drip lines. Then, lift the plants out of the bed and place them on the tarp. If you won't be completing the project within a few hours, cover the roots with wet newspaper to protect them from wind and sun, and keep them watered.*

If the project is going to take a few days, heel in your plants: Dig a shallow trench approximately 10 inches deep, then lay each plant on its side with the rootball in the trench, and cover the roots with soil and mulch (inset). Plants can often remain heeled in for several weeks as long as they receive sufficient water and light. The sooner your plants can be set in place, however, the better they'll keep their health and vigor.

2. Break up the bed's soil with a spading fork. *If the soil has become very compacted, you may want to use a mattock. Apply a 4- to 5-inch layer of a mixture of leaf mold and compost, and work it into the soil to a depth of one spade length (above). This is also a good opportunity to adjust your soil's pH level by adding limestone to overacid soil or gypsum to very alkaline soil. Follow package directions, and work in small sections, moving from one end of the bed to the other. When working inside the bed, stand on a flat board to distribute your weight more evenly and thus minimize any soil compaction.*

3. Situate your plants on the bed's surface to visualize the design. *When digging holes for your old plants and for new ones purchased in containers, make the holes slightly larger than the plant's rootball. Gently remove each plant from its container and loosen any compacted soil around the rootball; place the plant in the hole, spreading the roots out evenly. The planting depth of both the container plants and your old plants should be the same as it was previously in the container or in the garden (above). If you are setting in new bare-root plants, soak their roots in lukewarm water for an hour before planting—longer if they were fairly dry when they arrived in the mail. To plant, dig a hole as deep and as wide as the plant's longest roots. Then mound up some soil in the center of the hole. Set the plant on top of the mound and spread the roots out evenly all around (inset). Make sure that the plant's crown—where the stems and roots meet—is flush with the soil's surface. Holding the plant in place, fill the hole with soil and firm it in.*

Limiting Your Garden Water Needs

Undemanding plants in this easy-care garden include Tilia cordata, the ornamental grass, Miscanthus sinensis 'Gracillimus' and barberry. Low-growing Juniperus 'Blue Rug' provides an attractive, low-maintenance groundcover.

Watering is the most important gardening chore, and one that hardly any gardener can trust to nature alone. Erratic rainfall patterns or extended droughts during the growing season are the rule rather than the exception for most of the United States *(map, page 124)*.

When it comes to water, working with nature is far more rewarding and less complicated than trying to outwit it. And, if you design your garden to make it not only beautiful but also as self-sufficient as possible, you can reduce the time you spend on watering and on maintenance in general. This sensible, less adversarial approach to gardening is called xeriscaping.

The Xeriscape Approach

Xeriscaping is a term that derives from *xeros*—the Greek word for dry and also the botanical term for drought—and from *landscape*. This new way of thinking about gardening originated in the semi-arid West in the early 1980s, but it is equally applicable to virtually every part of the United States.

There are seven basic guidelines for establishing a water-thrifty garden, all of which make good gardening sense:

- Plan and design comprehensively, taking your area's climatic conditions into account at every stage.
- Analyze your garden's soil and improve it to increase water retention.
- Create lawn areas of manageable sizes and shapes, and plant them with grasses that are suited to the climate.
- Select plants that are well adapted to your area and group them according to their water needs.
- Irrigate efficiently by applying the right amount of water at the right time, and by using the right equipment for the task.
- Use mulches to keep the soil moist and cool and to reduce the growth of weeds.
- Adopt routine maintenance practices that conserve water. These include mowing turf grass high, weeding regularly so that ornamental plants don't compete with weeds for moisture, and fertilizing sparingly.

The Benefits of Xeriscaping

Efficient watering, in itself a timesaver, also has timesaving consequences. Because the excessive growth that often results from overwatering is curtailed, a plant's need for nutrients—and therefore the need for fertilizer—is reduced. Also curbed is the production of excessively soft, waterlogged tissue that is prone to attack by insects, so fewer applications of pesticides may be necessary. And since efficient irrigation practices concentrate water where ornamental plants need it most instead of applying it wastefully to the whole garden, another consequence is fewer weeds. Weed seeds that germinate readily in moist soil have difficulty surviving the xeriscape garden's generally drier conditions.

The April display put on by a mixed planting of drought-tolerant perennials and shrubs includes (clockwise from lower right) pink-and white-flowered Santa Barbara daisies; Jerusalem sage, with yellow flowers; the pink Mexican evening primrose; sweet pea shrub, with small pinkish purple blooms; yellow daylilies; and a pale-flowered, stiffly upright westringia.

Drought Potential in the Continental United States

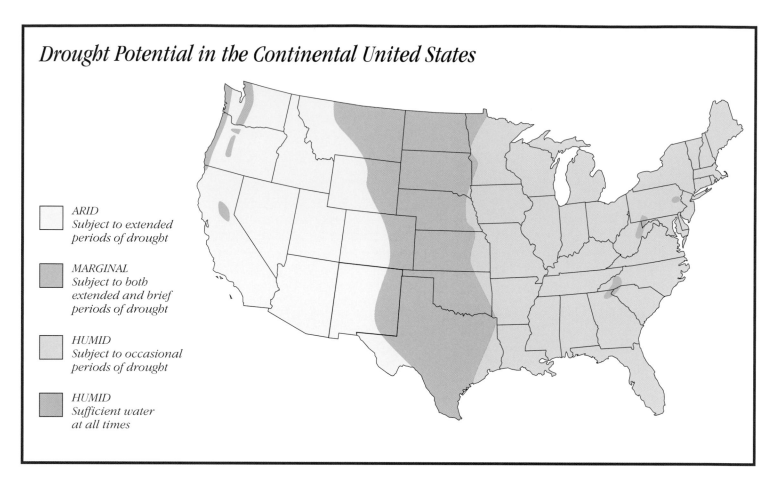

ARID
Subject to extended periods of drought

MARGINAL
Subject to both extended and brief periods of drought

HUMID
Subject to occasional periods of drought

HUMID
Sufficient water at all times

Besides the practical benefits of xeriscaping, there are aesthetic ones as well. When there's a good match between plants and their environment, there's a much better chance of strong, healthy growth and a fine display of flowers. In addition, a well-designed xeriscape remains in good condition even in the heat of summer, when more conventional landscapes frequently look parched and droopy.

Getting Started

Converting your garden to a xeriscape doesn't necessarily mean starting over, a prospect that is daunting to most gardeners. It may simply mean taking a close look at your garden's moisture supply and demand and replanting an area or two where those factors are out of balance. For instance, you may decide to plant daylilies or creeping mahonia on a steep, dry bank where keeping turf grass in decent condition has been a losing battle. Or you might remove the solitary but thirsty rosebush growing in the midst of trailing lantana, which blooms less profusely with frequent waterings.

Water-thrifty plants such as Russian sage, core-

opsis, cotoneaster, catmint, and yucca are classic choices for a xeriscape. But there's no reason to restrict yourself solely to plants that tolerate drought. High-maintenance, water-demanding varieties can be part of a xeriscape without a burdensome amount of work as long as you plant them together instead of scattering them about *(opposite)*.

Creating Zones

Grouping plants with similar cultural and maintenance needs—a procedure known as zoning—is one of the surest ways offered by the xeriscape approach to cut work time in the garden. The major factor in dividing a garden into zones is water. You'll want to consider how convenient it is to irrigate different parts of your garden and whether you'll do it manually or with an automatic system. And, since the water-retentive capacity of soil varies greatly according to its structure and organic content, you'll need to familiarize yourself with your soil. Other factors to assess include soil pH and the distribution of light and shade.

Unless a garden is unusually large, three zones—for high, moderate, and low water use—

In the northern California hillside garden at left, rose-pink sea thrift and white and pale blue Douglas irises bloom luxuriantly during the dry season.

should suffice. The fewer zones you have, the easier watering will be. Too many zones also increase the chance of giving less thirsty plants too much water, which harms plants as much as not enough water. When you are blocking out your garden's zones and considering plant choices, keep these guidelines in mind:

- Limit the number of different kinds of plants.
- Keep lone specimen plants to a minimum.
- Group plants in well-defined beds.
- Link zones by using transitional plants that tolerate different moisture levels.
- Use patios and other paved areas to separate zones. Place drought-resistant plants next to pavement, which heats up in sunlight and causes the soil to dry out faster.

Sites for High Water Use

You may want to put your oasis, or zone of high water use, in an area close to the house, where plants will be both easier to water and harder to overlook. If your ground slopes, you can take advantage of water's natural downward flow and place moisture-loving plants near the foot of the slope. Alternatively, site these plants in partial shade, which will shield them from heat and direct sunlight and help reduce their water needs. But be flexible: If the best place for water- and sun-loving favorites such as roses lies at the periphery of your yard, and if you are willing to spend the extra time and effort it will take to maintain them, then situate the oasis zone there.

CHAPTER FIVE

Growing a Healthy Lawn

The perfectly manicured lawn is an American institution. Nowhere else in the world do people devote so much effort to maintaining a large expanse of smooth green turf. In an effort to cultivate an unblemished carpet of grass, many homeowners put higher concentrations of chemicals on their lawns than American farmers apply to their crops. And yet, all that pampering doesn't necessarily improve the lawn's appearance. Large chemical doses can kill useful creatures such as earthworms and beneficial insects and microorganisms. Frequent fertilizing and watering make the grass grow faster, leading to more mowing, and close mowing encourages problems such as weeds, pests, and diseases.

The good news is that you can create a lawn that is both beautiful and undemanding, such as the lush, easy-care Baltimore lawn at left. On the following pages you'll learn how to choose the right grass for your site's conditions; how to care properly for your soil as well as your grass to keep it green and vigorous; and how to spot trouble and manage it in ways that are not only effective but also kind to the environment.

Lawn-Care Basics and Preventive Measures

The most important component of a healthy lawn is the grass itself. Traditionally, American lawns have been made up of old varieties of grass that require considerable care to keep healthy. Recently, however, breeders have created improved grasses that need much less maintenance. A number are disease resistant, many are drought tolerant, and some even repel insects. Other varieties require less fertilizer and less frequent mowing.

Whether you are starting a new lawn, are overseeding an existing one, or simply want to make the most of what's now growing on your property, it helps to know something about the different types of grasses that are available, what their particular needs are, and which variety best suits your area.

What Is Turf Grass?

Unlike most other plants, which grow from the tips, turf grasses grow from the base—a feature that endows a lawn with the durability to survive heavy foot traffic and frequent mowing. Turf grasses are usually classified by the season and the part of the country in which they grow best, as indicated in the chart at right. Perennial ryegrass and Kentucky bluegrass, for example, are known as cool-season grasses; they are planted primarily in northern areas and grow most vigorously in spring and fall. Warm-season grasses—Bermuda and St. Augustine, for instance—grow actively in the hot summer temperatures of the South before going dormant in the fall and turning brown.

Turf grasses are also classified by their growth habits, which can be either creeping or bunching. Creeping varieties—also known as sod-forming—spread relatively quickly by sending out horizontal shoots, called stolons when above ground and rhizomes when underneath the soil (box, page 130). Bunching grasses send up blades, called tillers, from a single crown, forming clumps and spreading slowly. If you live in the North, it's better to mix creeping and bunching grasses or two bunching varieties than to plant a single species. Combining cool-season species with different habits makes your lawn hardier and more resistant to stress. Warm-season grasses don't mix well, however, because they grow more aggressively; lawns in the South are usually just a single species.

Different species of grass vary in their appearance by blade width and color. To Americans, the narrower the blade and the deeper the green, the more elegant the lawn. But the best lawns combine good looks with good growth characteristics. In

GRASSES		CHARACTERISTICS				
		Texture & Appearance	Growth Habit	Drought Tolerance	Heat Tolerance	
COOL SEASON	Bent grass	Very fine bladed; bright green	Bunching	Very low	Low	
	Kentucky bluegrass	Medium- to fine-bladed; medium to dark green	Creeping, rhizomes	Moderate	Moderate	
	Fine fescue	Very fine bladed; medium to deep green	Bunching or creeping, rhizomes	Moderate to high	Moderate	
	Tall fescue	Medium- to coarse-bladed; light to medium green	Bunching	High	High	
	Perennial ryegrass	Medium-bladed; shiny; medium to dark green	Bunching	Moderate to low	Moderate to low	
WARM SEASON	Bahia grass	Tough, coarse-bladed; light green	Creeping, rhizomes	High	High	
	Bermuda grass	Fine- to medium-bladed; medium to dark green	Creeping, rhizomes and stolons	High	High	
	Blue grama grass	Medium-bladed; grayish green	Bunching	Very high	High	
	Buffalo grass	Fine-bladed; light green to grayish green	Creeping, stolons	Very high	High	
	Centipede grass	Medium- to coarse-bladed; light green	Creeping, stolons	Moderate	High	
	St. Augustine grass	Coarse-bladed; bluish green to medium green	Creeping, stolons	Moderate	High	
	Zoysia	Coarse- to medium-bladed; medium green	Creeping, rhizomes and stolons	Moderate to high	High	

Know Your Turf Grass

The chart below describes 12 common lawn grasses—five cool-season varieties, which thrive in spring and fall, and seven warm-season grasses, which perform best in summer. The growing zones recommended for each grass appear on the map at right. At zone borders, you can grow both cool- and warm-season grasses.

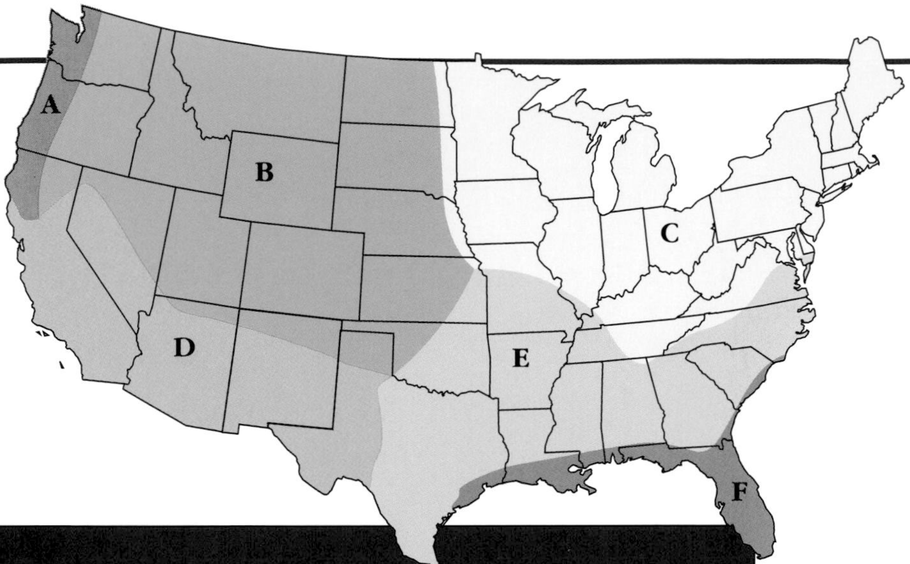

Cold Tolerance	Light Requirements	Propagation & Rate of Establishment	Lateral & Top Growth Rate	Soil Requirements	Fertilizer Needs	Wear Tolerance	Thatching Potential	Disease Susceptibility	Zones
Very high; thrives in cool, humid climates	Full sun; tolerates some light shade	Seed (germinates 5-12 days); moderate to slow	Fast; mow often to ¾ inch	Moist, fertile; compaction-intolerant; pH 4.5-6.7	High; 4-6 lbs. N per 1,000 sq. ft. per year	Moderate to low	High	Very high	A, northern parts of C
High	Full sun; some cultivars tolerate some shade	Seed (germinates 14-21 days), sod; moderate to slow	Moderate	Moist, fertile, well-drained; compaction-tolerant; pH 6-7	Moderate to high; 3-5 lbs. N per 1,000 sq. ft. per year	Moderate to high	Moderate to high	Moderate	A, B, C
High	Full sun to medium shade	Seed (germinates 10-14 days); moderate	Moderate	Silt, clay; tolerates sandy, infertile; compaction-intolerant; pH 5.5-6.5	Low; 0-2 lbs. N per 1,000 sq. ft. per year	Low	High	Moderate to high	A, B, C
Moderate	Full sun to medium shade	Seed (germinates 7-10 days) or sod; moderate	Very fast top growth	Silt, clay; tolerates sand, heavy clay, compaction; pH 4.7-8.5	Low to moderate; 2-4 lbs. N per 1,000 sq. ft. per year	Moderate	Low	Moderate	A, B, C, western parts of D
Moderate	Full sun to light shade	Seed (germinates 5-7 days); very fast	Fast	Fertile; tolerates moderate compaction; pH 6-7	High; 4-5 lbs. N per 1,000 sq. ft. per year	High	Low	High	Northern parts of D and E, southern parts of B and C
Low	Full sun to part shade	Seed (germinates 21-28 days); moderate to slow	Slow	Tolerates sand to clay, infertile, coastal areas; pH 6.5-7.5	Moderate; 2-4 lbs. N per 1,000 sq. ft. per year	Moderate to low	Low	Low	F, southern parts of E
Moderate to low	Full sun	Seed (germinates 10-14 days), sod, sprigs, plugs; all fast	Fast; invasive	Sand, silt; tolerates clay, compaction; pH 5.5-7.5	Moderate to high; 3-6 lbs. N per 1,000 sq. ft. per year	High	High	Moderate	D, E, F
High	Full sun	Seed (germinates 15-30 days); moderate to fast	Moderate	Tolerates all conditions but acidity and compaction; pH 7-8	Very low; 0-1 lb. N per 1,000 sq. ft. per year	Moderate to low	Low	Low	B, D, western parts of C and E
Moderate to high	Full sun; some hybrid cultivars tolerate light shade	Seed, sod, plugs; slow to moderate from seed, fast from plugs	Fast; invasive	Tolerates silt, clay, sand, alkalinity, compaction; pH 6-7.5	Low; 0-2 lbs. N per 1,000 sq. ft. per year	Moderate to low	Low	Moderate	B, D
Moderate to low	Full sun to part shade	Seed (germinates 14-20 days), sod, sprigs, plugs; slow to moderate	Slow	High tolerance; prefers infertile, acid; salt-intolerant	Low; 0-2 lbs. N per 1,000 sq. ft. per year; may need iron	Moderate to low	Moderate; avoid overfertilizing	Low	F, southern parts of E
Very low	Full sun to part shade	Sprigs, plugs, sod; all fast	Fast	Well-drained, fertile, sandy; tolerates salt, compaction; pH 6-7.5	Moderate to high; 3-5 lbs. N per 1,000 sq. ft. per year	Moderate to low	High	Moderate	D and F, southern parts of E
Moderate to high	Full sun to part shade	Sprigs, plugs, sod; slow	Slow lateral; moderate top	High tolerance; prefers well-drained, fine-textured; pH 5-7	Low; 0-3 lbs. N per 1,000 sq. ft. per year	Very high	Moderate; high if too much nitrogen	Low	D, E, F

the North, for example, Kentucky bluegrass makes a very attractive, cold-hardy lawn, but it needs full sun and much tending. Tall fescue is not as fine textured in appearance, but it requires much less fertilizer and resists weeds. A mixture of the two would provide the advantages of both. In a single-species southern lawn, zoysia may be the best choice for areas that experience frequent drought and other difficult weather conditions.

Soil: A Healthy Lawn's Foundation

Turf grass grows best in loamy soil that is well drained, slightly acidic, and rich in organic matter. A soil test will reveal your soil's pH level, the available nutrients, the presence of organic matter, and the soil's texture—determined by the proportions of sand, silt, and clay particles it contains. The chart opposite, which lists the characteristics of different soil types, will help you plan a maintenance strategy for your lawn.

Regardless of soil or turf-grass type, the ground under any established lawn becomes dense and hard over the years. As a result, air, water, and fertilizer cannot reach the plants' roots. Adding to the problem are excessive applications of chemicals. These can kill the beneficial microorganisms that break down the soil and produce humus and earthworms, which are natural soil aerators.

You can restore health to your lawn by aerating the soil yourself. This means removing small soil plugs—about ½ inch in diameter and 3 inches deep—at regularly spaced intervals. If your lawn is small, you can use an aerating fork—a manual tool with hollow tines that pulls up soil plugs. For larger areas, you may want to rent an aerating machine from your local garden center.

Aerate your lawn once a year, while the turf is actively growing, but not in hot weather. And be sure the soil is moist before you begin. Then, after you've removed the soil plugs, spread what is called a top dressing over the lawn and into the holes. The type of top dressing you use will vary according to your soil type. For a fast-draining sandy soil, spread ½ to 1 inch of finely screened shredded compost. This will not only help improve the soil's water-holding capacity over time, it will also replenish vital nutrients. For clay soils, which are often compacted and drain poorly, top-dress with sand or compost, or a mixture of both.

Most turf grasses grow best in soil with a slightly acid pH of 6 to 6.8. If your soil tests too acidic, you can correct it—or raise the pH—by adding lime. For an alkaline soil, you can lower the pH with elemental sulfur. Refer to the pH chart opposite to determine how to adjust your soil's pH.

Fertilizing the Lawn

Turf grass needs a slow and constant supply of nutrients, especially the major elements nitrogen, phosphorus, and potassium. Nitrogen is the most important for steady and vigorous growth of the grass. If plants receive too little, they will look light green or yellow and be vulnerable to pests and dis-

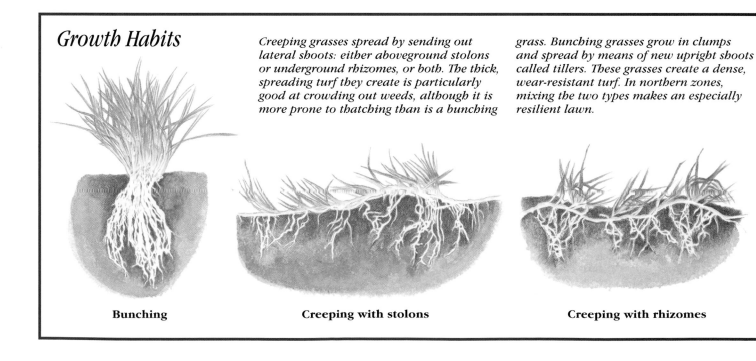

Growth Habits

Creeping grasses spread by sending out lateral shoots: either aboveground stolons or underground rhizomes, or both. The thick, spreading turf they create is particularly good at crowding out weeds, although it is more prone to thatching than is a bunching grass. Bunching grasses grow in clumps and spread by means of new upright shoots called tillers. These grasses create a dense, wear-resistant turf. In northern zones, mixing the two types makes an especially resilient lawn.

Bunching   **Creeping with stolons**   **Creeping with rhizomes**

eases. Too much nitrogen weakens the grass, which also invites trouble. Roots aren't forced to dig deep into the soil for nutrients, and the lawn then becomes dependent on regular doses of fertilizer. Also, because they are stimulated to grow quickly, overfertilized lawns need frequent mowing; this continually stresses the grass.

Lawn fertilizers are either synthetic or natural, or a combination of the two. Synthetics dissolve relatively quickly in the soil, especially the so-called fast-release types. As their name suggests, they work fast but disappear fast as well, subjecting the grass to stressful peaks and valleys of nutrient availability. They should be used only if your lawn needs an immediate dose of nutrients. Slow-release synthetics discharge their nutrients gradually, as do natural fertilizers. Although synthetics are cheaper, natural fertilizers have the additional benefit of adding bulk to the soil in the form of organic matter. There are many blended natural fertilizers on the market, which may contain combinations of dried poultry manure, blood meal, cottonseed meal, alfalfa meal, and seaweed. Commercial mixtures of organic and slow-release synthetic fertilizers also work well.

If you live in the northern regions of the United States, you need to fertilize only once in early fall and again 6 to 8 weeks later, before the grass goes dormant. Southern lawns require one to three applications a year, depending on the species of grass; they need fertilizing most in late spring and summer. The chart on pages 128-129 lists the needs for each turf species.

If you are applying dry or granular fertilizer to a

How Your Soil Affects Your Grass

Soil is the foundation of a lawn's health. The chart at right describes the characteristics of different soil types and will help you determine what amendments you need to incorporate into your soil as part of your lawn's regular maintenance program. If your soil is too acidic or too alkaline, the chart at lower right will guide you in correcting it.

Plant roots can absorb essential nutrients most easily from soil that is slightly acidic (pH 6 to 6.8); an improper pH not only impairs your lawn's capacity to extract nourishment, it also leaves it open to any number of problems. Don't make the recommended adjustments all at once, though; instead, gradually apply a fraction of the needed lime or elemental sulfur every 3 to 6 months, during any season and under any condition except on top of snow. Continue adjusting the soil—no more than 1 point in a year—until it has reached the right pH.

SOIL	CHARACTERISTICS						
	Texture	Drainage	Water Retention	Nutrient Retention	Organic Amendment Needs	Spring Warm-Up Rate	Compaction Potential
Clayey	Heavy, sticky when wet	Very slow	High	Very high	Compost, peat moss or humus, organic matter; sand for drainage	Slow	High
Silty	Silty or powdery	Slow	High	Moderate	Well-rotted compost or manure, peat humus	Moderate	High
Sandy	Light, dry, gritty	Fast	Low; needs frequent watering	Low; needs frequent fertilizing	Organic matter and fertilizer; peat humus and compost	Fast	Low
Loamy	Crumbly	Moderate	Moderate to high	Moderate to high	Compost, peat humus, any organic matter	Moderate	Moderate

ADJUSTING YOUR pH LEVEL

To Raise pH					To Lower pH				
Total lbs. of lime (calcium carbonate) needed per 1,000 sq. ft. to raise pH to 6.5					Total lbs. of elemental sulfur needed per 1,000 sq. ft. to lower pH to 6.5				
Soil pH	Clayey	Silty	Sandy	Loamy	Soil pH	Clayey	Silty	Sandy	Loamy
4.5	195	125	100	135	8.5	50	40	35	40
5.0	155	90	75	105	8.0	40	30	25	30
5.5	110	65	50	80	7.5	25	20	15	20
6.0	55	35	25	40					

large lawn, you can quickly cover a lot of ground with a broadcast spreader, which throws out the pellets in 6- to 8-foot swaths. Another device, the drop spreader—which drops the fertilizer in a 2-foot-wide path—can be calibrated to spread the amount recommended on the fertilizer bag. To ensure thorough coverage, first apply half of the recommended amount over the entire lawn, then make a pass in a perpendicular direction to spread the rest. Apply a liquid fertilizer with a hose-end sprayer or with a lawn sprinkler that has been out-

fitted with a fertilizing siphon. This device will siphon fertilizer from a container and direct it to the sprinkler.

How and When to Mow

A lawn needs mowing to stay healthy, not just to keep it neat. Cutting off older growth at the top of the grass plant stimulates root growth and encourages new top growth that fills in bare spots and makes the lawn thicker and more cushiony. There is a right way and a wrong way to mow, however, and improper mowing can actually damage your lawn. Whenever the tips of the grass plants are cut, the roots are weakened to some degree, and if more than 40 percent of the blades' length is removed, root growth is drastically slowed. A rule of thumb is to never remove more than a third of the grass blade at any one time. If the grass gets too tall, don't try to cut it back to its proper height all at once. First, give it a light cut, then let it recover for a few days before cutting again. Continue to alternate cutting with periods of rest until the grass is the proper height. (See the chart opposite for correct mowing heights.)

Tailor your cutting schedule to conform to the growth of the lawn, mowing often when the grass

A lawn mower with dull blades can damage grass tips, causing yellowing and ragged edges (near right) that are entry points for disease. By contrast, a sharp mower blade makes a clean, straight cut that keeps grass healthy and gives the lawn a trim look (far right).

When grass is continually cut short, root growth slows and may stop entirely (near right). But when it is mowed at the higher end of its preferred range, the plant suffers less shock, allowing the roots to branch and grow deep to make a stronger plant (far right)

is growing most vigorously, and less frequently as growth slows. While you are cutting, make sure to overlap the previous swath by about one-third with each pass so as not to miss any grass blades. Grass blades tend to lean in the direction the mower travels, so vary your pattern every three or four times you mow; this helps the grass stand upright and also keeps ruts from forming in the lawn.

When it comes to lawn mowers, reel mowers—either manual or powered—make the cleanest cuts. However, they have been eclipsed over the years by the rotary power mower, which is faster and allows you to mow the grass higher. Mulching mowers offer the bonus of chopping up grass clippings and forcing them down to the soil line, thus returning nutrients to the soil. Clippings from any mower, however, will benefit the grass if left in place, although they won't break down quite as fast as those at soil level. Leaving the clippings also eliminates the task of raking and bagging the shorn grass. Be sure to remove the clippings from the first spring mowing and the last fall mowing, though, to discourage disease. And regardless of the type of mower you use, keep the blades sharp by taking the mower to a hardware store or other service shop at least once a season.

Watering the Right Way

During its active growing season, turf grass needs 1 to 2 inches of water a week. Much of that amount may come from rainfall, but in many parts of the country you'll have to provide the water yourself. When lawns are dry, they lose their resiliency: They wilt and are slow to spring back when you walk on them. Also, the blades may look dull and take on a blue tint.

Watering correctly is important. When a lawn is overwatered, the grass blades grow more rapidly than the roots, weakening the whole plant. Not only will you have to mow such a lawn more often, but a constantly moist turf encourages weeds and—worse—fungal diseases. On the other hand, watering too lightly results in shallow root growth. Without adequate root length and branching to anchor the plant and tap into stores of water and nutrients deeper in the soil, the grass has a hard time combating drought, disease, and pests.

The best way to water is slowly and deeply, allowing the fluid to penetrate 6 to 8 inches into the soil. In clay soil, it may take hours for an inch of water to percolate that deeply. If you have clay soil, it's a good idea to water in cycles of perhaps 10 minutes on and 50 minutes off to allow the soil time to take up the water.

GRASSES		MOWING HEIGHTS		
		Cool Weather	Hot Weather	Last Mow
COOL SEASON	Bent grass	½" - ¾"	¾" - 1"	½" - ¾"
	Kentucky bluegrass	2" - 2½"	3"	2"
	Fine fescue	1½" - 2"	2"- 2½"	1½"- 2"
	Tall fescue	2" - 2½"	2½"- 4"	2½"
	Perennial ryegrass	1½" - 2"	2"- 2½"	1½"- 2"
WARM SEASON	Bahia grass	2" - 3"	3" - 3½"	2½" - 3"
	Bermuda grass	½" - 1½"	¾"- 3"	¾"- 1"
	Blue grama grass	2" - 4"	3" - 4"	2"- 3"
	Buffalo grass	2" - 5"	2" - 5"	2"- 4"
	Centipede grass	1" - 2"	1½" - 2"	1½" - 2"
	St. Augustine grass	2"- 3"	3"- 3½"	2½"
	Zoysia	½" - 1½"	1" - 2"	1" - 1½"

Controlling Thatch

Even the best-maintained lawn eventually accumulates a layer of dead but undecomposed plant material, called thatch, on the soil surface. In a natural system, this material—fibrous roots, stolons, rhizomes, and clippings—is quickly broken down by soil microorganisms. Chemicals that are applied to the lawn slow that process. And some grasses are just naturally thatch builders. While a layer of thatch less than half an inch thick will do no harm, anything more not only blocks the flow of water, air, and nutrients into the soil but also provides a home for pests and diseases. Warm-season lawns should be dethatched once or twice a year, in spring or fall, and cool-season grasses once every 3 years in late spring or summer. If your lawn is small, you can use a metal thatch rake to scratch the matted plant material out. If you have a very large lawn, however, you may want to consider renting a gasoline-powered dethatcher. Minimizing your use of chemicals and aerating the lawn will help keep thatch under control.

Identifying and Solving Lawn Problems

Despite the best care and attention, any number of things can still go wrong with your lawn, especially if it hasn't been converted to a low-maintenance system. Before assuming that a pest or disease is causing a particular problem, consider whether environmental or cultural conditions might be responsible. Such problems can often be easily fixed, and doing so promptly may prevent the invasion of pests or diseases.

Recognizing Common Problems

Brown spots, though they can be a sign of possible infestation or infection, may also be a symptom of something less troublesome, such as chemical spills, dog-urine damage, or nutrient deficiency *(chart, below)*. Other problems have their own telltale signs. If the lawn appears yellow or grayish, for example, you've probably mowed it with a dull blade. Let it grow out, then mow lightly with a blade that is sharp. Compacted, moist, shady areas often provide the perfect environment for algae, which may appear as a green to black slimy scum on the soil and grass. Spray the area with copper sulfate, aerate the soil, and do what you can to improve drainage and increase the amount of light the site receives. A low pH level may exacerbate the problem; check to be sure your soil pH is in the 6 to 6.8 range.

Moss also settles on shady, infertile, acidic soils. Rake it up and, if necessary, apply iron sulfate at a dose of 3 tablespoons per 1 to 2 gallons of water to cover 1,000 square feet of turf. Afterward, correct your soil by raising the pH to the proper level and adding the right amount of organic fertilizer to make sure the moss doesn't return. Aerating and improving drainage will also help.

Controlling Weeds

A lawn doesn't have to be entirely weed free to be healthy and attractive, so it's up to you to decide how many uninvited guests you will tolerate. The stricter you are about weeds, the more time and money you will need to spend to thwart them—

Brown spots on the lawn (above) aren't always caused by pests or diseases. The chart at right lists five common environmental causes of such problems—including nutrient deficiencies and drought—and ways to recognize and treat them.

ENVIRONMENTAL CAUSES OF BROWN SPOTS AND HOW TO FIX THEM			
Damage	**Problem**	**Cause**	**Solution**
Salt	Grass slowly turns brown and dies, especially in lowest areas; soil may have white or dark brown crust.	Salt buildup from natural level in soil, or residue from excess fertilizer. Possibly poor drainage.	If drainage is good, water heavily. Aerate soil, add sand. Fill in low spots. Fertilize in correct amounts.
Fertilizer Burn	Patches, stripes, or curves of dead grass that do not spread or enlarge; appear 2-5 days after fertilizing.	High level of nitrogen due to misuse of fast-release synthetic fertilizer, especially in warm weather.	Water thoroughly after fertilizing. Replace soil under spots that are bare after 3-4 weeks and replant.
Dog Urine	Circles of dead or brown grass, surrounded by healthy green grass; may appear as dark green patches.	Nitrogen and salts in dog urine burn or kill grass; especially damaging in hot, dry weather.	Water immediately. If grass dies, allow grass to fill in area, dig up and reseed, or patch with sod.
Drought/Heat	Grass wilts; becomes dull, bluish, or grayish green to brown. Footprints show. Areas thin out.	Symptoms appear first in hottest and driest areas: along sidewalks, driveways, sunny and sandy areas.	Mow cool-season grasses ½" higher. Water; check soil moisture. Overseed with drought-tolerant grass.
Nutrient Deficiencies	Lawn turns slightly yellow, purplish, or reddish brown; grows slowly; leaf tops wither, grass thins.	Lawn needs to be fertilized, or improper soil pH is keeping grass from taking up nutrients.	Have soil tested for nutrient levels; correct with recommended fertilizer. Adjust pH, if necessary.

and the more likely you'll be to resort to chemical herbicides to get rid of them.

You can rid your lawn of most weeds—and prevent them, too—using both cultural and mechanical methods. Turf that is growing vigorously and steadily will crowd out the lion's share of weeds. To that end, light fertilizing at the right time strengthens the grass and allows it to beat out the competition. And don't forget that weeds can be a sign that something else is wrong. Certain weeds thrive in compacted soil, for example, while others like wet conditions; the chart at right describes specific weeds and the environmental problems they may indicate.

Lawn weeds may be annual or perennial, broadleaf or grassy, and warm- or cool-season. Identifying them and understanding their habits can help to control them (pages 152-155). For example, if you cut and remove annual weeds such as crab grass before they set seed, you'll go a long way toward eradicating them. However, perennial weeds, such as dandelion, must be removed roots and all to prevent them from spreading. Low-growing, spreading lawn weeds may be discouraged by continued high mowing of the grass.

Sometimes the best way to control lawn weeds is with plain old elbow grease. There are many effective weed knives, diggers, pullers, and poppers on the market. Taking them in hand for an hour or so every week will reduce your weed population dramatically. Pulling weeds can leave bare spots in your lawn, however, and new weeds will move in unless you take steps to foil them. After digging

Weeds in a lawn sometimes serve as warnings of underlying trouble. The perennial weed curly dock (top), for example, with its red-tinged leaves and seeds, can be a sign of excessive moisture. Annual bluegrass (bottom), an unwelcome Kentucky bluegrass relative, thrives in compacted, moist soils, especially when the turf is mowed too closely. Good weed control includes correcting those conditions to prevent recurrence.

WEEDS THAT SIGNAL TROUBLE

Name of Weed	Conditions Indicated
Annual bluegrass	Compaction; high moisture; shade; infertile soil; low mowing
Black medic	Dry, infertile soil; drought
*Common chickweed	Compaction; thinning turf; excessive moisture; highly fertile or acid soil; moist shade
Clover	Thinning turf; low fertility; drought conditions; compaction
*Crab grass	Thinning turf; frequent, light, shallow watering; low mowing; compaction; low fertility; poor drainage; drought
Curly dock	Poor drainage; excess moisture; turf stressed by hot, dry weather
*Dandelion	Thinning grass; overwatering; low mowing; low fertility; drought; highly opportunistic
*Goose grass	Compaction; high moisture; poor drainage; low mowing; frequent or light watering; highly fertile soil
Ground ivy	Shade; moist soil; poor drainage; highly fertile soil
Henbit	Excessive moisture; highly fertile soil; thinning or new turf
Lespedeza	Dry, infertile, acid soil; drought
Plantain	Dense soil; excessive moisture; low fertility; low mowing
Prostrate knotweed	Compaction, especially in heavily traveled areas; drought; thinning turf
Red sorrel	Low pH (under 5); infertile soil; poor drainage
*Spurge	Sand or gravel soils; dry soil; drought stress; thin, undernourished, infertile turf; also found on well-maintained lawns subject to low mowing
Wild garlic	Thinning turf; tolerates almost any environment in cool seasons, including heavy, wet soil or sandy soil with low humus
Wild onion	Thinning turf; tolerates almost any environment in spring and fall
Wild violet	Shade with cool, moist soil; poor drainage
*Wood sorrel	Drought; highly opportunistic in many situations

*See also Guide to Common Garden Weeds, pages 152-155.

weeds up, fill in any spots with a bit of topsoil, put down some grass seed, and scratch the seeds into the soil with a rake.

If your lawn is more than 25 percent weeds, pulling and cutting won't do the trick. Such a large infestation results from faulty maintenance practices such as improper fertilizing, or an underlying problem such as the wrong kind of grass, too much shade, or poor soil. Start by overseeding your lawn with an improved grass variety, and consider what maintenance habits or environmental conditions might be allowing weeds to take hold.

As a last resort, you can try a selective herbicide, but be aware that while it may remove the weeds, it won't solve the problem that may be inviting them. In the worst cases, you might consider starting over entirely by removing the lawn, correcting the soil, and replanting with a better turf variety.

The Problem of Pests

Pests are less likely to attack a healthy lawn, but they may show up occasionally, especially when their natural enemies aren't present or when the grass is stressed by harsh weather. Like weeds, pests sometimes signal environmental problems, such as poor soil or improper mowing or fertilizing.

The damage often appears as discolored grass or brown and dying patches. You can usually get rid of the pest by using one of several natural insecticides, such as *Bacillus thuringiensis* (Bt). Check with your local Cooperative Extension Service for the right time to apply insecticides, and follow all package directions. Chemical pesticides should be used very carefully and only as a last resort.

Some of the pests most commonly found in lawns are the following:
- Armyworms are serious pests of warm-season grasses, especially Bermuda grass, although they can attack any species. The caterpillars are 1 to 2 inches long, striped, and yellow to brownish green; fall armyworms have an inverted Y on their heads. Active in the heat of summer, they chew grass blades to skeletons, leaving patches of ragged grass. Use Bt to control them.
- The white grubs of Japanese and other beetles attack the roots of many grasses, including Kentucky bluegrass, bent grass, and fescues. As the grubs feed, the turf loosens from the soil and turns brown. Many grubs can be controlled with neem and beneficial nematodes. Milky spore disease will control Japanese beetle grubs. For complete descriptions

When Japanese beetle larvae feed underground on grass roots, the lawn develops brown patches as grass plants die (above). The turf eventually becomes loose and can be lifted from the soil. Mole crickets (left) tunnel about an inch below the surface of the ground, feeding on roots and leaving raised mounds of soil and wilted brown grass.

TIPS FROM THE PROS

Overseeding for a Better Lawn

You don't have to go to the trouble of digging up your entire lawn and starting over to grow any of the new disease- and insect-resistant or low-maintenance grasses that are now on the market. A technique called overseeding allows you to sow them right over your existing turf. Because the new varieties are more vigorous than the older ones, they will eventually take over the lawn.

You'll get the best results if you overseed at a time when the lawn is not under stress from excessive heat or drought. To start, mow your existing grass to about half the normal mowing height. Then rough up the turf with a garden rake to expose a good deal of soil. Select seed that is appropriate for your local conditions (consult the chart of turf grasses on pages 128-129), and sow it at one-and-one-half times the rate that is recommended on the package. Although seed can be sown by hand, for complete, even coverage it's best to use a drop spreader or a broadcast spreader.

Rake the area again, then water well and keep it moist until the new grass begins to sprout. Stay off the area during this period, and don't mow for a few weeks—until the new grass reaches its maximum recommended height. (See box on page 133 for mowing heights.)

of the damage, detection, and control of various species of beetle grubs, see pages 301-324 of the Encyclopedia of Beneficials, Pests, and Diseases at the back of this book.

- Adult billbugs are dark, snouted beetles that eat grass leaves and burrow in stems; root-eating grubs are legless and white with yellowish to reddish brown heads. They leave behind yellow or brown patches of turf that can be pulled up from the soil. Early-summer treatment with beneficial nematodes will control these pests.

- Chinch bugs feed on many grass varieties from early spring to late autumn, causing the turf to yellow and die in patches. Young nymphs—bright red with a white stripe—cause most of the damage. They prefer sunny lawns during hot, dry weather. See page 304 of the encyclopedia for a comprehensive list of control methods.

- Cutworms are minor pests unless their populations become large. The caterpillars are usually smooth and can be brownish, grayish white, or green tinged. They feed at night from spring through summer on grass stems and leaves. Control them with neem.

- Greenbugs are light green aphids that feed on grass blades—especially underwatered or overfertilized Kentucky bluegrass—in early summer and late fall, turning affected areas a rusty color. They can be controlled with insecticidal soap.

- Mites are minute spider relatives that usually attack Bermuda grass or Kentucky bluegrass, sucking the juice out of the blades and turning them yellow. Most active during hot, dry weather, mites can be controlled with insecticidal soap.

- Mole crickets—winged relatives of the grasshopper that are brown and 1½ inches long—cause problems in all types of southern lawns from April to October. They feed on grass roots as they tunnel beneath the lawn, causing the soil to dry out. Control them with *Nosema locustae* or beneficial nematodes.

- Sod webworms attack Kentucky bluegrass, bent grass, fescues, and zoysia. The light brown, spotted caterpillars feed at night in the thatch layer from late spring through summer. For more information on detecting and controlling sod webworms, see page 319 of the encyclopedia.

A surface examination of your lawn may reveal adult or larval insects on the grass, but certain pests—such as sod webworms, cutworms, and chinch bugs—are hard to spot because they live in

Pest-Resistant Grasses

These cultivated endophytic turf grasses resist attack from many common lawn pests. The percentages given indicate the proportion of the turf that will not be affected if a pest attempts to invade your lawn. Because endophytes are living organisms in the grass seed, the seed must be handled carefully. Be sure to buy fresh seed—the maximum shelf life is 2 years—and store it at 50° to 60°F.

Perennial Ryegrass

HIGH ENDOPHYTE LEVEL (80-100%):
'Commander'
'Pennant'
'Pinnacle'
'Repell'
'Saturn'
'Saville'

MODERATELY HIGH ENDOPHYTE LEVEL (60-80%):
'Accolade'
'Citation II'
'Cowboy'
'Omega II'
'Stallion'

MODERATE ENDOPHYTE LEVEL (30-60%):
'Caliente'
'Delray'
'Palmer'
'Premier'
'Vintage'

Tall Fescue

HIGH ENDOPHYTE LEVEL (80-100%):
'Bonsai'
'Shenandoah'
'SR 8200'

MODERATE ENDOPHYTE LEVEL (30-60%):
'Phoenix'
'Pixie'

Fine Fescue

HIGH ENDOPHYTE LEVEL (80-100%):
'Aurora' with endophytes
'Discovery'
'Jamestown II'
'Reliant' with endophytes
'Shadow' with endophytes
'SR 5000'

thatch or at the soil surface. You can force them into the open by thoroughly drenching the soil with a solution containing 2 to 3 tablespoons of liquid dish detergent to every gallon of water.

Other pests, such as beetle grubs, live below the soil surface. If you can roll up the turf like a carpet, you will probably see grubs at work. If the turf doesn't roll but you suspect underground pests, check by digging up a few 1-foot-square, 2-inch-thick slabs of sod and searching the soil. Afterward, replace and thoroughly water the sod, and it will regrow.

If your lawn suffers from chronic problems, consider overseeding with an insect-resistant grass. Many new varieties of perennial ryegrass, tall fescue, and fine fescue resist damage from pests such as sod webworms, armyworms, cutworms, billbug larvae, chinch bugs, and greenbugs. Known as endophytic grasses, they host a beneficial fungus in their leaf and stem tissue that repels or kills these common lawn insects. See the list above for recommendations.

Treating Turf Grass Diseases

Turf diseases are often a side effect of high-maintenance lawn programs. High temperatures and humidity, inadequate air circulation, poor soil, and too much shade also increase the chance that disease will strike your lawn, especially if your grass variety does not tolerate these conditions.

Most diseases are caused by fungi that live in the soil and the thatch layer. Many are choosy about climate and temperature and will appear only under the right circumstances. Also, some diseases are species specific, targeting only particular types of grass. When disease does strike, diagnosis can be difficult. General symptoms range from striped blades to brown patches of turf to a water-soaked appearance. The most reliable way to identify a disease is to send samples of your turf and soil to your local Cooperative Extension Service or a university's plant pathology lab.

To combat a disease, you'll need to assess and repair the cultural and environmental conditions that may be giving it a foothold. In almost all cases, dethatching and aerating will help, as will watering the lawn deeply and only in the morning. Top-dressing with compost can slow some diseases. You may need to use a light application of a fast-release synthetic fertilizer to get nutrients to ailing grass plants quickly. Also, consider overseeding with one of the newer grass varieties that are resistant to a specific disease.

Descriptions of 10 common lawn diseases and the conditions that trigger them are profiled here. See pages 324-339 of the Encyclopedia of Beneficials, Pests, and Diseases at the back of this book for information about other diseases that affect a wide range of plants, including turf grasses.

1. BROWN PATCH (Rhizoctonia solani)

This summertime disease strikes most turf grasses at some point. Leaves appear dark and water-soaked, then become dry and brown, creating irregular or circular patches as large as several feet across. It occurs primarily when temperatures and humidity are high; excessive nitrogen exacerbates the problem. Avoid heavy fertilizing, and don't overwater. Raise the mowing height, and apply the beneficial microorganism Trichoderma, neem, fungicidal soap, or garlic oil.

2. DOLLARSPOT (Sclerotinia homoeocarpa)

Most grass species are susceptible to this disease, which causes straw-colored spots that range from the size of a silver dollar to 6 inches across. Blades die from the tip down. Dollarspot is most common in late spring to early summer and again in early fall, in dry soil and high humidity. Control it with light, frequent applications of nitrogen fertilizer; water deeply, at most once a week; and use neem, fungicidal soap, or garlic oil.

3. FAIRY RINGS (Marasmius oreades)

This disease occurs most often in areas of high rainfall. Dark green circles or arcs of grass appear in spring; later, mushrooms may sprout. Deprived of water and nutrients, the grass within the ring dies. Fertilize with nitrogen, aerate the rings, keep the area watered, and mow frequently. There are no chemical controls. Complete eradication may mean replacing the turf and soil.

4. MELTING OUT (Drechslera poae)

This disease may attack Kentucky bluegrass during cool, moist spring and fall weather. Blades first develop tan spots with purplish brown borders. Later, lesions appear water-soaked, and the entire plant rots. Avoid synthetic nitrogen fertilizers, water deeply and infrequently, and mow high. Overseed the lawn with a resistant variety.

5. NECROTIC RING SPOT
(Leptosphaeria korrae)

Often found in Kentucky bluegrass, bent grass, and creeping red fescue, necrotic ring spot usually begins during cool, wet weather. The disease strikes plant roots. Circles of dead grass with living plants at the center, often greater than a foot in diameter, may appear; individual plants look purple. Avoid summer fertilizing, mow on schedule at the proper height, and overseed with perennial ryegrass or tall fescue.

6. PARASITIC NEMATODES

Of the thousands of nematode species, about 50 are turf grass parasites that feed on roots. Damage—yellowing, wilting, and thinning—is difficult to distinguish from environmental stress. Dig soil samples from several spots on the lawn where the damage borders healthy grass, keep the samples moist, and take them to a Cooperative Extension Service for treatment recommendations based on the species. Mow the grass high, water properly, and fertilize.

7. PYTHIUM BLIGHT
(Pythium species)

High humidity and warm nights, paired with excessive fertilizing and mowing and poor drainage, are ideal conditions for pythium blight. It appears first in shady areas as light brown or reddish brown patches, circles, or streaks. Leaf blades may look watery, and thin, cottony webbing may be evident early in the day. Good preventive maintenance is essential; once it strikes it is impossible to eradicate.

8. RED THREAD
(Laetisaria fuciformis)

This disease most commonly attacks fine fescue, perennial ryegrass, and Kentucky bluegrass during cool, wet, overcast weather. Infected blades in the final stage display reddish threads of cottony webbing; circular patches of infection may measure up to 2 feet across. Apply a synthetic fertilizer lightly and frequently; water deeply and regularly. Check soil pH. Plant a resistant variety.

9. SNOW MOLD (Microdochium nivale; Typhula species)

Snow mold can be active at temperatures just above freezing and most often strikes dormant grass. Moist soil, deep snow, and lush grass encourage the disease, which appears as 2- to 3-inch round patches that expand up to 2 feet. Inside the patch, the grass appears water-soaked; outside, there may be a pink or grayish ring around the patch. Monitor pH, improve drainage, and prune nearby trees and shrubs to increase air circulation.

10. STRIPE SMUT
(Ustilago striiformis)

A foe of Kentucky bluegrass, bent grass, and perennial ryegrass, stripe smut is most noticeable during spring and fall. Plants turn yellow or light green, grayish to black streaks appear on blades, and eventually blades shred and curl. The disease occurs most often when turf is treated with large doses of nitrogen. Mow high during summer, water deeply to avoid drought stress, and apply a balanced fertilizer in fall.

139

CHAPTER SIX

Controlling Weeds

Weeds are the most diverse of all plant groups—inch-high creepers, 40-foot-tall trees, perennials with beguiling flowers, rangy thistles with finger-pricking spines. Their common trait is not a fixed one, like color or size. Instead, it is a matter of definition: If a plant is growing in the wrong place, it is a weed. Queen Anne's lace, for example, is welcome in the informal garden at left, where it mingles demurely with red valerian. However, this Eurasian native has colonized American fields and roadsides and can be a nuisance where it is not wanted.

The guide on pages 152-155 will help you identify the irksome plants before eradicating them becomes an arduous task. With concern for the environment on the rise, chemical methods of controlling weeds have given way to nonchemical ones whenever feasible. Earth-friendly measures described in this chapter include hoeing and mulching, as well as designing gardens to be weed resistant. For the times when herbicides are the only answer to a weed problem, you'll need to learn the proper methods for handling and applying the chemicals (pages 150-151).

Defending the Garden against Weeds

As a gardener, you can view weeds in two ways: as benefactors in some situations and as opponents in others. Paradoxically, the very traits that make a plant a headache in a garden often make it valuable in a natural plant community.

When a fire, flood, or some other disturbance strips away vegetation in the wild, weeds are among the pioneers that recolonize the denuded soil. Those with long taproots pull up nutrients from below the surface. Canada thistle's roots, for instance, grow down as far as 20 feet. When the weed dies and decomposes, the nutrients enrich the soil, and the remains of the foliage and stems increase its organic content. Also, taproots break through the underlying hardpan that, in many areas of the United States, prevents water from sinking deep into the soil. Once the weeds have cracked the hardpan, other plants can flourish there. Ragweed, annual morning glory, and clover—all weeds, to gardeners—are known to agronomists as soil improvers. Purslane spreads its rooting stems across eroded hillsides, netting organic particles and rebuilding the soil.

The weeds that take root in your garden say something about the characteristics of its soil and can therefore help you decide what steps to take to improve it. Sorrel, knapweed, coltsfoot, and hawkweed, for instance, are sure indicators of acidic soil, while Joe-Pye weed, buttercups, moss, and dock spring up where drainage is poor. A flourishing crop of mustard, bindweed, or quack grass may be evidence of a thin, hard surface crust or of a hardpan lying below the surface that will discourage other plants.

Weeds as the Gardener's Enemy

Whatever their usefulness in some situations, weeds must nevertheless be viewed as the enemy, and for several excellent reasons that have to do both with aesthetics and with the health of your plantings. First, their straggly or obtrusive shapes spoil the look of the garden. Second, their vigorous roots spread rapidly, depriving ornamental plants and vegetables of soil nutrients and moisture, and competing with them for space and light. Third, weeds may harbor plant diseases that destroy cultivated plants, and they also attract pests to the garden. Sorrel, dock, and groundsel, for example, are favorite breeding grounds of the tarnished plant bug, which does serious damage to hundreds of different species, including most vegetables and many perennials, trees, and shrubs.

Life Cycles of Herbaceous Weeds

Weeds fall into many of the same categories as ornamentals—woody plants, vines, and herbaceous annuals, biennials, and perennials. Annual weeds, which account for about 80 percent of common garden weeds, germinate, grow, bloom, set seed, and die in one growing season. Most of these are shallow-rooted sun lovers that set vast numbers of seeds. A single redroot pigweed, for instance, may scatter more than 100,000 seeds, whereas one witchweed plant can produce five times that number.

Just as impressive as the sheer number of weed seeds is the length of time they can remain dormant when conditions are unfavorable, then germinate and produce healthy plants when conditions improve. Lamb's-quarters seeds unearthed at an archaeological site, for example, sprouted after 1,700 years. The best strategy for combating annual weeds, then, is to get rid of them early in the season, before they bloom and drop those enduring seeds.

A few weed species, such as Queen Anne's lace, are biennials, which means that they begin growth one year, then flower, set seed, and die the next. Like annuals, these plants can be prodigious seed producers—a biennial mullein may scatter as many as 223,000 seeds. Handle biennials as you would annuals: Cut or pull them the first season and you won't have to look for them again.

The Tenacious Perennials

While not as common in the garden as their annual counterparts, the perennial weeds that pop up among your plantings are potentially even more of a nuisance because they may live and reproduce for many years. Poison ivy, dandelion,

SELECTING A WEED-CONTROL STRATEGY

Weed Habitat	Solution	Comments
Ground cover	Mulch; hand pull or hoe; apply herbicide.	Lay mulch only 2 inches deep to allow ground cover to spread. Shield the ground cover from herbicide as shown on page 151.
Lawn	Hand pull or hoe; raise blade of mower.	Close mowing and a constantly moist soil encourage weeds.
New garden area	Plant cover crop; solarize *(pages 203-204)*; till repeatedly.	Plant the area promptly so weeds won't recolonize it. Control any that appear with hand pulling or cultivation. Mulch the newly installed plants.
Perennial or annual bed	Mulch; hand pull or hoe; install an edging.	If the area has poor drainage, underplant with ground cover or mulch with stone.
Rose bed	Mulch; cultivate shallowly.	Do not use an organic mulch if the area is prone to black spot or mildew.
Tree set in lawn	Mulch; plant ground cover.	Keep mulch several inches away from tree trunks.
Under shrubs	Mulch; plant ground cover.	Keep mulch several inches from stems; use a coarse mulch on slopes to prevent washing; use easily controlled species such as ice plant or ajuga.
Terraces, walks	Pour boiling water on weeds; install pavers over landscape fabric or tarpaper; plant low-growing plants between pavers; spray with herbicide.	Use herbicide sparingly to minimize runoff.

Designing Defenses against Weeds

Your garden will be far easier to maintain if you take principles of weed control into account when you are laying out beds and borders, selecting and siting plants, and choosing mulches. Several methods of weed prevention that are not only utilitarian but also aesthetically pleasing have been incorporated into the garden shown below:

- The fence surrounding the garden and the dense shrubs planted at the perimeter block many airborne seeds.
- Where the perennial bed in the foreground abuts the lawn, plastic edging keeps grass rhizomes from creeping into the bed. Such a barrier must extend at least 4 inches underground to prevent frost from heaving it out of place.
- The woodchip mulch covering the planting bed discourages weed seeds that need light to germinate. The mulch also keeps soil moist, making it easier to pluck out unwanted seedlings.
- The lawn is a manageable size, which makes it easier to control any weeds that may crop up in the turf. A small-size lawn is also easier to keep healthy, and grass that is growing vigorously will resist the spread of weeds.

and pokeweed send roots deep into the soil. Cutting their tops off early in the season keeps them from blooming and spreading, but the roots will send up foliage repeatedly. Many other perennial species, including quack grass, henbit, and comfrey, sprout anew from even small fragments of root or stem. To get rid of these weeds, you must destroy them, roots and all. With repeated cutting or heavy mulching, you may be able to starve the roots, since a plant deprived of either leaves or sunlight can't manufacture food.

Keeping Weeds Out

The best way to deal with weeds of any type is to keep them out of your garden in the first place or, if they do find their way in, to make their stay less agreeable. Although it is easiest to do this when you're working with a new garden, there are reliable techniques for reducing or eliminating the weed population in mature gardens.

One proven way to prevent weeds is to choose plants well suited to your climate and your property's various microclimates, soil conditions, and drainage patterns. Vigorous plantings resist competition from stray weeds and are less likely to succumb to the pests they attract. For instance, a rugosa rose planted on a dry, windy slope can spread quickly and shade out weeds. A rhododendron planted in the same spot will be a much poorer competitor because it needs more moisture and shade to thrive; weed seedlings will flourish around and beneath it.

Getting Rid of Weed Seeds

When you create a new flower bed or lawn, allow the extra time it takes to give the soil a weedless start. If your garden has only a thin layer of topsoil, spend a season digging in organic materials to enrich it. Resist the quick but risky alternative of buying merchandise that's advertised as topsoil. Far too often such an offering is a poor substitute at best, lacking the nutrients, organic content, and microorganisms that characterize genuine topsoil. Soil you buy may also be full of weed seeds waiting to germinate on your property. At the same time, be wary of soil said to be weed free; it may have been heavily treated with herbicides that will allow nothing at all to grow for years. Either way, commercial "topsoil" is a bad bargain.

Once the organic content of the soil has been boosted, the second step is to eliminate any weed seeds. One way of doing this is by solarization *(pages 203-204)*, a process that takes several weeks. Alternatively, if you are able to reserve an entire growing season for preparation, you can remove the weeds and greatly improve the soil at the same time by tilling the ground and sowing what is called a cover crop.

A Clean Start with Cover Crops

Begin the process in early spring, sowing the tilled ground with buckwheat, hairy vetch, or another cover crop recommended for your area. If you are using buckwheat or vetch, apply seed at the rate of 4 pounds per 1,000 square feet. As the crop sprouts and grows, so do the weeds, but most of them get shaded out before they set seed. Before the crop flowers, till it under completely—the decaying plants now act as "green manure"—then plant another batch of seed. Again, till the crop under before it flowers. For the third and last crop of the year, use annual ryegrass to carry on the weed-shading work from late in the growing season until the following spring. Once more, till the crop under before it flowers. These cover-crop cycles will eliminate nearly all the weeds on the site, both annual and perennial, and after the last tilling, your garden or lawn will be ready to plant.

A cover crop is feasible for virtually any size plot. In a small area, you won't need a rotary tiller to break up the soil. Simply spade the ground and rake it before seeding. Then, when the time comes, use a garden fork to turn the crop under. Whether you till by hand or by machine, the relatively weed-free condition of the soil—plus the nutrients and organic matter furnished by the cover crop—will give a new bed or lawn a wonderful boost.

Barring Weeds from Entry

Even if you've eliminated weeds from your soil, the wind, birds, wild animals, and roving pets can carry seeds from neighboring properties and deposit them in your yard. Fences, walls, and hedges are effective barriers against airborne seeds and those carried by animals. Among fences, a solid, stockade type is best, but even lattice fencing offers significant protection. A row of closely planted shrubs with dense foliage will also intercept would-be weed invaders. Such barrier plantings can even be seasonal. A strip of tall annuals or perennials, for instance, will protect your vegetable garden but will disappear when frost arrives, leaving the way clear for you to do cleanup chores.

Weed seeds sometimes hide in the containers and rootballs of plants you buy at garden centers. Examine your purchases carefully to avoid inadvertently transporting weeds home to your garden. And if you go camping or hiking, look over your gear and brush yourself off on the way back, so that weed seeds from the wilderness won't come home with you.

Mulches for Weed Control

Mulch acts as an excellent ground-level barrier against weeds. By restricting the amount of light reaching the soil surface, mulch prevents many weed seeds from germinating. In addition, it can smother any seedlings that do get started before they become large enough to be troublesome. Both organic materials, such as leaves, bark, or newspaper, and inorganic materials, such as stone or landscape fabric, are effective weed blockers.

Using an Organic Mulch

Plant-material mulches, such as leaves, shredded bark, buckwheat hulls, wheat or oat straw or salt hay, and woodchips, are widely available and convenient to use. They also have the added advantage of improving the soil as they decay. Plan on replenishing the mulch occasionally to replace material that has decomposed. Most leaf and shredded-bark mulches must be renewed annually; for longer-lasting mulch, use bark chips or pine needles, which take longer to decompose. *(Caution: Orchard grass should never be used, because it contains seeds that will sprout into hummocks that are very difficult to get rid of.)*

The recommended depth of the mulch depends on the size of its particles. A layer 2 to 3 inches deep for a finely textured mulch, such as compost, or 4 to 6 inches deep for a bulkier one, such as pine bark, is usually sufficient for weed control; laid deeper, the mulch may keep oxygen, water, and nutrients from reaching the roots of garden plants. Lay mulch thickest in areas between plants. Avoid piling it directly against the stems, as this encourages disease. Mulch piled against the base of a tree or shrub is a favorite nesting place for rodents, so leave a bare ring of soil around those plants. If you are mulching with fresh woodchips, be sure to scatter a slow-release nitrogen fertilizer over the soil before spreading the chips; otherwise, microorganisms breaking down the wood will draw nitrogen from the soil.

Inorganic Mulches

Gravel, marble chips, lava rock, and other stone mulches are good choices for small formal areas, desert gardens, and rock gardens. In areas where slugs, snails, or mildews and other fungus diseases are a serious problem, stone is preferable to organic materials, which foster the moist conditions these pests and diseases require.

For maximum protection against weeds, you can combine a top layer of stone with an underlay of woven landscape fabric, black plastic sheeting, or newspaper spread several sheets thick (don't use colored pages, however—the inks can be toxic). Some gardeners use these materials alone, but aside from the fact that they're uniformly unattractive, they have some practical drawbacks. Black plastic and landscape fabric deteriorate when they are exposed to sunlight, and newspaper and plastic are prone to being blown out of place unless they're weighted down.

Landscape fabric is the most expensive of the underlays, but it can last 5 years or more. Water and nutrients easily pass through it, and its rough texture helps keep the overlaid mulch in place. Newspaper and black plastic excel at blocking weeds, but they also block the downward movement of moisture and fertilizers. If you use such an underlay, you'll need to punch several holes through it where it surrounds each plant.

With any of the underlays, pile on at least 2 inches of decorative mulch. If the layer is too thin, you'll have to spend gardening time putting it back in place over the bare patches that will inevitably appear.

Ground Covers for Weed Control

If you prefer to suppress weeds with an attractive blanket of plants rather than one of woodchips or stone, consider a perennial ground cover with dense foliage. Just make sure you don't plant one that will become a weed itself. English ivy has this potential, especially in the warmer parts of the country. Play it safe by choosing shallow-rooted, easily controlled ground covers such as periwinkle,

Mother-of-thyme in full rosy purple bloom fills the crevices of this northern California terrace and spills down the steps between billowy white mounds of snow-in-summer. Both of these plants grow densely enough to outcompete weeds.

Invasive Exotic Plants

Some plants that are harmless in their native habitats can be disastrous when introduced into a new area. There are many instances of plants from abroad that have become all-but-invincible weeds in the American landscape, overrunning gardens and escaping into the countryside because they've been freed from factors such as climate or pests that had kept them within bounds. A well-known example is the kudzu vine *(below),* native to China and Japan, which can grow stems up to 60 feet long in a single season.

Unfortunately, many nurseries continue to market troublesome exotics without any cautionary advice, even though experience has shown how ill suited the plants are for certain parts of the United States, or even the entire country. Watch out for so-called "miracle plants" touted for their rapid growth. The weedy Japanese rose, for example, has become naturalized in much of the country.

Below is a list of exotic plants that you should investigate carefully before planting. A reputable local nursery, horticulturists at nearby public gardens, or your Cooperative Extension Service agent are good sources of information about a plant's weed potential in your area.

hypericum, sedum, moneywort, plumbago, and creeping phlox. When you plant a ground cover, remember that until it spreads and fills out, it's a good idea to mulch the bare spaces between plants to discourage weeds. With ground covers like periwinkle that colonize by runners or rooting stems, lay mulch no more than 2 inches deep; a thicker layer will prevent the plants from spreading.

Once your ground cover becomes established, hand pulling or digging should take care of the few weeds that come up. If stubborn perennial weeds make it necessary for you to use a herbicide spray, protect the plants carefully, as shown on page 151.

A Temporary Ground Cover

A creative way to keep weeds from sprouting before the ornamentals in your garden have filled out and can shade the soil is to set out a temporary ground cover of fast-growing leaf lettuce, radicchio, or other early-season salad greens. By the time you've harvested and enjoyed the last of your crop, the perennials will have grown large enough to minimize late-appearing weeds.

Exotics with Weed Potential

Aegopodium podagraria
(goutweed, bishop's weed)
Ailanthus altissima
(tree-of-heaven)
Celastrus orbiculatus
(Oriental bittersweet)
Eichhornia crassipes
(water hyacinth)
Hedera helix
(English ivy)
Houttuynia cordata
(houttuynia)
Lathyrus latifolius
(perennial pea)
Lonicera japonica
(Japanese honeysuckle)
Lythrum salicaria
(purple loosestrife)

***Morus* spp.**
(mulberry)
***Phyllostachys* spp.**
(running bamboo)
Pueraria lobata
(kudzu vine)
Rosa multiflora
(Japanese rose)

Note: The abbreviation "spp." stands for the plural of "species"; where used in lists it means that many, but not all, of the species in a genus meet the criterion of the list.

Kudzu vine
(Pueraria
lobata)

Combating Weeds

Despite the best preventive measures, weeds will inevitably appear in a garden. Hand pulling, digging, hoeing, and mowing are, in environmental terms, the safest means of eliminating the pesky plants. If you keep an eye out for weed seedlings and attack them before they develop extensive root systems, weeding won't be an onerous, back-straining chore, and you can reserve herbicides for serious problems.

The Best Time to Weed and How to Do It

Pulling or digging weeds is easiest when the soil is moist. The roots are more likely to come up intact, with fewer fragments left behind to resprout. If you have just watered the garden or if you've had heavy rain, however, wait a day or two before you weed to give the soil surface time to dry out. Walking on wet soil compacts it, and you run a greater risk of transferring disease organisms from one plant to another when foliage is wet.

For small weeds, you'll need a trowel and a hand fork. For dandelions and other weeds with taproots, use a dandelion weeder (also called an asparagus knife). There are short-handled and long-handled versions of this tool; if you get one with a long handle, you won't have to kneel to do your weeding. For larger weeds or weed-infested areas, useful tools include hoes and long-handled garden forks to dig the weeds, and lawn mowers and power trimmers with whipping filaments to cut off weeds before they go to seed.

Cultivating the garden with a hoe—that is, working the soil to destroy weeds—is an art that becomes easier with practice. Hold the hoe so that the blade, kept well sharpened as shown at right, cuts through the soil in a shallow arc and goes no deeper than about 1 to 1½ inches below the surface. Avoid turning over clods of soil, as this may expose buried weed seeds and encourage sprouting. And most important, hoe regularly. Annual weeds may be killed on your first pass, but perennial weeds may take repeated cutting.

When you are confronted with a large weed, the garden fork is the best tool for the job. Thrust the tines deep into the soil beside the weed, and rock the fork back and forth. When the roots are well loosened, lift them out and shake off the soil. Finally, be sure to gather up and discard any root fragments to prevent the weed from resprouting.

A string trimmer works well in tight spots a lawn mower can't reach, such as along the bottom of a fence, around a mailbox post, or along the edge of a bed or border. Be extremely careful when using this tool, or you may cut down a favorite ornamental by accident. And never use a string trimmer on a weed growing against a tree trunk; the filament can cut the bark, opening a pathway for disease organisms and pests. Mowing larger expanses of weeds before they go to seed will keep them in check. This may not kill them but will prevent most of them from spreading further.

Proper disposal of weeds is vital, since they have remarkable powers of regeneration. Try to gather up everything—foliage, seed heads, bits of stems and roots. Compost weeds only if your pile heats up to 140°F at its center and is turned regularly. Otherwise, dispose of weeds in accordance with local ordinances for plant debris.

Selecting and Maintaining a Hoe

When shopping for a new hoe, look for one with a blade and shaft—which fits onto the wooden handle—that are cast from a single piece of metal. If the two parts are cast separately and welded together, they are likely to break at the weld. Make sure the blade's bevel runs along the inner side, as shown below.

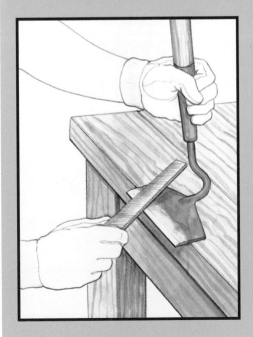

Keeping your hoe sharp greatly reduces the time and effort you spend on weeding. Use a mill bastard file to sharpen it; although a whetstone is faster, it produces an edge that is too fine and brittle and thus easily chipped. File across the bevel in one direction only, from the edge of the blade toward the shaft.

When mechanical methods of weed control fail despite your best efforts, you may decide the problem is severe enough to warrant using a herbicide. If you do, be sure to choose the right product and use it responsibly, for your own sake and for the sake of the environment.

Choosing a Herbicide. There are two basic types of herbicides for the home garden—preemergent herbicides, which prevent seeds from germinating, and postemergent herbicides, which kill plants that are actively growing. Postemergents work in one of two ways. One kind kills foliage on contact and is a good choice for annual weeds. The other kind, called systemic, is drawn into the plant's tissues, disrupting natural functions and destroying the plant from within. Use systemic herbicides on herbaceous perennial weeds or woody weeds; a contact herbicide may cause damage but fail to kill them.

The Importance of Labels. A herbicide label indicates the types of plants for which the product is formulated, when and how to apply it, and the period of effectiveness. Such information is vital. For instance, if you sow seeds in a bed recently treated with a preemergent herbicide that persists in the soil for months, the seeds won't germinate and you will have wasted your time and money. (See the guide to reading herbicide labels below, left.)

Taking Site and Weather into Account. If a weed is growing among ornamental plants, you'll need to protect them from the chemical *(opposite)*. Don't use a granular herbicide on a slope, since it is likely to wash downhill and do unintentional damage. Be especially cautious with herbicides near a vegetable garden, drainage field, wetland, stream, or garden pool; the chemicals can drift or wash onto other plants, kill fish, or pollute water supplies. You also need to exercise care in the root zone of a tree or shrub, which can be harmed if the roots absorb a systemic herbicide.

Never apply herbicides when it is rainy or windy; wait until a dry, calm day.

Heeding Precautions. While working with herbicides, don't drink, smoke, eat, touch your face, or use the bathroom. Keep pets and children away from treatment areas. (Follow this precaution if a neighbor's property is sprayed, whether by the homeowner or by a commercial service.)

Before you fill a sprayer with herbicide, test the nozzle's spray pattern with plain water so you'll know how to aim; for a ready-mixed spray product, spray newspaper to check the pattern. For liquids that are diluted before application, avoid disposal problems by preparing only a small quantity; if necessary, mix a second batch to finish the job. The herbicide should wet the foliage and stems well without dripping; using an excessive amount increases the risk of environmental damage.

To check a granular herbicide spreader's rate of application, mark out a measured area on a driveway or sidewalk and run the spreader over it. Sweep up and measure the herbicide, and adjust the spreader if necessary.

When finished, rinse all equipment with three changes of water. Wash your clothes and take a shower. Store the herbicide in its original container, preferably under lock and key.

Reading a Herbicide Label

Herbicide labels, which are regulated by the Environmental Protection Agency, contain information that will help you choose the right product for the job and use it properly. For the best results, read the entire label and follow the instructions to the letter. A typical label includes the following kinds of information:

- **Uses.** Plants that the herbicide controls; may also list plants on which the herbicide should *not* be used. Areas where the product can safely be used; other areas where it should *not* be used, such as near vegetable gardens or water sources.
- **Cautions and Hazards.** Specific dangers to users and the environment; emergency procedures to follow in case of accidents with the herbicide.
- **Directions for Use.** Dilution formulas as necessary; amount to use per unit area; details of application, such as appropriate methods and equipment, and weather conditions not conducive to safe use; clothing and safety wear, such as goggles.
- **Contents.** The product's chemical name and its chemical formula; the common name; percentages of ingredients in the formulation.
- **Storage and Disposal.** Specific directions for correct handling of the container and any unused portions.

Protecting Ornamentals from Herbicides

Many postemergent herbicides are so potent that even a small amount will kill any plant tissue it touches. Easy ways to protect ornamentals with newspaper and cardboard are shown below, along with a method for applying the herbicide to woody weeds with a brush instead of a spray. Even if you are spraying just a single weed, don't neglect to shield valuable plantings, and be sure to wear sturdy waterproof gloves. When the job is finished, leave the newspaper or cardboard in place until it is dry. Handle it carefully when you remove it; dropping it spray-side down on a plant could kill it. Be equally careful with a chemical-laden brush.

Store any brushes or shields contaminated with herbicide in a secure, dry place. Be scrupulous about following any local regulations when you dispose of them.

PROTECTING LOW-GROWING PLANTS
To spray a weed surrounded by low-growing plants, cover all the plants you want to save with three layers of newspaper and weight down their edges. Stretch a vining weed out across the paper (below); hold an erect weed against the paper with a stick. Spray the foliage and stems until they are barely wet. Remove the paper when it dries; remove the weed when it withers, in a week or so.

SPRAYING WEEDS NEAR LARGE ORNAMENTALS
Lay newspaper three sheets deep around the weed. Put a large piece of cardboard cut from a carton between the weed and the ornamental, then spray (above). Make sure the cardboard screen is tall enough to shield the ornamental's top growth.

GETTING RID OF AN UNWANTED SHRUB OR SAPLING
1. Cut the plant's stems or trunk off as close to the ground as possible (near right).

2. Choose a herbicide, such as a product containing triclopyr, that is licensed for application with a brush. Pour a very small quantity into a glass container with a wide mouth. Dip a brush into the herbicide, barely moistening it to avoid drips, and brush the cut surfaces (far right). When you're finished, wash the brush well in a bucket of soapy water. Follow directions on the product label for disposing of unused portions. Reserve the brush for herbicide use only.

Guide to Common Garden Weeds

1. AMARANTHUS RETROFLEXUS (Redroot Pigweed)

This annual produces as many as 200,000 seeds per plant. Some western pigweeds break loose from their roots and roll like tumbleweeds across the land, scattering their seeds as they go. Control pigweed by uprooting young plants or cutting the stems off at ground level.

2. AMBROSIA ARTEMISIIFOLIA (Common Ragweed)

Although the seed is a favorite food of birds, ragweed pollen is the bane of hay fever sufferers. The seeds need light for germination, so a layer of mulch is a good preventive. The shade cast by larger plants will also discourage growth. Mow or cut plants down before they go to seed.

3. BRASSICA KABER (Wild Mustard)

Introduced to the Americas as a seasoning, wild mustard has spread to become a pest species. Dig out or cut plants to the ground before they flower to prevent seeds from forming. The seeds are numerous and remain viable for years.

4. CENCHRUS SPECIES (Sandbur)

The spiny seeds of these annual or biennial grasses are painful for humans and animals alike and, if plentiful enough, can make a yard unusable. As the name implies, sandburs prefer sandy soils. When they invade a lawn, their blades are camouflaged and hard to see. Hand pull or dig, taking care not to touch the seeds.

5. CENTAUREA SOLSTITIALIS (Star Thistle)

Fast becoming a serious pest in California, Washington, and Oregon, star thistle usually grows as an annual but sometimes acts like a biennial. Cut it down before the flowers form; the bracts around the flowers bear sharp spines.

6. CERASTIUM ARVENSE (Field Chickweed)

This perennial weed grows in gardens throughout the United States. Destroy it with shallow cultivation before it can flower and go to seed. Gather up all the stems you've cut, since each one can form roots and develop into a new plant.

7. CHENOPODIUM ALBUM (Lamb's-Quarters)

An annual that appears early in the season, lamb's-quarters grows in gardens all over the United States. Mulch beds to discourage germination, and pull out or cut down any plants that appear before they flower.

8. CIRSIUM ARVENSE (Canada Thistle)

Despite its name, this perennial weed is a Eurasian native. A single plant can extend its root system over a large area, sending up numerous stems to create a massive stand. Cut stems down but don't hoe the plants, since root pieces start new plants. Treat persistent stands with a systemic herbicide.

9. CONVOLVULUS ARVENSIS (Field Bindweed)

This perennial has a huge root system that makes an established plant almost impossible to get rid of. Avoid tilling near the roots; severed pieces will produce new plants. Control with regular hoeing. Never allow plants to go to seed. Thick mulches help suppress germination.

10. CYPERUS ESCULENTUS (Nut Sedge, Nut Grass)

Nut sedge, a perennial, is usually found in moist or poorly drained soil. Its roots send up new shoots whenever the main stem is cut. Dig up the roots or cut off new growth as it appears; this will eventually kill the plants. Use landscape fabric, not woodchips or other organic mulches, to block the foliage.

11. DATURA STRAMONIUM (Jimson Weed)

All parts of this annual are poisonous, so remove it as soon as you see it. Most herbicides don't affect it; hoe it or hand pull it, wearing gloves to protect against the spines that form on the flower capsules. Because of its poisons, jimson weed should be disposed of according to local ordinances for plant debris.

12. DIGITARIA ISCHAEMUM, D. SANGUINALIS (Crab Grass)

Crab grass, an annual, is well known for its unsightly, sprawling presence in lawns, especially in places where the soil is compacted. Aerate the lawn and let turf grass grow taller than usual so it can shade out crab grass. In flower beds, dig it out before it sets seed; mulch to prevent seeds from sprouting.

Guide to Common Garden Weeds

13. ELEUSINE INDICA (Goose Grass)
Goose grass is an annual that commonly takes hold in a sparse lawn growing in compacted, nutrient-poor soil. Aerating the soil, fertilizing, and mowing the lawn higher all help to control the weed. Remove plants from the lawn by hand before they flower, and mulch beds to discourage seedlings.

14. EUPHORBIA MACULATA (Spotted Spurge)
This annual, which often takes root in pavement cracks, grows so low that the blades of a lawn mower pass above it, leaving the weed intact. Pull it out by the roots before it produces its tiny, pink-white flowers and thousands of seeds.

15. HORDEUM JUBATUM (Foxtail Barley, Wild Barley)
Foxtail barley grows to 2 feet and has sharp awns (bristles) on its seed heads that pose a danger to animals, since they can lodge in the ears, mouth, and eyes or be drawn into the lungs. Mow this perennial low or dig it out. Don't compost it; awns may not decompose completely.

16. OXALIS STRICTA (Wood Sorrel, Sourgrass)
This annual weed and its look-alike relative, the perennial O. corniculata, have seed capsules that explode and shoot seeds as far as 6 feet from the mother plant. Mulch to smother seeds or dig out the taproots.

17. PHYTOLACCA AMERICANA (Pokeweed)
Most pokeweed plants are seeded by birds, which relish pokeberries. If you can dig up this perennial's long taproot, do so. Otherwise, keep the stems cut to the ground; this will eventually starve out the plant.

18. POLYGONUM PERFOLIATUM (Mile-a-Minute)
A native of Asia, this fast-spreading vine thrives in many different habitats in the United States. If you discover no more than a plant or two in your garden, dig them out, taking care to avoid the sharp thorns. If the vines are more numerous, treat them with a systemic herbicide.

19. PORTULACA OLERACEA (Purslane)

Purslane lives on such a compressed schedule that there can be several generations of this drought-tolerant annual in a single growing season. Hoe regularly to destroy new plants, or pull them up by hand. Dispose of purslane promptly; left lying on the ground, it can go to seed or reroot weeks later.

20. RHUS DIVERSILOBA (Poison Oak)

This West Coast native produces an oil that causes a bad rash in most people. It may grow as a shrub or a vine. Dig out by the roots or use a systemic herbicide if the site allows, following the precautions recommended for poison ivy (right). Handle eastern poison oak (R. toxicodendron) in the same way.

21. RHUS RADICANS (Poison Ivy)

Another cause of nasty rashes, poison ivy varies in form but generally has leaves arranged in threes. Dig out the roots or use a systemic herbicide if the site allows. Wear protective clothing, and wash it and tools well afterward. Never compost or burn poison oak or poison ivy; inhaling the smoke is dangerous.

22. ROSA MULTIFLORA (Multiflora Rose)

Once sold as a decorative hedge plant, this tough perennial spreads by seeds and rooting stems, and takes hold tenaciously in uncultivated areas. Dig small plants up by the roots. Cut larger ones to the ground and treat the stubs with a systemic herbicide.

23. RUBUS SPECIES (Wild Bramble)

In time, the thorny canes of brambles such as raspberry, dewberry, and blackberry create impassable thickets. If you get at a plant when it is still young, however, digging out as much of the roots as you can and cutting new shoots to the ground, it will eventually die. This may take more than a year.

24. TARAXACUM OFFICINALE (Dandelion)

Dandelion's long taproots nourish it through many a beheading, so for effective removal, dig out the root. Try to get it all: New shoots spring from root pieces left in the ground.

CHAPTER SEVEN

Coping with Garden Pests

Insects are everywhere, in astonishing variety and equally astonishing numbers—worldwide, there are some 2 million species. Fortunately, only about 1,000 of these qualify as pests. Moreover, fewer than a dozen species are likely to feed destructively on the plants growing in a particular garden. For the knowledgeable gardener, controlling that handful of pests is a manageable business rather than an unending battle.

This chapter describes fundamental good-gardening practices and smart plant selection, both of which help keep pest problems to a minimum. Learning to recognize undesirable insect species is essential, as is the ability to identify beneficial creatures such as the cardinal at left, shown feeding her offspring one of the garden's most voracious pests—a tomato hornworm. Once you know the enemy, you can choose from among an array of control methods, from handpicking caterpillars off plants to spraying with pesticides. If you decide to use chemicals, follow the recommendations in this chapter to ensure your personal safety and the health of your garden.

Creating a Pest-Resistant Garden

No matter what you do in your garden, insects will always be among the creatures sustained by its elements—soil, mulch, water, turf, the compost pile, the flowering annuals and perennials, the shrubs and trees. How you approach the ones that can eat their way through your thoughtfully chosen plants is an important matter. Whatever steps you take against the destructive few will also affect the garden's benign creatures, from invisible soil microbes to pest-eating ladybird beetles to the songbirds that enliven the scene.

Tolerance in the Garden

The most sensible course is to accept insects, including the pests, as a fact of garden life. Trying to eradicate them with a chemical assault is a losing battle. More important, such an aggressive approach is environmentally unsound.

A corollary of tolerating a varied population of insects is learning to live with imperfection. Tolerating a certain amount of pest damage is fundamental to the environmentally friendly philosophy of pest control known as Integrated Pest Management, or IPM. It calls for using a variety of cultural, physical, biological, and chemical methods that work together to keep the damage done by pests at an acceptable level while preserving the overall health of the garden environment.

When you practice the cultural measures described on the following pages, you do not compromise the attractiveness of your garden. On the contrary, the basics of good gardening are also the basics of sensible pest control. Providing good growing conditions has two significant advantages: Your plants will be far more likely to reach their full potential in beauty, and they will be healthy. By keeping your plants strong and vigorous, you will maximize their natural ability to withstand pests and diseases.

Doing the Essential Groundwork

The single best guarantee that your plants will be healthy is soil of the highest quality. For the most complete picture of your garden's soil, have it professionally tested. When the soil is reasonably dry, dig up samples to about 4 inches deep from several spots around the garden. Combine them and send about 1 pint of the mixture to your local Co-operative Extension Service or any private soil-testing lab. The results will reveal your soil's pH level, available nutrients, the presence of organic matter, and the soil's texture, determined by the proportions of sand, silt, and clay particles it contains. The ideal soil type is loam—a crumbly, loose combination of sand, silt, and clay that drains well and contains sufficient organic matter, nutrients, air, and water.

You may be lucky enough to have loamy soil. It's more likely, however, that you'll need to amend your soil to bring it closer to the ideal. A heavy clay soil must be amended to let air, water,

---

How to Buy a Healthy Plant

Follow these guidelines when you purchase new plants, to avoid importing problems into your garden:

- Shop at a garden center or nursery known for the quality of its plants, the expertise of its salespeople, and a fair return policy in case a plant proves unsatisfactory.
- Check a plant for the presence of pests and for pest damage, such as webs or egg masses on stems or leaves, or holes chewed in the leaves. Be sure to examine the undersides of the foliage.
- Look for foliage with good color and form. Reject plants that show wilting, curling, spotting, or yellowing.
- Carefully lift a container plant out of its pot to check that roots are white and moist, not brown or soggy. They should fill the soil ball but not encircle it.
- Look for plants that have good branch structure, with no broken stems or bark wounds.
- Choose plants with full, healthy buds or, if the growing season has begun, new foliage and stems.

Drawing on Nature's Diversity

A garden abounding with plants of different kinds—exotics, natives, perennials, annuals, broadleaf evergreens, conifers, flowering shrubs and trees—is far less vulnerable to devastating infestations of pests than a garden designed with a more restricted plant palette. Selecting a garden's principal furnishings from only a handful of plant families—roses, boxwood, iris, and dogwood, for instance—is risky business, since an equally small handful of pest species has the potential to devastate your entire garden.

In short, the closer a garden comes to monoculture, the more it is deprived of the protective mechanisms that exist in natural plant communities, which are characteristically rich in species. A garden like the one shown here is attractive to pest predators such as birds, beneficial insects, lizards, and toads. It supplies many different food sources such as nectar, pollen, fruit, and seeds over a long season. And its range of trees, shrubs, and herbaceous plants of varying sizes and densities creates habitats for a variety of species. With good planning, the elements that make the garden beautiful will also discourage pests, and at no environmental cost.

The Myth of Companion Planting

Many gardeners wouldn't think of planting a vegetable garden without including lots of aromatic plants reputed to keep insect pests away from their crops. Nevertheless, research suggests that this so-called companion planting doesn't deserve the faith that gardeners place in it. It is true that certain plants hinder the proliferation of undesirable organisms. For instance, it has been shown that marigolds can control pest nematodes, tiny worms that live in soil and infest plants. The problem is that the marigolds suppress the nematodes only when the plants are spaced so densely that there is virtually no room left in the garden for a food crop. The pest-repelling abilities of other favorite companion plants have been tested under controlled conditions and have been just as disappointing.

and nutrients penetrate it more easily and reach plant roots. To lighten clay, mix it half-and-half with coarse sand or organic matter such as peat moss or compost. These materials can also be used to improve the structure of dense, silty soil, which, like clay, is prone to waterlogging. In light, porous, sandy soils, water drains away quickly and takes plant nutrients with it. The solution in this case is to dig in clayey topsoil or an organic material such as composted manure to improve the soil's capacity to hold moisture.

It is also important to keep your soil's pH within a healthy range. Most plants will grow well in soil that is slightly acid, with a pH between 6 and 7. When the pH is too high or too low, plants aren't able to draw essential nutrients from the soil, and as a result they grow poorly. You can correct a soil that is too acidic by digging in dolomitic limestone, which is alkaline. When a soil is too alkaline, on the other hand, use iron sulfate to increase its acidity. Test your soil's pH every year or two to be sure that it remains within a desirable range.

Supplying Nutrients

A soil test will also reveal whether your soil provides enough of the three nutrients essential for healthy plant growth—nitrogen, phosphorus, and potassium. Garden fertilizers are labeled to show what percentage they contain of each of these elements, and the numbers are always arranged in the same order. Thus a fertilizer designated "12-4-4" is by weight 12 percent nitrogen, 4 percent phosphorus, and 4 percent potassium; the remaining 80 percent is made up of inert fillers.

You have a choice of using either a chemical fertilizer, which is manufactured or mined, or an organic fertilizer, which is derived from plant or animal material. The two types are equally nourishing to plants and equally convenient to use. However, the organic fertilizers have an important advantage: The nutrients they contain are released gradually over a period of time. Chemical nutrients, by contrast, are often immediately available to the plants, increasing the risk of burning plant roots if you happen to overfertilize.

Not all plants thrive on the same regimen of nutrients. The nitrogen-rich diet that turf grasses demand, for instance, would stimulate rapid, floppy growth if it were applied to herbaceous perennials, making them targets for aphids. A general-purpose fertilizer will suffice for most plants, but be sure to accommodate those plants that have special needs. To help you recognize the symptoms of several deficiency diseases that can be corrected with the right fertilizer, see pages 330-331 of the Encyclopedia of Beneficials, Pests, and Diseases at the back of this book.

Plants to Suit the Site

Choosing the plants that will fulfill your vision for your garden is an intensely personal, aesthetic exercise—and an eminently practical one as well. As you're making decisions on such matters as flower season and color, the height of a shade tree, or the combination of foliage textures for a mixed hedge, you will want to compare each plant's cultural requirements with the general conditions your garden offers. You'll also want to identify any microclimates on the site, such as a sunny corner sheltered from winter winds.

In creating a profile of your garden conditions, you'll need to consider several things:

- The hardiness zone of your area, based on the average minimum temperature.
- Temperature and humidity in summer. Are nights cool or hot? Plants adapted to cool nights often do poorly where summers are muggy.
- The average amount of rainfall and its distribution over the course of the year. If your area has dry spells lasting 2 weeks or so, as much of the United States does during summer, drought-tolerant plants would be likely candidates for your garden.
- The hours of sun and shade that different parts of the garden receive in different seasons of the year, and the quality of that shade—dappled or dense?
- Soil composition, acidity, and drainage in various parts of the garden.

Once you have collected this information, you can determine whether there is a good match between a plant's cultural requirements and your garden's environment. What you learn from your analysis may also help explain why certain plants in your garden, or in nearby gardens that are similar to yours, have flourished while others have grown poorly or died.

Pest-Resistant Plants

In addition to a plant's visual appeal and its ability to thrive in your garden, you will want to consider how vulnerable it is to pests. Some species are naturally resistant to pest damage, and in some cases horticulturists have developed new hybrids and cultivars offering such resistance. Some popular pest-resistant deciduous shrubs and small trees are listed on page 162.

Plants actively counter pests with a variety of mechanical and physiological measures. Two examples of mechanical, or physical, defenses are tough outer membranes that prevent insect pests from feeding on leaves or pods, and needlelike thorns that discourage browsing animals, such as deer. (See pages 190-191 for a list of deer-resistant plants.) A covering of hairs on stems and leaves, which on some plants can be sticky, traps pests that land on them and prevents the insects from feeding. Physiological defensive tricks include releasing toxic or repellent compounds to deter pests. Oak trees, for example, contain bitter-tasting compounds called tannins that thwart bark beetles and boring insects, and geraniums contain a chemical that paralyzes Japanese beetles.

Plants are classified according to the degree of resistance they possess. "Immune" means that a plant cannot be harmed by a particular pest; "resistant" identifies plants that are rarely infested by specific pests and suffer only minor damage if they are attacked; "tolerant" describes a plant that is subject to infestation but does not suffer any permanent damage. Finally, the word "susceptible" is a red flag for gardeners because it indicates that a plant is highly vulnerable to one or more pests. There are also species and cultivars that are innately resistant to disease *(lists, pages 198-199)*.

Native Plants, Native Pests

Plants that grow naturally in your geographical area can usually be counted on to perform reliably in the garden, since they are adapted to the prevailing climate and soil. Many of these native species are also resistant to native pests. Over eons of coexistence, plants that evolved effective defenses against the indigenous pests were more likely to succeed than their susceptible cousins.

Parrotia persica (Persian parrotia) adds a touch of yellow to this lush autumnal garden. Naturally resistant to pests, it can withstand attacks that would cause serious damage to more vulnerable trees.

Not all natives are trouble free, however. In the eastern United States, for example, native cherries are often beset by ugly masses of tent caterpillars, while some of the exotic species imported from Asia are less attractive to these pests. And, of course, every part of the country has its share of imported pests, and native plants have no defense against these.

For information on ornamentals native to your area, contact your local Cooperative Extension Service. Numerous mail-order nurseries also specialize in native plants, and more and more retail nurseries are stocking natives. See the box on page 158 for buying guidelines.

Maintenance Practices That Foil Pests

Proper techniques for watering, fertilizing, and sanitation keep a garden growing well and also help fend off pests and diseases. How often you need to water depends on the amount of precipitation your garden receives and on soil type—sandy soils dry out quickly, clayey soils more slowly. To determine whether it's time to water, check the soil's moisture level by digging down 3 to 4 inches with a trowel or soil auger; if the top 1½ to 2 inches are dry, the garden is due for a watering.

In the absence of sufficient rainfall, a rule of thumb is to provide at least 1 inch of water per week, dispersed slowly and evenly during one long soaking. When plants are watered deeply at long intervals instead of frequently and lightly, they develop tougher outer layers that protect them from moisture loss and discourage pests from feeding. In addition, root systems are encouraged to grow downward to soil levels that retain moisture. As a result, the plants develop a greater tolerance for drought. For additional information on good watering practices, see page 200.

A 2- to 4-inch layer of organic mulch such as shredded bark or compost will help conserve soil moisture, suppress weeds and, especially when compost is used, provide a slow-release source of plant nutrients. Mulch also helps keep the soil rich in the microorganisms that break down fallen leaves, dead animals, and other kinds of organic matter into humus—the single most vital ingredient of high-quality soil.

Weeds compete with ornamentals and vegetable crops for space, light, water, and nutrients. And since weedy areas frequently harbor crickets, grasshoppers, slugs, snails, stink bugs, and other pests that damage plants, eliminating weeds eliminates a source of trouble.

Clear garden beds of spent flowers, fallen leaves and fruit, weeds, and other debris that could harbor pests, and add them to the compost pile. In the case of diseased plant materials or weeds that have gone to seed, dispose of them in the trash or incorporate them into a compost pile that gets hot enough to render them harmless—at least 140° F.

Pest-Resistant Shrubs and Trees

DECIDUOUS FLOWERING SHRUBS

Abeliophyllum distichum
(white forsythia)
Acanthopanax sieboldianus
(five-leaf aralia)
Berberis thunbergii
(Japanese barberry)
Buddleia davidii
(butterfly bush)
Calycanthus floridus
(Carolina allspice)
Caragana arborescens
(Siberian pea shrub)
Chionanthus virginicus
(fringe tree)
Clethra alnifolia
(sweet pepperbush)
Cytisus scoparius
(Scotch broom)
Deutzia gracilis
(slender deutzia)

Deutzia x rosea
(deutzia)
Enkianthus campanulatus
(red-veined enkianthus)
Euonymus alata
(winged euonymus)
Forsythia x intermedia
(border forsythia)
Fothergilla major
(large fothergilla)
Hippophae rhamnoides
(sallow thorn)
Hypericum prolificum
(shrubby St.-John's-wort)
Jasminum nudiflorum
(winter jasmine)
Philadelphus spp.
(mock orange)
Potentilla fruticosa
(bush cinquefoil)
Spiraea spp.
(bridal wreath)
Stewartia ovata

(mountain camellia)
Symphoricarpos spp.
(coralberry, snowberry)
Viburnum sieboldii
(Siebold viburnum)
Weigela florida
(old-fashioned weigela)

Note: The abbreviation "spp." stands for the plural of "species"; where used in lists it means that many, but not all, of the species in a genus meet the criterion of the list.

ORNAMENTAL TREES LESS THAN 30 FEET HIGH

Carpinus caroliniana
(American hornbeam)
Cornus mas
(cornelian cherry)
Elaeagnus angustifolia
(Russian wild olive)
Franklinia alatamaha
(franklinia)
Koelreuteria paniculata
(golden rain tree)
Lagerstroemia 'Natchez', 'Biloxi', 'Muskogee'
(crape myrtle)
Magnolia stellata
(star magnolia)
Myrica pensylvanica
(bayberry)
Parrotia persica
(Persian parrotia)
Pistacia chinensis
(Chinese pistachio)
Stewartia pseudocamellia
(Japanese stewartia)
Styrax japonicus
(Japanese snowbell)

Deutzia x rosea (deutzia)

Identifying Insect Pests

Sometimes even a culturally pest-resistant garden comes under attack by insects. If they inflict damage on your plants that is beyond your threshold for tolerance, you will want to deal with them quickly and effectively. To do this, you must first identify the insects, then choose an appropriate method of control. Since every pest-control method involves time, effort, money, and environmental risk, it's important to have a good understanding of the several types available—physical, biological, and chemical *(pages 169-185)*—before you make your choice.

This may seem like a straightforward approach, but it all hinges on a somewhat complex task—correct identification of a pest and its stage in the life cycle. Identification is easier with a basic understanding of insect anatomy *(right)*. Since the aim is not to eliminate every creeping creature in your garden, learning about anatomy and life cycles will also help you distinguish between the pest insects and the beneficials *(pages 174-179)*. Most beneficial insects feed on pests or use them as hosts for their young. In this way, they are a naturally assertive biological control, keeping pest populations in check.

One key to avoiding major pest problems is to monitor your garden regularly. This means checking your plants weekly for signs of pests and pest damage. At the height of the growing season, you may want to check as often as once a day.

Keep a garden diary. When you see pest damage, record the date, the approximate number of leaves or plants infested, and the location of the damage on the plant. If you can see the pest, note the type of insect, if you know it, and how many there are; this will help you detect changes in the population from day to day or from week to week. Also make note of any unusual environmental conditions such as unseasonable temperatures, drought, or extra rainfall; these can affect pest populations as well as the plants themselves.

Remember, too, that not all plant damage can be blamed on pests. Nutritional deficiencies, diseases, or environmental stresses such as pollution can weaken a plant. But if your once-thriving plants are failing and you can rule out stress, soil problems, and weather-related hardships, chances are that pests are to blame.

With any pest problem, 90 percent of the solution lies in identifying the culprit. The clearest evidence you can get is to observe the insect feeding on your plant. If you can't see the pest, however, you will have to base your diagnosis on the damage it has done *(page 164)*.

Whatever region, climate, or zone you live in, you face a fairly limited number of insect pests. Learn to recognize the usual suspects by anatomy, habit, and damage pattern. To find out which pests you are likely to see, use the *Range* and *Host* information given at the top of each entry on pages 301-323 of the Encyclopedia of Beneficials, Pests, and Diseases at the back of this book. When examining insects, it's useful to look at them through a hand-held 10-power magnifying lens, the kind available for around 15 dollars through well-stocked garden centers or

Head

Thorax

Abdomen

Like this chinch bug, all insects have four distinct features: three body sections—head, thorax, and abdomen—and six legs. Many also have antennae, which help them find food, and wings. Variations in the colors or sizes of these features will help you identify the particular insects in your garden.

Common Plant Pests

Identifying the damage pests inflict on your garden is often a confusing task. However, there are some telltale indications that will quickly enable you to zero in on your plants' attackers. The havoc wreaked by several of the more commonly found insect pests and insect relatives is illustrated below.

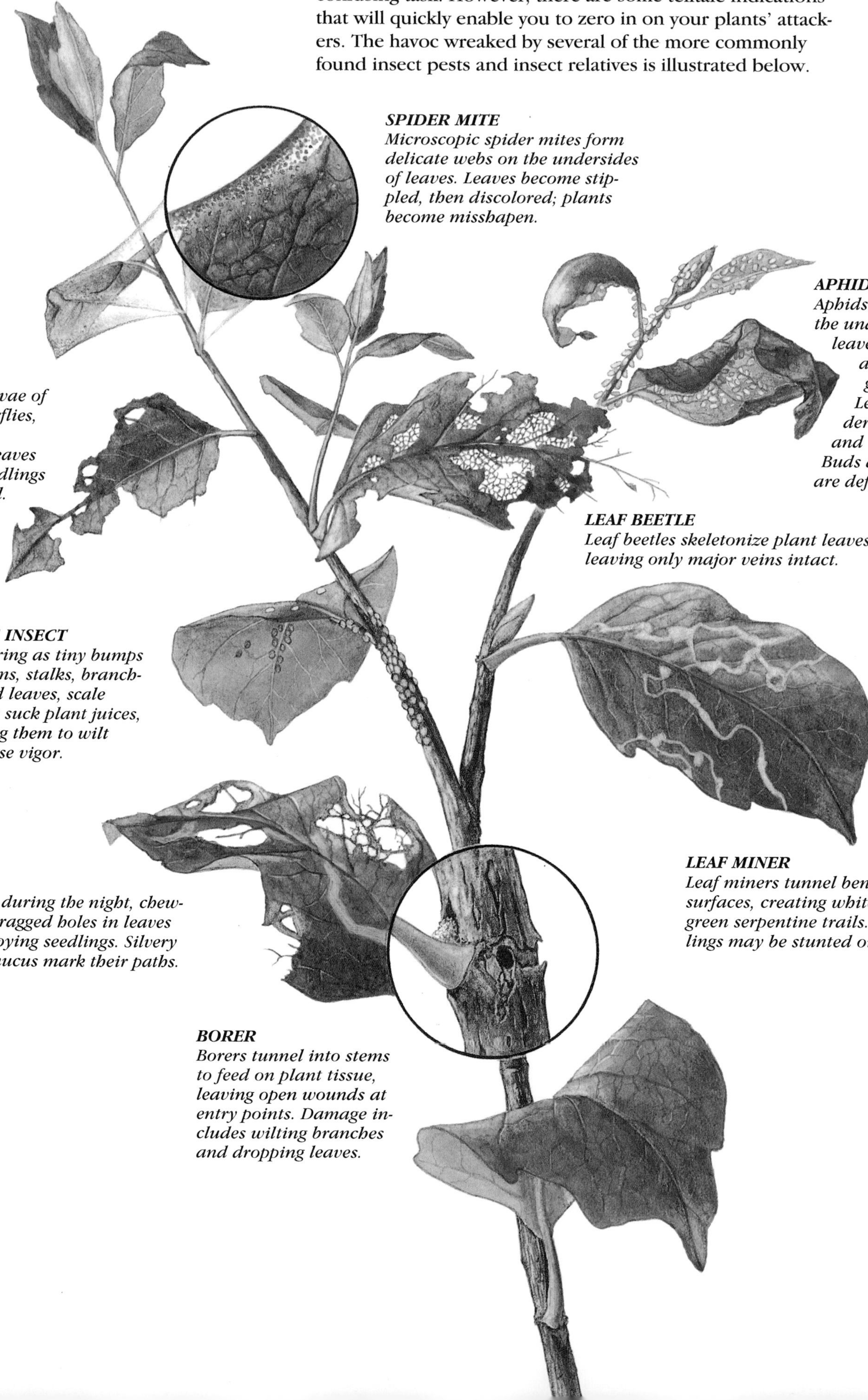

SPIDER MITE
Microscopic spider mites form delicate webs on the undersides of leaves. Leaves become stippled, then discolored; plants become misshapen.

APHID
Aphids cluster on the undersides of leaves, usually attacking new growth first. Leaves curl under at the edges and turn brown. Buds and flowers are deformed.

CATERPILLAR
The wormlike larvae of moths and butterflies, caterpillars chew ragged holes in leaves and often eat seedlings down to soil level.

LEAF BEETLE
Leaf beetles skeletonize plant leaves, leaving only major veins intact.

SCALE INSECT
Appearing as tiny bumps on stems, stalks, branches, and leaves, scale insects suck plant juices, causing them to wilt and lose vigor.

LEAF MINER
Leaf miners tunnel beneath leaf surfaces, creating white or light green serpentine trails. Seedlings may be stunted or die.

SLUG
Slugs feed during the night, chewing large, ragged holes in leaves and destroying seedlings. Silvery trails of mucus mark their paths.

BORER
Borers tunnel into stems to feed on plant tissue, leaving open wounds at entry points. Damage includes wilting branches and dropping leaves.

Look-Alike Insects

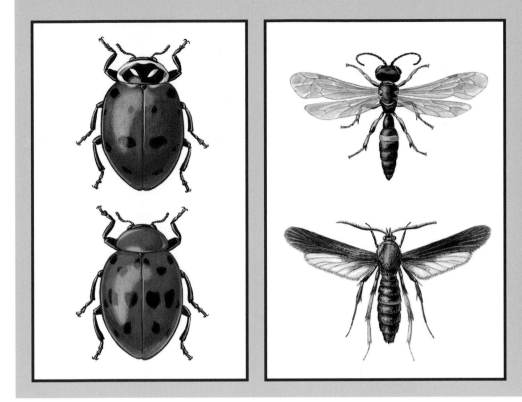

Many insect pests have markings and body shapes similar to those of beneficial insects, and even the most knowledgeable gardener will have to take a closer look to tell plant friend from foe. It is especially easy to confuse the destructive Mexican bean beetle *(far left, bottom)* with the helpful ladybird beetle *(far left, top)*. The trick is to count spots: The number will vary from one ladybird beetle to another, but all Mexican bean beetles have exactly 16 spots. In the case of the destructive peach tree borer moth *(bottom left)* and the digger wasp *(top left)*, a beneficial that preys on caterpillars and other pests, the difference lies in body contour: The troublesome moth has a thick middle, while the wasp has a narrow waist.

mail-order catalogs. Once you've become familiar with the local troublemakers, any newcomer will be obvious to your trained eye.

Many people lump all garden creatures that creep, crawl, and fly into a single category, called bugs. True bugs, however, are only one of the 28 orders in the class Insecta, and account for just a tiny fraction of the more than 2 million insect species. All insects, bugs included, share a unique anatomy: They have three body sections—head, thorax, and abdomen—and six legs, arranged in three pairs *(page 163)*. An insect body is exoskeletal—that is, the skeleton is on the outside, much like a suit of armor—and most are less than ¾ inch long. Some insects have antennae, which they use for smelling or tasting. Most insects have one pair of compound eyes, one on either side of the head; many have additional, simple eyes, on the upper part of the face. They have no lungs but breathe through tiny holes along the sides of the body, taking in oxygen directly to various internal organs. Much of an insect's internal equipment is geared toward reproduction.

Most insects also have wings. Their ability to fly lets them travel great distances, especially if drawn by an attractive host plant. This, coupled with their prodigious reproductive powers, explains how pest populations can explode overnight. Insect life cycles are short, allowing some species to produce 25 generations in a season; many lay eggs by the hundreds. This is another reason to deal quickly with any pest infestation.

Feeding Habits as Evidence

Insects live to eat, and they do so in a variety of ways. Some chew, some suck, and some bore through leaves, roots, stems, and even thick tree bark. As you become better acquainted with different pests and their habits, you'll quickly recognize the damage they create and be able to match it to the offending pest.

Sucking insects such as aphids, cicadas, leafhoppers, lace bugs, psyllids, and whiteflies feed on a plant by inserting a feeding tube in a leaf and sucking the juice out. This causes the leaves to discolor and eventually fall off. Chewing insects eat holes in the leaves, stems, and flowers of plants, marring their appearance. Among the chewers are beetles, caterpillars, crickets, grasshoppers, and weevils.

Borers, the other large group of insect pests, eat away at the insides of plants through feeding tunnels. Borers are hard to detect because you can't see them until the damage is done, when plants yellow and wilt or, in more advanced cases, branches and stems die back. This group includes bark beetles, tree borers, stalk borers, and wood wasps.

When you see the insects themselves in your garden, their numbers are another clue to their identity. Most pest insects tend to act in groups when they attack a plant. By contrast, most of the beneficial insects are predators that feed on the pests, so they usually appear in smaller numbers in your garden.

Knowing When an Insect Becomes a Pest

Other clues to identifying insect pests lie in knowing which plants they attack and at what stage of their life cycle they act as pests. For example, the sod webworm and the tomato hornworm are both larval stages of moths, and feed on grass and tomato plants, respectively. These and other pest species inflict damage only as larvae; in other species, the adult is the pest, and in a few species, the insect is damaging in all of its life stages.

Knowing the life-cycle stages in which a pest feeds on your plants will help you spot a troublemaker more quickly, because you'll know what kind of creature—adult or larva—to be looking for. Complete identification of your pest will also help you apply the most effective control at the life stage—dormant, larval, or adult—when the pest is most susceptible to attack. For more information on the life cycles of pests and the best time to apply controls, see pages 301-324 of the Encyclopedia of Beneficials, Pests, and Diseases at the back of this book.

Metamorphosis: Simple or Complete

On their way to adulthood, insects not only grow, they also undergo a transformation called metamorphosis. This transformation can be either simple or complete. In simple metamorphosis *(right),* insects such as aphids, crickets, and plant bugs alter very little as they grow from eggs to adulthood. This contrasts with complete metamorphosis *(far right),* in which insects such as beetles, butterflies, and wasps experience drastic physical changes before emerging as adults.

Unlike animals that nurture their eggs until they hatch, insects commonly lay their eggs and leave them to gestate on their own. Insect eggs come in many shapes and sizes, and because they are independent, they are often covered with a protective layer of tiny hairs or a shellaclike coating. The eggs are normally laid on or near the plants or host insects that will provide food for the nymphs or larvae. Some insects lay eggs singly; most deposit them in batches ranging from 50 to hundreds of eggs.

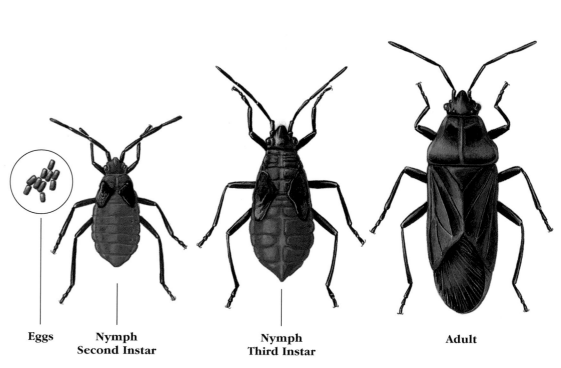

Eggs   **Nymph Second Instar**   **Nymph Third Instar**   **Adult**

Some insects, like the box elder bug shown above, develop by simple metamorphosis, changing little as they grow. Emerging from nearly microscopic eggs laid on leaves or in small crevices in the ground, the immature insects, or nymphs, are each covered with a rigid shell, or exoskeleton. As a nymph grows, its exoskeleton becomes too tight, forcing the nymph to shed, or molt, its outer layer and grow a larger one. Immediately after a molt, the insect is soft bodied and pale, but within a couple of hours, the new exoskeleton hardens and begins to take on color. Typically, an insect's development involves four to eight molts, or instars. A box elder bug undergoes five instars during its early life.

Insect Relatives

Insects are often grouped with certain other garden pests and beneficials that seem related but belong to no insect order. These include spiders and mites—known by their four pairs of legs—as well as centipedes, millipedes, slugs, snails, and roundworms. These so-called insect relatives have feeding habits similar to those of the insects inhabiting your garden. As with insects, you'll want to take care not to eliminate them indiscriminately, since not all are harmful. (Mammal pests include moles, gophers, mice, squirrels, rabbits, woodchucks, and deer. They can devastate a garden within hours and obviously call for control methods that differ from those for insect pests. See pages 186-191.)

Snails and Slugs

Snails and slugs hide during the day and feed on low-hanging leaves and fruits at night or on overcast or rainy days. They prefer damp soil in a shady location and are most damaging in summer, especially in wet regions or during rainy years. For details on coping with these elusive garden pests, see box on page 172.

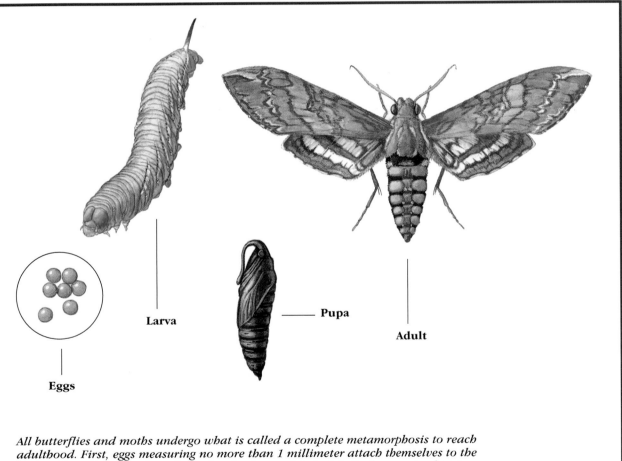

Eggs

Larva

Pupa

Adult

All butterflies and moths undergo what is called a complete metamorphosis to reach adulthood. First, eggs measuring no more than 1 millimeter attach themselves to the undersides of leaves, where they take about a week to hatch. Each emerging larva, or caterpillar, feeds voraciously for 2 to 4 weeks, shedding its skin several times, until it is fully grown. To advance to the next stage and become a pupa, the mature caterpillar attaches itself to a plant or other object and spins a cocoon around its body. Inside the cocoon, the pupa's body changes dramatically over the next 10 to 15 days into a winged, six-legged adult. The adult butterfly or moth breaks out of the cocoon and, by mating to produce eggs, perpetuates the life cycle.

Graceful Adult, Voracious Larva

Butterflies are among the most spectacular and colorful creatures in your garden. In their larval state, however, many of these elusive beauties can munch your plants down to nubs. By growing species that the larvae prefer *(below, left)*, you can nourish these soon-to-be butterflies while minimizing the damage to your other plants.

To keep your garden attractive to the adult butterflies as they emerge from their cocoons, grow plants of various heights with colorful, nectar-bearing flowers from which butterflies can sip *(below, right)*. Butterflies also need to bask in sunlight to keep their body temperatures up, so be sure to locate these plants in a sunny spot. Forgo pesticides; the chemicals will turn all butterflies away from your garden, no matter how many attractive plantings you provide.

Plants to Nourish Larvae

Anethum graveolens
(dill)
Artemisia spp.
(wormwood)
Barbarea
(winter cress)
Cirsium spp.
(thistle)
Daucus carota
(Queen Anne's lace)
Dicentra spp.
(bleeding heart)
Foeniculum vulgare
(sweet fennel)
Nasturtium
(nasturtium)
Pastinaca sativa
(parsnip)
Petroselinum crispum
(parsley)
Populus spp.
(poplar, aspen, cottonwood)
Ruta graveolens
(common rue)
Sedum spp.
(stonecrop)

Note: The abbreviation "spp." stands for the plural of "species"; where used in lists it means that many, but not all, of the species in a genus meet the criterion of the list.

Black Swallowtail Butterfly Larva

Black Swallowtail Butterfly

Plants to Attract Butterflies

Artemisia spp.
(wormwood)
Asclepias spp.
(milkweed)
Aster spp.
(aster)
Buddleia spp.
(butterfly bush)
Centaurea spp.
(knapweed)
Cephalanthus spp.
(buttonbush)
Coreopsis spp.
(tickseed)
Echinacea purpurea
(purple coneflower)
Lantana spp.
(lantana)
Lonicera spp.
(honeysuckle)
Mentha spp.
(mint)
Rudbeckia hirta
(black-eyed Susan)
Salix spp.
(willow)

Note: The abbreviation "spp." stands for the plural of "species"; where used in lists it means that many, but not all, of the species in a genus meet the criterion of the list.

Dealing with Pests on the Spot

For the gardener who wants to avoid overkill, a simple physical control is the first line of defense when a pest threatens to do serious damage. Most of these measures—barriers, traps, and the like—rely on common sense and traditional techniques of good gardening. However, discoveries in insect behavior and reproduction have provided several technological twists in the area of physical controls that have proven to be enormous boons.

As a rule, physical controls pose no environmental hazards and are inexpensive. Used singly or in combination, they offer you sensible options for managing pest problems.

Protecting Seedlings

An obvious way of heading off trouble is to erect a barrier that stops pests from getting to your plants. Seedlings are especially vulnerable to attack. Because of their small size, they can be chewed to the ground in no time and have little or nothing in the way of food reserves to help them replace shoots or leaves.

Plant collars and row covers are two easy ways of protecting seedlings until they are established. Collars, which are slipped around individual seedlings as shown in the illustration at far right, keep crawling pests like cutworms from reaching tender stems and foliage. Row covers, made of transparent fabric that allows sunlight to reach young plants, are most often used in the vegetable garden as barriers against birds and flying insects. The covers' edges are buried in the soil to keep crawling insects from wiggling underneath them.

Blocking Pests on Trees

Tree bands, a variation of the plant-collar idea, can be used to block gypsy moth caterpillars, webworms, root weevils, and other crawling pests that make their way up a tree trunk to feed on the foliage. Garden centers and mail-order catalogs carry bands, but it's easy and much less expensive to make them yourself. Using burlap or another sturdy fabric, cut a strip 8 to 12 inches wide and several inches longer than the tree trunk's circumference. Cut a piece of heavy string a foot or so

Barriers and Traps

The seedling above is shielded from crawling pests with a plant collar, here an inverted paper cup. You can also use sections of cardboard from a roll of paper towels. At left, burlap tied around the tree and folded down over the string stops gypsy moth larvae and other pests from climbing the trunk to feed on foliage. Sticky glue painted above the burlap catches any pests that elude the barrier.

Placed near plants that would otherwise be attacked, the sticky trap at right lures aphids and several other flying pests that share a strong attraction to yellow objects. Insects landing on the surface of the trap become mired in its adhesive coating and suffocate. White and blue traps are effective with other species of pests.

169

longer than the circumference. At a point several feet above the ground, wrap the strip of fabric around the trunk. Center the string on the fabric and tie it firmly in place. Then fold the top portion of the fabric down over the string to make a flap.

Some of the pests that wander into this dead end will find their way out and crawl back down the trunk. Others will remain trapped, and some, such as gypsy moths, may enjoy the shelter from sun and rain and pupate there. Check the bands about once a week, or more frequently in the case of heavy infestation. Wearing gloves, pick off any trapped pests and drop them into a bucket of soapy water to kill them.

Leaf-eating pests are especially hard on young trees, but established trees can also be vulnerable in years when a pest's population explodes. Install bands before the threatened trees produce new foliage in the spring.

Mulching for Pest Control

Among its many virtues, mulch helps combat pests in a variety of ways. A coarse organic mulch such as cocoa hulls discourages slugs and snails because their bodies are soft and scratch easily *(pages 172-173)*. A thick layer of shredded bark or other mulch

prevents overwintering pests like beetle grubs from finding food as they emerge from the soil. And black plastic, which is impenetrable as long as it isn't torn, disrupts the life cycles of thrips, leaf miners, and other pests that lay their eggs in soil or overwinter in a dormant stage. A newspaper mulch works much the same way but is effective for only one season, since it is biodegradable.

Aluminum to Foil Flying Pests

The light rays bouncing off a reflective mulch confuse aphids, thrips, and other flying pests and keep them from locating their target plants. You can buy aluminum-coated kraft paper insulation or aluminized plastic at home and garden centers, but ordinary aluminum foil works just as well. Given the utilitarian appearance of these materials, they are best reserved for the vegetable garden or a nursery bed tucked out of sight.

Lay strips of the reflective mulch under the leaf canopy, leaving spaces between the strips and near the plant's stem so that water can reach the soil. Since the aluminum reflects enough heat to scorch plants, especially tender seedlings, it should be removed before the weather becomes

Luring Pests with Sex Chemicals

During mating season, some insect pests release a pheromone—an airborne chemical signal that lets the opposite sex of the species know where to find them. Each species has its own unique pheromone, and its members have a remarkable ability to detect it, even at extremely low concentrations and over a distance of several miles. Insects are indifferent to alien pheromones.

The ability to produce synthetic versions of insect pheromones has resulted in a highly targeted technique of pest control. A trap impregnated with a pheromone catches males of one species only, eliminating them from the mating game and thus reducing the size of the next generation.

The traps come in a number of different shapes; the triangular or delta trap and the wing trap are shown at right. These two traps have sticky inner surfaces that hold insects fast. Other traps have a funnel-

shaped entrance that prevents escape.

In addition to serving as control devices, some pheromone traps are used for monitoring changes in a given pest population. If the number of pests captured begins to rise sharply, the gardener can take appropriate measures to short-circuit trouble, perhaps by using physical controls more diligently or by taking advantage of one of the biological controls described on pages 174-179.

Before you buy a pheromone trap, make certain the pest attacking your garden belongs to the species for which the trap was designed. Follow the directions for replacing the pheromone lure and cleaning the trap.

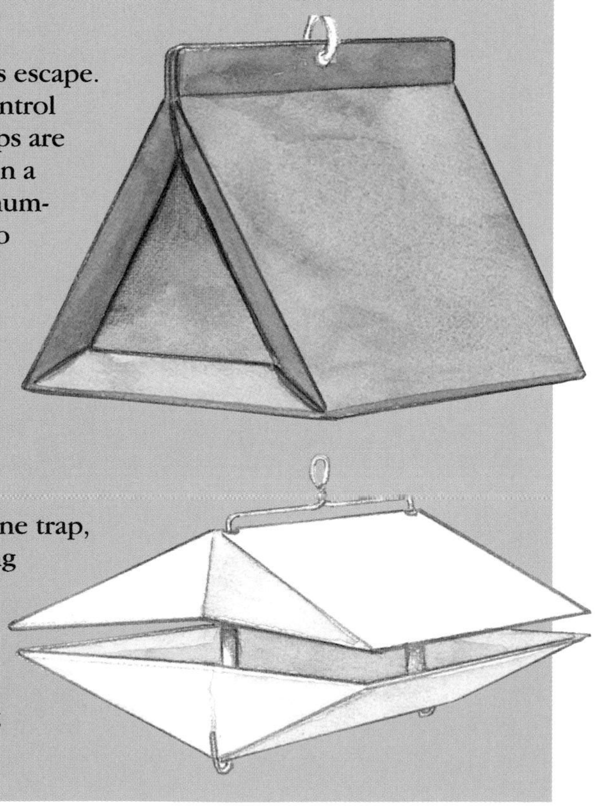

170

hot. A good practice is to remove the mulch as soon as young plants have become established.

Traps for Flying Pests

Along with barriers and mulches, traps are one of the most effective physical controls for the home garden. There are many types of traps on the market, almost all of which are designed to catch flying insects of a specific kind. Be sure to identify the pest you're targeting so that you'll select the right kind of trap. In addition to drawing pests away from your plants, the traps help you monitor changes in the size of a particular pest population. If the number of trapped pests begins to rise sharply, you can take defensive measures before a lot of plant damage is done.

Avoid using any type of electric-light trap. None of these traps discriminates between victims, killing all insects, pests and beneficials alike. Moreover, they are expensive.

Luring Pests with Scent

One popular type of trap uses a scented lure, which, in most cases, is designed to catch a particular insect. For apple maggot flies, for example, the traps contain fruit and floral scents. The traps that attract adult Japanese beetles use two different lures—a floral scent for the females and, for the males, a synthetic scent that mimics a sex pheromone females produce to attract a mate. (For more about pheromone traps, see the box on the opposite page.)

Unless it is used properly, a Japanese beetle trap can be counterproductive, actually attracting more insects to the plants you are trying to protect than would have appeared had you done nothing at all. Be sure to position the traps on nonhost plants such as pines, or on a structure like a fence post, at least 20 to 30 yards away and downwind from vulnerable plantings. If your area is suffering from an unusually large influx of Japanese beetles, it is probably better not to use the traps at all, or the pests might swarm to your garden from neighboring yards.

To protect a quarter-acre garden, set out at least one trap; a half-acre will need two or more. The smell of accumulated dead beetles keeps live ones from entering traps, so it's important to empty them at least twice a week. A trap that lets rainwater drain away quickly minimizes the odor. After a month or 6 weeks, if the influx of pests has not diminished, install a fresh lure.

A trap set amid cucumber plants is peppered with pests that were drawn to its color and became entangled in its coating. Yellow sticky traps snare numerous small insect pests, including aphids, whiteflies, and leafhoppers.

Luring Pests with Color

Some traps, like the one shown above, combine an alluring color with a sticky surface. Different insects are drawn to different colors. Aphids, leafhoppers, and whiteflies are partial to yellow, for instance, whereas tarnished plant bugs, flea beetles, and rose chafers prefer white, and most thrips flock to blue. When the pest lands on the trap's colored panel, it becomes entangled in the coating of glue covering the surface. Unlike Japanese beetle traps, these sticky traps, as they are called, should be placed near the plants you want to protect. Position the traps at about the same height as the plants.

Homemade Sticky Traps

Although sticky traps can be bought through many mail-order catalogs or at any well-stocked garden center, you can make one easily at home. Cut scrap wood into rectangles measuring about 6 by 6 inch-

Coping with Slugs and Snails

Snails and slugs are elusive pests, feeding at night and taking refuge during the day under rocks, boards, leaves, or dense ground cover, or in other moist, shaded spots. Their presence in the garden is betrayed by the silvery trails of mucus they leave behind and the large, ragged holes they chew in stems, bulbs, fruits, and leaves. Hostas, iris, and succulents are among their favorite plants, and in the vegetable garden, they nibble on tomatoes, lettuce, strawberries, and the pungent leaves of onions.

Gardeners have a number of effective options for fighting snails and slugs, including those illustrated at right—two kinds of traps and a barrier that exploits these pests' aversion to copper. Your level of squeamishness will influence which of the following methods you choose:

• Handpicking is most productive at night, when snails and slugs are actively feeding. Equip yourself with a flashlight and a pail of soapy water to dispose of the pests as you find them. Since their mucus is difficult to wash off, you may want to wear thin surgical gloves or use large tongs to pick the pests up.

• Salt sprinkled on slugs kills them by drawing fluid out of their bodies. However, repeated use of this technique carries the risk of making your soil salty enough to injure plants. This method is less successful with snails because their shells shield them from the salt.

• Place inverted flower pots or melon or grapefruit rinds in a shady spot to trap slugs or snails seeking daytime shelter.

• Sink a shallow can or pie tin to its rim in soil and fill with beer or other yeasty liquid. Empty every few days and replace the liquid.

• Spread a band of an abrasive material on the soil around plants as a deterrent; diatomaceous earth, sand, sawdust, and wood ashes are effective, but only when dry.

COPPER BARRIERS
The most reliable barriers against slugs and snails are made of copper, which is toxic to these mollusks. Thin sheets of copper, available at hardware stores, are easily cut in strips to use as barriers. For a raised bed, fasten strips at least 4 to 5 inches wide to each side (above). To edge a bed, cut strips 4 to 6 inches wide and install them with the top 2 inches above the soil line. As an extra deterrent, bend the strip's upper edge outward to form a lip.

es and paint them yellow, white, or blue, depending on the pest. You can buy a weather-resistant adhesive designed for coating traps or make the glue yourself. Simply combine equal parts of petroleum jelly or mineral oil and liquid dishwashing soap or laundry detergent and mix well. Spread the glue on the painted rectangles and hang them in the garden. In an exposed place, homemade glue should last about 2 weeks. When the trap is no longer sticky, remove the old glue and pest remnants with a paint scraper and apply a fresh coat of glue.

In addition to spreading it on traps, you can paint a stripe of glue around a tree trunk to catch crawling insects. If you've put a fabric trap on the tree *(page 169),* apply the sticky glue just above it.

Catching Pests in the Act

With traps, the need to actually handle pests is kept to a minimum. But if you're a gardener who doesn't mind the closer contact required, hand-

picking crawling creatures such as hornworms, cutworms, and Colorado potato beetles off leaves and stems is a very effective method of control. There are only a few plant pests that will cause you any discomfort if they come into contact with bare skin, and even then it is usually temporary. These include blister beetles, whose body fluids can irritate skin; caterpillars with stinging hairs; and black flies, which inflict bites like those of a mosquito. As a precaution, you should always wear garden gloves when handpicking pests. You can also use kitchen tongs instead of your fingers to grasp them. To kill handpicked pests, drop them into a container filled with soapy water. Dispose of them in the trash or your compost heap.

Techniques for Dislodging Pests

If you prefer to place a bit of distance between you and your garden pests, a stream of water from

AN UNBAITED BOARD TRAP
Nail two strips of wood about an inch thick to one side of a board. Set the board strip-side down on the ground. After a night of feeding, snails and slugs will collect in the dark, moist space beneath the board to escape drying heat and sunlight. Check the trap early each morning. Pick or scrape off any slugs and snails you find, and dispose of them in a pail of soapy water.

BAITED TRAPS
Designed for use with bait, the plastic trap illustrated below has a removable lid and a small, lightweight door that swings inward only, preventing the snails and slugs that crawl in from escaping. If you use a poison bait, a trap with a tight-fitting lid like this one reduces the risk of harm to pets. The lid also makes it easy to dump out the dead snails and slugs and to clean the trap's interior. The trap is partially buried to make it easier for the pests to enter.

a hose is often sufficient to remove invaders from plants. Be sure to spray the underside of the foliage, where aphids, whiteflies, mites, and other pests frequently feed, as well as the upper surfaces. If a plant's stems are fragile, hold them firmly with one hand as you wash the pests off. Make sure, however, not to turn the water on so high that the jet rips off leaves or damages new shoots.

If stems and branches are strong and resilient, vigorous shaking is enough to make many kinds of pests, including leaf-eating beetles and black vine weevils, fall to the ground. Place an old sheet or a tarpaulin around the base of the plant to collect the falling pests. When you are finished, shake the pests into a pail of soapy water.

Vacuuming pests off plants is another option, but only when it's done with a machine that has been made specifically for this purpose and has a gentle sucking action. Don't use a household vacuum, which is powerful enough to cause damage to the plant. Since the vacuum will pick up any insect in its path, it's important to distinguish pests from harmless or beneficial insects when using this technique.

Pruning Infested Plants

The best way to deal with some pests is to prune off the part of the plant that is afflicted. Fall webworm caterpillars, for example, hatch inside a gauzy-looking nest the female spins in susceptible trees. To rid the tree of the pests, crush the caterpillars or tear the bag open to expose the larvae to the elements. Then use sharp, well-made shears or a pruning saw and sever the infested stem or branch cleanly with a slanting cut about ¼ inch above a bud, as shown on page 204.

Insect-egg masses on foliage or stems can be pruned off; when you see leaf-miner trails on a susceptible plant, pinch off the infested leaves promptly. Add them to a hot compost pile—one that reaches at least 140°F—or put them in a tightly sealed plastic bag and place it in the trash.

Exploiting Natural Checks and Balances

In nature, the predator-prey system does a good job of keeping the size of pest populations within bounds. Even though a garden is an artificial environment, in which planting and cultivation practices can tip the balance in favor of pests, the checks and balances that operate in the wild can be adapted as a powerful and environmentally sound weapon against them.

The arsenal borrowed from nature includes predatory vertebrates, insects, insect relatives such as spiders and mites, beneficial nematodes, and bacteria that attack garden pests. Organisms that benefit the garden by feeding on pests are referred to as biological controls.

By encouraging the beneficial predators that already inhabit your garden and introducing others to augment its defenses, you can keep the pest population at a level that doesn't threaten the health or good looks of your plants. Moreover, this natural defensive system may become largely self-perpetuating, requiring little more of you than occasional tinkering. It is important to recognize, however, that biological controls are not over-night solutions to pest problems. Nor are they always complete solutions by themselves. An excellent way to apply them is in conjunction with many of the physical and cultural controls described on pages 158-162 and 169-173.

You must also recognize that biological controls function properly only if you minimize or even abandon the use of broad-spectrum pesticides. These products, which include most synthetic chemical pesticides as well as certain natural ones, such as pyrethrin and rotenone, kill many kinds of insects, including beneficials. At best, such pesticides provide you with a short-term solution to your pest problem.

Creating a Hospitable Environment

Just as there are conditions that make your garden attractive to pests, there are things you can do to attract and keep pest predators. A steady source of water such as a small pool is sure to draw benefi-

An insatiable predator, this convergent ladybird beetle eats its way along an aphid-infested plant stem. An adult beetle of this species can consume more than 30 of the insects a day; during its 3-week larval stage, the predator's intake can total 400 aphids. Other species of ladybird beetles, which are also known as ladybugs, feast on scale insects, mealybugs, whiteflies, and mites.

How a Parasitoid Destroys a Pest

The body of an insect selected by a parasitoid is both a protective habitat and a food supply for developing offspring. The drawings below illustrate this sequence in the life of a typical parasitoid, the braconid wasp. At far left, the female wasp injects an egg into its victim through a tube called an ovipositor **(A)**. The egg-laying process usually paralyzes the host but does not kill it immediately.

The egg quickly develops into a larva **(B)**. By the end of this life stage, which lasts 8 to 10 days, the larva's feeding activity has killed the host aphid. The larva metamorphoses into a pupa **(C)**, which continues to develop within the aphid's dry shell. At the end of pupation, the braconid wasp has attained its adult form and cuts a neat escape hatch to emerge from the host's remains **(D)**.

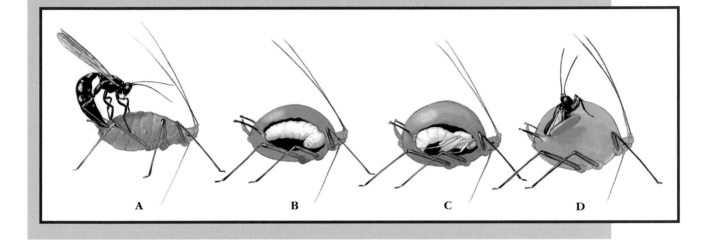

cial vertebrates, including frogs, toads, snakes, lizards, and birds. Toads also appreciate shelter in the garden—perhaps an overturned flower pot with a chipped rim for an opening. Fruiting shrubs and trees are magnets for birds, providing both shelter and food. The species that are mainly fruit or seed eaters in maturity catch prodigious numbers of insects to feed their young.

Insects, spiders, and other small predators can also be drawn to your garden by water and shelter; some types gravitate to shrubs, others to tall herbaceous plants or to a moist, cool layer of organic mulch. The more varied your landscape, the greater the chance that these creatures will find appropriate niches.

Spiders have an undeservedly bad reputation, for only a few species are dangerous to humans and none to plants. The wise gardener suppresses the impulse to kill spiders, since they are among the most efficient biological controls in the garden, consuming a wide variety of common garden pests. They are also present in great numbers in most areas. According to one study, for example, a typical 1-acre suburban plot has more than 60,000 spiders. Clearly, spiders play an important part in nature's system of checks and balances.

Purchasing Biological Controls

If the naturally occurring population of beneficials in your garden doesn't adequately contain pest outbreaks, it may be because they are too few in number or because they don't prey on the particular species of pest causing the trouble. In such cases, you can buy beneficials from a mail-order insectary for release in your garden. The information on the following pages and in the section of the encyclopedia that begins on page 294 will help you choose the beneficials you need.

Predatory Insects

Beneficial insects can be divided into two groups according to their feeding habits—predators and parasitoids. A predator's diet consists of other, usually smaller, insects. Green lacewings, ground beetles, ladybird beetles, rove beetles, and praying mantises are typical of these hunters. Some feed indiscriminately on a wide range of pests, including aphids, whiteflies, flea beetles, and spider

Predators for Sale

Many beneficial insects and other predators are available from mail-order insectaries. Before placing an order, identify your target pest. If you're uncertain of its type, send a specimen to your local Cooperative Extension Service. Or you may want to talk to a customer-service representative at a reputable insectary.

When your shipment of predators arrives, attend to it promptly. All predators need careful handling, and most must be released at a certain time. Read and follow all instructions. Three common mail-order predators are shown below in various life stages; since they'll be garden friends, you'll want to recognize them in all their various forms.

The convergent ladybird beetle, shown as a larva above left and as a pupa at center, is sold in its adult form (above, right).

Green lacewings are typically sold as eggs (above, left). The larva is at center and the adult appears at right.

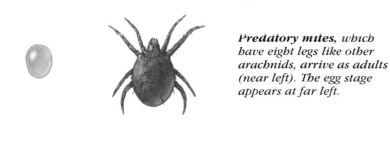

Predatory mites, which have eight legs like other arachnids, arrive as adults (near left). The egg stage appears at far left.

mites. Others are very specific about their food choices. Aphid midges, for example, feast on aphids and nothing else.

Most predators are voracious eaters. In its larval stage, for example, the green lacewing can devour 100 aphids in a day. But a shortcoming of predatory insects is that they also prey on other beneficials. Praying mantises, for instance, hunt down and devour their own kind.

Parasitoid Insects

Parasitoids, whose name means parasite-like, lay their eggs on or in a living insect host. After hatching, the larvae feed on the host, usually remaining attached to it until they have developed into adults *(diagram, page 175)*. Unlike a true para-

How to Release Beneficial Nematodes

Because of their ability to destroy more than 400 different soil-borne pests, beneficial nematodes are a popular biological control. The wormlike creatures are easy to handle and easy to apply to the soil. They arrive on sponges that usually measure about 5 by 7 inches, each of which has been saturated with a solution containing nearly 1 million nematodes—an amount sufficient to treat three or four large patio pots or window boxes. Before you can know how many nematodes to order, you'll need to determine the severity of your infestation and the size of the area to be treated. For a quarter-acre garden with a moderate infestation, you'll need around 25 to 30 million nematodes.

When the nematodes are delivered, immediately remove them from their packaging and inspect them *(Step 1, right)*. Apply them only during warm months, when temperatures range between 65° and 78° F. Wait until after sunset to release them into the garden, otherwise, ultraviolet rays from the sun can kill them. Nematodes work best in moist, loamy soil. If you are applying them to turf that has a thick mat of thatch, dethatch the lawn *(page 133)* so that the nematodes can easily penetrate the soil.

site, which feeds on its host but doesn't kill it, a parasitoid eventually kills the host.

Most parasitoid species target a particular type of pest and often only at one life-cycle stage. The trichogramma wasp, for instance, lays its eggs exclusively inside the eggs of specific butterfly and moth pests, thereby preventing the host eggs from hatching into troublesome caterpillars. Other pests controlled by parasitoids include aphids, whiteflies, and scale insects. Because the parasitoids are so selective, they are useful only when their chosen host infests your garden; without the host, the beneficial won't survive. This underscores the importance of learning to recognize garden pests, so that you'll be able to pick an appropriate control.

At least a dozen different parasitoids are widely available for purchase through the mail. Some species are shipped as adults, others in earlier stages of development. In the case of trichogramma wasps, the package you receive may contain a 1-inch-square card that holds up to 5,000 wasp eggs. Be sure to carefully read all instructions for unpacking, handling, and dispersing parasitoids. For further information and details on specific parasitoids available commercially, see the chart on page 179.

Predatory Mites

Like spiders, mites are arachnids rather than insects. The mite family includes several species of beneficials that prey on pests such as thrips and pest mites—for example, the spider mites and cyclamen mites that frequently cause serious dam-

1. **Look over the sponges.** They should feel damp and, to the naked eye, should appear to be coated with a cream-colored film. Using a magnifying glass, look to see if the nematodes are alive (they'll be wriggling). Proceed to Step 2, or reseal the sponges in their original plastic bag and store for no longer than 1 week in a refrigerator set at 40° to 50°F. (Caution: Because food refrigerators must be set lower than this to keep food from spoiling, do not store nematodes in them.)

2. **Fill a bucket with 1 gallon of lukewarm distilled water or rainwater.** Do not use chlorinated water, which can kill the nematodes. Wearing gloves, rinse the sponges in the water for a few minutes to release the nematodes into the water. Lightly squeeze the sponges, then dispose of them in the trash.

3. **Pour the nematode solution into a watering can and apply evenly to the soil.** Saturate the area but do not overwater; excess water can deplete the oxygen in the soil and kill the nematodes.

age to vegetables as well as many herbaceous ornamentals, trees, and shrubs.

Measuring less than 1/50 inch in length, the predatory mite species are often smaller than their prey, which can include adult mites as well as mite eggs, larvae, and nymphs. Under optimal environmental conditions, the beneficials can go from egg hatching to egg laying in a week, outstripping the reproductive rate of the pests. Because their population can increase so rapidly, predatory mites are a particularly effective biological control. Unlike predatory insects, they do not attack beneficial insects or insect relatives. And because they are harmless to humans and so tiny as to be no annoyance at all, they can be used indoors safely and conveniently to control houseplant pests.

A Benevolent Snail

The decollate snail is a Mediterranean native that appeared in this country over a century ago and has since become widespread in the southern states and in California. A nocturnal hunter, this predator feeds voraciously on pest snails, eggs and adults alike. The decollate snail is useful for controlling the common brown garden snail, which chews holes in a wide variety of plants, especially those in warm, moist climates.

This benevolent creature does have its drawbacks, however. It feeds on the seedlings of a wide variety of plant species and can do serious damage to several succulents and other low-growing plants. You should also check local ordinances before ordering a supply of decollate snails. In some parts of California, buying these predators for release in the garden is illegal because they can pose a threat to benign native mollusk species.

Beneficial Nematodes

Barely large enough to be seen with the naked eye, beneficial nematodes are microscopic roundworms that live in the soil. Unlike pest nematodes *(page 196),* which cause lesions and galls as they feed on plant stems and roots, beneficial nematodes destroy certain species of caterpillars, cutworms, borers, grubs, and beetle larvae. Like the parasitoids, beneficial nematodes are specialists: Certain species target certain pests. They do not damage plants, nor do they attack earthworms, which are natural aerators and essential to the health of the soil.

Applied to the soil *(pages 176-177),* beneficial nematodes locate their prey by following the trail of carbon dioxide released by the pest as it moves through the ground. The nematodes then invade the pest's body. One species has a dorsal "tooth" that it uses to pierce the epidermis of a pest; the creatures can then enter the host through its vascular system. Once inside, nematodes release fast-multiplying bacteria that can kill the host within 24 to 48 hours. The nematodes feed on the host and also eat the lethal bacteria, then lay hundreds to thousands of eggs inside the host. When the food supply is exhausted, the new generation of nematodes begins searching for insect hosts on their own. As long as the soil remains moist and the temperature is somewhere between 65° and 78°F, the reproductive cycle continues uninterrupted; thus a single application of beneficial nematodes may be effective for up to one year. If soil-borne pests are a persistent problem in your area, however, you may need to replenish the nematodes once or twice a year. The nematodes will die out once the pests have been eradicated.

Beneficial Microbes

Microorganisms even smaller than nematodes are also being exploited as pesticides. The most popular of these are two bacteria strains that are extremely effective against particular target insects. Virtually nontoxic to other insects, animals, or humans, these controls are inexpensive, easy to mass-produce, and easy to apply.

The bacterium *Bacillus thuringiensis* (Bt) is lethal to leaf-eating caterpillars. There are 30 different strains of Bt, each of which infects only one host species. Other serious garden pests controlled by a strain of Bt include the elm leaf beetle and the larvae of the Colorado potato beetle. Given the specificity of Bt, correctly identifying the type of pest that is causing damage in your garden is essential. Bt can be purchased in a variety of forms—dusts, powders, liquids, and sprays—at most home and garden centers and from mail-order companies. As with all pest-control agents, read the instructions carefully before use.

The second bacterium widely used to control pests causes an infection called milky spore disease, which attacks Japanese beetle grubs, or pupae. Japanese beetles commonly lay their eggs just below the surface of a lawn. As the grubs develop there, they feed on the roots of the grass or on thatch, a matted accumulation of grass debris. When the bacterial spores are dusted onto the lawn, they attack the grubs and multiply inside their bodies. The grubs die, releasing the spores into the soil and continuing the cycle of infection.

BENEFICIAL INSECTS AND THEIR TARGETS

Beneficials	Target Pests	Comments
Braconid wasps	Aphids, beetle larvae, moth larvae	Overwinter as newly hatched larvae inside living hosts. Adults feed on nectar and pollen.
Flower flies, hover flies	Aphids, mealybugs, mites, thrips	Black-and-yellow-banded bodies resemble bees or hornets. Adults feed on nectar and pollen of daisylike flowers.
Green lacewings, brown lacewings	Aphids, thrips, mealybugs, scales, moth eggs, mites, small caterpillars, soft-bodied insects	Eggs overwinter on plants. Adults feed on nectar and pollen. To prevent cannibalism in larvae, distribute purchased eggs widely.
Lady beetles, ladybugs	Aphids, whiteflies, mealybugs, spider mites, scales	Adults overwinter in leaf litter. The migratory convergent ladybeetle overwinters in large groups.
Praying mantises	Aphids, beetles, bugs, caterpillars, flies, leafhoppers, wasps. Mantises also prey on butterflies, bees, and other desirable insects and on one another.	Eggs overwinter in a frothy gray case attached to stems or twigs. Mantises are highly territorial and feed mostly on large insects.
Predatory bugs: assassin bug, ambush bug, big-eyed bug, minute pirate bug, spined soldier bug	Aphids, beetle larvae, leafhopper nymphs, spider mites, thrips	Prefer permanent beds and garden litter for shelter.
Predatory mites	Citrus red mites, cyclamen mites, European red mites, rust mites, two-spotted spider mites, thrips	Found in soil, moss, humus, manure, and on plants. Thrive in high humidity; cannot survive at low humidity. Low temperature slows reproduction rate.
Rove beetles	Aphids, fly eggs, maggots, mites, nematodes, slugs, snails, springtails	Found in a wide variety of habitats. Prefer permanent beds for overwintering.
Soldier beetles	Aphids, beetle larvae, butterfly larvae, caterpillars, grasshopper eggs, moth larvae	Adults are nectar and pollen feeders; prefer goldenrod. Eggs laid in soil or ground cover. Both larvae and adults are predators.
Trichogramma wasps	Cabbage worms, cutworms, eggs of 200 moth species, leaf-roller caterpillars	Larvae parasitize and kill pest eggs. Adults feed on nectar; prefer the daisy family and Queen Anne's lace and other members of the carrot family.

Buying Pesticides

Confronting the myriad bottles and containers in the pesticide aisle of the local garden center can be a bewildering experience for a gardener. Your first impulse may be to reach for the familiar package with the well-known manufacturer's name. But before you purchase your next pesticide, take a moment to consider the differences between an organic pesticide and a synthetic one.

Organic pesticides, as the name implies, are made from naturally occurring ingredients. They are effective against a wide range of pests and break down easily, with little effect on the environment. Although some organic pesticides have harmful effects on humans, bees, ladybird beetles, and other benign creatures, the danger is short-lived and can be minimized by proper handling. The chart on page 185 lists eight organic pesticides, the pests they target, and any precautions to follow in using the pesticide.

Synthetic pesticides are derived from both naturally occurring and manufactured materials. They are similar in chemistry to what are called persistent insecticides, which have been banned because of their damaging residual effects on the environment and all life forms. Synthetic pesticides can be highly toxic and tend to remain active for much longer periods of time than organics.

The product label will not tell you straight out whether the pesticide is organic or synthetic; you'll need to know the names of the botanical insecticides and the chemical names of the various synthetic products. Three groups of synthetics are widely available—organochlorines, organophosphates, and carbamates. Organochlorines contain carbon, chlorine, and hydrogen, in addition to pesticides such as chlordane and methoxychlor. Both chemicals are toxic to aquatic life if released into the water supply. Organophosphates, the most common of the synthetic pesticides, are derived from phosphoric acid and control a wide variety of garden pests. Although toxic to vertebrates, organophosphates break down quickly and have little residual effect. This group includes malathion, trichlorfon, and Diazinon. Carbamates are derived from carbamic acid; one of the best known is carbaryl, which is used to control lawn and garden pests as well as ticks and cockroaches. Carbaryl is highly toxic to natural predators, bees, and aquatic invertebrates, and moderately toxic to fish.

With both organic and synthetic pesticide products, it is imperative that you read the label and follow all instructions for applying the pesticide and disposing of it.

If you've given milder pest-control measures a fair trial and been disappointed with the results, you may decide to opt for a chemical control. As with other techniques, the prudent approach is always to use the pesticide least likely to harm humans, pets, or the environment. In practice, this means giving preference to pesticides derived from natural materials—principally minerals, plants, soaps, and oils—over the more toxic synthetics.

The reason that natural pesticides are relatively benign is that they generally target specific insects. These pesticides also break down into harmless substances shortly after they are applied; synthetic pesticides, on the other hand, may remain toxic far longer.

The fact that natural pesticides lose their potency quickly shouldn't mislead the gardener into underestimating their lethal capabilities. For instance, two of the most venerable botanicals—rotenone and pyrethrins—are powerful broad-spectrum poisons, killing a wide range of insects, including aphids, spider mites, and other serious pests, as well as some beneficials, such as honeybees, lacewings, spiders, and braconid wasps.

Higher animals, including humans, aren't immune to natural pesticides, either. Carelessly handled, these products can make a gardener very ill. And different creatures have peculiar sensitivities. While pyrethrins earn good marks for doing little harm to most mammals, cats are highly susceptible to pyrethrin poisoning.

Judging a Product's Safety

Many pesticides have not been fully tested, and being registered with the Environmental Protection Agency (EPA) does not necessarily mean they are safe. In fact, no pesticide on the market is designated "safe" on its label. Even the chemicals of low to moderate toxicity must be labeled with the word caution because they have the potential for doing serious harm to humans. Ingesting even a fraction of an ounce of one of the milder pesticides can be fatal, and long-term exposure also has been known to kill.

A pesticide's label spells out the product's appropriate uses, its toxic effects on humans and the environment, methods of application, directions for storage and disposal, and other critical information. The guide on page 184 will help you interpret this information so you'll get full benefit from the pesticide with the least possible harm.

How Natural Pesticides Work

If you decide to use a pesticide, identify the pest first, then choose a chemical that targets your problem. There is no one cure-all; your natural arsenal will have a range of weapons. Some of them, including Bt, are stomach poisons and work only when an insect ingests a bit of a treated plant. Overall, chewing insects—beetles, caterpillars, and the like—are more vulnerable to stomach poisons than sucking insects. In fact, sucking insects may not be affected at all, since they pierce the leaf surface and suck out the sap rather than eat the pesticide-coated surface itself.

Contact poisons, as their name suggests, must make direct contact with the pest. They are best sprayed onto the pest—a technique that is easiest to carry out on eggs, pupae, slow-moving crawling insects, and insects such as scales, whiteflies, and aphids. Flying insects can be felled unintentionally by drifting spray, and creeping or crawling pests can pick up a poison on their feet or antennae as they make their way over the surface of a treated plant. When you apply a contact pesticide, don't neglect crevices and the undersides of stems or foliage *(page 183)*.

Using Soap Sprays

Insecticidal soap sprays are contact poisons that are absorbed through the cuticle covering the pest's body. Once inside, they make cell membranes leaky, causing severe dehydration. Most vulnerable to soap sprays are aphids, scales, mites, and other soft-cuticled pests. Beetles, grasshoppers, and other pests with hard cuticles are much less susceptible.

The soap sprays remain potent only as long as they are wet, so spray in the early morning or in the evening, when lower temperatures and higher humidity slow the rate of evaporation. To avoid killing beneficials, keep the pesticide aimed specifically at problem species. Also, test-spray a few leaves and inspect them for yellowing or other symptoms of injury before treating the entire plant.

Horticultural Oils

These pesticides are sprayed on infested plants, smothering pests in a fine film. Eggs are especially

vulnerable, as are soft-bodied mites and insects, including scales, mealybugs, and whiteflies. Beneficials coated by the spray may also be killed, but once the treated plant dries, beneficials aren't in danger. The oils are available as dormant oil, for use when plants are dormant, and as superior oil, for use during the growing season. Avoid using any oils when temperatures exceed 90°F, and spray in early morning or late evening when the sun is at its weakest. For details, see pages 182-183.

A Pesticide from Seeds

Neem is a remarkably versatile botanical insecticide extracted from the seeds of the neem tree and first registered by the EPA in the 1980s. It has been found to combat more than 200 species of pests, including gypsy moths, whiteflies, mealybugs, Japanese beetles, leaf miners, and the Colorado potato beetle. For some leaf-eating insects, the repellent is so powerful that they completely shun plants they would otherwise defoliate. Other leaf eaters may begin to feed but stop immediately. Neem can also halt a larva's metamorphosis at the pupal stage. Since fewer individuals mature and reproduce, the pest population declines.

Neem is available as a foliar spray and as a soil drench. When taken up by a plant's roots and transported throughout its tissues, neem protects the plant from voracious insects for as long as 2 months. Judged safe for use on vegetables and fruits by the EPA, neem has an extremely low toxicity rating for humans and other mammals. It does not harm butterflies, honeybees, or ladybird beetles, and it does not accumulate in soil or water.

A Variety of Pesticide Forms

Pesticides are available in a number of different forms—liquid, granular, or dust. Whatever a pesticide's formulation, use a delivery device that allows the maximum possible precision to protect yourself from exposure and the environment from contamination.

An aerosol can filled with a premixed pesticide is an easy-to-use, surefire applicator (and also the most expensive). More important, it eliminates the risk of accidental spills. Equally convenient and somewhat more economical are the small trigger sprayers that contain premixed pesticide. At a still lower cost, you can mix a small quantity of liquid concentrate or wettable powder with water in a small pail reserved for this specific purpose. Carefully pour the mixture into a small trigger sprayer for application.

When you have a large job to do—spraying a lawn, for instance, or a number of trees or shrubs—the best device for applying a liquid pesticide is a compressed-air sprayer *(below)*. On a well-designed sprayer, the trigger that controls the spray is far enough from the nozzle that there is little danger of the pesticide dripping or spilling onto your hand.

That's not the case with hose-end sprayers, which are notorious drippers and splashers. Not only is it difficult to calibrate them to get the right proportion of pesticide to water, but if the sprayer lacks a backflow-prevention filter, the pesticide may flow backward into the hose—or even into the domestic water supply. For all of these reasons, you should avoid using hose-end sprayers to apply pesticides.

Soil infested with pests is commonly treated with granular pesticides, which can be applied with a drop spreader or sprinkled directly from the container onto the soil. However, birds can be killed by eating granules. A better dry pesticide choice is a dust, which can be safely spread with a bulb duster.

How to Use Horticultural Oils

Horticultural oils are safe and effective pesticides if you observe the following guidelines:
- Use either dormant oil or superior oil on plants that are in dormancy. In spring and summer, when plants are in active growth, use superior oil only.
- Choose the right strength. A 3-percent solution for dormant plants and a 2-percent solution in spring and summer are safe for the majority of plants. If the oil makes leaves burn or blister, try a 1-percent solution.
- Shake the sprayer occasionally to keep the oil and water solution well mixed.
- Apply horticultural oil early in the day in sunny, dry conditions so the oil will dry quickly.
- Spray each plant until every exposed surface—trunk, stems, branches, both sides of the leaves, and flowers—is wet.
- Allow at least 2 weeks between applications, and longer when plants are stressed by drought. Most species can be sprayed up to four times a year.

1. Before mixing or spraying horticultural oil, *put on a face mask and goggles to prevent oil particles from getting into your lungs and eyes. Wearing rubber gloves, unscrew the top of a 1-gallon compression sprayer. Measure the amount of oil according to the strength of the solution needed and pour it into the sprayer. Recap the bottle of oil. Fill the sprayer with water.*

Applying a Pesticide

A critical first step when working with a pesticide is to read the label thoroughly, even for a product that you have used before. Pay close attention to instructions for application, as well as any precautionary statements about the use of the chemical. Then, though it may be inconvenient, wait for a day when there is no wind to apply the pesticide. If it is imperative to go ahead with the job and no more than a slight breeze is stirring the air, proceed with caution, making sure that you keep your back squarely to the wind while you work; otherwise, you risk exposing yourself to the chemical.

In addition to being windless, the weather should be mild; low temperatures slow the breakdown process and pesticides remain toxic for a longer time. If the pesticide you are using is toxic to bees, apply it early in the morning or in the evening when they aren't active. Never apply a pesticide where it can run off into a drain, storm sewer, or stream. Treat only the plants or the parts of plants that are troubled by the pest, and use the lowest recommended dose. Because many natural pesticides are slow acting, you should give them several days to work before reapplying.

Spraying for Total Coverage

To ensure that a contact poison hits all target pests on a plant, begin spraying at its base and work up to the top, aiming the sprayer at the undersides of the leaves, as shown at left. Spray each surface, including stems and leaf axils, until the pesticide just begins to drip off. Next, spray the upper surfaces of the leaves, working from the top of the plant down.

2. Replace the top of the sprayer and screw it on tightly. Hold the container steady with one hand and pump the handle until you cannot pump it anymore (right). Shake the sprayer vigorously to make sure the oil and water are thoroughly mixed.

3. Spray an even coat of the oil solution on the entire plant (above). Shake the container occasionally to mix the oil and water. When you have finished, release the pressure valve on your sprayer, or carefully unscrew the sprayer's top. Dispose of any unused solution according to the pesticide label directions.

Dressing for the Job

The label of every pesticide describes any special protective equipment you will need, so read it carefully before you begin, and follow the directions scrupulously. With even the least toxic pesticide, you should always wear a long-sleeved, loose-fitting shirt; long pants; rubber work gloves (dishwashing gloves are not adequate); and nonporous shoes or boots (pesticides can soak into leather or fabric). As insurance against eye or lung irritation, you may also want to wear a mask and goggles. For more toxic chemicals, however, goggles and a respirator that has been specially designed for the chemical you are using are absolute necessities for ensuring your safety.

Once you begin handling a pesticide, do not smoke, drink, eat, or use the bathroom until the job is completed and you have washed your hands thoroughly. When you are preparing a mixture for spraying, measure out precisely the prescribed amount of pesticide. Be very careful not to splash the material on yourself, your clothes, or the surrounding area.

To avoid disposal or storage problems, mix only as much pesticide as you need for a single spraying. Should there be any left over at the end of the job, spray out the excess on other plants that can be treated, or follow the instructions on the label for proper disposal of unused material.

Cleaning Up

When you've finished applying the pesticide, wash the sprayer and mixing implements thoroughly with soap and water, rinse, and repeat. Store pesticides and any implements used with them in a cool, dry place, preferably a toolshed or garage rather than in the house. They should be out of a child's reach. Finally, wash your clothes separately from the rest of the laundry; dry them on high heat or outdoors in the sun.

Reading Pesticide Labels

The label on a pesticide container is your most complete source of information about a product. Although the words may be in microscopic type, it is important to read them before you buy. Each label has certain information required by law. It will inform you of the relative hazards of the material and how it may legally be used, along with any precautions you should take. Below are explanations for some of the most important components of a pesticide label:

- **Signal Word:** This is the most critical word—and the largest one—on the label. It reveals the relative acute toxicity of the pesticide, which is the measure of damage done if a product is ingested, inhaled, or absorbed through the skin. The least toxic materials are labeled with the word "Caution." The word "Warning" means the pesticide is moderately toxic. "Danger" or "Poison" on the label means the pesticide is highly toxic; this designation may also be accompanied by a skull-and-crossbones symbol. If there is no signal word on the package, the pesticide is relatively nontoxic. These signal words refer only to immediate damage sustained from one-time exposure to the pesticide; they reveal nothing about possible chronic effects.
- **Precautionary Statements:** These are the possible chronic effects, if any, including the chemical's ability to poison components of the nervous system (neurotoxici-

ty), cause cancer (carcinogenicity), have adverse effects on the reproductive process, and create mutations in genetic structure (mutagenicity). Also under this heading are precautions that should be taken when applying the pesticide, such as protective clothing that must be worn. The amount of time that must pass before you harvest food crops that have been sprayed with the product, sometimes listed as "reentry times required," is also included here.

- **Active Ingredient:** The pesticide's chemical composition and the percentage of it contained in the mixture.
- **Inerts:** A general term for all fillers and inactive ingredients, listed by percentage.
- **Statement of Practical Treatment:** Emergency first-aid measures if you are exposed to the pesticide.
- **Environmental Hazards:** Includes effect on beneficial insects such as bees, waterfowl, and other wildlife.
- **Directions for Use:** How to mix the pesticide, and when and how to apply it. You are required by law to follow these directions to the letter.
- **Storage and Disposal:** States whether the material must be kept from heat or freezing, and how to dispose of packaging and unused material.
- **Crops and Insects Controlled:** Includes a list of plants this pesticide may be used on and pests for which it has been approved. By law, the product may not be used on any crop or against any pest not listed on the label.

CHOOSING A BOTANICAL PESTICIDE

Pesticide	Target Pests	Comments
Citrus oils	Spider mites, aphids	Relatively nontoxic to humans and other mammals. May cause an allergic reaction.
False hellebore	Beetles, caterpillars, grasshoppers, sawflies	Highly toxic if ingested.
Neem	Aphids, flea beetles, gypsy moths, leaf miners, thrips, whiteflies	Relatively nontoxic to humans and other mammals and to beneficial insects.
Pyrethrins	Aphids, leafhoppers, spider mites, thrips, whiteflies	Toxic to fish, aquatic insects, and ladybeetles. Moderately toxic to bees and mammals. Pest insects may appear dead but revive after metabolizing pyrethrin.
Quassia	Aphids, caterpillars, sawflies	One of the safest botanical insecticides. Nontoxic to ladybeetles and bees.
Rotenone	Aphids, flea beetles, leafhoppers, spider mites, whiteflies, and other sucking and chewing insects	Highly toxic to fish, aquatic insects, and birds. Moderately toxic to humans and other mammals. May cause an allergic reaction.
Ryania	Aphids, Japanese beetles, lepidopterous larvae including codling moths, painted lady butterflies, and sunflower moths	Low toxicity to humans and other mammals and to beneficial insects.
Sabadilla	Aphids, blister beetles, chinch bugs, citrus thrips, grasshoppers, harlequin bugs, tarnished plant bugs, webworms	Toxic to humans and other mammals and to bees. May cause an allergic reaction.

Nuisance Mammals

Wildlife in the garden can be a mixed blessing. Many gardeners enjoy having chipmunks and cottontail rabbits around; the animals are fun to watch, and the damage they do, although it can be annoying, is almost always minor. Moreover, fences and chemical repellents do a good job of minimizing their impact on the garden.

Then there are the animals that do so much harm to the garden even the kindliest of gardeners cannot tolerate their presence. Although it isn't easy, it is possible to rid a garden of such pests by depriving them of food and water and eliminating their access to shelter. Nuisance animals can also be captured in live traps or, more drastically, in lethal traps.

Several mammals are especially notorious for damaging American gardens. Moles dig underground burrows that disturb plant roots and disfigure lawns. Voles, pocket gophers, ground squirrels, and woodchucks also tunnel extensively,

feeding underground on roots and bulbs, and making aboveground forays for leaves and stems. Jack rabbits, hares, rats, mice, and deer graze on shrubby ornamentals, fruit trees, and perennials. Skunks pockmark lawns in search of grubs and insects, and tree squirrels eat bulbs, fruits, and nuts.

Moles

Members of the shrew family, the seven species of moles found in the United States are torpedo-shaped creatures weighing about 4 ounces. Outfitted for digging with strong forepaws splayed outward, they can tunnel as far as 200 feet a day. Gardeners rarely see moles, which emerge from their network of burrows and feeding tunnels only to gather nesting materials. Active day and night year round, moles search constantly for the insects, slugs, and grubs that make up their diet; af-

The star-nosed mole pictured below has 22 fleshy pink appendages around its nostrils that it uses like fingers to explore the soil for grubs and insects. Like all moles, this species has large-toed, spade-shaped forepaws that are well adapted for efficient digging.

ter only a few hours without food they starve to death. They use their snouts, which have a highly developed sense of touch, to locate their prey.

Moles make their presence known by the small cones of loose soil—or molehills—around the openings to their burrows and by the telltale ridges made by shallow tunnels. The ridges are primarily an aesthetic problem, as are the molehills, although they can be high enough to damage a lawn mower.

Since moles devour soil pests such as cutworms and white grubs in large numbers and don't feed on plants at all, it makes sense to be as tolerant of their objectionable habits as possible. You can minimize the impact of their tunneling by tamping down raised strips of soil and watering them well to ensure that disturbed plant roots don't dry out.

Moles have hearing so acute that you may be able to get rid of them with a level of noise that is tolerable to human ears. A simple technique is to push the shaft of a plastic pinwheel down into a tunnel until you feel it touch the tunnel's floor. As it turns in the wind, the pinwheel may transmit vibrations strong enough to force the moles to abandon the tunnel. Partially buried bottles, which whistle and vibrate in the wind, may also help rid your garden of the pests.

Lethal traps are undoubtedly the most effective means of managing moles. Harpoon, scissor-jaw, or choker-loop traps should be set over frequently traveled tunnels in early spring or early fall. These devices kill quickly and are considered more humane than a live trap, since a mole could easily starve to death before the well-meaning gardener had a chance to check the trap.

Bury a dead mole where you trap it. Its remains will discourage other moles from reinfesting that part of your garden.

Voles and Pocket Gophers

Voles and pocket gophers are small rodents that deface lawns and beds with mounds of soil and feed on an entire range of plant materials. Voles, also called meadow or field mice, are found across the northern tier of the United States and as far south as northern Florida. About 6 inches long including their tails, they live in abandoned mole burrows, thick blankets of mulch, dense weeds, and grassy areas. They eat seeds, fruits, grasses, tender bark, and other soft plant materials, digging 1- to 2-inch-wide surface runways where they feed on roots. These runways crisscross a lawn like a brown maze. A vole eats twice its weight every

The meadow vole (left) feeds on strawberries and other fruits, seeds, and grasses, and in winter it strips bark from trees and shrubs. The lawn shown below has been ruined by the maze of runways made by voles.

A pocket gopher emerging from its tunnel (right) displays the sickle-shaped claws it uses for digging. On its aboveground forays, the pocket gopher fills its expandable cheek pouches with food and nesting materials.

Found in most parts of the United States, the striped skunk (above) digs holes and damages garden plants in its search for insects and grubs. When this pest is alarmed, the noxious, malodorous liquid it sprays to a distance of 10 feet or more can cause temporary blindness.

Adopting an erect posture meant to intimidate an enemy, the wood-chuck at right may eat more than 1½ pounds of vegetation a day, including leaves, blossoms, and tougher fare such as woody stems. The woodchuck's sharp incisors grow at a rate of 14 inches a year to replace the portions worn away by incessant gnawing.

day but tends to destroy much more than it eats.

Reproducing at a rate of 10 litters of five off-spring per year, voles tend to be so numerous that a gardener's options for control are few. A house cat that is a diligent mouser is a help, but traps scarcely make a dent in the population. Modifying the garden habitat by weeding, mowing the lawn often, and removing thick mulches deprives voles of favorite habitats. You can erase their runways by tilling the soil and replanting the area; you will likely kill some of the population in the process.

Pocket gophers, unlike voles, lead solitary lives. Named for the pocketlike cheek pouches in which they carry vegetation for food and nesting, pocket gophers are common throughout the West and Midwest. Like moles, they are active at all hours and in all seasons, and tunnel underground. You can easily distinguish the entrance of a pocket gopher's tunnel from the opening of a mole's burrow: Instead of a cone, the soil is arranged in a fan-shaped mound.

Pocket gophers feed both above ground and below. If you see a plant wiggle, then disappear beneath the soil's surface, a pocket gopher is at work. Besides destroying vegetation, these animals also chew through plastic irrigation lines.

Fumigating a pocket gopher's tunnel with smoke or gas cartridges, flooding it with water, dumping used kitty litter into it, or placing a few tablespoons of strychnine-laced bait in the tunnel are sometimes suggested as controls, but none of them is completely reliable. If you have a severe infestation, you may have to resort to a lethal trap. The best type for pocket gophers is the two-pronged pincher trap. Always wear gloves when checking traps, since pocket gophers are hosts to lice and external parasites. Stuffing a dead pocket gopher into the tunnel will discourage reinfestation.

Rats, Mice, and Squirrels

Together, these three groups of rodents account for nearly 40 percent of all mammalian species. They breed prolifically, can be found in all climates except the polar regions, and continuously compete with people for food and space.

Rats and mice dig up seeds and eat seedlings and fruits. Ground squirrels, which live in underground burrows, are omnivores. They eat seeds, fruits, grasses,

Commonly Used Controls

Prevention is the best way to control animal pests. Choose shrubs and perennials animals shun. To prevent pests from burrowing, lay down wire mesh before spreading topsoil and planting. Use fencing in your design. When damage occurs, identify the animal causing it. If possible, first make changes in the garden's habitats—remove brush piles, control weeds, fill in boggy areas, store firewood on pallets—to eliminate sources of food, water, and shelter. If this doesn't work, choose controls from the chart at right. The following controls help to exclude animals, manipulate their behavior, or reduce their population:

- Fences and protective guards: The height of a fence and whether it should extend underground depend on the ability of the pest to jump or burrow. Guards include metal flashing, wire mesh, and netting.
- Repellents: Chemical taste and odor repellents such as thiram, ammonium salts, and putrescent egg solids, sprayed directly on plants, can be effective if applied weekly.
- Scare tactics: Noise, the scent of natural predators (including people), and lifelike owl, snake, and cat decoys can ward off pests.
- Live and lethal traps: Live traps include baited cages and boxes. Spring-loaded snap, skewer, scissors, and choke traps kill the animal.

PESTS	CONTROLS					
	Habitat Alteration	Fences/Protective Guards	Repellents	Scare Tactics	Live Traps	Lethal Traps
Deer		✔	✔			
Ground Squirrels			✔	✔		✔
Jack Rabbits/Hares		✔	✔	✔	✔	
Meadow Voles	✔	✔				✔
Moles		✔	✔	✔		✔
Pocket Gophers	✔					✔
Rats/Mice	✔			✔		✔
Skunks	✔	✔	✔		✔	
Tree Squirrels		✔	✔		✔	
Woodchucks	✔	✔		✔	✔	

insects, and lizards, and raid birds' nests for both eggs and hatchlings. Tree squirrels, which have long, bushy tails and usually nest in trees, feed on buds, nuts, fruits, and the tender stems of woody plants. They strip bark from trees and gnaw through irrigation lines and telephone cables.

The yard cleanup recommended for discouraging voles may also work with rats and mice. Spread mothballs around the bases of shrubs and trees to repel both ground and tree squirrels. Two types of lethal traps—snap traps and jaw traps—are effective against ground squirrels, mice, and rats.

Using a Live Trap

You can also catch mice, rats, and squirrels in a live trap, either a box or a cage type. Special caution is called for, however, since these rodents can transmit viral diseases to humans. Decide beforehand where you will release any animal you catch, and

At home in rural, suburban, and urban areas, the highly adaptable American gray squirrel (left) eats buds, seeds, nuts, and fruits of ornamental plants; gnaws through the bark of trees to reach the edible inner layers; and chews holes in irrigation lines.

Deer-Resistant Plants

While only a handful of ornamentals are truly deer-proof, there are many that deer shun unless preferred food sources are scarce. Characteristics likely to make a plant deer resistant are thorns, tough or fuzzy leaves or stems, and strong flavors and aromas.

GROUND COVERS

Ajuga reptans
(carpet bugle)
Asperula odorata
(sweet woodruff)
Convallaria majalis
(lily of the valley)
Lamium 'Beacon Silver'
(dead nettle)
Pachysandra
(pachysandra)
Vinca minor
(periwinkle)

PERENNIALS

Achillea spp.
(yarrow)
Astilbe spp.
(false spirea)
Coreopsis spp.
(tickseed)
Dianthus spp.
(garden pink)
Echinacea spp.
(purple coneflower)
Eupatorium purpureum
(Joe-Pye weed)

Geranium spp.
(cranesbill)
Helleborus spp.
(hellebore)
Iberis spp.
(candytuft)
Liatris spicata
(spike gay-feather)
Linaria spp.
(toadflax)
Lychnis coronaria
(rose campion)
Perovskia atriplicifolia
(Russian sage)
Rudbeckia spp.
(coneflower)
Solidago spp.
(goldenrod)
Veronica officinalis
(speedwell)

VINES

Celastrus spp.
(bittersweet)
Clematis spp.
(clematis)
Hedera helix
(English ivy)
Lonicera spp.
(honeysuckle)

Wisteria spp.
(wisteria)

SHRUBS

Buddleia davidii
(butterfly bush)
Buxus sempervirens
(common boxwood)
Calycanthus occidentalis
(sweet shrub)
Ceanothus sanguineus
(wild lilac)
Cephalotaxus fortunei
(Chinese plum yew)
Cornus stolonifera
(red-osier dogwood)
Corylus americana
(American hazelnut)
Enkianthus campanulatus
(enkianthus)
Hibiscus syriacus
(rose of Sharon)
Ilex x meserveae
(blue holly)
Ilex glabra
(inkberry)
Leucothoe fontanesiana
(leucothoe)
Mahonia bealei

White-Tailed Deer Fawn

check the trap at least once a day. When you catch an animal, calm it by covering the trap with a tarpaulin or blanket before moving it; wear heavy gloves and keep children away from the trap. When you are ready to release the animal, back away from the trap as soon as you open it.

Skunks can also be controlled with live traps, but because of their offensive smell when they are alarmed, this is a job best left to a pest-control professional. Besides doing damage with their digging, skunks are undesirable because they can carry the rabies virus.

The Rabbit Family

Jack rabbits and snowshoe hares are far more destructive than cottontail rabbits because of their greater size and fecundity: The average female produces four litters of eight kits annually. These prolific pests consume up to 1 pound of vegeta-

tion each day, feasting on flowers, turf grass, foliage, shoots, stems, and the tender bark of young trees and shrubs.

Physical barriers and repellents are effective against jack rabbits and hares. These animals are stopped by a 3-foot-high fence of ¾-inch wire mesh, which need not extend underground, since these pests do not normally burrow. You can also protect a tree with a collar of sheet-metal flashing that extends 2 feet above the snow line. Commercial repellents containing thiram, ammonium soaps, putrescent egg solids, lime sulfur, copper carbonate, or asphalt must be reapplied to plants weekly or after a heavy rain.

Woodchucks

Although woodchucks (also known as groundhogs) are far less numerous per acre than the animals described so far, their size—as much as 20 pounds—and voracious appetite can create a serious problem for the gardener: These large rodents can devastate new plantings in a few hours. They dig burrows up to 50 feet long on two or

(leatherleaf mahonia)
Philadelphus spp.
(mock orange)
Spiraea spp.
(bridal wreath)
Syringa vulgaris
(common lilac)
Viburnum carlesii
(Koreanspice viburnum)
Viburnum opulus
(snowball bush)
Yucca filamentosa
(yucca)

TREES

Acer platanoides
(Norway maple)

Acer saccharinum
(silver maple)
Betula papyrifera
(white birch)
Crataegus spp.
(hawthorn)
Cryptomeria japonica
(Japanese cedar)
Lithocarpus densiflorus
(tanbark oak)
**_Metasequoia
glyptostroboides_**
(dawn redwood)
Parrotia persica
(Persian parrotia)
Picea abies
(Norway spruce)

Picea glauca
(white spruce)
Pinus sylvestris
(Scotch pine)
Pinus thunbergii
(black pine)
Tsuga canadensis
(Canadian hemlock)

*Note: The abbreviation
"spp." stands for the plural
of "species"; where used in
lists it means that many,
but not all, of the species in
a genus meet the criterion
of the list.*

Clematis (clematis)

*Rudbeckia hirta
(black-eyed Susan)*

Syringa vulgaris (common lilac)

more levels. The apron of dirt at each of the two or three entrances serves as a sentry post and a safe spot for sunning and grooming. Slow-moving and easily frightened, woodchucks rarely venture far from their underground homes.

Because of their timidity, woodchucks prefer the protection of tall grass or undergrowth, so clearing away such vegetation may effectively discourage them. If this tactic fails, a sturdy fence that extends 3 feet above ground level and at least 2 feet below will keep a woodchuck out of a garden plot. You can also capture the animal in a baited box or cage trap. Release it more than 5 miles from its burrow; otherwise, it may find its way back home. A lethal trap can be used, of course, but you may not want to handle a dead mammal of this size.

Deer

Deer can pillage a garden even faster than woodchucks. The two species common to the United States—the white-tailed deer in the East and the mule deer in the West—strip shrubs and trees of foliage and devour perennials and vegetables in record time. While deer usually live at the edge of woodlands, they also roam suburban areas.

The same commercial repellents that succeed with jack rabbits and hares work with deer if plants are sprayed at the first sign of new growth in spring and at weekly intervals thereafter. Fences must be at least 7 feet high to prevent deer from leaping over them, and ideally they should slant outward from the protected area at a 45° angle. Another tactic is to fill your garden with plants that deer generally ignore; a list of these appears above. Keep in mind, though, that when the deer population in an area outstrips the available food supply, the hungry animals will eat virtually any kind of vegetation.

*Betula papyrifera
(white birch)*

CHAPTER EIGHT

Preventing Plant Disease

At one time or another even the most conscientious gardener is likely to discover a plant with signs of disease. In the lovely spring garden at left, for example, blemished petals and leaves on the red tulips betray the presence of botrytis blight, a fungal disease. The outdoors is teeming with billions of microorganisms, and although most of them are beneficial, a few—called plant pathogens—feed on and damage living plants.

Instead of relying primarily on synthetic chemicals to prevent disease or restore plants to health, many gardeners have begun to adopt a more sophisticated, environmentally friendly strategy. It calls for selecting disease-resistant plants suitable for a garden's particular environment and keeping the soil in good condition. Cultural, physical, and biological means of preventing and controlling disease, many of which are described on the following pages, are the gardener's first choice. Chemical controls (pages 206-207) are reserved for use only when simpler, safer methods prove ineffective.

Identifying Diseases

It is impossible to predict when disease will strike the garden. A plant that grew vigorously one year may have wilting leaves or inferior blooms the next, for no apparent reason. With a little knowledge, however, the gardener can learn to detect signs of disease early on and may be able to prevent a small problem from turning into a large one.

An essential first step to knowing your garden is identifying your plants. Since different genera and species are vulnerable to different diseases, a plant's botanical name is an important diagnostic clue. Keep a list of your plants in a diary and update it with each acquisition. In addition, use the diary to note such events as the date you set out a new plant or transplanted an old one, and how a new disease-resistant cultivar is performing. Also note any periods of unusual weather and the application of fertilizers or other chemicals.

The more observant you are in the garden, the more likely you'll be to notice when your plants deviate from the norm. Make it a habit to stroll through the garden once a week to examine your plants, looking at the undersides of leaves and checking stems; a 10-power hand lens will help you inspect them more closely. Keep track of your observations, recording any unusual symptoms you may find. Some common symptoms of disease are illustrated on page 197. Typically, diseases are seasonal, so if there's an outbreak one year, your diary will remind you when to be on the alert in coming years for a recurrence.

If you have difficulty pinning down a plant's problem, ask the local Cooperative Extension Service or a reputable nursery for help. Your diary, along with a fresh specimen of the plant, will provide the expert with information needed to make an accurate diagnosis.

The Varieties of Diseases

Plant diseases are divided into two broad categories—infectious and noninfectious. Among the agents responsible for infectious diseases are a number of invasive, parasitic pathogens that include certain fungi, bacteria, viruses, and even a few plants. Noninfectious diseases, on the other hand, arise from environmental problems such as mineral deficiencies, severe weather, and overwatering. Understanding these causes should be the first line of defense for your garden.

Fungi

Approximately 80 percent of the infectious diseases you are likely to encounter in your garden are caused by various types of fungi. Most fungi are beneficial: They live off dead leaves and other organic matter, decomposing it in the process. Disease-causing fungi, by contrast, feed on living plants and release toxins as they spread over the plant's surface or invade its tissue. Some fungal infections, such as powdery mildew, are mainly a cosmetic problem, while others, such as root rot, can do serious damage and even kill the plant.

Fungi reproduce by releasing spores, which can be spread by water, wind, insects, birds, animals, or humans. Some spores can survive a trip of hundreds of miles, then germinate within minutes when deposited in a hospitable place. Spores need moisture to germinate, so dry weather will suppress fresh outbreaks of fungal disease.

Bacteria

As with fungi, most species of bacteria in the garden are valuable organisms, releasing nitrogen into the soil and breaking down dead plant and animal tissue. The species that cause plant diseases are most frequently transmitted by water, but can also be carried by foraging insects, or wind, or on gardening tools.

Some bacteria enter a plant by penetrating cells on its surface, while others invade through pores or other natural openings, or through wounds in stems or bark. An insect carrying a bacterium can inject it directly as it feeds. Once inside, bacteria may clog a plant's water-conducting system or drain nutrients from its cells. The symptoms of a bacterial disease often resemble those produced by a fungus, such as rotting tissue. If the rotted portion is slimy and smells foul, however, the cause can only be a bacterium; fungi don't produce either symptom.

Viruses

A plant that has stunted foliage, abnormal leaf curling, mosaic-like patterns on its foliage, or color changes such as yellow rings or lines may be in-

The owner of this lush Chapel Hill, North Carolina, garden shuns chemicals. She credits the garden's health to well-prepared soil and to disease-resistant shrubs, grasses, and perennials such as the Joe-Pye weed blooming at right.

fected with a virus. Most viruses travel among plants in the saliva of insects, but nematodes—microscopic, wormlike creatures—are also carriers. In addition, a gardener can transmit viruses via hands, shoes, or tools, especially those used for cutting. Thus pruning, grafting, dividing, and taking cuttings all carry a risk, however minimal, of exposing plants to viruses.

Viral diseases are the hardest to diagnose. A single virus may have a variety of symptoms, which often closely resemble those produced by a nutrient deficiency. The only sure way to diagnose a virus is to have the plant analyzed by experts in a laboratory. The simpler course is to maintain an adequate supply of nutrients in your soil; if the problem persists even after you have added nutrients to the soil, you can assume that a virus is the cause. Since there is no known cure of any kind for viral diseases, the prudent move is to destroy the infected plant.

Nematodes

Although most species of nematodes are harmless or even beneficial to plants *(page 178),* some are destructive. Most parasitic nematodes feed on roots, stunting the plant and causing wilting and yellowing. A few species feed inside stems, while others damage leaves and sometimes blossoms. The damage done by nematodes, viruses, and cultural disorders can look very similar, but laboratory analysis of a soil sample or a plant can pinpoint the exact cause.

Cultural Problems

Mineral deficiencies, unsuitable light conditions, poor drainage, too much or too little water, air pollution, and injury can also be responsible for plant disorders. These can be hard to distinguish from infectious diseases, but one helpful clue is the way a problem is distributed in the garden. If all of the plants in one area share the same symptom, an environmental factor is likely to be at fault; infectious diseases, on the other hand, tend to be randomly distributed or to attack one plant at first, then spread to others. Again, noting the pattern of distribution in a garden diary can be an invaluable diagnostic tool.

Keeping an Eye on Trees

Many gardeners assume that trees can take care of themselves, especially if the plants have been around for a long time. In reality, the unnatural conditions of the garden, such as the lack of accumulated leaf litter, soil compaction, and inept pruning, are hazardous to trees. For this reason, the plants should be examined from time to time for signs of environmental stress or disease. This is especially important for a tree beyond the sapling stage. A tree slows its growth rate as it ages, but a slowdown that is too abrupt is a sign of declining health. A technique for tracking a tree's health from year to year is described at left.

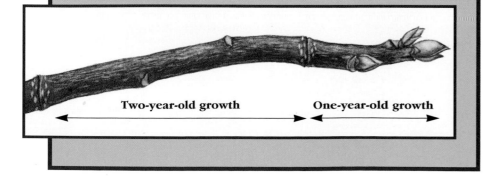

Disease Families and Their Symptoms

Plant diseases are commonly grouped by the kinds of symptoms they produce. Illustrated here are the eight symptoms that appear most frequently in home gardens, and the popular terms for the diseases involved. However, no single pathogen is responsible for each symptom. For instance, the wartlike swellings known as galls may be caused by a bacterium or by fungi.

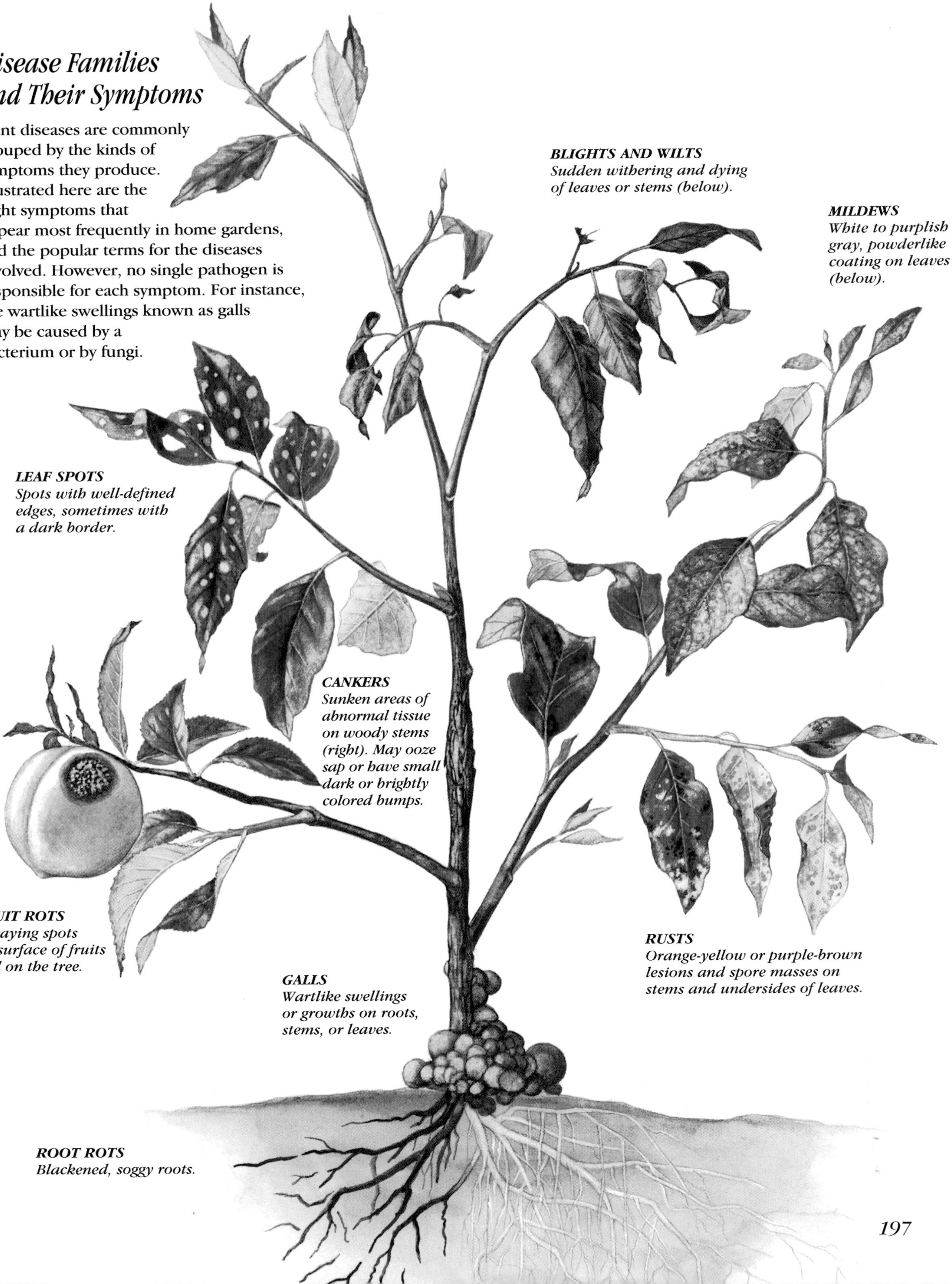

LEAF SPOTS
Spots with well-defined edges, sometimes with a dark border.

BLIGHTS AND WILTS
Sudden withering and dying of leaves or stems (below).

MILDEWS
White to purplish gray, powderlike coating on leaves (below).

CANKERS
Sunken areas of abnormal tissue on woody stems (right). May ooze sap or have small dark or brightly colored bumps.

FRUIT ROTS
Decaying spots on surface of fruits still on the tree.

RUSTS
Orange-yellow or purple-brown lesions and spore masses on stems and undersides of leaves.

GALLS
Wartlike swellings or growths on roots, stems, or leaves.

ROOT ROTS
Blackened, soggy roots.

Preventive Medicine for Plants

Every day, plant pathogens find their way into your garden, within striking distance of your favorite plants. But a well-planned garden—one that optimizes growing conditions for plants and discourages the presence of pathogens—has a much better chance of avoiding infection. Gardening defensively is a much more effective way of managing plant diseases than attempting to cure them. The techniques and approaches described here will help keep your garden disease free, and they can also prevent the recurrence of diseases that have been troublesome in the past.

The Right Plants

Plants have evolved to adapt to particular environments, and a gardener should strive to make a suitable match between the physical needs of plants and the physical conditions of the garden. Trying to fight the environment is a losing battle for gardener and plant alike, so before you buy a plant, make sure your garden will offer it what it needs to grow vigorously. If you are replacing a plant that has died, do not get an identical variety; chances are good that the same problem would beset the replacement plant, creating unnecessary work and expense for you.

Disease-Resistant Species and Cultivars of Popular Shrubs

The following shrubs are resistant to one or more diseases—listed after the plant's common name—that typically attack other members of the genus:

Chamaecyparis lawsoniana 'Ellwoodii' (false cypress)—armillaria

Cotoneaster adpressus, C. apiculatus, C. praecox (cotoneaster)—fire blight

Euonymus alata (winged euonymus)—crown gall, scale

Juniperus chinensis 'Femina', 'Keteleeri'; J. communis 'Aureo-spica', 'Depressa', 'Suecia'; J. conferta; J. sabina 'Broadmoor', 'Knap Hill', 'Skandia' (juniper)—phomopsis, cedar-apple rust

Pyracantha 'Apache', 'Fiery Cascade', 'Mohave', 'Navaho', 'Pueblo', 'Rutgers', 'Shawnee', 'Teton' (firethorn)—scab, fire blight

Rhododendron 'Copperman', 'Fashion', 'Pink Gumpo' (azalea)—phomopsis; *R. poukhanense, 'Corrine', 'Fakir', 'Formosa', 'Fred Cochran', 'Glacier', 'Hampton Beauty', 'Hi-gasa', 'Merlin', 'Polar Seas'* (azalea)—phytophthora; *R. delavayi; R. occidentale; R. sanctum; R. simsii, 'Caroline', 'Martha Isaacson', 'Pink Trumpet', 'Red Head'* (rhododendron)—phytophthora; *R. 'Boursault', 'Cunningham's White', 'English Roseum', 'Le Bar's Red', 'Roseum 2'* (rhododendron)—botryosphaeria

Rosa 'All That Jazz', 'Carefree Wonder', 'Pascali', 'Peace', 'Queen Elizabeth', 'Sutter's Gold', 'The Fairy', 'Tropicana' (rose)—black spot

Thuja occidentalis 'Ellwangeriana', 'Lutescens' (arborvitae)—phomopsis, tip blight

Viburnum burkwoodii 'Mohawk'; V. carlcephalum 'Cayuga' (viburnum)—bacterial leaf spot, powdery mildew

Euonymus alata (winged euonymus)

Shopping for Disease-Resistant Plants

Some plants are naturally resistant to infection, possessing toxic compounds or physical features, such as a thick, impenetrable outer coating, to repel pathogens. Other resistant plants are the product of crossbreeding programs that seek to combine naturally occurring protective chemicals with outstanding ornamental features.

More and more attractive cultivars of virtually every kind of plant are being bred for disease resistance. Before you undertake a planting project, find out whether there are resistant varieties that would work well in your garden. On the opposite page and below are lists of some desirable species and cultivars of shrubs and trees that will outperform their unimproved relatives where the diseases indicated are a problem. Check with your Cooperative Extension Service agent for a list of diseases that commonly occur in your area.

When you are shopping at a nursery, read plant labels to see if they contain information about the plant's resistance to disease. This often takes the form of coded abbreviations—for example, "DMPM" means that the plant is resistant to downy mildew and powdery mildew. Also desirable, though their level of natural protection is somewhat less, are plants described as "tolerant" of a certain disease. This means that although the plant may become infected, it won't be significantly damaged by the disease.

Immunity vs. Resistance

A resistant plant is just that: It is unlikely to be infected by a pathogen, but it isn't totally immune. If a serious disease is widespread in your area, you

Malus 'Donald Wyman'
('Donald Wyman' crab apple)

Disease-Resistant Species and Cultivars of Popular Trees

The following trees are resistant to one or more diseases—listed after the plant's common name—that typically attack other members of the genus:

Acer platanoides 'Jade Glen', *'Parkway'* (maple)—verticillium wilt

Cornus kousa; C. florida x *kousa hybrids* (dogwood)—Discula anthracnose

Ficus carica 'Kadota', 'Mission' (fig)—armillaria

Fraxinus pennsylvanica (ash)—anthracnose; *F. velutina 'Modesto'*—armillaria

Ilex cornuta, 'Meserve', 'Blue Prince', 'China Boy', 'China Girl' (holly)—black root rot; *I. aquifolium*—armillaria

Lagerstroemia 'Acoma', 'Apalachee', 'Biloxi', 'Choctaw', 'Comanche', 'Hopi', 'Lipan', 'Miami', 'Natchez', 'Osage', 'Pecos', 'Sioux', 'Tonto', 'Tuskegee', *'Wichita', 'Zuma', 'Zuni'* (crape myrtle)—powdery mildew

Malus 'Beverly', 'Dolgo', 'Donald Wyman', 'Liset', 'Naragansett', 'Red Jewel', 'Snowdrift' (crab apple)—gymnosporangium rust, fire blight, frogeye leaf spot, rust, scab

Pinus nigra (Austrian pine)—armillaria; *P. palustris* (longleaf pine)—fusiform rust

Platanus 'Columbia', 'Liberty' (plane tree)—anthracnose

Populus 'Assiniboine' (poplar)—canker, rust

Quercus coccinea; Q. palustris; Q. rubra; Q. velutina (oak)—anthracnose

may want to restrict yourself to plants that are never harmed by that particular pathogen. For instance, where flowering crab apples are plagued by apple scab (which defaces foliage and makes leaves and fruit drop prematurely), you might choose a redbud, Kousa dogwood, or serviceberry instead of a crab apple if you want a small ornamental tree that flowers in spring.

Choosing a Healthy Specimen

When you have decided what kind of plant to buy, select the individual specimen carefully. Use the guidelines on page 158 to examine a nursery plant for diseases and pests. If possible, check the root system by gently lifting the plant out of the pot. If the roots are dark, soggy, or malodorous, choose another plant. Also reject a plant that has a wound on it; nicked or torn bark or a broken branch provides an entry point for disease.

Some nurseries sell plants labeled "certified disease-free." These plants have been grown under carefully controlled conditions, protected from insects, and determined by a plant pathologist to be free of infection. Although such certification adds to the price of the plant, the expense may be well worth it in the long run.

Optimizing Growing Conditions

Relying heavily on resistant and tolerant cultivars is an essential tactic in creating a garden as free of disease as possible. Equally important is maintaining the health of your plants with proper cultural and physical practices: The more vigorous plants are, the less likely they'll succumb to disease.

Observing Good Planting Practices

Resist the temptation to crowd your plants together to achieve the effect of dense foliage and lush blooms. Instead, space them generously, following the recommended planting distances. This reduces competition for nutrients, water, and sunlight, and permits air to circulate freely around stems and leaves. Good air circulation is especially vital for preventing the humid conditions in which fungi thrive. The spores of botrytis blights and powdery mildews, for instance, are present in the air, the soil, or plant debris in most gardens, but they can't infect plants unless the environment is warm and moist.

Amending the Soil

Healthy soil leads to healthy plants that can fend off all but the most persistent diseases. If the soil has a proper balance of nutrients and a hospitable pH range, and is well drained, plants will develop good root systems and make efficient use of nutrients and water.

You will need to amend the soil in your garden every year to replenish nutrients consumed by growing plants. Compost is the most effective all-around amendment; you can make it yourself (pages 106-107) or buy it in bags. In the fall, spread a 2-inch layer over the soil and dig it in.

The Art of Watering

The following techniques will keep your plants well watered while making the garden less hospitable to disease organisms:

- When planning a garden, group plants according to their water needs.
- Most gardens need 1 to 1½ inches of water every 7 to 10 days. Install a rain gauge so you can measure how much rainfall your garden receives. If it is insufficient, make up the deficit with a single, slow soaking.
- Use soaker hoses or install an underground drip-irrigation system. Unlike sprinkling, these watering methods keep foliage dry and eliminate splashing, reducing the likelihood of fungal infections.
- If you do use a sprinkler, water early in the day so that the sun can quickly evaporate the moisture on the leaves. If your system is automated, be sure it does not automatically water when it's raining.
- After watering, use a trowel or a soil auger to check that the water has penetrated to a depth of 8 to 12 inches. If it hasn't, apply the water at a slower rate.
- Between waterings, dig down 6 to 8 inches with a spade or trowel to check the soil moisture. Don't water again until the top 1½ to 2 inches of soil begin to dry out.
- If the soil in one area is much slower to dry out, test the drainage (page 202) and, if necessary, take steps to improve it.

Overall soil fertility can also be enhanced with fertilizer. You can choose an inorganic, chemical-based fertilizer or one made from natural materials, such as dehydrated manure, cottonseed meal, dried blood, bone meal, or rock phosphate. Chemical fertilizers are often less expensive to use and may act more quickly, but they will burn a plant's roots if applied too heavily. An organic fertilizer, on the other hand, may take a little longer to work but has less chance of burning plant roots. Also, it won't harm the soil microbes that help control plant diseases.

If the soil has been well prepared, an application of fertilizer before the growing season begins will probably be sufficient for the year. Be moderate, though, especially when applying nitrogen; too much of this element can promote rapid leaf and stem growth, which is often soft and susceptible to pathogens.

Plants grown in a soil that lacks one or more nutrients will eventually show symptoms of deficiency—usually stunted growth and yellowing leaves. On pages 330-331 of the Encyclopedia of Beneficials, Pests, and Diseases at the back of this book are descriptions of four of the most frequently encountered deficiencies—iron, magnesium, nitrogen, and potassium. If you suspect a nutrient imbalance, have your soil tested. Your local Cooperative Extension Service can recommend a kit you can use to administer the test yourself or, if you prefer, a laboratory where you can send a soil sample for analysis. Ask the laboratory to recommend the appropriate organic fertilizer and the rate at which it should be applied if there is a nutrient imbalance.

The Plant's Restorative: Manure Tea

Another environmentally safe way to give plants a mild dose of nutrients is by spraying them with manure tea. This homemade brew is easy to concoct: Just wrap 1 gallon of manure-based compost or well-rotted manure in burlap or some other coarse cloth and secure it at the top. Place the bag in a 5-gallon bucket and fill it with water. Leave the mixture in a warm place for at least 3 days, but preferably for a week. Then fill a spray applicator with the liquid and spray the plants well. Repeat every 3 to 4 days. You can also use manure tea for watering plants and to provide some protection against fungal diseases. For example, soaking seeds overnight in manure tea has been found to reduce the incidence of damping-off (box, right).

Finding the Correct Soil pH

Most plants absorb nutrients and grow best in slightly acid soil, with a pH of around 6.5. There are a few exceptions to this rule—azaleas, for instance, prefer a more acidic soil—so you'll need to find out whether any of your plants have different pH requirements. Some soil-borne pathogens such as *Pythium*, a fungus that causes damping-off and root rot, are very sensitive to minor fluctuations in pH levels. These pathogens can be controlled simply by lowering the pH level with additions of lime or raising it with sulfur. If your plants have been infected by a soil-borne pathogen before, ask your Cooperative Extension Service agent if it would make sense to adjust the pH.

Rotating Annuals and Vegetables

Despite your best efforts at controlling soil-borne pathogens, they will thrive as long as a preferred food supply is present. In a fairly short time, they can multiply from negligible numbers to a population capable of launching a devastating attack. For instance, vinca is highly susceptible to root rot, which is caused by a fungus found in small numbers in most soils. If allowed to feed on vinca for several years in a row, however, the fungus will become rampant. To eliminate a pathogen that is partial to only one or a few species, try rotating your plants. This solution isn't practical for perennials and other plants in permanent locations, but it is easily accomplished with annuals and vegetables. Instead of planting them in the same spot year after year, skip at least 2 years before repeating an annual or vegetable in a site.

The Importance of Soil Drainage

Many fungi flourish in waterlogged soil, so it's wise to test how well your soil drains, especially if it is largely composed of clay. Dig a hole 10 inches deep and 12 inches in diameter and pour in 1 gallon of water. If any water remains in the hole after 10 minutes, the drainage needs to be improved. You may be able to correct the problem merely by digging in generous amounts of organic matter and coarse sand. Other solutions to try when simpler ones are inadequate include building a raised bed or installing drainage pipes.

Watering to Promote Garden Health

How and when one waters also plays an important role in whether disease takes hold in your garden. The powerful stream of a hose, for instance, can splash pathogens that are on or near the soil's surface onto leaves and stems. When humidity is high, overhead watering with a sprinkler can leave foliage wet for long periods, providing a favorable environment for fungi to germinate. The best method for discouraging disease is ground-level watering, whether through soaker hoses or through an underground system. For more tips on acquiring good watering habits, see the box on page 200.

Since pathogens spread most easily in moist environments, it is important to avoid working in the garden soon after a rainfall or a watering. You could inadvertently pick up the pathogens on your hands, shoes, clothing, or tools and transport them to other parts of the garden.

The Benefits of Mulching

Another way to keep soil-borne pathogens away from plant stems and leaves is to lay down a protective barrier of mulch. A 2- to 4-inch layer of compost, shredded bark, or other organic material not only blocks disease-causing pathogens, it also introduces into the soil various kinds of microorganisms that promote a healthy garden. Composted pine bark, for example, is particularly rich in beneficial nematodes and bacteria that prey on parasitic nematodes and other pathogens. Other microorganisms keep down the pathogen population by outcompeting them for food and habitat.

Mulch also helps keep plants in good health by conserving moisture and adding nutrients as it decays. And a circle of mulch at least 4 feet in diameter around the trunk of a tree will prevent the lawn mower from inflicting nicks and cuts that would expose the inner layers of living tissue to disease organisms. (When spreading the mulch, remember to keep it a few inches away from the trunk—it should surround the trunk but not touch it.) The tree will be even better protected if all of its roots that protrude above the soil are mulched.

Biological and Chemical Preventives

The microorganisms in decaying mulch are an example of biological disease control, which lets living organisms destroy harmful ones either by eating them or by appropriating their food and territory.

Besides the biological controls that are naturally present in a garden, there are also a handful of commercial fungicides and bactericides. If you have had trouble with a disease in the past, check with your local nursery to see if a biological fungicide or bactericide has been developed for home gardens. Apply the control to all susceptible plants to prevent a recurrence, following the instructions on the label.

Controlling Diseases

Once you've diagnosed a plant disease, there are often several ways to get rid of it or prevent a recurrence. Some of these methods, such as pruning, involve virtually no risk to your plants or to the environment. Earth-friendly sprays and dusts of low or no toxicity *(page 206)* offer another avenue of attack. For truly stubborn or serious diseases, you may decide to use one of the more toxic chemical controls *(pages 206-207)*.

But before you do anything, keep in mind that many diseases are merely cosmetic problems and will run their natural course without doing serious damage to the infected plant. If you feel you must take action in such instances, limit yourself to cultural or physical controls; these diseases don't warrant the use of toxic chemicals.

Destroying Pathogens with Sunlight

Solarization is a reliable, environmentally safe way to rid a garden plot of soil-borne diseases as well as weeds. Clear plastic is spread on the ground to trap the sun's heat, which raises the temperature of the top 3 to 5 inches of soil to 120°F or above, roasting microorganisms and weed seeds buried in it. The technique must be carried out in the

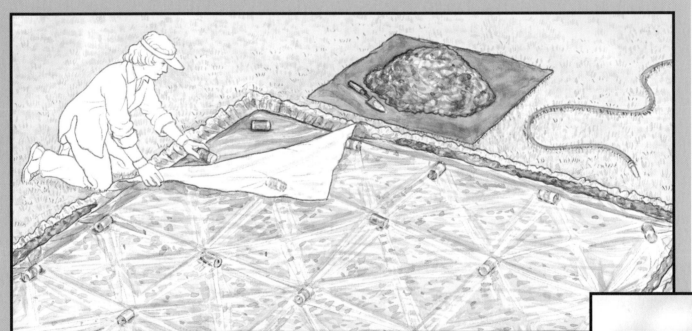
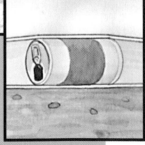

Solarizing Soil Pathogens

1. Clear a sunny plot of existing vegetation, rocks, and other debris, and dig in any soil amendments needed. Rake the soil smooth and dig a trench a few inches deep around the plot. Water the soil to a depth of at least 12 inches. Next, using clear plastic measuring 3 to 4 mils thick, cut two sheets large enough to cover the plot.

2. Spread one sheet smoothly on the soil. Lay empty soda cans about 2 feet apart on the sheet, then spread the second sheet over the cans (above and inset). Tuck the edges of the plastic sheets into the trench and pile soil on them to make a seal; this will trap heat and moisture in the air space between the sheets. After a rain, sweep off any water.

3. To check soil temperature, fold back a corner of the plastic and insert a soil thermometer; reseal the sheets afterward. Leave the sheets in place for several days after the temperature remains at 120°F or above; it may take 4 to 8 weeks for the bed to heat to this point.

Pruning Diseased Wood

Stems showing signs of disease should be pruned back promptly to healthy tissue to prevent further infection. (However, if the weather is rainy, wait for a dry day, since pathogens are easily transmitted by water.) To remove a stem completely, make the cut at its base, flush with the parent stem so there won't be a stub. If you are shortening a stem rather than removing it, prune back to a healthy bud. Cut the stem at a 45° angle in the same direction that the bud points, so that water will drain away from the bud.

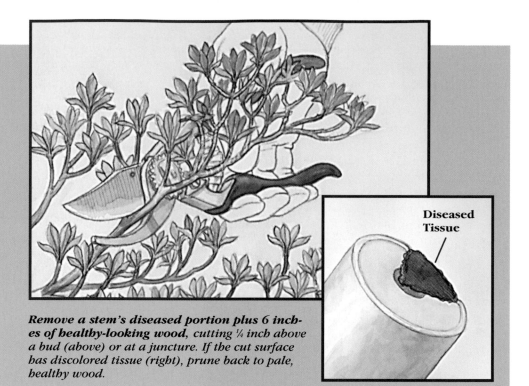

Remove a stem's diseased portion plus 6 inches of healthy-looking wood, cutting ¼ inch above a bud (above) or at a juncture. If the cut surface has discolored tissue (right), prune back to pale, healthy wood.

Pruning Large Branches

The bulge at the base of a tree branch, called the branch collar, is a protective zone that helps heal the wound created when the branch is removed, whether naturally or by pruning. This specialized tissue produces a callus that seals the wound's surface, preventing wood-decay fungi from infecting the trunk.

When you prune, be very careful to leave the branch collar intact so that healing will take place. For the same reason, never cut into a callus, even to remove a rotted or diseased section of a trunk. The tree itself will seal off the dead tissue.

*A **single pruning cut** made flush with the trunk (A) removes the branch's collar and tears bark, exposing wood to infection. Cutting too far from the trunk leaves a disease-prone stub (B). For good healing (C), use a series of three cuts (D). First, saw halfway through the branch from the underside, 8 to 12 inches from the collar (1). Then saw through the branch from above, a few inches beyond the first cut (2). Saw off the resulting stub just forward of the collar, following its natural angle (3).*

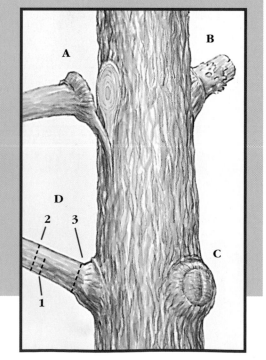

hottest, sunniest season and is suitable only for plots that are in direct sun for most of the day. Also, the soil must be bare—that is, unplanted.

How long the process takes depends on weather and climate. Solarization is complete in about 4 weeks when daytime temperatures average 90°F; it can take up to 8 weeks if temperatures average in the 70s. Fungi, nematodes, and weed seeds are killed when the soil temperature exceeds 120°F. At 160°F and above, some viruses and bacteria will also be destroyed. Unfortunately, solarization kills beneficial microbes as well, so be sure to dig a material rich in microbes, such as aged manure or compost, into the plot later to repopulate it. Earthworms survive the process by tunneling deeper into the soil.

After solarization, take care to cultivate the soil very shallowly; if you dig too deep, you may reinfest the plot with pathogens and seeds that survived in the cooler soil below.

Pruning

Some tree diseases, such as fire blight and twig canker, can be controlled by pruning out infected branches. You can also use pruning as a method of prevention. Thinning a plant—that is, removing some stems or branches from its center—discourages diseases that thrive in stagnant conditions, by improving air circulation and reducing humidity.

When pruning, take care not to inadvertently increase a shrub's or tree's vulnerability to disease with badly executed cuts *(opposite, below)*. Use a high-quality tool that is large enough to cleanly cut the wood you're working on. To keep from spreading disease as you work, some horticulturists recommend carrying along a pail containing a solution of 1 part household bleach to 9 parts water so that you can disinfect your clippers after each cut. Leave the clippers in the solution for 15 seconds. When you are finished pruning, sterilize them again, rinse in clean water, and dry, then coat the metal parts with a light oil to prevent rusting.

When to Prune a Tree

The timing of tree pruning is very important. Done in the wrong season, it can actually increase problems. Trees respond to pruning either by releasing sap or by quickly producing a burst of new growth, both of which attract pests and diseases. Most trees do best when pruned during their dormant stage, so you should postpone the job until then, if possible. Pruning diseased wood is an exception to this rule: It should be removed as soon as you notice it, unless the weather is wet, since pathogens spread easily in water.

Horticulturists now advise against using tree paint on pruning cuts. Not only does it have no known benefit, it may actually promote some wood rots by preventing the wound from drying, which is a natural protection against infection.

Removing Diseased Plants

For some diseases, there is no known cure. In these cases, the plant should be pulled up and disposed of as soon as possible. If the plant has a soil-borne disease such as nematodes or crown rot, dig it out, roots and all, being careful not to knock any soil off the rootball. Put everything in a plastic garbage bag and seal tightly. Replace the diseased plant with a resistant variety. Once the pathogens have lost their hosts, they will eventually die out.

Handling diseased plant material properly is crucial in preventing the further spread of pathogens. When you garden, keep a plastic bag with you for collecting clippings and other material. Fungus spores can spread in the garden as quickly as dandelion seeds in the breeze. Dispose of the bagged plant material with your household trash, or bury it in an out-of-the-way place. You can also compost it, but only if you are certain that your pile will heat up to a minimum of 140°F.

Although spot anthracnose can spoil the looks of a flowering dogwood's blossoms, as shown above, the tree suffers no serious or long-lasting effects. However, another fungal disease with similar symptoms, Discula anthracnose, is fatal to this species of dogwood.

A Safe, Simple Spray

Baking soda is a natural fungicide that is nontoxic to the environment. When sprayed on plants, it prevents fungal spores from penetrating plant tissue. In addition, it can halt the spread of an established infection. The box below gives directions for making and using baking soda spray.

Horticultural Oils

Spraying infected trees and shrubs with horticultural oils prevents the fungi responsible for rusts and mildews from germinating. These oils are even more widely used to control pests such as mites, plant bugs, and psyllids *(page 181)*. The sprays aren't toxic to mammals.

Horticultural oils are applied in two different concentrations depending on the season. The stronger of the two is applied in winter, while plants are dormant. For warmer weather, when plants are in active growth, a diluted solution is used to avoid damaging foliage *(pages 182-183)*.

Chemical Controls

When milder measures prove to be useless, the gardener must weigh the risks posed by a more potent method of control. If the disease's only effect on the plant is a less-than-perfect appearance, you may feel that a fungicide, which can kill beneficial microorganisms along with plant pathogens, is not warranted. Moreover, many fungicides harm wildlife, especially fish. Fortunately, the question of whether or not to spray rarely, if ever, arises with most ornamentals. For a handful, however, such as

hybrid tea roses, chemicals are essential for the plant to grow and bloom well. In such cases, you'll have to decide whether the plant is worth the risks, the expense, and the effort of spraying.

If disease symptoms are far advanced, it's probably too late for a spray to be effective, at least during the current season. If so, wait until the following year, then spray shortly before the season and the conditions—muggy, hot weather, for instance—are ripe for a renewed outbreak. In short, think in terms of prevention, and plan ahead.

Fungicides

Since fungi cause about 80 percent of the diseases that affect ornamental plants, most of the chemicals available for treating plant diseases are fungicides. Fungicides work in two ways. Most of them are surface protectants, which means they keep spores from germinating on or penetrating a plant. These fungicides prevent disease, but they cannot cure it. Apply these sprays when conditions favor infection. For example, in the case of garden phlox, which is susceptible to powdery mildew, spray shortly before the days turn warm and sunny but when nights are still cool.

The second group of fungicides are the systemics, which prevent disease and also cure it. A systemic penetrates a plant's tissue, where it interferes with the growth of the pathogen. Unlike most surface protectants, which prevent a wide range of diseases, systemics generally have a narrow spectrum, making accurate diagnosis especially important. Systemics are much less likely than surface protectants to injure plant tissues, and they seldom leave a visible residue.

The chart at right lists the most common fungicides available to home gardeners in ascending order of toxicity, with the safest one appearing first. Pick the least toxic product available for your disease problem. All of these fungicides are considered organic because they are active for only one day, unlike some other fungicides that persist in the environment.

Taking Precautions

Before you buy a fungicide, and again when you are preparing to use it, read the label carefully to make sure it is an appropriate chemical for the plant and the disease you are treating. Follow all instructions to the letter, and handle the fungicide with as much care as you would a pesticide or herbicide *(pages 150-151 and 180-185)*.

Baking Soda Spray

1 tablespoon baking soda
1 gallon water
⅛ to ¼ teaspoon insecticidal soap

Dissolve the baking soda in the water, then add the soap, which helps the solution spread and stick to the foliage. Fill a spray can or bottle with the solution and spray all of the leaves on both sides. Repeat every 5 to 7 days until the symptoms disappear.

To prevent another outbreak the following year, begin spraying in spring and continue until the fall. This spray is effective against powdery mildews, leaf blights, and leaf spots.

RECOMMENDED FUNGICIDES

Type	Diseases Controlled	Precautions and Hazards
Fungicidal soap. Surface protectant.	Black spot, brown canker, leaf spot, powdery mildews, and rust.	Before treating a plant, test a few leaves for browning or other symptoms of sensitivity.
Copper hydroxide, copper tanate. Surface protectants.	Many fungal and some bacterial leaf spots, botrytis, downy mildews, and powdery mildews.	Spray early on a dry, sunny day. Copper hydroxide is less expensive than copper tanate but may burn foliage in damp weather and leaves a visible residue. Both are eye irritants and toxic to wildlife.
Copper sulfate and hydrated lime (Bordeaux mixture). Surface protectant.	Many fungal and some bacterial diseases, including anthracnose, bacterial leaf spots, black rot, blights, fruit scab, septoria leaf spot, and wilts.	Spray on a windless evening, when no bees are active. Do not use in damp or humid weather if the temperature is below 50°F. Never use with other pesticides or fungicides.
Sulfur. Surface protectant.	Black spot, brown rot, powdery mildews, rusts, scabs, and other fungi. Also controls mites.	To avoid damaging foliage, do not apply when the temperature exceeds 85°F. Do not apply to open flowers, because bees will be harmed. Wait a month to use after applying horticultural oil.
Lime sulfur. Surface protectant.	Anthracnose, powdery mildews, rusts, and scabs.	Use only in cold weather on dormant plants. Lime sulfur is more caustic and thus more likely to damage plants than plain sulfur. Toxic to fish.
Horticultural oils. Surface protectant.	Powdery mildews, puccinia rust, and septoria leaf spot.	Do not use when temperatures exceed 90°F or when plants are water stressed. Do not use if a fungicide containing sulfur has been applied within the last month.
Captan. Surface protectant.	Damping-off fungi (used on seed).	Leaves visible residue. Causes spotting, yellowing, or defoliation if used in cool, moist weather on young leaves of roses and stone fruits. Eye irritant; wear goggles. Toxic to soil microorganisms.
Chlorothalonil. Surface protectant.	Blights, botrytis, leaf spots, and powdery mildews.	Eye irritant; wear goggles. Slightly toxic to wildlife and soil microorganisms.
Mancozeb. Surface protectant.	Blights, botrytis, downy mildews, and leaf spots.	Use sparingly on foliage only. Store in a cool, dry location in an airtight container; heat and moisture may decompose it. Toxic to soil microorganisms.
Propiconazole. Systemic.	Many diseases of ornamentals and turf grasses, including Discula anthracnose of dogwood, blights, leaf spots, powdery mildews, and rusts.	Severe eye irritant; always wear goggles and rubber gloves. Toxic to soil organisms.
Thiophanate-methyl. Systemic.	Many blights, black spot, Discula anthracnose of dogwood, and leaf and fruit spots.	Irritant to eyes, nose, and throat; always wear respirator, goggles, rubber gloves, and rubber boots.
Triadimefon. Systemic.	Powdery mildews, rusts, and a variety of leaf spots and blights.	Avoid contact with powder when mixing. Toxic to soil organisms.
Triforine. Systemic.	Powdery mildews and a variety of leaf spots and blights, including brown rot of stone fruit.	Resistance to this fungicide has appeared in some strains of fungi that cause black spot on roses. Toxic to soil organisms.

Garden Plans for Difficult Areas

A beautiful yard is every gardener's dream. But unless you have a garden plan, that dream could dissolve into chaos. A plan is particularly important if the site presents special challenges—a steep slope subject to erosion, for example, or a curbside plot along a busy street.

The five simple plans shown on the following pages were created by either professional landscape architects or homeowners. Each design is presented in a watercolor rendering of the garden, a schematic drawing to identify the plants, and an overhead planting plan.

The plans illustrate a variety of imaginative solutions for difficult areas, from a windy site by a lake to a dry, sunny spot such as the one at right. Use the plans to re-create these gardens in toto or in part, adapting them to your particular climate and conditions, or use them as a starting place for your own creative designs.

A. *Achillea x 'Moonshine' (yarrow)* (1)
B. *Dianthus armeria (pink)* (3)
C. *Stokesia laevis 'Blue Danube' (Stokes' aster)* (1) **D.** *Stachys officinalis (betony)* (1) **E.** *Geranium sanguineum var. striatum (bloody cranesbill)* (1)
F. *Rosa 'Gruss an Aachen'* (1) **G.** *Alstroemeria Ligtu Hybrids (Peruvian lily)* (1) **H.** *Phlomis lanata (Jerusalem sage)* (1) **I.** *Anemone coronaria* (6)
J. *Chrysanthemum parthenium (feverfew)* (1) **K.** *Centaurea dealbata (knapweed)* (1) **L.** *Lavandula dentata (lavender)* (2) **M.** *Dietes vegeta (African iris)* (1) **N.** *Daucus carota (Queen Anne's lace)* (2) **O.** *Verbena bonariensis (Brazilian verbena)* (4)
P. *Rosa 'Iceberg'* (1) **Q.** *Salvia greggii (autumn sage)* (1)

Perennial Border for a Dry, Sunny Site

A neat white fence sets off a profusion of pastels in this sunny front border, created jointly by the owner and her landscape architect in La Jolla, California. Designed to capture the chaotic charm of an English cottage garden, the border blends soft colors and evokes a cool mood in this hot region located near the ocean.

Although the temperature here is tropical, it is not accompanied by tropical moisture levels. In fact, since rainfall normally occurs only in brief periods in the fall and spring, salt tends to build up in the adobe clay soil. To improve this unpromising soil, the owner amends it with compost and mulches the garden frequently with fir bark and rotted horse manure.

Adaptable, drought-tolerant flowers such as *Salvia greggii* fill the border. The plants grow rapidly and to a good size, and the garden is almost constantly in flower. Alstroemeria blooms not only in spring but again in fall, while *Verbena bonariensis, Achillea* x 'Moonshine', and roses show their colors nearly year round. The mounded shapes of the plants, occasionally punctuated by tall, flower-topped stems of verbena, echo the undulating horizontal line of the fence.

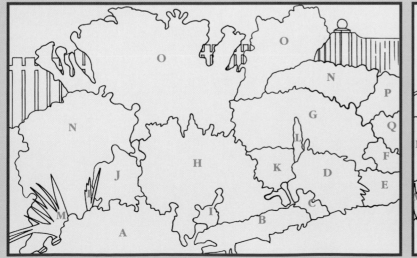

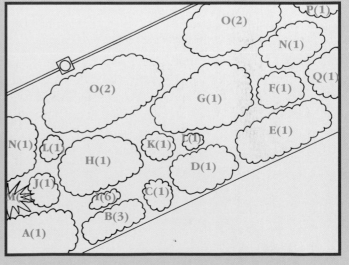

Terraced Hillside Garden

This garden plan was chosen to solve a number of problems on a property in a Maryland suburb of Washington, D.C. First, the land sloped and was subject to erosion. In addition, the site lay partly in shade, and the roots of two large Norway spruce trees obtruded on the area. The most obvious solution would have been a simple ground cover. Instead, the owners built a series of terraces and raised beds—eight in all. These not only put a stop to the erosion while improving drainage, but they also allowed the owners to experiment with different light and moisture conditions. No longer constrained by the site, they could indulge their desire to combine different kinds of plants.

The garden blends subtle foliage colors and textures, such as the fuzziness of gray lamb's ears *(Stachys byzantina)* and the silver of dusty-miller *(Senecio cineraria)* with the lacy greenery of Christmas fern *(Polystichum acrostichoides)* and the broad, flat foliage of hosta. By interspersing these plants with brightly flowering perennials such as geranium, begonia, and iris, the design invites the eye to linger. A brick walkway rising with the terraces creates leisurely opportunities for visitors to pause and enjoy the view.

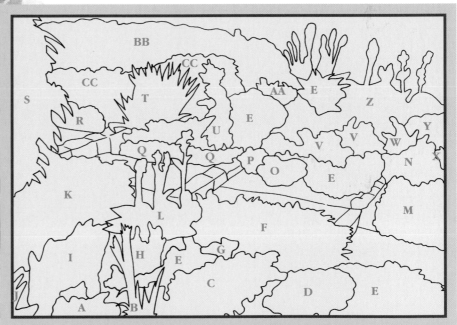

A. *Viola 'Royal Robe'* (6) **B.** *Mentha x 'Grapefruit Mint'* (1) **C.** *Senecio cineraria* (6) **D.** *Asteromoea mongolica* (5) **E.** *Catharanthus roseus* (many) **F.** *Stachys byzantina* (8) **G.** *Asarum canadense* (5) **H.** *Dianthus* (10) **I.** *Nepeta faassenii* (3) **J.** *Polystichum acrostichoides* (11) **K.** *Geranium* (7) **L.** *Hosta decorata* (1) **M.** *Begonia grandis* (10) **N.** *Allium senescens* (12) **O.** *Artemisia schmidtiana 'Silver Mound'* (3) **P.** *Spiraea japonica* (5) **Q.** *Sedum spurium 'Dragon's Blood'* (6) **R.** *Aquilegia flabellata 'Pumila'* (3) **S.** *Vernonia noveboracensis* (5) **T.** *Iris x germanica* (4) **U.** *Lilium auratum* (3) **V.** *Spiraea japonica 'Little Princess'* (6) **W.** *Artemisia ludoviciana 'Silver King'* (3) **X.** *Calamintha grandiflora 'Bert's Beauty'* (3) **Y.** *Aquilegia canadensis* (8) **Z.** *Hosta elegans* (7) **AA.** *Impatiens x New Guinea* (9) **BB.** *Polygonatum odoratum thunbergii 'Variegatum'* (4) **CC.** *Hypericum* (12)

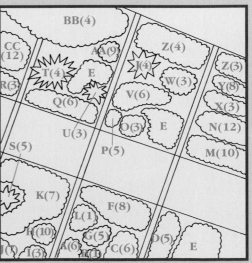

Lakeside Grass Garden

Designed by a landscape architect for the owner of an inland lakeshore site near Milwaukee, Wisconsin, this island bed of ornamental grasses sways delicately with every passing breeze, adding motion to the more usual garden attractions of plant color and form. The clump-forming, noninvasive grasses, chosen primarily for their color, textural appeal, and adaptability, are virtually maintenance free, needing only to be cut back to about 2 inches high in early spring.

Throughout the year the grasses present an ever-changing but consistently beautiful display, which is particularly valuable in a region where winter is 6 months long. The 'Haense Herms' switch grass, for example, produces showy red seeds in autumn, then turns a soft, tawny beige for the winter. The fountain grass keeps much of its mass year round, turning a lovely bright almond color in the coldest months.

The height and growing habit of each plant also played a role in the garden's design. Graceful maiden grass, the tallest of the grasses chosen, was placed in the center of the bed. Surrounding it are feather reed grass, standing bold and upright; dwarf fountain grass, which is pendulous and arching; and switch grass, whose form is delicate, light, and airy.

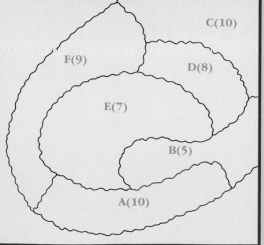

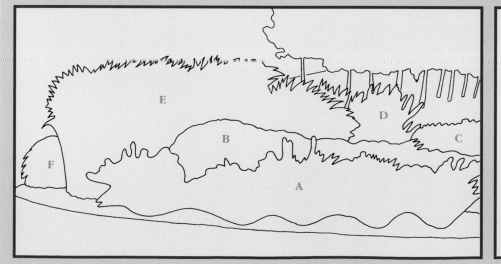

A. *Pennisetum alopecuroides 'Hameln' (dwarf fountain grass) (10)*
B. *Panicum virgatum 'Strictum' (switch grass) (5)*
C. *Schizachyrium scoparium (bluestem) (10)*
D. *Calamagrostis acutiflora 'Stricta' (feather reed grass) (8)*
E. *Miscanthus sinensis 'Gracillimus' (maiden grass) (7)*
F. *Panicum virgatum 'Haense Herms' (red switch grass) (9)*

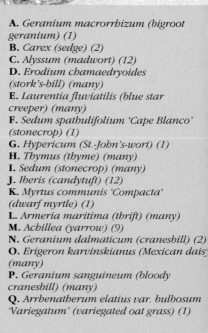

A. *Geranium macrorrhizum (bigroot geranium) (1)*
B. *Carex (sedge) (2)*
C. *Alyssum (madwort) (12)*
D. *Erodium chamaedryoides (stork's-bill) (many)*
E. *Laurentia fluviatilis (blue star creeper) (many)*
F. *Sedum spathulifolium 'Cape Blanco' (stonecrop) (1)*
G. *Hypericum (St.-John's-wort) (1)*
H. *Thymus (thyme) (many)*
I. *Sedum (stonecrop) (many)*
J. *Iberis (candytuft) (12)*
K. *Myrtus communis 'Compacta' (dwarf myrtle) (1)*
L. *Armeria maritima (thrift) (many)*
M. *Achillea (yarrow) (9)*
N. *Geranium dalmaticum (cranesbill) (2)*
O. *Erigeron karvinskianus (Mexican dais) (many)*
P. *Geranium sanguineum (bloody cranesbill) (many)*
Q. *Arrhenatherum elatius var. bulbosum 'Variegatum' (variegated oat grass) (1)*

Rock Garden

By tucking sturdy, low-growing plants like sedum, armeria, and hypericum into small pockets in steps made of chunks of broken sidewalk, the creator of this unusual plan has built a rock garden that leads up to a home in Pasadena, California. The plants, which can withstand light foot traffic, have been allowed to spread, producing a delightful wandering effect.

The designer selected plants with a variety of foliage textures and flower colors. Purple *Geranium sanguineum* cascades over the top step, leading down to the rose-colored *Armeria maritima*, with its narrow, grasslike leaves. Yellow-flowering sedum backs a mass of white iberis flowing over the bottom step, where a topiary of dwarf Greek myrtle adds vertical interest on the right. Although the garden's peak blooming season runs from March through May, the plants have been chosen so that something is in bloom every day of the year. And many of the plants—including the armeria, the sedum, and the Mexican daisy—have evergreen foliage, providing consistent color.

The site needs little maintenance beyond removing dead flowers, cutting back when plants spread too much, and watering regularly. The plants grow in a mixture of peat moss and sand, with a top dressing of finely textured "bird shot" gravel to promote good drainage.

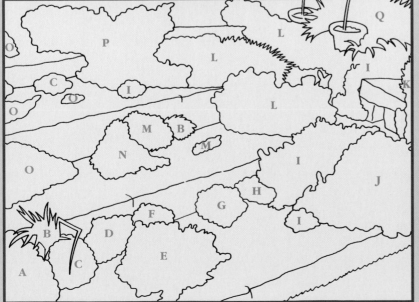

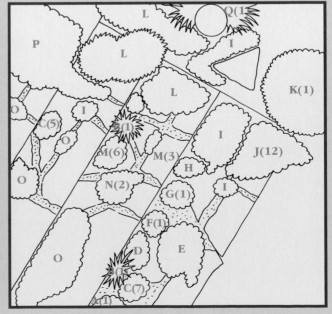

A. *Trachelospermum asiaticum* (Asiatic jasmine) (4) B. *Lantana 'New Gold'* (shrub verbena) (9) C. *Lantana montevidensis* (shrub verbena) (6) D. *Rosemarinus officinalis* (rosemary) (2) E. *Dasylirion wheeleri* (Wheeler's sotol) (2) F. *Salvia greggii* (autumn sage) (2) G. *Hesperaloe parviflora* (red yucca) (1) H. *Raphiolepis indica 'Clara'* (dwarf indian hawthorn) (3) I. *Leucophyllum frutescens 'Compactum'* (compact Texas sage) (2) J. *Yucca recurvifolia* (yucca) (3) K. *Muhlenbergia capillaris* (muhly grass) (1) L. *Sophora secundiflora* (mescal bean) (2) M. *Plumbago auriculata* (Cape leadwort) (1)

216

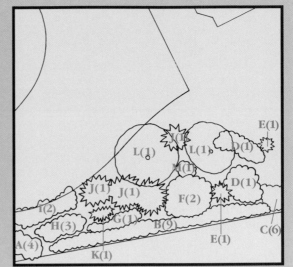

Curbside Planting

Mixing sedate plantings with something a bit on the wild side was the objective of the landscape architect who created this curbside garden in San Antonio, Texas. The designer achieved the effect by combining, for example, the manicured look of Asiatic jasmine ground cover with billowy, untrimmed golden and purple trailing lantanas and pink and purple salvias.

To ensure a continuous flow of color through the seasons, the designer included native Texas plants like muhly grass, which changes from a beige-brown in summer to a heathery pink in the fall. For variety in texture and growth habit, he included such bold plants as the cactuslike *Yucca recurvifolia,* with its towering plumes of white blossoms, and the spiky Wheeler's sotol, which he contrasted with soft, silvery Texas sage and fine-textured rosemary.

Meant primarily to add beauty to this highly visible house on a corner lot, the tall, dense plantings in this garden also serve to totally conceal a front driveway, which can be seen in the overhead planting diagram above.

Problems/Solutions

One side of our patio is quite open to view from several neighbors' yards, and we'd like more privacy. The patio is screened off with shrubs on the other open sides, but I was wondering if there are any annuals that could function as screening?

Annual vines such as *Humulus japonicus* (Japanese hopvine) and *Lagenaria siceraria* (calabash gourd) can be grown on 2-by-3-inch wood poles set in the ground and strung with durable twine or plastic fishline for plant supports. These plants, which can be grown in pots that are set on the edge of the patio, have dense enough foliage to block the view from outside.

One of my great joys is attracting wildlife to my garden. What are the most alluring annuals for butterflies and humming-birds? Do any annuals produce seed that birds can feed on over the winter?

Of the long list of annuals on the butterfly hit parade, the best are *Cosmos bipinnatus* (garden cosmos), *Gaillardia pulchella* (Indian blanket), *Helianthus* (sunflower), *Heliotropium arborescens* (cherry pie), *Hesperis matronalis* (dame's rocket), *Limonium sinuatum* (notchleaf statice), *Rudbeckia hirta* (black-eyed Susan), *Tithonia rotundifolia* (Mexican sunflower), *Verbena* (vervain), and *Zinnia elegans* (common zinnia). Hummingbirds will flock to *Alcea rosea* (hollyhock), *Antirrhinum majus* (common snapdragon), *Dianthus barbatus* (sweet William), *Digitalis purpurea* (common foxglove), *Ipomopsis aggregata* (scarlet gilia), and *Salvia* (sage). For seed heads that will feed a variety of birds during the cold months, plant *Amaranthus* (amaranth), *Coreopsis* (tickseed), *Cosmos, Gomphrena, Helianthus annuus* (common sunflower), *Rudbeckia hirta,* and *Verbena bonariensis* (Brazilian verbena).

We own a seaside cabin where we spend our summers, and I'd like to put several beds of annuals around it. What plants will do best in the conditions found at the beach?

Even in this trying environment of wind and salt-laden air, a fairly large variety of annuals will succeed. You can choose with confidence from among *Ageratum houstonianum* (flossflower), *Antirrhinum majus* (common snapdragon), *Calendula officinalis* (pot marigold), *Dimorphotheca* (Cape marigold), *Lavatera trimestris* (tree mallow), *Lobelia erinus* (edging lobelia), *Lobularia maritima* (sweet alyssum), *Pelargonium* (geranium), *Phlox drummondii* (annual phlox), *Portulaca grandiflora* (moss rose), *Salvia argentea* (silver sage), *Senecio cineraria* (dusty-miller), *Tagetes patula* (French marigold), and *Verbena* (vervain).

Because we can almost never find time to tend our garden except for a bit on weekends, we're looking for flowers that can get along pretty well on their own. Are there any annuals that will bloom nicely from spring to frost without assistance?

Once you've gotten them off to a good start in well-prepared soil, you can expect self-sufficient performance from *Begonia* x *semperflorens-cultorum* (wax begonia), *Catharanthus roseus* (Madagascar periwinkle), *Heliotropium arborescens* (cherry pie), *Pentas lanceolata* (Egyptian star-cluster), *Petunia* x *hybrida* (common garden petunia), and *Salvia splendens* (scarlet sage).

There's a patch of ground out near my property line facing the road where the soil is rather infertile, dry, and sandy. I'd like to dress up the area a bit, but without putting in a lot of effort. Are there any annuals that would work in such soil?

Happily, a wide variety of annuals will do well in these unpromising conditions. You can choose from *Arctotis* (African daisy), *Calendula officinalis* (pot marigold), *Callistephus chinensis* (China aster), *Clarkia amoena* (farewell-to-spring), *Coreopsis tinctoria* (tickseed), *Dyssodia tenuiloba* (Dahlberg daisy), *Euphorbia marginata* (snow-on-the-mountain), *Gaillardia pulchella* (Indian blanket), *Kochia scoparia* (burning bush, summer cypress), *Lobularia maritima* (sweet alyssum), *Phlox drummondii* (annual phlox), *Portulaca grandiflora* (moss rose), *Tithonia rotundifolia* (Mexican sunflower), and *Verbena* x *hybrida* (vervain).

I have a little rill running through a corner of my property that I can see from my kitchen window, and I would like to brighten up its banks with annuals. Can you recommend some that will adapt to damp sites?

The versatile clan of annuals includes species that will be right at home in very boggy conditions, including *Limnanthes douglasii* (meadow foam), *Mimulus* x *hybridus* (monkey flower), and *Myosotis sylvatica* (forget-me-not). In soil that is not boggy but is generally moist, you can grow *Caladium* x *hortulanum* (fancy-leaved caladium), *Catharanthus roseus* (Madagascar periwinkle), *Cleome hasslerana* (spider flower), *Coleus* x *hybridus* (coleus), *Exacum affine* (Persian violet), *Impatiens, Torenia fournieri* (bluewings), and *Viola* x *wittrockiana* (garden pansy).

My favorite kind of foundation planting is an annual border, but I know from soil testing that the foundation of my house leaches limestone into the soil, keeping it on the alkaline side. What annuals are best for alkaline soil?

Within reasonable limits—say, a pH of no more than 8—you can confidently expect the following annuals to adapt comfortably to the soil around your foundation: *Calendula officinalis* (pot marigold), *Catharanthus roseus* (Madagascar periwinkle), *Dianthus barbatus* (sweet William), *Gaillardia pulchella* (Indian blanket), *Gypsophila elegans* (baby's-breath), *Iberis umbellata* (globe candytuft), *Lathyrus odoratus* (sweet pea), *Papaver rhoeas* (corn poppy), *Pelargonium* (geranium), *Phlox drummondii* (annual phlox), *Scabiosa atropurpurea* (pincushion flower), *Senecio cineraria* (dusty-miller), *Tropaeolum majus* (garden nasturtium), *Verbena* x *hybrida* (vervain), and *Zinnia elegans* (common zinnia).

I buy annuals at the home and garden center, and they look great, but when I plant them, they soon poop out. Am I doing something wrong?

To entice buyers, home and garden centers and roadside stands often display lushly blooming annuals—particularly tender annuals—several weeks before the ground is warm enough to accommodate them. Many of these plants have been forced into early bloom and may also have had extra applications of chemical fertilizers. Plants that have been raised like this are liable to suffer severe transplant shock when set out in the garden, especially if it's done too early in the season. To avoid this kind of frustration, buy plants that are not yet in full bloom and safeguard them under cover or in a cold frame until it is safe to set them out.

I would like to grow bulbs in partial shade, but I understand they don't do well under some trees. Which kinds of trees should I avoid?

Maples, beeches, and other trees with shallow, fibrous roots are the ones to avoid. Bulbs and most other kinds of plants have a hard time competing with them for nutrients, water, and growing space. Also avoid evergreens and other trees with low canopies that prevent at least a half-day of filtered light from getting through.

I have more bulbs than I need for this fall. Can I hold some to plant next fall?

Unlike some seeds, bulbs cannot be held from one year to the next, because the moisture in their tissues will dry out and they will die.

We have had a mild winter so far, and my daffodils and tulips are coming up too early. Now we are expecting some hard freezes. How do I protect my bulbs?

The surprisingly tough foliage of these plants can take temperatures down to around 15°F. Below that point, the leaves may be "burned"—dried out by the cold—unless you cover or surround the plants with a light mulch. Even if the foliage is damaged, however, it doesn't seem to greatly affect later bloom and overall plant performance.

I think my newly planted bulbs must have frozen, because we had a very cold winter and they didn't come up this spring. When I dug them, they were soft and mushy. How can I keep this from happening again?

You can do several things: Plant your bulbs early, and at a depth at least 3 times their height; water well after planting to initiate root growth, because well-rooted bulbs resist frost damage better; mulch after planting to keep the soil temperature stable while the bulbs are rooting; and make sure the area is well drained, because soil that holds too much moisture is more likely to freeze and to encourage rot.

My double daffodils send up nice big fat buds that never open. What is the problem?

Your plants are experiencing "blasting." Double daffodils are especially susceptible to blasting, which happens when the plump buds are subjected to sudden freezing, high temperatures, or insufficient moisture. Protect buds from temperature extremes and water well. Some new cultivars have been developed that are blast resistant.

My bulb foliage gets too long and flops over, leaving an unsightly mess in my garden. How can I keep my plants from getting so tall?

Plants grow too tall and leggy when they do not have enough light. Most bulbs that do not get at least a half-day of sun not only flop over but also have sparse blooms. Transplant the bulbs to a sunnier location; fertilize and water well; and thin out overhanging vegetation to let in more light. For future plantings on this site, choose cultivars that are more shade tolerant.

How can I figure out where to put down fertilizer for my bulbs in fall when there is no remaining foliage to guide me?

Plant *Muscari* (grape hyacinth) bulbs around the edges of your other bulbs; the foliage will emerge in the fall and show you where to fertilize. Or place markers such as vinyl plant labels or even golf tees around the edge of your planting in the spring; they will stay around to show you the way. Finally, you could take photographs of your plot in the spring and use them as a guide.

I use bone meal to fertilize my bulbs, as the old gardening books advise. But the bulbs just aren't blooming well. What's going wrong?

Bone meal is not a complete fertilizer; it supplies only phosphorus and calcium. Bulbs also need nitrogen, potash, and trace elements. If you wish to fully fertilize your bulbs using only organic nutrient sources, you must add blood meal or cottonseed meal for nitrogen and "New Jersey Greensand" or wood ashes for potash and trace elements. Or you can use a ready-formulated fertilizer made just for bulbs. A 9-9-6 slow-release formula is best for tulips and members of the lily family but can be used for all bulbs. A 5-10-20 slow-release formula with trace elements is best for daffodils and members of the amaryllis family.

Many of my bulbs have stopped blooming, and others aren't blooming as well as they used to. Do I need to dig them up and divide them?

That is one solution, but perhaps an easier and more efficient way would be to fertilize the clumps to resupply the nutrients the bulbs have used up as they multiplied over the years. Once they have enough nutrients, along with moisture and sunshine, most of those old clumps will bloom gloriously.

Something is eating my tulip and crocus bulbs underground. Could it be moles, and how do I deal with this problem?

Moles are carnivorous and do not eat plants. The underground bulb monster is more than likely a vole, also known as a field mouse. One way to protect your bulbs is to plant them a bit deeper than normal; voles work in the top 3 to 4 inches of soil. Another is to put a handful of sharp-edged, crushed gravel—pieces about the size of a fingernail—around each bulb; voles do not like to dig through or move around in gravelly soil.

PERENNIALS

I have a perennial border with lots of bold colors like red, orange, and yellow. These colors are compatible, but my garden seems to lack continuity. What can I do?

Tie your bold colors together by introducing perennials with blue flowers. Leadwort *(Ceratostigma)*, globe thistle *(Echinops)*, flax *(Linum)*, Siberian iris *(Iris sibirica)*, Russian sage *(Perovskia)*, false indigo *(Baptisia)*, and blue cultivars of moss phlox *(Phlox subulata)* are a few of the best. You may also want to try plants with silver or gray foliage, such as lavender *(Lavandula angustifolia)*, lamb's ears *(Stachys byzantina)*, or *Artemisia* 'Silver Mound'. For best results, repeat your selections along the length of the border, and remember to mass blue-flowered plants as much as possible because blue is a receding color.

I have tried unsuccessfully over the years to grow delphiniums in my garden. Plants that I purchase from nurseries will flourish for the summer and then fail to return the following year. Are delphiniums really perennials?

Most gardeners plant various forms of the Pacific Coast hybrids. Members of this strain do exceptionally well in climates where cold winters and cool summers prevail. But they do not do well in areas where winter temperatures fluctuate above and below freezing and where summer temperatures are hot. If you live in a less-than-perfect delphinium climate, you might try *Delphinium bellamosa, D. belladonna,* or *D. chinense* and their cultivars, which are more forgiving.

I'm having trouble establishing Oriental poppies despite planting them the recommended 2 inches deep and in ideal growing conditions. Any suggestions?

Most Oriental poppies prefer the colder regions (Zones 5-7). Where winter temperatures fluctuate, poppies may break dormancy during warm periods, only to be struck down a few days later by a frost. Winter mulching can sometimes protect them, but don't mulch during the rest of the year, or you'll invite crown rot. Also, poppies hate wet feet during their late-summer dormant period, so don't water them in late spring when their foliage begins to brown.

A lot of perennials in my garden need staking in late summer. This requires a good bit of work on my part, and the result looks rather artificial. Is there any way to avoid this tedious task?

First of all, if you know that a favorite plant is going to need support, put a protective hoop around it or make a frame of stakes and string as the plant is coming up; the developing foliage will soon hide the supports. Second, perennials require less staking if you select cultivars that are naturally more compact; if you space your plants far enough apart so that sunlight and circulating air reach all the foliage; and if you feed them a low-nitrogen organic fertilizer. Pinching back your unruly plants also helps.

How do I prepare soil in the different sections of my garden to accommodate various perennials I want to plant? It seems that some species like more acid soil and some like more alkaline soil.

Of the thousands of perennials to select from, only a few have pH requirements that fall outside the average range for most garden soils. Maintain a pH between 6 and 7, and almost any perennial will do well. For those plants that require more alkalinity, dig dolomitic limestone into the soil at the planting location; it won't leach out into the surrounding soil. In the case of acid-loving plants, try adding peat moss to the planting site.

My perennial bed gets 6 hours of morning sun. Will my plants thrive with this amount of light?

Plant requirements for sun are determined by the intensity and duration of sunlight. For sun-loving perennials, 6 hours of sun is adequate only when it occurs at midday or in the afternoon. In other words, when picking plants for a garden with morning sun and afternoon shade, you should opt for shade plants. If, on the other hand, your garden is shaded all morning but gets afternoon sun, pick plants that require full sun.

I'd like to grow perennials under a large Norway maple tree. What are some good choices?

Norway maples have a network of surface roots that can rob plants of moisture. Plants that can tolerate these dry shade conditions include violets *(Viola)*, woodland strawberries *(Fragaria)*, dead nettle *(Lamium)*, *Hosta, Epimedium,* and leadwort *(Ceratostigma)*.

One of my perennials has yellow, stunted foliage. When I dug it up, it had nodules all over the roots. What is the problem?

More than likely your plant has root knot nematodes. You can control this pest by using a nontoxic material made from ground crab shells that is available at better garden centers.

I have a bed of irises that is overrun with iris borer. What should I do?

First, establish a new iris bed in another location. Then dig up and divide irises from your infested bed in mid to late summer, selecting only healthy, young rhizomes. Throw away all the old rhizomes and plant debris. Dip the transplants in a solution of 1 part chlorine bleach to 9 parts water, and let them dry in the shade before planting. Keep the new bed clear of decaying foliage to discourage the adult moths from laying their eggs in the vicinity.

My peonies have petals that are brown all over, and they don't open properly. What is wrong and how can I correct it?

One of three things could be happening. First, your flower buds could be suffering from excessive heat—more than 85°F—at bloom time (called bull-heading). Second, your peonies could have a fungal disease called botrytis blight. Third, the damage you describe could be caused by tiny sucking insects called thrips.

ROSES

We have a summer place right on the ocean in Massachusetts. Are there any roses that will grow in this setting?

Any of the rugosa species and most hybrid rugosas, such as 'Blanc Double de Coubert' or 'Belle Poitevine', will grow and bloom in your situation. Rugosas tolerate salt spray and will grow in sand dunes unattended. In fact, the Japanese native species has naturalized on beaches in the northeastern and northwestern United States.

My yard has a lot of shade. Are there any roses that will grow in it?

Roses need sun to perform well. The best ones to try under your conditions would be the modern hybrid musks, such as 'Ballerina', 'Belinda', 'Buff Beauty', or 'Prosperity'. If they don't grow and bloom there, no rose will.

I get black spot on my roses every year. I really don't want to use chemical fungicides, but I'm getting desperate. Is there any way I can keep the disease from ruining my plants without adding toxic chemicals to the garden?

Try this year-round preventive program that uses nonharmful products: Before the first frost, spray your roses with a commercial antidesiccant, according to label directions, to keep any fungus spores off the leaves during the winter. Then, while the plants are still dormant in the spring, spray them with wettable or liquid sulfur fungicide, followed by a thorough spray of dormant oil. Keep applying the sulfur periodically until frost—every week to 10 days at most. Don't spray sulfur, though, when the temperature is 85°F or higher, because it may burn the foliage, and keep it away from rugosa roses and their hybrids altogether; rugosas are damaged by sulfur—but they're immune to most fungi in the first place. This treatment will control not only black spot but also rust and powdery mildew, as well as infestations of aphids, thrips, and mites.

Are there any roses that deer do not eat?

Probably not. Try planting companions that deer dislike, such as rosemary or artemisia. Sometimes people put wire and fencing around their roses to keep deer from browsing, but this defeats the purpose of roses beautifying the garden. Instead, lay wire mesh on the ground near and in the rose bed, and plant ground covers such as ivy, phlox, or dianthus, making the mesh invisible. Deer will not step into these areas.

WILDFLOWERS

I have a traditional landscape that includes an evergreen foundation planting, a number of specimen shrubs, and a large lawn. Is there some way I can incorporate wildflowers into existing plantings, or will I need to tear them out and start from scratch?

You don't need to do anything drastic to incorporate wildflowers into your garden. Many of them are perfectly appropriate in a traditional garden that has a large proportion of nonnative plants. Your major concern will be to choose plants whose moisture, light, and soil requirements match the conditions of your site.

One of my gardening goals is to have color throughout the year. Is that possible with wildflowers?

With careful planning, year-round color is certainly possible. Just be sure to pick species with bloom periods that overlap each other; as one species completes its life cycle, another species will begin to bloom and will take its place. Also, be sure to plant a mix of perennials and annuals. The annuals will bloom for many weeks or even all season, providing continuous color and interest to fill any intervals between waves of perennial flowers. In fall and winter, foliage, fruits, and seed pods will offer a beauty unique to those seasons.

Four years ago I planted a small meadow of wildflowers and native grasses from a commercial seed mix. It's beautiful, but some of the plants that bloomed heavily the first season aren't as dominant anymore. Is it normal for a meadow to change like this from year to year?

Yes. A wildflower meadow is a complex, interactive plant community that evolves over time. Annuals are its main source of color until the slower-developing perennials mature. Also, the species that are best adapted to a particular site will eventually come to dominate. In time the balance of species will tend to stabilize, but there will always be differences from year to year because of weather conditions such as a mild winter or a wet summer.

My yard is rather small, and it's already so full of plants that I'm not sure I can fit in any wildflowers. Is it worth trying to grow some in pots or in window boxes?

Growing wildflowers in containers is a wonderful way to enjoy the benefits of native plants where space is at a premium, and they are just as appropriate as other annuals and perennials. They provide concentrated splashes of color and can be moved as light conditions change or retired to an unobtrusive spot when their blooming season ends. They are also a great way to introduce children to the pleasures of growing plants. Among the many attractive natives for container plantings are baby-blue-eyes, bitterroot, clarkia, common stonecrop and wild stonecrop, California poppy, Drummond's phlox, mealy blue sage, purple saxifrage, and Tahoka daisy. Water plants suited to container gardening include fragrant water lily and pickerelweed.

224

My family enjoys watching the birds that visit our garden, and we also value them as a natural means of pest control. We already have a number of trees and shrubs with fruits that attract birds and would like to plant some wildflowers that would increase the food supply. What are some especially good choices for this purpose?

You can attract a variety of birds with an array of different seed- or fruit-producing annuals, perennials, and grasses, such as asters, compass plant, fire pink, goat's-rue, goldenrod, jack-in-the-pulpit, mountain mint, partridgeberry, pickerelweed, purple coneflower, rudbeckia, Rocky Mountain bee plant, sideoats grama, spikenard, sunflowers, switch grass, tickseed, and wild geranium. Hummingbirds are attracted to nectar-producing flowers such as bee balm, cardinal flower, copper iris, columbine, lupine, monkshood, penstemon, fire pink, sage, spider lily, spigelia, verbena, wild four-o'clocks, wild hyssop, and yucca.

Are there any wildflowers that I could use as a ground cover to control soil erosion on a slope in my side yard?

New England aster, lanceleaf coreopsis, Indian blanket, and Rocky Mountain penstemon are all excellent choices for solving this problem.

Which wildflowers are suited to an exposed spot in a desert garden that is in full sun almost all day in summer?

Southwestern verbena, desert marigold, and desert mallow are just three of the many attractive wildflowers that will thrive in this hot, dry microhabitat.

Water drains from several neighboring properties into my backyard, so the soil is often damp and the lawn is growing poorly. Are wildflowers a sensible alternative to turf grass?

Although the majority of wildflowers would do no better than your lawn, some tolerate or even demand the soggy conditions you describe, including such fine ornamentals as sweet flag, swamp milkweed, rose mallow, blue flag, and cardinal flower.

How can I get my wildflowers to bloom for a longer period?

Deadheading—that is, removing blossoms that are past their prime—encourages wildflowers to bloom longer and more profusely, and it also keeps the plants looking fresh and tidy. However, this practice isn't appropriate if you want to collect seed from your wildflower garden for propagating, because it prevents seed production.

LAWN CARE

I am confused about which lawn-grass mixture I should buy for easy care. How can I decide among "playground mix," "park mix," or "estate mix" when those terms do not apply to my little yard?

The complex process of selecting the proper grass mix is not helped by the sales jargon you mention. There is no one lawn grass that can be planted throughout the United States. Like other perennials, grass species have unique requirements for moisture, light, temperature, and so on. The fine-bladed grasses that give the thick, luxurious lawns that most people prefer are bluegrass, Chewings and red fescues, and some of the new perennial ryegrasses. Find out what will grow in your area, and choose a grass mixture that includes those types. A combination of grasses in a mixture is best because some varieties will survive even if others have difficulty taking hold.

I love my lawn, but weed control is driving me crazy. What can I do to make things easier?

In temperate climates, cut your grass high. This promotes much deeper roots and a greener lawn, and the taller grass shades out many weeds such as crab grass. Also, keep the soil pH level between 6 and 6.8 to encourage grass growth and discourage weeds, and apply the appropriate amounts of fertilizer for your grass type. Leave lawn clippings in place to recycle into the ground.

One spot in my lawn stays wet, and I am always getting my riding lawn mower stuck in it. Is there anything I can do short of putting in a tile drain?

There are many trees that thrive in wet areas, where they take up lots of water, thus drying the area. Some members of the willow family—pussy willow *(Salix discolor),* weeping willow *(S. babylonica),* and the corkscrew willow *(S. matsudana* 'Tortuosa')—are good choices. Be sure, though, that there are no walkways, terraces, or drainfields close by; willow roots are extremely invasive and can damage them.

SHADE GARDENING

My outside sitting area is shaded by day, but I enjoy it the most at night during the hot summer months. How can I add horticultural interest for this very special time?

A few wonderful shade garden plants are perfect for these conditions. The pure white lilylike flowers of *Hosta plantaginea* open fully at night to release a honey-scented fragrance. Nicotianas are also fragrant at night. If you have a spot nearby that receives several hours of sun, be sure to put in the hauntingly fragrant *Ipomoea alba* (moonflower) vine, with its enormous white blossoms that open around sunset and glow in the moonlight. Look also for new *Hemerocallis* cultivars called nocturnal bloomers, which keep their blossoms open into evening, and extended bloomers, whose flowers stay open for up to 2 days.

I built a shaded flagstone terrace where the roots of a nearby maple restricted my gardening efforts. Now I spend too much time pulling weeds between the stones. Can I plant anything in these spaces to reduce maintenance and add interest?

Plant the narrowest crevices with *Sagina subulata* (Corsican pearlwort), a fine plant for paving areas with its creeping, mossy evergreen foliage and tiny white spring flowers. In wider spaces you can establish *Mentha requienii* (Corsican mint), with ground-hugging leaves that emit a delicious fragrance of peppermint when trod upon occasionally, and *Mazus reptans,* a creeper with purple-blue to white flowers. For extra interest, but not to be walked on, consider *Lysimachia nummularia* 'Aurea' (creeping Jenny), with rounded yellow leaves and yellow blossoms in summer, or one of the several cultivars of *Ajuga,* with colored or variegated foliage.

What can I plant to give me lots of fragrance in my shade garden?

You should rely upon a succession of plants through the seasons and avoid the many species that are fragrant only at close range. From late winter to early spring, cultivars of *Hamamelis mollis* and *H.* x *intermedia* waft their enticing fragrance over the awakening landscape. As spring progresses, *Viburnum carlesii* (Koreanspice viburnum) will add its own tangy scent. Few plants are more fragrant from midspring to early summer than azaleas. One of the best is *Rhododendron arborescens* (sweet azalea). In summer, mass plantings of night-fragrant *Hosta plantaginea* and annuals such as *Lobularia maritima* (sweet alyssum) and the night-fragrant nicotianas are very effective. Finish up in autumn with another native, *Hamamelis virginiana.*

What is the longest-blooming perennial I can plant in my shade garden?

In all but the hottest, driest parts of the country, the plant you seek is undoubtedly *Corydalis lutea*. It starts to bloom fairly early in spring and continues producing its small clusters of pendant, tubular yellow flowers until the onset of hard frost.

My shade garden really goes into the doldrums in summer. Although I plant drifts of impatiens and begonias, I miss the individuality and charm of blooming perennials and shrubs at this time. What can I plant to enliven the scene?

In addition to the unlimited potential of daylilies, here are a dozen stalwart perennials to bridge your early-to-late-summer flower gap: *Aconitum napellus*, *Astilbe* x *arendsii* cultivars, *Chelone lyonii* (pink turtlehead), *Chrysogonum virginianum*, *Cimicifuga racemosa* (black cohosh) and *C. americana* (American bugbane), *Dicentra eximia* cultivars and hybrids, hosta, *Ligularia dentata* 'Desdemona', *Lilium* (lily), *Physostegia virginiana* (false dragonhead) cultivars, *Stokesia laevis* (Stokes' aster), and *Thalictrum rochebrunianum* (lavender mist meadow rue). Two very hardy native shrubs for outstanding blossoms in July are *Aesculus parviflora* (bottlebrush buckeye) and *Rhododendron prunifolium* (plum-leaved azalea), a real beauty with blossoms of glowing orange-red.

I've had no luck luring hummingbirds to my shade garden. Most plants recommended for this purpose seem to be sun lovers, and others bloom only briefly. Do you have any suggestions?

One of the best plants for attracting hummingbirds is *Lonicera sempervirens* (trumpet or coral honeysuckle). It is also one of the most beautiful and longest-flowering vines you can bring into the garden. Train it up a trellis, where it will grow 10 to 15 feet high. The 2-inch-long blossoms are scarlet with orange throats and appear in great numbers from midspring to fall. The plant succeeds in partial shade, although it will blossom better in full sun. It is hardy to Zone 4.

The potted plants I grow on my shaded terrace never have that lush, overflowing look that I see in pictures in books and magazines. What am I doing wrong?

The secret is to be *very* generous initially with the number of plants used in each pot; regularly pinch back new buds on plants that require it to promote bushy growth; never let the soil dry out completely; and use a freely draining potting mix that contains a slow-release fertilizer. After 2 months, start applying a liquid fertilizer every 10 to 14 days. By early to midsummer your containers should be spilling over with lush growth.

I'm starting a woodland shade garden, but the site has lots of poison ivy. How should I get rid of it?

Use great caution when removing this plant; even people who have always been immune to it can develop a sensitivity. Avoid direct contact, contaminated clothing or pet fur, and even smoke from burning plants. With a long-handled hoe, uproot small plants as soon as you notice them. Spray larger plants with the herbicide glyphosate; repeat if necessary. If the poison ivy has ascended a tree, cut its stems near the base with a long-handled pole saw and treat the basal portions with herbicide. Wearing washable cloth gloves or a double layer of disposable latex gloves, dig a hole about 2 feet deep and bury all pruned and dead plant parts. If you are particularly sensitive or if the infestation is large, seek professional help to eradicate the plants.

Some of my rhododendrons have become overgrown. Can I cut them back? If so, when can I do this?

Rhododendrons usually need little or no pruning unless they get out of bounds, or if the growth becomes sparse, with long stretches of stem devoid of leaves. Then they will require drastic action. Cut back entire branches to within 2 feet of the ground, all at one time, just after the flowers have faded. You should see new sprouts from previously dormant buds on the old stems in about 4 to 8 weeks, but sometimes resprouting does not occur and the entire plant is lost. If this causes concern with a choice cultivar, you can take a more conservative approach by removing one-third of the branches at a time over a 3-year period.

How can I prevent red spider infestations on my astilbes? A miticide I used killed most of the foliage.

Moisture-retentive soil and an inch of water a week during drought are essential for astilbes, especially in warm climates. Dryness and sun are an open invitation to red spider infestations. If dull green leaves and characteristic webbing show that an infestation has occurred, spray the undersides of the leaves often with a forceful stream of water to knock off the pests.

GARDEN DESIGN

I have many garden ideas for different parts of my property, but I have a hard time visualizing how they might all fit together. How can I work them out?

Go out into the landscape and try them. Place tall stakes where you think you would like trees; use hose, string, or powdered lime to define lawn shapes, paths, and beds; string up lines to represent fencing; spread out sheets or blankets where you might like a small paved area. Set outdoor furniture in places where you might want seating. Then look at these elements from different angles and keep making adjustments until you feel satisfied.

I've recently bought an older home with a rather boring landscape. I can't afford to redo the entire property at once. How can I develop the garden gradually over a period of, say, 5 years? In what order should I proceed?

Spend the first year getting to know your garden. Keep a notebook to record such data as when the plants bloom and how the sun strikes different areas throughout the day and in different seasons. Test the soil, and begin correcting any deficiencies. Bring in an arborist to evaluate the trees. The autumn and winter of the first year is a good time for removing diseased or poorly placed trees and planting new ones. The second year, put your money into "hardscape" items—an irrigation system, if needed, and patios, walkways, retaining walls, and fences. Protect trees during the construction process by surrounding the root zone with temporary fencing. During the third year, concentrate on shrubbery—thinning, transplanting, and adding color and texture. Use the fourth year to establish herbaceous beds. By the fifth year you should be ready to add the finishing touches—a sundial, perhaps, or garden art to serve as focal points.

I have planted different gardens in our large suburban lot over the years, but now I don't have the time to keep up all the areas as well as I would like to. How can I revamp the gardens so they will look good with less maintenance?

Categorize the different garden areas according to the levels of maintenance needed to keep each looking good: intensive, moderate, or casual. Are the intensive areas too many, too scattered, and too far away to be noticed or enjoyed? If so, concentrate your efforts where they matter. Let the farther reaches revert to woodland. Turn a mixed border into a low-maintenance shrub border. Replace a struggling woodland garden with a hardy ground cover. Put your main effort into pruning a few key specimen trees and shrubs for shape and intensively maintaining a close-in flower border.

I loved a planting scheme I saw in a garden book, but when I tried to copy it in my garden it didn't look right. How can I tell what will work in my garden?

Apart from incompatible cultural requirements among plants, the most common cause for an unsuccessful duplication of a garden scheme in another location is the difference in scale, proportion, and conformation of the surrounding space. When you see a design that you like, check to determine whether the setting of the locale where you want to duplicate it is similar to that of the original. You're almost certain to be disappointed, for example, if you pick out an arrangement set against a fenced-in corner for reproduction at the edge of a lawn opening onto woods.

Many design books emphasize the importance of shape and mass in planting design, but I can't seem to get past the flower colors when I am making plant arrangements. How can I begin to see plants the way designers see them?

To see shape only, first try to look at your plant groupings as if they were all one color. Use a black-and-white photocopy of a garden view and trace an outline of trees, shrubs, and groups of smaller plants in the picture. Don't try to follow the outline shape in detail; generalize as much as possible, so that you end up with a diagram of circles, ovals, cones, horizontal lines, and so on. If the diagram turns out to be a series of boring circles, try adding vertical spikes or a taller cone shape to vary the composition. Once you have hit upon a pleasing combination of shapes, use this as the basis for working out a detailed planting plan that will include texture and color.

I need immediate screening from my neighbors. Should I put in a fence along my property line?

This only makes sense when you want to mark your property or keep out intruders and animals. A more effective way of screening unwanted views is to place a fence or screen where it gives you the greatest protection. On a sloping lot, for example, a screen placed at the edge of an elevated terrace will be more effective than one at the property line, where you may be able to see over the fence from where you sit. Also, fences and screens are expensive garden elements, and you should take full advantage of their architectural features by locating them where you gain the most from the definition they provide, such as near a terrace.

The back of my lot slopes down so steeply from my house that the soil is washing away. I want to terrace the land for planters, but I'm concerned because the area is large and I might be creating a monster in terms of maintenance. What do you suggest?

Why not terrace the upper portion closest to your house and clothe the lower part in shrubs and ground covers? Plants with dense root systems, such as cotoneaster, *Hypericum calycinum* (St.-John's-wort), or juniper, will help prevent erosion. You would be well advised to call a landscape architect to prepare a plan for the terraced portion. A professional can help you select the most cost-effective material for a retaining wall and can engineer the wall to stand up to the force of soil and water pushing against it.

What are some good trees to plant in front of a new two-story townhouse on a very small lot?

Choose deep-rooted species; avoid such trees as sweet gum and Norway maple, which have greedy, shallow roots that compete with nearby shrubbery and make it impossible to grow grass. In the past few years nurseries have introduced several narrow-crowned, upright selections of familiar shade trees suitable for use in small gardens and as street plantings. Trees with less than a 15-foot spread include *Pyrus calleryana* 'Chanticleer' (Callery pear), pyramidal *Carpinus betulus* 'Fastigiata' (European hornbeam), *Quercus robur* 'Fastigiata' (English oak), and one of the several red maples selected for upright form, such as *Acer rubrum* 'Armstrong'.

I have a tiny city garden that is walled in on all sides with almost no planting space around the patio. How can I make it a year-round garden that is full of plants that bloom in succession?

If you can't go outward go up: Plant the space thickly with climbers. Combine vines so that when one is finished, another will bloom—for example, a planting of *Clematis montana*, 'New Dawn' climbing roses, and *Clematis paniculata (C. maximowicziana)* to cover spring, summer, and fall. Use bold foliage plants like *Yucca filamentosa* and *Mahonia bealei* for accents. Make a dense evergreen background by planting ivies or *Clematis armandii*. On the patio, set pots of annuals and bulbs in groups, or arrange them on a baker's rack for even more planting space.

I've tried lots of plant combinations but am still not satisfied that I've hit on one with exquisite beauty. How do I get beyond pretty to truly beautiful?

The foremost quality of any beautiful plant combination is simplicity. You may be using too many different plants or arranging them in a way that makes them hard to read visually. Some of the best ways to achieve simplicity include limiting your palette to just two or three kinds of plants (although you may use several of each kind in a massed effect); limiting your flower colors to variations on a single color theme; and planting them so that there is open space around or between them, even when they grow to full, mature size. Simple, beautiful combinations possess restraint, yet enough contrast in form, foliage, and color to stir the viewer's interest.

I try to put together perennials and annuals with matched flower colors, but the effect is rather haphazard. What's the secret to making good-looking color combinations?

The problem you describe is usually caused by too few plants in the combination. Single plants tend to recede to mere points of color when viewed from even a short distance. Try using drifts rather than just one, two, or three plants. A drift is a group of five to nine plants, all of the same variety, usually arranged in a shape with tapered ends. Drifts will give you broad swaths of color that can be combined by weaving their tapered ends into one another. These generous areas of color will have much more impact than the spotty color afforded by single plants.

Most days I get to enjoy my garden only in the evening, after work, when the light is low and failing. Are there any plants that I can combine to add interest to the evening garden?

As daylight fails, the cones, or color-sensing cells in the eye, begin to stop functioning in favor of the rods, or light-sensing cells. Colors on the red end of the spectrum appear to darken first, and eventually red looks black. The violet- and lavender-sensing cones are the last to lose their function in the dimming light. Thus, planting lavender or violet flowers will give you a startlingly fluorescent display as this shift occurs in the eye. Among perennials, a combination of *Platycodon grandiflorus* 'Blue' (balloon flower), *Adenophora confusa* (ladybells), and *Linum perenne* (blue flax) is an excellent choice for an evening garden.

Along the foundation of my house I have combinations of evergreens, both needled and broadleaf, that tend to look like big lumps of green rather than a designed grouping. How can I create a more dramatic effect?

Select the most interesting evergreens as the basis for a revamped design—that is, the ones with the most distinct shape, foliage texture, or colors—and transplant to other areas the shrubs that have less character. If the open space is appealing, either keep it open and cover it with a mulch or plant it with a low ground cover whose color contrasts with the evergreens around it. If the open space calls for a plant, consider a deciduous one with twisting, sinuous trunks or branches, or one whose form or texture strongly contrasts with the plants around it.

I have a spot on a rise where the sun sets—a perfect place for backlighting plants with the late afternoon sun. What plants would look good with backlight?

The Japanese maple *Acer palmatum* with *Imperata cylindrica* 'Rubra' (Japanese blood grass) in front makes a great combination for backlighting, especially in fall, when the maple is turning color. Grapevines, black locust, and many other thin-leaved plants are also beautiful when the sun shines through them.

What designs would you advise for someone who has a limited budget as well as a limited amount of time?

After you decide which low-maintenance trees, shrubs, and evergreens you like, repeat them throughout your garden. The same holds true for herbaceous perennials: Limit the types of plants you choose, and plant more of them. However, you'll want to have a certain amount of plant diversity so that if disease strikes, you won't lose everything. Select and site your plants carefully to ensure against cultural, disease, or insect problems.

PLANTING AND MAINTENANCE

What's the easiest way to tackle the job of planting a steep bank?

Soil preparation is a must, since most banks have inadequate soil. For each plant, dig a deep hole and add amendments to the soil; stagger the placement of the holes to achieve a less linear effect. To control the growth of weeds on a slope, lay down landscape fabric and put the plants into the ground through slits cut in the fabric. Spread pine needles or shredded bark on top of the fabric; these materials tend to stay in place, whereas a chunky mulch like pine bark nuggets will slide off a steep slope. Terracing with landscape timbers or stone reduces potential erosion and increases moisture retention but requires a bigger investment of both labor and money.

Plant choices aside, are there certain garden designs that are more maintenance free than others?

Garden styles definitely affect maintenance requirements. In general, the more formal your design, the more upkeep the garden will need, because formality requires balance, symmetry, and exactness, which means more pruning and trimming of shrubs and trees. Informal designs, on the other hand, allow plants more freedom to follow natural growth patterns.

231

How can I prevent winter damage to my broadleaf evergreens—rhododendrons, azaleas, and hollies—and also to evergreen perennials such as bergenia and Christmas and Lenten roses?

Sun and wind are usually the culprits in winter injury to evergreen plants. Leaves are most susceptible to damage when the plant becomes dehydrated, and drought conditions can often exist in the winter garden. Even though your neighbors may think you're crazy, water your evergreen plants in winter to help prevent injury to leaves and tender twigs. If you know that a plant is susceptible to winter damage, select a sheltered site that will provide some protection from wind and afternoon sun, such as against the north wall of the house or on the shady side of a tall hedge.

What is the least time-consuming way to fertilize a garden?

Blended organic fertilizers are the backbone of any fertilizing program for low maintenance. They contain a great variety of mineral nutrients and organic molecules that are released slowly into the soil. Gardeners can also turn to timed-release fertilizer pellets; when applied in late winter, the pellets deliver nitrogen, phosphorus, and potassium evenly over an entire growing season.

Are there any shrubs that don't have to be pruned?

Unfortunately, no. You can start by buying shrub cultivars that have been selected specifically for their compact growth form and neat branching habits. But in any event, the conscientious gardener should follow the three Ds of pruning: Remove dead, diseased, and deformed branches at any time in a plant's life. To reduce the amount of pruning that you have to do, plant shrubs in a space large enough to allow them to achieve their mature dimensions without becoming obstacles. Also, try to remove no more than a third of the top growth at any time; this will limit the amount of suckering that occurs. Also, let shrubs assume their natural shape rather than pruning them into geometric globes and boxes.

I have tried to garden organically, and I compost all my plant debris—trimmings, old foliage, and weeds that I hoe from the garden—but it seems I have more weeds, disease, and insects every year. I thought organic gardening was going to be beneficial; what's wrong?

You are probably composting weeds that have seeds, giving them a fertile place to germinate before returning them to the garden to grow strong. Instead, put weeds that have gone to seed into the trash. Also, take care not to compost any diseased plant foliage. Many disease-causing organisms have resistant spores or go through resting stages that can survive the rigors of the composting process, particularly if your pile doesn't heat up sufficiently. Lacing your compost with 5-10-5 fertilizer or a compost activator, and turning it so that the outer, cooler portions are moved inward will help generate the heat necessary to kill insect larvae and disease organisms that may find their way into your compost pile.

I am continually mulching my garden to keep down weeds and conserve moisture. It not only costs a lot of money but is also very time-consuming. Do I have any alternatives?

One alternative is to switch from an organic mulch, which needs to be replenished periodically, to a stone mulch. Although stone doesn't have the soil-enhancing properties of an organic mulch, it is fairly permanent: One to 2 inches of uniform-size stones in earth colors provide a good-looking mulch that will last for decades. The best fertilizer to use for stone-mulched beds is one of the blended organics.

I would like to mulch all of my plants—trees, shrubs, and flower beds. When is the best time to do this?

Mulching after a recent rainfall would be ideal, and the best months are those during which the garden is dormant. Mulching later may bury and damage young bulb and perennial foliage. If you wait until the garden is actively growing to mulch, you'll spend a lot of extra time and effort working around your growing foliage so that you can apply the mulch evenly. The ground should be weed free before mulch is applied.

I'm a person who hates to weed. What can I do to keep weeding to a minimum?

It is much easier to remove a tiny weed seedling than a full-grown weed that has had time to develop long, tough roots. By weeding when the plants are young, you also remove them before they have a chance to go to seed, a situation that makes your weeding problems even worse.

How can I prepare a soil that will suit a wide number of plant varieties?

Every species of plant has its own range of tolerance for environmental factors such as pH, moisture, and nutrients, and it is impossible in a mixed planting to provide the ideal conditions for each one. Instead, try to achieve a happy medium by creating conditions that most plants can put up with. A pH of 5.8 to 6.5 will benefit the widest number of garden plants, and good drainage usually benefits all of them. Prepare a soil that is loose and crumbly and rich in nutrients; add organic matter in the form of compost and blended organic fertilizers.

My soil is a heavy clay. What amendments should I add to improve the structure of my soil?

Your first impulse might be to add sand, but while sand will loosen your heavy clay, it is not enough to transform it into a good garden soil. You will need to add lots of organic matter as well. Compost is an excellent choice; you can also use peat moss, leaf mold, bark chips or ground bark, sawdust, or well-rotted animal manure.

Do you recommend using traps to catch insects like Japanese beetles?

Insect traps today are quite improved over the ones on the market a few years ago. Be sure not to place them directly in the garden, however, because you will only attract insects from outside areas to the very plants you are trying to protect.

For insect problems in my garden, including aphids, thrips, and whiteflies, can you recommend a spray that will not harm the environment—or me?

All sprays can be harmful if not properly used, but one relatively safe kind is marketed under different brand names as insecticidal soap. Made up of various formulations of potassium salts of fatty acids, they kill by penetrating the shells of soft-bodied insects, causing dehydration and rapid death. They cannot penetrate eggs already laid, so a few repeat sprayings at 7- to 10-day intervals are necessary to kill emerging larvae and achieve complete control.

Zone and Frost Maps of the U.S.

To determine if a plant will flourish in your climate, first locate your zone on the map below and check it against the zone information given in the Easy-Care Plant Selection Guide that begins on page 236 or in the encyclopedia entries that begin on page 242. For annuals and biennials, planting dates depend on when frosts occur: Hardy annuals can be safely sown 6 weeks before the last spring frost, whereas tender annuals should be sown only after all danger of frost is past. Also, while cool-season annuals can withstand some frost, warm-season plants can be grown without protection only in the frost-free period between the last and first frosts. Used together, the zone map and the frost-date maps shown opposite will help you select plants suited to your area and determine when to plant them. Frost dates vary widely within each region, however, so check with your weather service or Cooperative Extension Service for more precise figures, and record the temperatures in your own garden from year to year.

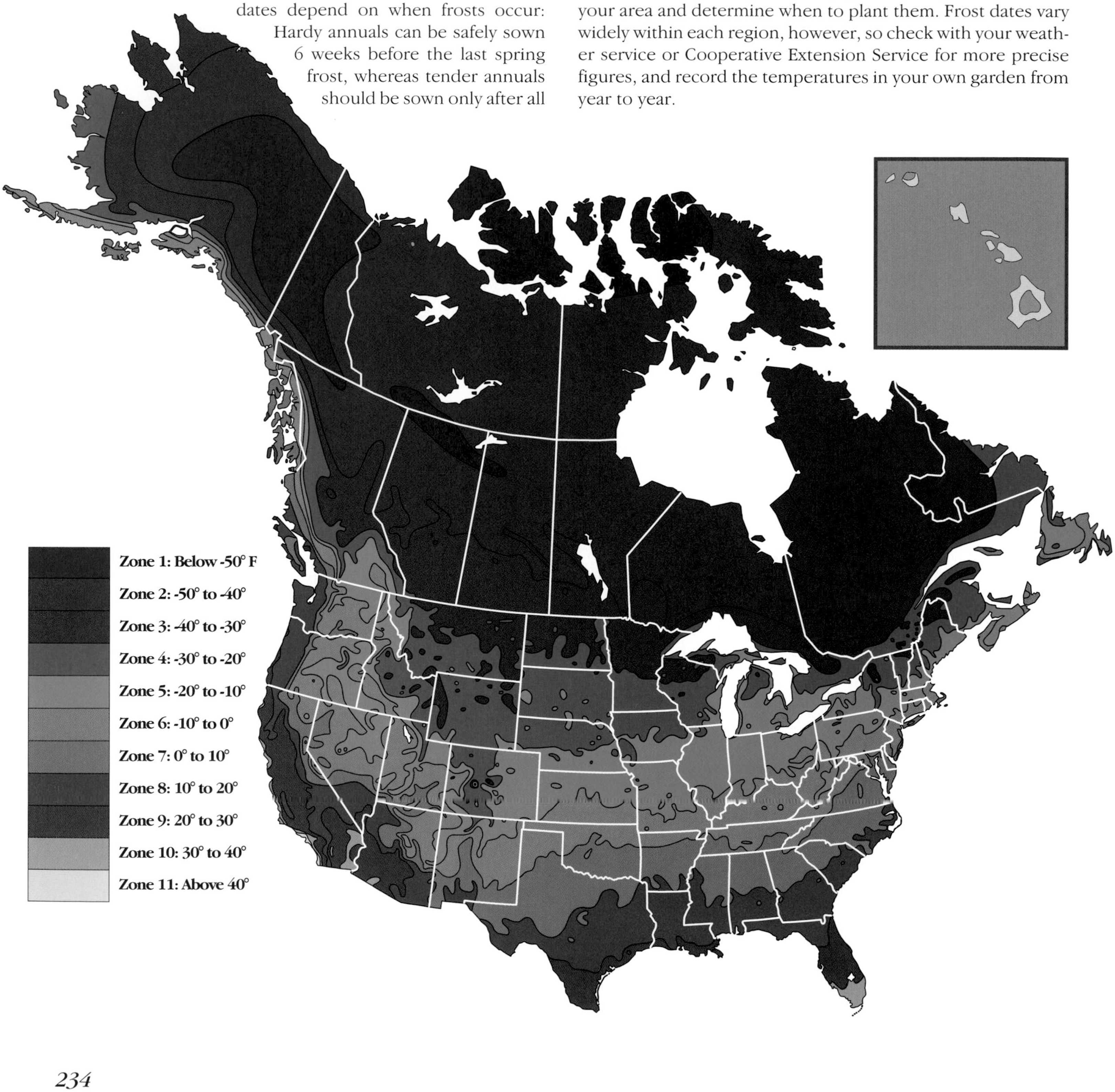

Zone 1: Below -50° F
Zone 2: -50° to -40°
Zone 3: -40° to -30°
Zone 4: -30° to -20°
Zone 5: -20° to -10°
Zone 6: -10° to 0°
Zone 7: 0° to 10°
Zone 8: 10° to 20°
Zone 9: 20° to 30°
Zone 10: 30° to 40°
Zone 11: Above 40°

AVERAGE DATES OF LAST SPRING FROST

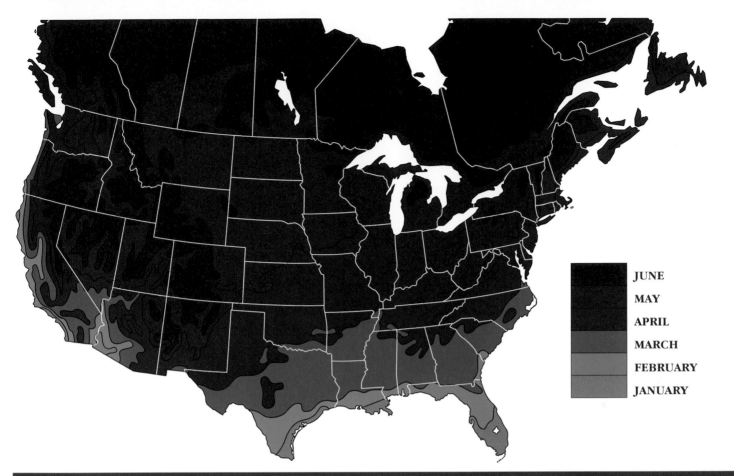

JUNE
MAY
APRIL
MARCH
FEBRUARY
JANUARY

AVERAGE DATES OF FIRST FALL FROST

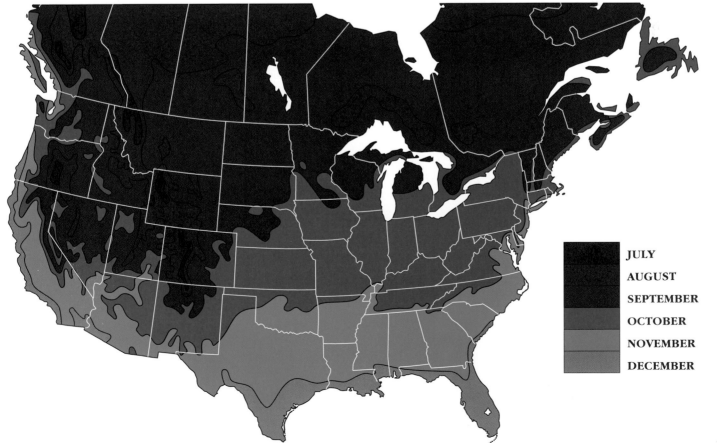

JULY
AUGUST
SEPTEMBER
OCTOBER
NOVEMBER
DECEMBER

Easy-Care Plant Selection Guide

Organized by plant type, this chart provides information needed to select species and varieties that will thrive in the particular conditions of your garden. For additional information on each plant, refer to the Encyclopedia that begins on page 242.

Plant	Zone 3	Zone 4	Zone 5	Zone 6	Zone 7	Zone 8	Zone 9	Zone 10	Zone 11	Dry	Moist	Full Sun	Partial Shade	Shade	Pests/Diseases	Drought	Pollution	Under 1	1-3	3-6	6-10	10-20	Over 20	Foliage	Flowers	Fruit	Form
GROUND COVERS																											
AJUGA REPTANS	✔	✔	✔	✔	✔	✔	✔	✔			✔	✔	✔	✔			✔							✔	✔		
ARCTOSTAPHYLOS UVA-URSI	✔	✔	✔	✔	✔					✔		✔	✔			✔	✔							✔	✔	✔	
CERATOSTIGMA PLUMBAGINOIDES			✔	✔	✔	✔				✔		✔	✔		✔		✔							✔	✔		
CHRYSOGONUM VIRGINIANUM		✔	✔	✔	✔	✔				✔		✔	✔	✔	✔		✔							✔	✔		
ECHEVERIA AGAVOIDES					✔	✔	✔	✔		✔		✔				✔		✔						✔	✔		✔
EPIMEDIUM GRANDIFLORUM		✔	✔	✔	✔						✔	✔	✔	✔			✔							✔	✔		
GERANIUM MACRORRHIZUM		✔	✔	✔	✔							✔	✔			✔	✔							✔	✔		
HEDERA CANARIENSIS					✔	✔					✔	✔	✔	✔			✔							✔			
HEDERA HELIX		✔	✔	✔	✔	✔	✔				✔	✔	✔	✔			✔							✔			
IBERIS SEMPERVIRENS		✔	✔	✔	✔						✔	✔				✔								✔	✔		✔
LAMIUM MACULATUM 'BEACON SILVER'		✔	✔	✔	✔					✔	✔		✔	✔	✔		✔							✔	✔		
LIRIOPE MUSCARI 'MONROE'S WHITE'		✔	✔	✔	✔	✔	✔	✔		✔	✔	✔	✔	✔	✔				✔					✔	✔	✔	
LIRIOPE SPICATA		✔	✔	✔	✔	✔	✔	✔		✔	✔	✔	✔	✔	✔		✔							✔	✔	✔	
OPHIOPOGON JAPONICUS			✔	✔	✔						✔	✔	✔			✔		✔						✔	✔		
OSTEOSPERMUM FRUTICOSUM 'HYBRID WHITE'					✔	✔				✔		✔				✔		✔						✔	✔		
PACHYSANDRA PROCUMBENS		✔	✔	✔	✔	✔					✔		✔	✔	✔		✔							✔	✔		
PHLOX STOLONIFERA	✔	✔	✔	✔	✔						✔		✔				✔							✔	✔		
PHLOX SUBULATA	✔	✔	✔	✔	✔	✔				✔		✔				✔								✔	✔		
STACHYS BYZANTINA 'HELENE VON STEIN'		✔	✔	✔	✔	✔				✔		✔	✔			✔			✔					✔			
VINCA MINOR	✔	✔	✔	✔	✔	✔	✔				✔	✔	✔	✔			✔							✔	✔		
PERENNIALS AND GRASSES																											
ACHILLEA MILLEFOLIUM 'ROSEA'	✔	✔	✔	✔	✔	✔	✔			✔		✔				✔			✔					✔	✔		
ACONITUM NAPELLUS	✔	✔	✔	✔	✔	✔					✔		✔							✔				✔	✔		
AEONIUM ARBOREUM 'SCHWARTZKOPF'					✔	✔				✔		✔				✔		✔						✔	✔		
AGAVE AMERICANA			✔	✔	✔	✔	✔			✔		✔				✔				✔				✔	✔		✔
ALOE STRIATA						✔	✔	✔		✔		✔				✔			✔					✔	✔		✔
AMSONIA TABERNAEMONTANA	✔	✔	✔	✔	✔	✔	✔			✔	✔	✔	✔		✔			✔						✔	✔		
ANEMONE X HYBRIDA 'SEPTEMBER CHARM'		✔	✔	✔	✔	✔					✔		✔		✔				✔						✔		
AQUILEGIA CANADENSIS		✔	✔	✔	✔	✔					✔	✔	✔						✔					✔	✔		

PERENNIALS AND GRASSES

	Zone 3	Zone 4	Zone 5	Zone 6	Zone 7	Zone 8	Zone 9	Zone 10	Zone 11	Dry	Moist	Full Sun	Partial Shade	Shade	Pests/Diseases	Drought	Pollution	Under 1	1-3	3-6	6-10	10-20	Over 20	Foliage	Flowers	Fruit	Form
ASCLEPIAS TUBEROSA		✔	✔	✔	✔	✔	✔	✔		✔		✔				✔		✔							✔		
ASTILBE TAQUETII 'SUPERBA'		✔	✔	✔	✔	✔					✔	✔	✔						✔					✔	✔		✔
BAPTISIA AUSTRALIS	✔	✔	✔	✔	✔	✔	✔	✔		✔	✔	✔	✔		✔				✔					✔	✔		
BERGENIA CORDIFOLIA	✔	✔	✔	✔	✔	✔					✔	✔	✔		✔		✔							✔	✔		
BOLTONIA ASTEROIDES 'SNOW BANK'		✔	✔	✔	✔	✔				✔	✔	✔								✔					✔		
BRUNNERA MACROPHYLLA	✔	✔	✔	✔	✔	✔					✔	✔		✔		✔			✔					✔	✔		
CALAMAGROSTIS X ACUTIFLORA 'KARL FOERSTER'		✔	✔	✔	✔	✔				✔	✔	✔	✔		✔	✔			✔					✔	✔		✔
CAMPANULA PORTENSCHLAGIANA		✔	✔	✔	✔					✔	✔	✔			✔		✔							✔	✔		✔
CAREX MORROWII		✔	✔	✔	✔	✔				✔	✔	✔	✔	✔				✔						✔			
CIMICIFUGA SIMPLEX		✔	✔	✔	✔						✔		✔		✔				✔					✔	✔		
COREOPSIS ROSEA		✔	✔	✔	✔	✔					✔	✔			✔			✔						✔	✔		
DICENTRA EXIMIA	✔	✔	✔	✔	✔						✔		✔					✔						✔	✔		✔
DICTAMNUS ALBUS	✔	✔	✔	✔	✔						✔	✔	✔		✔			✔						✔	✔	✔	
ECHINACEA PALLIDA	✔	✔	✔	✔	✔	✔	✔			✔		✔	✔			✔			✔						✔		
EUPATORIUM FISTULOSUM 'GATEWAY'	✔	✔	✔	✔	✔	✔	✔			✔	✔	✔	✔						✔						✔		
EUPHORBIA COROLLATA		✔	✔	✔	✔	✔	✔	✔		✔		✔			✔	✔			✔					✔	✔		
EUPHORBIA EPITHYMOIDES		✔	✔	✔	✔	✔	✔			✔		✔			✔	✔			✔					✔	✔		✔
GAZANIA 'FIESTA RED'				✔	✔	✔				✔		✔			✔	✔	✔								✔		
GERBERA JAMESONII				✔	✔	✔	✔				✔	✔	✔		✔		✔								✔		
HELIANTHUS MAXIMILIANI	✔	✔	✔	✔	✔	✔	✔			✔	✔	✔			✔						✔				✔		
HELICTOTRICHON SEMPERVIRENS		✔	✔	✔	✔	✔				✔	✔	✔			✔				✔					✔	✔		
HELLEBORUS FOETIDUS			✔	✔	✔	✔					✔		✔						✔					✔	✔		
HEMEROCALLIS 'EENIE WEENIE'	✔	✔	✔	✔	✔	✔	✔			✔	✔	✔	✔		✔		✔							✔	✔		
HEMEROCALLIS 'INCA TREASURE'	✔	✔	✔	✔	✔	✔	✔	✔		✔	✔	✔	✔		✔				✔					✔	✔		
HEUCHERA MICRANTHA 'PALACE PURPLE'		✔	✔	✔	✔	✔	✔				✔	✔	✔		✔				✔					✔	✔		✔
HIBISCUS 'LADY BALTIMORE'		✔	✔	✔	✔	✔					✔	✔	✔							✔					✔		
HOSTA PLANTAGINEA	✔	✔	✔	✔	✔	✔					✔		✔	✔					✔					✔	✔		✔
IMPERATA CYLINDRICA RUBRA 'RED BARON'			✔	✔	✔	✔				✔		✔	✔		✔				✔					✔			
IRIS SIBIRICA		✔	✔	✔	✔	✔	✔				✔	✔	✔		✔				✔						✔		
LAVANDULA ANGUSTIFOLIA			✔	✔	✔	✔				✔		✔							✔					✔	✔		
LAVANDULA STOECHAS					✔	✔	✔			✔		✔							✔					✔	✔		
LIATRIS SPICATA	✔	✔	✔	✔	✔	✔	✔			✔	✔	✔	✔						✔						✔		

237

	ZONE 3	ZONE 4	ZONE 5	ZONE 6	ZONE 7	ZONE 8	ZONE 9	ZONE 10	ZONE 11	DRY	MOIST	FULL SUN	PARTIAL SHADE	SHADE	PESTS/DISEASES	DROUGHT	POLLUTION	UNDER 1	1-3	3-6	6-10	10-20	OVER 20	FOLIAGE	FLOWERS	FRUIT	FORM
PERENNIALS AND GRASSES																											
MISCANTHUS SINENSIS 'YAKU JIMA'			✓	✓	✓	✓	✓				✓	✓			✓	✓				✓				✓	✓		
PAEONIA 'KRINKLED WHITE'	✓	✓	✓	✓	✓	✓					✓	✓	✓						✓					✓	✓		
PAEONIA 'RASPBERRY SUNDAE'	✓	✓	✓	✓	✓	✓					✓	✓	✓						✓					✓	✓		
PANICUM VIRGATUM		✓	✓	✓	✓	✓				✓	✓	✓				✓	✓			✓				✓	✓		
PAPAVER ORIENTALE	✓	✓	✓	✓	✓						✓	✓	✓		✓				✓						✓		
PATRINIA SCABIOSIFOLIA		✓	✓	✓	✓	✓					✓	✓	✓						✓						✓	✓	
PENNISETUM ALOPECUROIDES		✓	✓	✓	✓	✓					✓	✓				✓	✓		✓					✓	✓		
PEROVSKIA ATRIPLICIFOLIA		✓	✓	✓	✓	✓				✓		✓				✓			✓					✓	✓		
PHLOX MACULATA 'MISS LINGARD'	✓	✓	✓	✓	✓	✓	✓				✓	✓							✓						✓		
PLATYCODON GRANDIFLORUS		✓	✓	✓	✓	✓				✓	✓	✓	✓						✓						✓		
POLYGONATUM BIFLORUM	✓	✓	✓	✓	✓	✓	✓				✓		✓	✓					✓					✓	✓	✓	
ROMNEYA COULTERI				✓	✓	✓	✓			✓		✓				✓					✓			✓	✓		
RUDBECKIA NITIDA 'HERBSTSONNE'		✓	✓	✓	✓	✓	✓			✓	✓	✓			✓						✓				✓		
SALVIA GREGGII			✓	✓	✓	✓	✓			✓	✓	✓				✓			✓					✓	✓		
SANTOLINA CHAMAECYPARISSUS			✓	✓	✓							✓				✓	✓		✓					✓	✓		✓
SEDUM X 'VERA JAMESON'	✓	✓	✓	✓	✓	✓	✓	✓		✓		✓	✓		✓	✓	✓							✓	✓		
SOLIDAGO 'GOLDEN FLEECE'	✓	✓	✓	✓	✓	✓	✓			✓		✓	✓						✓						✓		
SPIGELIA MARILANDICA		✓	✓	✓	✓	✓					✓		✓						✓						✓		
VERONICA INCANA		✓	✓	✓	✓					✓	✓	✓	✓		✓				✓					✓	✓		
ZANTEDESCHIA AETHIOPICA 'CROWBOROUGH'						✓	✓				✓	✓	✓						✓					✓	✓		
DECIDUOUS SHRUBS																											
ABELIA X GRANDIFLORA 'FRANCIS MASON'			✓	✓	✓	✓					✓	✓	✓							✓				✓	✓		
ABELIA X GRANDIFLORA 'PROSTRATA'			✓	✓	✓	✓					✓	✓	✓					✓						✓	✓		
ACANTHOPANAX SIEBOLDIANUS 'VARIEGATUS'		✓	✓	✓	✓	✓				✓	✓	✓	✓	✓	✓	✓	✓				✓			✓			
ARONIA ARBUTIFOLIA 'BRILLIANTISSIMA'		✓	✓	✓	✓	✓	✓			✓	✓	✓	✓								✓					✓	
BERBERIS THUNBERGII 'GOLDEN RING'		✓	✓	✓	✓	✓				✓	✓	✓	✓			✓	✓		✓					✓			
BERBERIS THUNBERGII 'ROSE GLOW'		✓	✓	✓	✓	✓				✓	✓	✓	✓			✓	✓		✓					✓			
CALYCANTHUS FLORIDUS		✓	✓	✓	✓	✓					✓	✓	✓		✓						✓			✓	✓		
CARYOPTERIS X CLANDONENSIS			✓	✓	✓	✓				✓		✓							✓					✓	✓		
CERATOSTIGMA WILLMOTTIANUM					✓	✓	✓			✓	✓	✓	✓			✓			✓					✓	✓		
CHAENOMELES SPECIOSA 'TEXAS SCARLET'		✓	✓	✓	✓	✓				✓	✓	✓	✓						✓						✓		
CISTUS X PURPUREUS					✓	✓				✓		✓				✓			✓					✓	✓		
CISTUS SALVIIFOLIUS					✓	✓				✓		✓				✓		✓						✓	✓		

DECIDUOUS SHRUBS

	ZONE 3	ZONE 4	ZONE 5	ZONE 6	ZONE 7	ZONE 8	ZONE 9	ZONE 10	ZONE 11	DRY	MOIST	FULL SUN	PARTIAL SHADE	SHADE	PESTS/DISEASES	DROUGHT	POLLUTION	UNDER 1	1-3	3-6	6-10	10-20	OVER 20	FOLIAGE	FLOWERS	FRUIT	FORM
CLETHRA ALNIFOLIA	✓	✓	✓	✓	✓	✓	✓				✓	✓	✓	✓						✓				✓	✓		
CLETHRA BARBINERVIS			✓	✓	✓	✓					✓	✓	✓	✓	✓					✓				✓	✓		
CORNUS ALBA 'SIBIRICA'	✓	✓	✓	✓	✓						✓	✓	✓							✓				✓			✓
CORNUS MAS		✓	✓	✓	✓						✓	✓	✓								✓			✓	✓	✓	
COTINUS COGGYGRIA 'ROYAL PURPLE'		✓	✓	✓	✓	✓	✓			✓	✓	✓									✓			✓	✓		
DEUTZIA GRACILIS 'NIKKO'		✓	✓	✓	✓	✓					✓	✓	✓				✓							✓	✓		✓
ENKIANTHUS CAMPANULATUS		✓	✓	✓	✓	✓	✓				✓	✓	✓								✓			✓	✓		
FORSYTHIA X INTERMEDIA 'SPECTABILIS'		✓	✓	✓	✓					✓	✓	✓								✓					✓		
FORSYTHIA VIRIDISSIMA 'BRONXENSIS'		✓	✓	✓	✓					✓	✓	✓				✓									✓		✓
FOTHERGILLA GARDENII		✓	✓	✓	✓	✓					✓	✓	✓		✓		✓							✓	✓		
FOTHERGILLA MAJOR		✓	✓	✓	✓						✓	✓	✓							✓				✓	✓		
HAMAMELIS X INTERMEDIA			✓	✓	✓	✓					✓	✓	✓		✓							✓		✓	✓		
HIBISCUS SYRIACUS 'DIANA'			✓	✓	✓	✓					✓	✓					✓			✓					✓		
HYDRANGEA ARBORESCENS 'GRANDIFLORA'	✓	✓	✓	✓	✓	✓	✓				✓		✓						✓						✓		
HYDRANGEA PANICULATA	✓	✓	✓	✓	✓						✓	✓									✓			✓	✓		✓
HYDRANGEA QUERCIFOLIA			✓	✓	✓	✓	✓				✓	✓								✓				✓	✓		✓
ILEX 'SPARKLEBERRY'		✓	✓	✓	✓						✓	✓									✓					✓	
ITEA VIRGINICA 'HENRY'S GARNET'			✓	✓	✓	✓	✓				✓	✓	✓	✓					✓					✓	✓		
KERRIA JAPONICA			✓	✓	✓	✓	✓	✓			✓		✓	✓					✓					✓	✓		
MALUS SARGENTII		✓	✓	✓	✓	✓				✓	✓	✓									✓				✓	✓	
MYRICA PENSYLVANICA	✓	✓	✓	✓						✓	✓	✓	✓			✓					✓			✓		✓	
NANDINA DOMESTICA			✓	✓	✓	✓					✓	✓	✓								✓			✓	✓	✓	✓
POTENTILLA FRUTICOSA	✓	✓	✓	✓	✓					✓	✓	✓				✓			✓					✓	✓		
RHODODENDRON CALENDULACEUM			✓	✓	✓						✓	✓	✓							✓				✓	✓		
RHODODENDRON VASEYI 'WHITE FIND'	✓	✓	✓	✓	✓	✓					✓	✓	✓							✓				✓	✓		
ROSA ALBA 'INCARNATA'		✓	✓	✓	✓	✓	✓	✓			✓	✓				✓			✓					✓	✓		
ROSA RUGOSA	✓	✓	✓	✓	✓	✓	✓	✓			✓	✓				✓			✓					✓	✓	✓	
ROSA VIRGINIANA	✓	✓	✓	✓	✓	✓					✓	✓				✓			✓					✓	✓		
SPIRAEA X CINERA 'GREFSHEIM'	✓	✓	✓	✓	✓						✓	✓							✓					✓	✓		
SPIRAEA NIPPONICA 'SNOWMOUND'	✓	✓	✓	✓	✓						✓	✓							✓					✓	✓		
STEPHANANDRA INCISA 'CRISPA'	✓	✓	✓	✓	✓	✓					✓	✓	✓		✓		✓							✓			
SYRINGA MICROPHYLLA 'SUPERBA'		✓	✓	✓							✓	✓								✓				✓	✓		

	ZONES									SOIL		LIGHT			RESISTANT TO			HEIGHT (IN FEET)						NOTED FOR			
	ZONE 3	ZONE 4	ZONE 5	ZONE 6	ZONE 7	ZONE 8	ZONE 9	ZONE 10	ZONE 11	DRY	MOIST	FULL SUN	PARTIAL SHADE	SHADE	PESTS/DISEASES	DROUGHT	POLLUTION	UNDER 1	1-3	3-6	6-10	10-20	OVER 20	FOLIAGE	FLOWERS	FRUIT	FORM
DECIDUOUS SHRUBS																											
SYRINGA PATULA 'MISS KIM'	✓	✓	✓	✓	✓	✓					✓	✓							✓					✓	✓		
VACCINIUM ANGUSTIFOLIUM	✓	✓	✓	✓							✓	✓	✓				✓	✓						✓	✓	✓	
VIBURNUM CARLCEPHALUM			✓	✓	✓	✓					✓	✓	✓	✓						✓				✓	✓		
VIBURNUM DILATATUM			✓	✓	✓						✓	✓	✓	✓						✓				✓	✓	✓	
VIBURNUM PLICATUM VAR. TOMENTOSUM 'ESKIMO'			✓	✓	✓						✓	✓	✓	✓					✓					✓	✓	✓	
EVERGREEN SHRUBS																											
ARBUTUS UNEDO 'COMPACTA'				✓	✓	✓				✓	✓	✓	✓						✓					✓	✓	✓	
ARCTOSTAPHYLOS DENSIFLORA				✓	✓	✓	✓			✓		✓	✓			✓			✓					✓	✓		
BERBERIS JULIANAE		✓	✓	✓	✓					✓	✓	✓	✓		✓					✓				✓	✓		
BUXUS MICROPHYLLA 'WINTERGREEN'			✓	✓	✓	✓					✓	✓	✓				✓		✓					✓			✓
BUXUS SEMPERVIRENS 'VARDAR VALLEY'		✓	✓	✓	✓	✓					✓	✓	✓				✓		✓					✓			✓
CAMELLIA JAPONICA					✓	✓	✓				✓		✓									✓		✓	✓		
CAMELLIA SASANQUA					✓	✓	✓				✓		✓								✓			✓	✓		
CEANOTHUS 'DARK STAR'						✓	✓	✓	✓			✓				✓			✓					✓	✓		
DAPHNE ODORA				✓	✓	✓					✓		✓						✓					✓	✓		
GREVILLEA ROSMARINIFOLIA							✓	✓	✓		✓					✓			✓					✓	✓		
HETEROMELES ARBUTIFOLIA					✓	✓	✓			✓	✓	✓				✓						✓		✓		✓	
ILEX CRENATA 'HELLERI'		✓	✓	✓	✓						✓	✓	✓				✓		✓					✓			✓
ILEX GLABRA 'COMPACTA'		✓	✓	✓	✓	✓					✓	✓	✓		✓				✓					✓			✓
ILEX VOMITORIA				✓	✓	✓	✓				✓	✓	✓									✓	✓		✓	✓	
JUNIPERUS CHINENSIS 'GOLD COAST'	✓	✓	✓	✓	✓	✓	✓			✓		✓					✓	✓						✓			
KALMIA LATIFOLIA		✓	✓	✓	✓	✓	✓				✓	✓	✓	✓							✓			✓	✓		
LEPTOSPERMUM SCOPARIUM						✓	✓				✓	✓	✓			✓					✓				✓	✓	
LEUCOTHOE FONTANESIANA		✓	✓	✓	✓	✓					✓	✓							✓					✓	✓		✓
LONICERA PILEATA			✓	✓	✓						✓		✓	✓	✓			✓									✓
MAHONIA AQUIFOLIUM		✓	✓	✓	✓	✓					✓		✓						✓					✓	✓	✓	
MAHONIA BEALEI				✓	✓	✓	✓				✓		✓							✓				✓	✓	✓	
NERIUM OLEANDER 'LITTLE RED'					✓	✓	✓			✓	✓	✓	✓			✓	✓		✓					✓	✓		
OSMANTHUS HETEROPHYLLUS				✓	✓	✓					✓	✓	✓							✓				✓	✓		
PIERIS FLORIBUNDA			✓	✓	✓	✓					✓	✓	✓						✓					✓			✓
PITTOSPORUM TOBIRA					✓	✓	✓			✓	✓	✓	✓	✓		✓						✓		✓	✓		
PLUMBAGO AURICULATA					✓	✓	✓	✓	✓		✓	✓	✓			✓					✓			✓	✓		
PRUNUS LAUROCERASUS 'OTTO LUYKEN'			✓	✓	✓	✓					✓	✓	✓	✓					✓					✓	✓		

		ZONES									SOIL		LIGHT			RESISTANT TO			HEIGHT (IN FEET)						NOTED FOR			
	Plant	Zone 3	Zone 4	Zone 5	Zone 6	Zone 7	Zone 8	Zone 9	Zone 10	Zone 11	Dry	Moist	Full Sun	Partial Shade	Shade	Pests/Diseases	Drought	Pollution	Under 1	1-3	3-6	6-10	10-20	Over 20	Foliage	Flowers	Fruit	Form
EVERGREEN SHRUBS	PYRACANTHA COCCINEA 'MOJAVE'			✓	✓	✓	✓					✓	✓									✓			✓	✓	✓	
	RAPHIOLEPIS INDICA 'SNOW WHITE'					✓	✓	✓			✓	✓	✓				✓			✓					✓	✓		
	RHODODENDRON 'BOULE DE NEIGE'		✓	✓	✓	✓						✓	✓	✓						✓					✓	✓		
	RHODODENDRON YAKUSIMANUM			✓	✓	✓	✓					✓	✓	✓						✓					✓	✓		✓
	TAXUS BACCATA 'REPANDENS'			✓	✓	✓						✓	✓	✓	✓					✓					✓		✓	✓
	TAXUS X MEDIA 'DENSIFORMIS'	✓	✓	✓	✓							✓	✓	✓	✓					✓					✓			
	YUCCA FILAMENTOSA 'GOLDEN SWORD'		✓	✓	✓	✓	✓				✓		✓			✓	✓			✓					✓	✓		
DECIDUOUS TREES	ACER GRISEUM	✓	✓	✓	✓							✓	✓											✓					✓
	ACER PALMATUM 'DISSECTUM ATROPURPUREUM'			✓	✓	✓	✓					✓		✓									✓			✓			✓
	AMELANCHIER ARBOREA	✓	✓	✓	✓	✓	✓					✓	✓	✓										✓		✓	✓	✓	
	CERCIS CANADENSIS	✓	✓	✓	✓	✓	✓					✓	✓	✓											✓	✓	✓		
	CERCIS RENIFORMIS					✓	✓					✓	✓	✓										✓		✓	✓		
	CORNUS KOUSA			✓	✓	✓	✓					✓	✓	✓		✓								✓		✓	✓	✓	✓
	CORNUS 'AURORA' CV. RUTBAN		✓	✓	✓	✓						✓	✓											✓		✓	✓	✓	
	CRATAEGUS VIRIDIS 'WINTER KING'	✓	✓	✓	✓						✓	✓	✓											✓		✓	✓	✓	
	KOELREUTERIA PANICULATA			✓	✓	✓	✓				✓	✓	✓				✓	✓	✓						✓	✓	✓		
	LAGERSTROEMIA INDICA 'NATCHEZ'				✓	✓	✓					✓	✓				✓							✓			✓		✓
	MAGNOLIA X 'GALAXY'			✓	✓	✓	✓					✓	✓	✓										✓		✓	✓		✓
	MAGNOLIA 'RANDY'			✓	✓	✓	✓					✓	✓										✓			✓	✓		✓
	MAGNOLIA VIRGINIANA			✓	✓	✓	✓					✓	✓	✓										✓		✓	✓	✓	
	MALUS X 'DONALD WYMAN'	✓	✓	✓	✓	✓					✓	✓	✓											✓		✓	✓	✓	
	OXYDENDRUM ARBOREUM			✓	✓	✓	✓					✓	✓	✓		✓									✓	✓	✓		
	PRUNUS 'HALLY JOLIVETTE'			✓	✓	✓						✓	✓											✓					✓
	PRUNUS SARGENTII	✓	✓	✓	✓							✓	✓												✓	✓	✓		✓
	PYRUS CALLERYANA 'CAPITAL'			✓	✓	✓	✓				✓	✓	✓					✓	✓						✓	✓	✓		✓
EVERGREEN TREES	AGONIS FLEXUOSA							✓				✓	✓	✓				✓							✓	✓	✓		✓
	CHAMAECYPARIS OBTUSA 'CRIPPSII'		✓	✓	✓	✓						✓	✓												✓	✓			✓
	ILEX X ATTENUATA 'FOSTER #2'				✓	✓	✓	✓				✓	✓	✓											✓	✓		✓	✓
	JUNIPERUS SCOPULORUM 'SKYROCKET'	✓	✓	✓	✓	✓					✓		✓					✓							✓	✓			✓
	MAGNOLIA GRANDIFLORA 'LITTLE GEM'				✓	✓	✓	✓				✓	✓	✓										✓		✓	✓	✓	✓
	MYRICA CALIFORNICA					✓	✓	✓			✓	✓	✓	✓											✓	✓		✓	
	PINUS BUNGEANA		✓	✓	✓	✓	✓				✓	✓	✓												✓	✓			✓

Encyclopedia of Easy-Care Plants

Presented here is a selection of plants that are relatively problem free. The plants are listed alphabetically by their Latin botanical names; common names appear in bold type beneath the Latin. If you know a plant only by its common name, check the name in the index.

A botanical name consists first of the genus name, such as Achillea, which is usually printed in italics. Within a genus are one or more species, whose names are also in italics but are not capitalized, as in Achillea millefolium. Many species contain one or more varieties, either naturally occurring or cultivated; these names are enclosed in single quotation marks, as in Achillea millefolium 'Cerise Queen'. An "x" in a name, as in Achillea x 'Paprika', indicates a hybrid. "Zones" refers to the U.S. Department of Agriculture Plant Hardiness Zone Map (page 234). Plants grown outside recommended zones may do poorly or fail to survive.

Abelia
(a-BEE-lee-a)
ABELIA

Abelia x grandiflora 'Dwarf Purple'

Hardiness: *Zones 6-9*
Plant type: *shrub*
Height: *1½ to 6 feet*
Interest: *foliage, flowers*
Soil: *well-drained, moist, acid*
Light: *full sun to partial shade*

The glossy, dark green leaves of abelia turn a lovely bronze in the fall; they are evergreen in warmer zones, semievergreen in cooler areas. From summer through late fall, small, fragrant white flowers with a delicate pink blush appear in abundance. Abelia is useful as a specimen with a long season of interest, as a dense hedge, or combined with other shrubs in a mixed border.

Selected species and varieties: *A.* x *grandiflora* 'Francis Mason'—4 to 5 feet tall, with foliage variegated deep green and yellow; 'Prostrata' is 1½ to 2 feet tall with a spreading habit, semievergreen even in mild climates, and effective as a ground cover. *A.* x 'Edward Goucher'—3 to 5 feet tall, with lavender-pink flowers.

Growing conditions and maintenance: Plant abelia in soil amended with organic matter. It flowers best in full sun, but can handle up to half a day of shade. It needs occasional selective pruning to maintain a neat form; do not shear. Remove cold-damaged stems in spring.

Acanthopanax
(a-kan-tho-PAN-aks)
FIVE-LEAF ARALIA

Acanthopanax sieboldianus 'Variegatus'

Hardiness: *Zones 4-8*
Plant type: *deciduous shrub*
Height: *8 to 10 feet*
Interest: *foliage*
Soil: *well-drained*
Light: *full sun to full shade*

Acanthopanax is an excellent plant for difficult sites. The arching, wide-spreading stems form a broad, rounded shrub, but it can be sheared to produce a dense hedge. Its bright green compound leaves appear in early spring and persist into fall. Slender prickles along the stems make acanthopanax an effective barrier.

Selected species and varieties: *A. sieboldianus*—an erect shrub with arching branches, five to seven leaflets per leaf, and light brown stems with slender prickles; 'Variegatus' stands 6 to 8 feet tall and has leaves with creamy white margins.

Growing conditions and maintenance: Acanthopanax is easy to transplant and adapts to nearly every site. It tolerates a wide range of soil types, from acid to alkaline and from sandy to clay, and it stands up well to air pollution and drought. As a hedge, it can be heavily pruned or sheared to encourage compact growth and maintain the desired height. In an informal, mixed planting, little pruning is necessary.

Acer
(AY-ser)
MAPLE

Acer palmatum

Hardiness: *Zones 4-8*

Plant type: *large shrub or small tree*

Height: *6 to 30 feet*

Interest: *foliage, bark*

Soil: *moist, well-drained*

Light: *full sun to partial shade*

The smaller species of maple provide year-round interest as understory plantings and specimens.

Selected species and varieties: *A. palmatum* 'Dissectum Atropurpureum'—6 to 12 feet tall, with deep red, finely cut leaves and a wide-spreading form with twisted branches that are attractive in winter; 'Bloodgood' grows 15 to 20 feet tall with reddish purple leaves; 'Senkaki', to 10 feet, with coral red branches that are outstanding in winter; Zones 5-8. *A. griseum* (paperbark maple)—20 to 30 feet tall, with leaves that turn orange in fall; its peeling bark is cinnamon brown, striking in winter; Zones 4-8. *A. japonicum* 'Aconitifolium'—8 to 10 feet tall, with an equal spread of soft green leaves that turn crimson in fall; 'Aureum' grows 10 to 20 feet tall, with golden yellow leaves throughout summer; Zones 5-7.

Growing conditions and maintenance: Plant *A. griseum* in full sun; the others prefer light shade and some protection from wind and late frost. All are slow-growing plants that benefit from liberal amounts of organic matter incorporated into the soil.

Achillea
(a-kil-EE-a)
YARROW

Achillea millefollium 'Fire King'

Hardiness: *Zones 3-8*

Plant type: *herbaceous perennial*

Height: *1 to 3 feet*

Interest: *flowers, foliage*

Soil: *average to poor, well-drained*

Light: *full sun to full shade*

Yarrow is a summer-blooming, drought-tolerant perennial suitable for a sunny border or wildflower garden.

Selected species and varieties: *A.* 'Coronation Gold'—2½ to 3 feet tall, with yellow flowers blooming over a long season and gray-green fernlike leaves; 'Hoffnung' grows to 1½ feet, with antique yellow flowers; 'Moonshine', to 2 feet, with pale yellow flowers good for cutting and gray leaves; *A.* x 'Paprika', to 1½ feet, with hot pink flowers fading to creamy yellow. *A. millefolium* 'Cerise Queen', cherry red flowers; 'Fire King', deep rose-red flowers; 'Rosea', to 2 feet, with dense pink flower heads from midsummer to fall; Zones 4-8.

Growing conditions and maintenance: Some yarrows are fast spreading and may become invasive. They tolerate considerable neglect and can withstand drought and infertile soils. When grown in rich soil with abundant moisture, they become weak-stemmed and produce poor-quality flowers. They are easily divided in spring or fall.

Aconitum
(ak-o-NY-tum)
MONKSHOOD

Aconitum napellus

Hardiness: *Zones 3-8*

Plant type: *herbaceous perennial*

Height: *2 to 4 feet*

Interest: *flowers, foliage*

Soil: *fertile, moist, well-drained, acid*

Light: *partial shade*

Monkshood produces lush, glossy green foliage that remains attractive throughout the growing season. Tall, upright stems of blue or purple helmet-shaped flowers appear from mid to late summer.

Selected species and varieties: *A. carmichaelii*—2 to 4 feet tall, with leathery, dark green leaves and deep blue flowers that bloom in late summer on strong stems. *A. napellus*—3 to 4 feet, with finely divided leaves and blue to violet flowers from mid to late summer. *A.* x *bicolor*—a hybrid between *A. napellus* and *A. variegatum* that has given rise to many attractive garden hybrids, including 'Spark's Variety', with deep violet-blue flowers.

Growing conditions and maintenance: Though it prefers partial shade, monkshood will tolerate full sun if it receives ample water. Plants should not be allowed to dry out. Taller types may need staking. They can remain undisturbed indefinitely. The leaves and roots are poisonous, so do not plant near a vegetable garden.

Aeonium
(ee-OH-nee-um)
AEONIUM

Aeonium arboreum 'Schwartzkopf

Hardiness: *Zones 9-10*

Plant type: *succulent perennial*

Height: *1 to 3 feet*

Interest: *flowers, foliage*

Soil: *light, well-drained*

Light: *full sun*

Aeoniums bear fleshy leaves in attractive rosettes on succulent stems. Flowers in shades of yellow develop in terminal pyramidal clusters. Aeoniums are prized for their long season of interest in West Coast gardens, where they are often used as accents in rock gardens, dry borders, and containers.

Selected species and varieties: *A. arboreum* 'Schwartzkopf'—2 to 3 feet tall, upright and shrubby, with golden yellow flowers and dark, shiny, purple-black leaves appearing in 6- to 8-inch rosettes on branched stems. *A. tabuliforme*—12 inches, with pale yellow flowers and leaves forming saucer-shaped, stemless rosettes 3 to 10 inches across.

Growing conditions and maintenance: Aeoniums thrive in California coastal conditions, and they enjoy high humidity and mild temperatures. They can be grown farther inland, but may require some shade for protection from midday heat. They do not tolerate frost.

Agave
(a-GAH-vay)
CENTURY PLANT

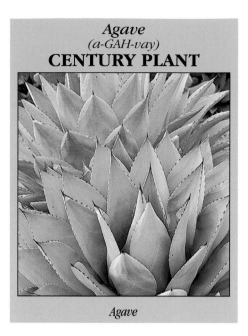

Agave

Hardiness: *Zones 9-10*

Plant type: *succulent perennial*

Height: *5 to 6 feet*

Interest: *foliage, flowers*

Soil: *sandy, well-drained*

Light: *full sun*

The century plant is an effective accent or barrier in warm, dry climates. Planted in groups, it will naturalize on dry banks.

Selected species and varieties: *A. americana*—leaves up to 6 feet long in a basal rosette; they are gray-green, succulent, stiff, evergreen, and armed with spines along the margin and tip; when plants reach 6 to 10 years of age, a branched flower stalk rises from the rosette and may grow 15 to 40 feet; the fragrant, yellow-green flowers appear in summer and last 1 to 2 months.

Growing conditions and maintenance: Good drainage is essential for the century plant. It is very drought tolerant; its leaves may shrivel under extremely dry conditions but will recover as soon as water is supplied. After flowering, the plant dies, leaving dozens of small plantlets around the base of the original rosette; these should be transplanted to separate locations when small.

Agonis
(a-GO-nis)
PEPPERMINT TREE

Agonis flexuosa

Hardiness: *Zone 10*

Plant type: *evergreen tree*

Height: *25 to 35 feet*

Interest: *foliage, bark, flowers*

Soil: *well-drained to dry*

Light: *full sun to partial shade*

The peppermint tree is a fast-growing evergreen for warm climates. Its leaves are willowlike and are borne on graceful, arching branches. It is a good choice for a wide-spreading lawn tree, street tree, or large container plant.

Selected species and varieties: *A. flexuosa*—to 35 feet, with an equal spread of deep green leaves that grow 3 to 6 inches long and are aromatic when crushed; small white, fragrant flowers appear in early summer, followed by woody capsules; has attractive reddish brown, vertically fissured bark.

Growing conditions and maintenance: The peppermint tree requires a nearly frost-free location; it will die back to the ground if temperatures fall below 25° F. It thrives in warm coastal locations and is tolerant of most soils and moisture conditions.

Ajuga
(a-JOO-ga)
BUGLEWEED

Ajuga reptans

Hardiness: *Zones 3-9*

Plant type: *herbaceous perennial*

Height: *6 to 9 inches*

Interest: *foliage, flowers, form*

Soil: *well-drained, acid*

Light: *full sun to partial shade*

Ajuga is an effective ground cover for sites under trees where grass will not grow. Its colorful foliage is effective year round, making it an excellent choice for the foreground of a shrub border or rock garden. The flowers are usually blue and are borne on short, erect stems from spring to early summer.

Selected species and varieties: *A. pyramidalis*—4 to 6 inches tall with blue flowers, it forms a neat clump and is slower spreading than other species; 'Metallica Crispa' grows 6 inches tall, with deep green to purple leaves of wrinkled texture. *A. reptans*—6 to 9 inches tall, it spreads fast to form a dense mat of deep green leaves, with violet-blue flowers; 'Bronze Beauty' has bronze leaves; 'Catlan's Giant' reaches 8 inches tall, with large green leaves; 'Silver Beauty', green-and-white variegated leaves.

Growing conditions and maintenance: Ajuga is adaptable to moist or dry soils. *A. reptans* spreads rapidly by stolons and may become invasive. Divide plants in spring or fall to prevent overcrowding.

Aloe
(AL-oh)
ALOE

Aloe striata

Hardiness: *Zones 10-11*

Plant type: *succulent perennial*

Height: *1½ to 3 feet*

Interest: *foliage, form*

Soil: *dry to well-drained*

Light: *full sun*

Aloes thrive in warm, dry climates. Although they are primarily grown for their attractive rosette-forming leaves, some species produce exotic flowers as well. They can be effectively used as specimens, ground covers, container plants, or in a rock garden.

Selected species and varieties: *A. striata* (coral aloe)—1½ to 3 feet tall, forming large clumps; grows thick, succulent, sword-shaped, gray-green leaves 15 to 20 inches long with pink margins, 12 to 20 per rosette; its flowers are tubular, coral red on well-branched stems; numerous hybrids are available.

Growing conditions and maintenance: Aloes tolerate seaside conditions, poor soil, and drought; excess water promotes root rot. They prefer a frost-free location; serious injury occurs at temperatures below 25° F. Once aloes are established, the only care they require is occasional deep watering.

Amelanchier
(am-el-ANG-kee-er)
SERVICEBERRY

Amelanchier alnifolia

Hardiness: *Zones 4-9*

Plant type: *large shrub or tree*

Height: *15 to 40 feet*

Interest: *foliage, flowers, fruit, bark*

Soil: *moist, well-drained, acid*

Light: *full sun to partial shade*

Serviceberry provides year-round landscape interest. White flower clusters appear in early spring; leaves emerge purplish gray and change to deep green in summer and to shades of yellow to apricot and red in fall. The smooth gray bark is attractive all winter.

Selected species and varieties: *A. arborea*—30 to 40 feet in the wild, rarely above 20 feet in cultivation; leaves grow 1 to 3 inches long, flowers form 2- to 4-inch pendulous clusters, and fruit is blueberry-like and attracts birds; it is useful in naturalized areas, woodland gardens, and mixed-shrub borders.

Growing conditions and maintenance: Serviceberry is often found growing wild beside stream banks, at the edge of woodlands, or along fence rows. In the garden, it tolerates a broad range of moisture conditions. Pruning is generally not necessary except to remove damaged wood.

Amsonia
(am-SO-nee-a)
BLUESTAR

Amsonia tabernaemontana

Hardiness: *Zones 3-9*

Plant type: *herbaceous perennial*

Height: *2 to 3 feet*

Interest: *foliage, flowers*

Soil: *moderately fertile, well-drained*

Light: *full sun to partial shade*

Amsonia produces pale blue, star-shaped blossoms. Appearing in late spring and early summer, they are particularly effective combined with more brightly colored flowers. The densely mounded, willow-like leaves remain attractive throughout the growing season, providing a lovely foil for later-blooming perennials.

Selected species and varieties: *A. tabernaemontana*—produces steel blue flowers in terminal clusters on 2- to 3-foot-tall, stiff, erect stems with many leaves 3 to 6 inches long that turn yellow in fall; *A. t.* var. *salicifolia* has longer and thinner leaves and blooms slightly later than the species.

Growing conditions and maintenance: Amsonias grown in shade have a more open habit than those grown in sun. In poor to moderately fertile soil, amsonia stems rarely need staking; avoid highly fertile soil, which produces rank, floppy growth. Except for propagating, division is usually not necessary.

Anemone
(a-NEM-o-nee)
WINDFLOWER

Anemone blanda

Hardiness: *Zones 3-8*

Plant type: *herbaceous perennial*

Height: *3 inches to 4 feet*

Interest: *flowers*

Soil: *fertile, moist, well-drained*

Light: *partial shade to full sun*

Anemones vary in habit, height, flowering season, and color. Spring-blooming species are suited for the front of a border or rock garden. Fall-flowering anemones are taller, more upright, and useful for the middle or back of a border.

Selected species and varieties: *A.* x *hybrida*—stems 2 to 4 feet tall, with fall-blooming pink or white, single, semidouble, or double flowers, Zones 4-8; 'Honorine Jobert' grows to 3 feet with white flowers; 'Margarete', 2 to 3 feet tall with semidouble pink blooms; 'September Charm', 2½ feet, with single silvery pink flowers. *A. hupehensis* var. *japonica*—similar to *A.* x *hybrida*, with pink to purple flowers; Zones 6-8. *A. vitifolia* 'Robustissima'—3 to 4 feet tall, with pink flowers in late summer and fall. *A. blanda*—3- to 8-inch midspring flowers in blue, red, white, or pink; Zones 5-8.

Growing conditions and maintenance: Although they prefer partial shade, anemones will tolerate full sun with adequate water. Incorporate generous amounts of organic matter into the soil. *A. blanda* is grown from tubers planted in fall. Fall-blooming types may need staking.

Aquilegia
(ak-wil-EE-jee-a)
COLUMBINE

Aquilegia canadensis

Hardiness: *Zones 3-9*

Plant type: *herbaceous perennial*

Height: *2 to 3 feet*

Interest: *flowers, foliage*

Soil: *moist, well-drained, acid*

Light: *full sun to partial shade*

Columbines are dainty plants bearing unusual spurred flowers and fernlike leaves. They are useful in the border, naturalized areas, and rock gardens.

Selected species and varieties: *A. canadensis*—2 to 3 feet tall, forming a rounded clump of finely divided leaves; in spring and early summer, each nodding stem produces several yellow-and-red flowers that attract hummingbirds and stay in bloom longer than many species with larger flowers; 'Corbett' has yellow flowers.

Growing conditions and maintenance: Columbine does not do well in dry soil; add organic matter to the soil before planting to help retain moisture. Though plants are generally short-lived (2 or 3 years), *A. canadensis* self-sows readily. Leaf miners often infest plantings; infected leaves should be removed.

Arbutus
(ar-BEW-tus)
STRAWBERRY TREE

Arbutus unedo

Hardiness: *Zones 7-9*

Plant type: *large shrub or small tree*

Height: *8 to 12 feet*

Interest: *foliage, bark, flowers, fruit*

Soil: *well-drained, acid*

Light: *full sun to partial shade*

The strawberry tree provides interest in southern and West Coast gardens throughout the year. The leaves are evergreen, the bark is deep reddish brown and exfoliates, and the branches become attractively gnarled with age. Small urn-shaped flowers grow in 2-inch clusters in the fall, and the orange-red berrylike fruit ripens the following season.

Selected species and varieties: *A. unedo* 'Compacta'—a slow-growing dwarf variety that eventually reaches 8 to 12 feet in height, it produces flowers, fruit, and dark green leaves almost continuously; useful as a hedge, as a specimen, or in a mixed-shrub border.

Growing conditions and maintenance: Plant where leaves will be protected from drying winds. The strawberry tree tolerates a wide range of soil conditions as long as drainage is good. It requires watering only during periods of drought. It is also tolerant of seaside conditions.

Arctostaphylos
(ark-toh-STAF-i-los)
BEARBERRY

Arctostaphylos densiflora

Hardiness: *Zones 2-10*

Plant type: *ground cover or shrub*

Height: *6 inches to 8 feet*

Interest: *foliage, flowers, fruit, bark*

Soil: *poor, sandy, acid*

Light: *full sun to partial shade*

Bearberry is an evergreen bearing tiny urn-shaped, spring-blooming flowers.

Selected species and varieties: *A. uva-ursi*—a ground cover that grows 6 to 12 inches high, with trailing stems up to 15 feet long and leathery, dark green leaves; it produces white flowers with a pink blush and, in late summer, bright red fruit that attracts birds; Zones 2-7. *A. densiflora*—grows 4 to 6 feet tall and equally as wide, with mahogany red bark and pink or white flowers in early spring; it is useful in a mixed-shrub border or as a specimen; Zones 7-10.

Growing conditions and maintenance: Both species require well-drained soil. They are drought resistant, though periodic deep watering is suggested during droughts. They are difficult to transplant except from containers. *A. uva-ursi* requires no pruning. *A. densiflora* is primarily grown on the West Coast. It may be pruned to reveal attractive bark and a branching habit.

Aronia
(a-RO-nee-a)
CHOKEBERRY

Aronia arbutifolia 'Brilliantissima'

Hardiness: *Zones 4-9*

Plant type: *deciduous shrub*

Height: *6 to 10 feet*

Interest: *fruit*

Soil: *well-drained*

Light: *full sun to partial shade*

Chokeberry bears a profusion of bright red berries in the fall that persist into winter and attract birds. It is an effective plant for massing or combining with other shrubs in a mixed border.

Selected species and varieties: *A. arbutifolia* 'Brilliantissima'—has dark green, lustrous leaves that turn scarlet in fall; flowers appear in spring in clusters 1 to 1½ inches in diameter; its flowers and fruit grow more abundantly than those of the species.

Growing conditions and maintenance: Chokeberry is easy to transplant and tolerant of almost any soil, but it will produce more fruit and better fall color in sun than in shade. Suckers growing from the base may become a nuisance.

Asclepias
(as-KLEE-pee-as)
BUTTERFLY WEED

Asclepias tuberosa

Hardiness: *Zones 3-9*

Plant type: *herbaceous perennial*

Height: *18 to 36 inches*

Interest: *flowers*

Soil: *dry, poor*

Light: *full sun*

Butterfly weed is a long-lived perennial that requires minimal care. Its flowers are usually vivid orange, though yellow and red flowers occasionally occur both in the wild and in cultivation. Flowering begins in late spring and may continue until late summer.

Selected species and varieties: *A. tuberosa*—stems are erect, to 3 feet, with thin pointed leaves along the entire length; individual flowers grow ¼ inch across in terminal clusters and are excellent for fresh or dried arrangements; the milkweedlike pods are also useful for dried arrangements.

Growing conditions and maintenance: Butterfly weed does not grow well in wet areas or where it must compete with tree roots. A taproot makes transplanting difficult, so once established the plant should be left alone; it will not spread invasively. It emerges late in the spring, so mark its location to avoid planting something on top of it.

Astilbe
(a-STIL-bee)
ASTILBE, FALSE SPIREA

Astilbe x arendsii 'Fanal'

Hardiness: *Zones 4-8*

Plant type: *herbaceous perennial*

Height: *8 inches to 4 feet*

Interest: *flowers, foliage*

Soil: *fertile, moist, well-drained*

Light: *full sun to partial shade*

Astilbes grace a garden with their mounds of fernlike foliage that range in color from deep green to bronze. Their plumelike flowers rise above the leaves in early to late summer. Astilbes are an excellent choice for the edge of a woodland garden, the front or middle of a border, or on the bank of a stream or garden pond.

Selected species and varieties: *A. taquetii* 'Superba'—to 4 feet tall, with pinkish purple flowers in late summer. *A. chinensis* 'Pumila'—8 to 15 inches tall, with a spreading habit and mauve-pink flowers in mid to late summer. *A.* x *arendsii* 'Fanal'—2 feet tall, with bronze leaves and carmine red flowers in early to midsummer.

Growing conditions and maintenance: Before planting astilbes, add generous amounts of organic matter to the soil to aid moisture retention. The foliage will shrivel and turn brown if allowed to dry out. Astilbe is a heavy feeder and should be divided every 3 to 4 years to maintain vigor and prolific flowering.

Baptisia
(bap-TIZ-ee-a)
WILD INDIGO

Baptisia australis

Hardiness: *Zones 3-9*

Plant type: *herbaceous perennial*

Height: *3 to 4 feet*

Interest: *flowers, foliage*

Soil: *well-drained to dry, sandy*

Light: *full sun*

Wild (false) indigo produces dainty, blue pealike flowers from midspring to early summer. Its blue-green leaves are an attractive foil for both its own blooms and those of surrounding plants. The leaves remain handsome throughout the growing season. The plant is useful for the back of a border or as a specimen; its pods are used in dried arrangements.

Selected species and varieties: *B. australis*—erect stems to 4 feet in height, producing compound leaves with three leaflets, each 1½ to 3 inches long, and indigo blue flowers in long, terminal racemes, good for cutting. *B. alba*—to 3 feet tall with white flowers; Zones 5-8.

Growing conditions and maintenance: Wild indigo adapts to almost any well-drained soil. It is slow growing and noninvasive. Tall selections may require staking. Remove faded flowers to extend the blooming season.

Berberis
(BER-ber-is)
BARBERRY

Berberis thunbergii 'Crimson Pigmy'

Hardiness: *Zones 4-8*

Plant type: *shrub*

Height: *3 to 10 feet*

Interest: *foliage, fruit*

Soil: *moist, well-drained, acid*

Light: *full sun to light shade*

Barberries are useful as foundation plantings, barriers, hedges, or specimens. Varieties with yellow or red foliage provide dramatic color contrast in the landscape and are good candidates for shrub borders and for combining with perennials. This genus includes both deciduous and evergreen species, which vary in height, form, and foliage color. All of the barberries produce spines along their stems, are adaptable to a wide range of growing conditions, and are extremely easy to cultivate.

Selected species and varieties: *B. thunbergii* 'Aurea'—deciduous, 3 to 4 feet tall, and slow growing, with bright yellow leaves when grown in full sun, yellow-green in shade; excellent for foliage contrast in mixed-shrub plantings; Zones 4-8. *B. thunbergii* 'Atropurpurea'—4 to 6 feet tall with an equal or greater spread and a dense, rounded habit; bears burgundy red foliage all season, yellow flowers in spring, and small, bright red berries in fall that persist into winter and keep the plant interesting after the leaves fall; 'Crimson Pigmy' grows 1½ to 2 feet tall by 3 to 5 feet wide, with a dense, moundlike

habit; 'Golden Ring', 4 to 6 feet tall with an equal or greater spread, and purplish red leaves with a green or yellow-green margin; 'Rose Glow', 4 to 5 feet tall with an equal spread and leaves that emerge rose-pink and become marbled with deeper pink and burgundy red as they mature; Zones 4-8. *B. julianae* (wintergreen barberry)—evergreen forming a dense mound that becomes 6 to 10 feet tall and equally as wide; it produces narrow, 2- to 3-inch-long leaves that are a lustrous dark green above and pale green below with spiny, serrated margins; clusters of yellow flowers bloom in early spring and are followed by blue-black fruit in summer that persists into fall; wintergreen barberry makes an impenetrable hedge or dense screen; Zones 5-8.

Growing conditions and maintenance: Barberries are tolerant of most soil conditions as long as good drainage is provided; they do not adapt well to a soil that is very moist. They withstand dry

Berberis thunbergii 'Aurea'

soils and urban conditions such as air pollution. Foliage color is best when they are grown in full sun. Pruning is generally unnecessary except to remove damaged branches.

Bergenia
(ber-JEN-ee-a)
BERGENIA

Bergenia cordifolia

Hardiness: *Zones 3-8*

Plant type: *herbaceous perennial*

Height: *8 to 18 inches*

Interest: *foliage, flowers*

Soil: *moist, well-drained*

Light: *full sun to partial shade*

The shiny evergreen leaves of bergenia, in their basal clumps, provide textural contrast to more delicately proportioned plants at the front of a herbaceous border or rock garden. They also create an interesting ground cover in front of shrubs. Their spring flowers are usually pink and are of secondary interest to the leaves.

Selected species and varieties: *B. cordifolia*—12 to 18 inches in height, with heart-shaped leaves and pink flowers. *B.* 'Abendglut'—9 inches tall, with maroon leaves and deep magenta flowers. *B.* 'Morgenrote'—grows 8 to 12 inches in height, with deep green foliage and carmine red blooms. *B.* 'Silberlicht'—produces white flowers that turn pink later in the season.

Growing conditions and maintenance: Although bergenias prefer a soil with abundant organic matter, they are tolerant of most soil conditions. They spread by rhizomes, and in fertile sites must be divided every 3 or 4 years, after flowering. In drier, less fertile situations, they can remain undisturbed for many years.

Boltonia
(bowl-TO-nee-a)
BOLTONIA

Boltonia asteroides 'Snowbank'

Hardiness: *Zones 4-8*

Plant type: *herbaceous perennial*

Height: *3 to 4 feet*

Interest: *flowers*

Soil: *moist, well-drained*

Light: *full sun*

Boltonia offers flowers from midsummer through fall, providing an extended display for the back of a mixed border or center of an island bed. Its daisylike blossoms appear above tall stems with narrow, gray-green willowlike leaves.

Selected species and varieties: *B. asteroides* 'Snowbank'—3 to 4 feet tall, with a compact, self-supporting habit; it produces white flowers ¾ to 1 inch across, borne profusely on branched stems.

Growing conditions and maintenance: Boltonia is adaptable to most sunny sites. In loose, moist soil it tends to spread more rapidly than in dry soil, but it is not generally invasive. Pinching off the tops of plants in late spring encourages bushy, compact growth. It can be divided in spring or fall.

Brunnera
(BRUN-er-a)
BRUNNERA

Brunnera macrophylla

Hardiness: *Zones 3-8*

Plant type: *herbaceous perennial*

Height: *12 to 18 inches*

Interest: *flowers, foliage*

Soil: *moist, well-drained*

Light: *partial shade*

Brunnera is a richly colored foreground plant or ground cover for a shady, moist area. Its dark green foliage contrasts well with the tiny deep blue flowers that are borne in branched clusters in spring and early summer.

Selected species and varieties: *B. macrophylla*—rounded habit, 12 to 18 inches tall and wide, with heart-shaped leaves up to 8 inches across and blue star-shaped flowers ⅛ to ¼ inch across.

Growing conditions and maintenance: Although brunnera prefers moist soil, it will tolerate dry soil as long as there is shade. For use as a ground cover, space plants 15 inches apart. When the clump shows signs of deterioration at the center (usually after several years of growth), dig it up and divide the vigorous outer portions for replanting, discarding the center.

Buxus
(BUK-sus)
BOXWOOD

Buxus sempervirens

Hardiness: *Zones 4-9*

Plant type: *shrub*

Height: *2 to 20 feet*

Interest: *foliage*

Soil: *well-drained*

Light: *full sun to light shade*

Boxwood is an elegant, long-lived evergreen shrub whose tiny leaves impart a fine texture to any planting. It is well suited for use as a hedge, an edging, or a foundation planting.

Selected species and varieties: *B. microphylla koreana*—to 2½ feet tall and twice as wide, hardy to Zone 4; 'Wintergreen' grows 2 feet tall and 4 feet wide, retains bright green leaf color throughout winter when many other varieties fade to brownish green, and is hardy to Zone 6. *B. sempervirens*—to 20 feet tall and wide, with a moundlike habit, hardy to Zone 5 or 6 depending on variety; 'Handsworthiensis' has handsome dark green leaves and a large, upright form, good for hedges; 'Suffruticosa' is a dwarf form, extremely slow growing to just 3 feet; 'Vardar Valley' also grows to 3 feet tall and spreads to 5 feet wide, with a flat-topped habit and dark blue-green leaves.

Growing conditions and maintenance: Plant boxwood in well-drained soil amended with organic matter in a site protected from drying winds. Mulch to help retain moisture. In warm climates, partial shade is beneficial.

Calamagrostis
(kal-a-ma-GROS-tis)
REED GRASS

Calamagrostis x acutiflora 'Karl Foerster'

Hardiness: *Zones 6-9*

Plant type: *ornamental grass*

Height: *4 to 7 feet*

Interest: *flowers, foliage*

Soil: *well-drained, acid*

Light: *full sun to partial shade*

Reed grass has a slender, erect habit that provides a vertical accent in the border. As one of the first grasses to bloom, it offers a long season of interest.

Selected species and varieties: *C.* x *acutiflora* 'Karl Foerster'—4 to 6 feet tall, with pink flowers maturing to golden tan from early summer to fall; 'Stricta', 5 to 7 feet tall, with greenish pink flowers appearing about 2 weeks later than those of 'Karl Foerster' and lasting through fall.

Growing conditions and maintenance: Reed grass is adaptable to a wide range of conditions, tolerating both heavy soils and poor, dry soils. It withstands moist to wet areas as well as drought. It is effective used as a garden accent, as a specimen, or massed beside ponds or streams.

Calycanthus
(kal-i-KAN-thus)
SWEET SHRUB

Calycanthus floridus 'Athens'

Hardiness: *Zones 4-9*

Plant type: *shrub*

Height: *6 to 9 feet*

Interest: *flowers, fragrance*

Soil: *moist, well-drained*

Light: *full sun to partial shade*

Sweet shrub is an adaptable plant that blends well with other shrubs in many garden settings. Its summer flowers are unusual looking and produce a delightfully fruity fragrance.

Selected species and varieties: *C. floridus*—6 to 9 feet tall and up to 12 feet wide, with long, dark green aromatic leaves that are deciduous but persist late into fall; rounded, fragrant, dark burgundy flowers with spreading, straplike petals blooming from late spring through early summer; and urn-shaped fruit persisting into winter; 'Athens' is a cultivar with highly fragrant yellow flowers.

Growing conditions and maintenance: Although it prefers moist, deep, well-drained soil, sweet shrub tolerates other soil conditions. It is easily transplanted. Suckers sometimes present a problem in beds.

Camellia
(kah-MEEL-ee-a)
CAMELLIA

Camellia japonica

Hardiness: *Zones 8-10*

Plant type: *shrub or small tree*

Height: *6 to 25 feet*

Interest: *flowers, foliage*

Soil: *moist, well-drained, acid*

Light: *partial shade*

Camellias are dense evergreens that produce very showy flowers in shades of pink, rose, white, and red. The flowers bloom from fall through spring and may be single, semidouble, or double.

Selected species and varieties: *C. japonica* (Japanese camellia)—grows 10 to 25 feet tall as a large shrub or a small tree, with a dense, upright habit, dark glossy evergreen leaves, and flowers 3 to 5 inches across from late winter through spring. *C. sasanqua* (sasanqua camellia)—6 to 10 feet tall, with a pyramidal habit, dark glossy evergreen leaves, and flowers 2 to 3 inches across blooming from fall to winter; varieties with increased cold hardiness include 'Polar Ice', 'Snow Flurry', 'Winter's Charm', 'Winter's Dream', 'Winter's Hope', 'Winter's Interlude', 'Winter's Rose', 'Winter's Star', and 'Winter's Waterlily'.

Growing conditions and maintenance: Camellias require protection from winter winds. They benefit from the addition of generous amounts of organic matter to the soil. Keep them continuously mulched, and do not overfertilize.

Campanula
(kam-PAN-ew-la)
BELLFLOWER

Campanula portenschlagiana

Hardiness: *Zones 3-9*

Plant type: *herbaceous perennial*

Height: *4 to 12 inches*

Interest: *flowers, foliage*

Soil: *moist, well-drained*

Light: *full sun to partial shade*

The Dalmatian and Serbian bellflowers, which are small with delicate blue flowers, are actually quite vigorous and well suited for rock gardens, dry walls, or the front of a border. They have a creeping, spreading habit and form attractive clumps of neat foliage. The flowers appear in sprays above the leaves.

Selected species and varieties: *C. portenschlagiana* (Dalmatian bellflower)—4 to 8 inches tall, spreading, with rounded, sharply serrated leaves and star-shaped, lilac-blue flowers blooming from late spring to early summer; hardy to Zone 5. *C. poscharskyana* (Serbian bellflower) —8 to 12 inches tall, up to 18 inches wide, with midsummer-blooming lilac flowers and roots that may become invasive; hardy to Zone 4.

Growing conditions and maintenance: Both species thrive when grown among rocks or cascading over walls. In warmer zones, they benefit from partial shade and supplemental moisture.

Carex
(KAY-reks)
SEDGE

Carex morrowii 'Variegata'

Hardiness: *Zones 5-9*

Plant type: *ornamental grass*

Height: *6 to 18 inches*

Interest: *foliage*

Soil: *moist, well-drained*

Light: *full sun to full shade*

Sedge is a clump-forming plant with grasslike leaves. Unlike most ornamental grasses, it can grow in the shade, making it a good choice for massing in the front of a shady border or edging a shady walk. Its leaves are arching and often unusually colored; the flowers are insignificant.

Selected species and varieties: *C. glauca*—6 inches tall, with blue-green leaves; good for rock gardens, massing, or containers. *C. morrowii* 'Variegata'—12 to 18 inches tall; the semievergreen leaves have a white stripe down the center; it makes an excellent ground cover or edging.

Growing conditions and maintenance: Although sedge thrives in shade, it adapts to full sun as long as it receives sufficient water. It produces such dense mounds of growth that few weeds are able to penetrate. The clumps can be divided in the spring.

Caryopteris
(kar-ee-OP-ter-is)
BLUEBEARD

Caryopteris x clandonensis 'Dark Knight'

Hardiness: *Zones 6-9*

Plant type: *shrub*

Height: *1½ to 4 feet*

Interest: *flowers, foliage*

Soil: *light, well-drained*

Light: *full sun*

Bluebeard is a small deciduous shrub with pleasantly aromatic flowers, stems, and leaves. The slender, upright stems form a rounded mound of gray-green foliage that is topped with blue flowers from mid to late summer.

Selected species and varieties: *C.* x *clandonensis* 'Blue Mist'—2 feet tall, with powder blue flowers; 'Dark Knight', 2 feet tall, deep purple flowers; 'Longwood Blue', 1½ to 2 feet tall, violet-blue flowers with dark stamens.

Growing conditions and maintenance: Although it produces woody stems, bluebeard is best treated as a herbaceous perennial; cut it back to the ground in the winter. When flower production wanes in the summer, a light pruning will often stimulate a second flush of blooms.

Ceanothus
(see-a-NO-thus)
WILD LILAC

Ceanothus 'Dark Star'

Ceratostigma
(ser-at-o-STIG-ma)
PLUMBAGO, LEADWORT

Ceratostigma plumbaginoides

Cercis
(SER-sis)
REDBUD

Cercis occidentalis

Hardiness: *Zones 9-11*

Plant type: *shrub*

Height: *4 to 15 feet*

Interest: *flowers, foliage*

Soil: *light, well-drained*

Light: *full sun*

Hardiness: *Zones 5-10*

Plant type: *herbaceous perennial or shrub*

Height: *8 to 48 inches*

Interest: *flowers, foliage*

Soil: *well-drained*

Light: *full sun to partial shade*

Hardiness: *Zones 4-10*

Plant type: *tree*

Height: *10 to 35 feet*

Interest: *flowers, foliage*

Soil: *moist, well-drained*

Light: *full sun to light shade*

The wild lilac is a free-flowering plant well adapted to the rugged coastal conditions of the West. It is useful planted in masses on dry, sunny slopes or as a screen. Individual plants make fine garden accents or specimens.

Selected species and varieties: *C.* 'Dark Star'—4 to 6 feet tall, 5 to 6 feet wide, with evergreen leaves ¼ to ½ inch long and cobalt blue flowers borne prolifically in spring; 'Gloire de Versailles' is deciduous and flowers late in the growing season; 'Ray Hartman' reaches 15 feet tall and 10 to 20 feet wide, and can be trained as a small tree; it has dark, glossy, evergreen leaves 1 to 2 inches long and spring-blooming, medium blue flowers in 3- to 5-inch clusters.

Growing conditions and maintenance: Wild lilacs thrive in hot, dry conditions and can withstand wind and drought. They do not tolerate heavy soils or overwatering. Plant them in fall and water occasionally, allowing the soil to dry out well between waterings. Once established, the plants generally require no supplemental moisture.

Plumbago develops shiny leaves and blue flowers that bloom late in the season. Low-growing species are effectively used as a ground cover for shrub borders, an edging for a garden walk, or creeping among stones in a rock garden. Taller types make attractive additions to a mixed-shrub border.

Selected species and varieties: *C. plumbaginoides*—8 to 12 inches tall and 18 inches wide, with leaves to 3 inches, turning bronze in fall in cool climates, and dark blue, saucer-shaped flowers in summer to late fall; hardy to Zone 6. *C. willmottianum*—to 4 feet, upright, deciduous; has 2-inch leaves and bears 1-inch bright blue flowers continuously from midsummer through fall; hardy to Zone 8.

Growing conditions and maintenance: Plumbago requires good drainage but is otherwise tolerant of most soils. It will die out in soils that remain wet over the winter, and it does not compete well with tree roots. Mark the location of *C. plumbaginoides* because it is slow to emerge in spring.

The redbud's early-season flowers signal the start of spring. It is effective as a specimen, in small groups, or in a woodland garden. Trees begin blooming when they are very young.

Selected species and varieties: *C. canadensis* (Eastern redbud)—20 to 30 feet tall with 25- to 35-foot spread, trunk often divided close to ground to produce interesting branching habit, leaves heart shaped, 3 to 5 inches across, flower buds reddish purple, opening to pink in early spring, Zones 4-9; 'Forest Pansy'—purple foliage. *C. occidentalis* (California redbud)—10 to 15 feet; Zones 8-10. *C. reniformis* (Texas redbud)—to 35 feet; Zones 8-9.

Growing conditions and maintenance: Redbuds tolerate most soils as long as they are well drained. They thrive in full sun or as understory trees in a woodland garden. They require occasional pruning to remove injured wood. Redbuds are short-lived, often surviving no longer than 10 to 15 years.

Chaenomeles (kee-NOM-e-leez) **FLOWERING QUINCE**	*Chamaecyparis* (kam-ee-SIP-a-ris) **FALSE CYPRESS**	*Chrysogonum* (kris-AHG-o-num) **GOLDENSTAR**

Chaenomeles speciosa 'Texas Scarlet'	*Chamaecyparis obtusa 'Crippsii'*	*Chrysogonum virginianum var. virginianum*

Hardiness: *Zones 4-8*

Plant type: *shrub*

Height: *3 to 10 feet*

Interest: *flowers*

Soil: *light to heavy, acid*

Light: *full sun to partial shade*

Flowering quince produces brightly colored flowers in early spring. Its dense growth habit makes it useful as a hedge or barrier.

Selected species and varieties: *C. speciosa* 'Cameo'—compact form, 3 to 5 feet, produces abundant, double, apricot pink flowers; 'Nivalis'—vigorous, large upright form with white flowers; 'Texas Scarlet'—3 to 5 feet tall, low-spreading habit, intense tomato red flowers.

Growing conditions and maintenance: Flowering quince is extremely easy to grow and will tolerate most soil and light conditions. It may become chlorotic in alkaline soil and require supplemental iron. When plants become leggy or flowering is reduced, prune the largest stems back to the ground, or cut the entire plant back to 6 inches immediately after flowering in the spring. Because they have a short flowering season and lose their leaves early in the fall, they are best used as a background plant, or in combination with other flowering shrubs.

Hardiness: *Zones 4-8*

Plant type: *tree or shrub*

Height: *3 to 60 feet or more*

Interest: *foliage*

Soil: *rich, moist, well-drained*

Light: *full sun*

False cypresses are evergreens that offer a wide range of growth habits, foliage colors, and garden uses. Juvenile plants display needlelike leaves; adult foliage is scalelike. Smaller varieties are useful as specimens in beds or rock gardens; taller ones make attractive screens or specimens.

Selected species and varieties: *C. lawsoniana*—40 to 60 feet or taller, with a pyramidal outline, horizontal drooping branches, and a massive trunk; Zones 5-7. *C. obtusa* 'Compacta'—3 to 5 feet tall, with blue-green leaves; 'Crippsii' grows to 30 feet tall with yellow-green leaves; 'Nana Gracilis', 4 to 6 feet with dark green leaves; Zones 4-8.

Growing conditions and maintenance: Although they prefer full sun, false cypresses will tolerate light shade. They thrive in humid areas and should be protected from hot, drying winds.

Hardiness: *Zones 5-9*

Plant type: *herbaceous perennial*

Height: *4 to 9 inches*

Interest: *flowers, foliage*

Soil: *well-drained*

Light: *full sun to full shade*

The deep green foliage of goldenstar provides a lush background for its bright yellow, star-shaped flowers, which appear from late spring into summer. Its low-growing, spreading habit makes it useful as a ground cover, for edging at the front of a border, or in a rock garden.

Selected species and varieties: *C. virginianum* var. *virginianum*—6 to 9 inches, with dark green, bluntly serrated leaves along upright spreading stems, and flowers 1½ inches across that bloom throughout the spring in warm areas, well into summer in cooler zones; var. *australe* is similar to var. *virginianum* but more prostrate.

Growing conditions and maintenance: Goldenstar grows well in most soils with average fertility. For use as a ground cover, space plants 12 inches apart. Divide every other year in spring.

Cimicifuga
(si-mi-SIFF-yew-ga)
BUGBANE

Cimicifuga simplex 'White Pearl'

Hardiness: *Zones 3-9*

Plant type: *herbaceous perennial*

Height: *3 to 8 feet*

Interest: *flowers, foliage*

Soil: *rich, moist, well-drained*

Light: *full sun to partial shade*

Bugbane is a graceful perennial for the rear of a shady border or wildflower garden. Its tall spires of white flowers, borne well above handsome dark green leaves, are a welcome sight in late summer and fall. It is also a fine choice to plant alongside a pond or stream.

Selected species and varieties: *C. racemosa*—4 to 8 feet tall, with deep green compound leaves and white flowers in 3-foot wandlike clusters on branched stems, blooming in midsummer; 'Atropurpurea' has purple foliage; Zones 3-9. *C. simplex*—3 to 4 feet tall, with attractive light green buds that open in fall to reveal 1- to 2-foot white flower spires; 'White Pearl' grows 3 to 4 feet tall, with a compact habit and pure white flowers; Zones 4-8.

Growing conditions and maintenance: Bugbane will tolerate full sun in cooler areas provided there is ample moisture. Incorporate generous amounts of organic matter into the soil prior to planting.

Cistus
(SIS-tus)
ROCKROSE

Cistus x purpureus

Hardiness: *Zones 9-10*

Plant type: *shrub*

Height: *18 inches to 4 feet*

Interest: *flowers, foliage*

Soil: *dry to well-drained*

Light: *full sun*

Rockrose is well suited to dry areas of the West Coast. It adds a long season of color to mixed-shrub borders, rock gardens, and dry banks. Its leaves are aromatic and nearly evergreen. The flowers, which resemble roses, last only one day but are prolific; flowering continues over several weeks in the spring and early summer.

Selected species and varieties: *C.* x *purpureus*—3 to 4 feet tall and equally as wide, with attractive 2-inch-long leaves that are dark green on top, gray-green below, and reddish purple flowers with a red spot at the base in early summer. *C. salviifolius*—18 to 24 inches tall and up to 6 feet wide, with gray-green textured leaves and white flowers with a yellow spot at the base in late spring.

Growing conditions and maintenance: Rockroses grow well in dry, windy areas, tolerating drought, seaside conditions, and poor soil. They are useful as a fire retardant.

Clethra
(KLETH-ra)
SUMMER-SWEET

Clethra barbinervis

Hardiness: *Zones 3-9*

Plant type: *shrub*

Height: *3 to 20 feet*

Interest: *flowers, fragrance, foliage*

Soil: *moist, acid*

Light: *full sun to full shade*

Summer-sweet is well named; its pink or white flowers appear in midsummer and are delightfully fragrant. Tolerant of most growing conditions, this deciduous shrub can easily be sited in any mixed border or moist woodland garden.

Selected species and varieties: *C. alnifolia*—3 to 8 feet tall and 4 to 6 feet wide, it produces deep green leaves that turn gold in fall and very fragrant white flowers in 2- to 6-inch-long clusters; 'Hummingbird' grows to 4 feet with a dense habit; 'Pink Spires' has deep pink buds that open to soft pink flowers. *C. barbinervis*—10 to 20 feet tall, with dark green leaves in clusters at branch tips, fragrant white late-summer flowers in 4- to 6-inch-long clusters, and beautiful gray to brown, smooth, exfoliating bark; Zones 5-8.

Growing conditions and maintenance: Summer-sweet tolerates most soil types as well as coastal conditions. It thrives in both sun and shade. Incorporate organic matter into the soil prior to planting. Prune in early spring.

Coreopsis
(ko-ree-OP-sis)
TICKSEED

Coreopsis verticillata 'Zagreb'

Hardiness: *Zones 4-9*

Plant type: *herbaceous perennial*

Height: *6 inches to 3 feet*

Interest: *flowers, foliage*

Soil: *well-drained*

Light: *full sun*

Coreopsis provides a long season of flowers both for the garden and indoor arrangements. The delicate appearance of the blossoms belies the sturdiness and dependability of the plant.

Selected species and varieties: *C. auriculata*—12 to 24 inches tall, with 2-inch yellow-orange flowers; suitable as an edging or a ground cover. *C. rosea*—15 to 24 inches, with needlelike leaves and pink flowers with yellow centers. *C. verticillata*—2 to 3 feet, with lacy, threadlike leaves and yellow flowers 1 to 2 inches across; 'Moonbeam' grows 18 to 24 inches tall, with a compact habit and pale yellow flowers; 'Zagreb', 12 to 18 inches, bears bright yellow flowers.

Growing conditions and maintenance: Coreopsis thrives in nearly any well-drained soil and can tolerate drought. (*C. rosea* is an exception, preferring a heavier, moister soil.) Continuous flowering throughout the summer can be encouraged by removing faded blossoms. For massing or for use as a ground cover, space plants 12 to 18 inches apart.

Cornus
(KOR-nus)
DOGWOOD

Cornus mas

Hardiness: *Zones 2-8*

Plant type: *tree or shrub*

Height: *5 to 30 feet*

Interest: *flowers, foliage, fruit, bark*

Soil: *moist, well-drained, acid*

Light: *full sun to partial shade*

Dogwoods are extremely ornamental and adaptable deciduous trees and shrubs. Some are best known for their flowers, others for their bark or twig color. Many display vibrant fall foliage and colorful fruit. Most offer year-round interest in the garden and are useful as specimens, understory trees, or shrubs, or in a shrub border.

Selected species and varieties: *C. alba* 'Sibirica'—an 8- to 10-foot-tall shrub, growing 5 to 10 feet wide, with an erect, open habit, green stems that take on a red tinge in summer and turn coral red in winter, leaves that turn reddish purple in fall, and modest-looking yellowish white flowers in late spring, followed by white to bluish fruit; Zones 2-8. *C. kousa*—a tree growing 20 to 30 feet tall with an equal spread; its exfoliating bark is mottled gray, tan, and brown on older specimens, and the leaves often turn red in fall; small yellow-green flowers surrounded by showy white bracts appear in late spring to early summer and persist for several weeks, followed by raspberry-like red fruit in fall; Zones 5-8. *C.* x *rutgersensis* hybrids (crosses between *C.*

kousa and native Eastern dogwood, *C. florida*, which is susceptible to pests and diseases)—*C.* 'Aurora' (cv. Rutban) has white flowers in late spring and resists leaf spot, canker, borer, and anthracnose; *C.* 'Ruth Ellen' (cv. Rutlan) is a low-spreading tree that blooms slightly earlier than 'Aurora'; hardy to Zone 6. *C. mas*—a small tree or large shrub, 10 to 25 feet tall, 15 to 20 feet wide, with exfoliating gray-and-brown bark, bright yellow flowers in very early spring, and red fruit in late summer; Zones 4-8. *C. sericea*—a shrub, 7 to 9 feet tall, with a 10-foot spread, multiple bright red stems that arise from the crown, leaves that turn red in fall, and modest white flowers in late spring, followed by white fruit; 'Flaviramea' has yellow stems; Zones 2-8.

Growing conditions and maintenance: Dogwoods prefer a soil with generous amounts of organic matter added prior to planting. *C. kousa* prefers full sun. Thin the lower branches of *C. kousa* to

Cornus kousa

reveal attractive exfoliating bark. Occasionally prune the oldest stems of red-stemmed dogwoods to 6 inches above the ground in late winter to encourage vigorous growth.

Cotinus
(ko-TY-nus)
SMOKE TREE

Cotinus coggygria

Hardiness: *Zones 5-8*

Plant type: *tree or shrub*

Height: *10 to 15 feet*

Interest: *foliage, flowers*

Soil: *well-drained*

Light: *full sun*

The smoke tree is valued for its attractive foliage and the unusual, wispy flower stalks that create a smokelike appearance and are effective throughout the summer. It can be grown as a large shrub with a width equal to its height, or pruned to a multiple-stemmed, small tree. It offers a colorful contrast to a green lawn when planted as a specimen or can be effectively combined with other shrubs in a mixed border.

Selected species and varieties: *C. coggygria* 'Royal Purple'—compact form, with unusual feathery, dark pink to purplish red, 8-inch fruiting stalks and oval, very dark, maroon-red leaves 2 to 3 inches long that maintain color through fall.

Growing conditions and maintenance: The smoke tree prefers a soil that is not too rich. It can be cut back to the ground in winter to encourage vigorous shoot growth. To grow it as a tree, remove all but three or four branches from the base and lower laterals.

Crataegus
(kra-TEE-gus)
HAWTHORN

Crataegus viridis 'Winter King'

Hardiness: *Zones 4-7*

Plant type: *tree*

Height: *20 to 35 feet*

Interest: *foliage, flowers, fruit*

Soil: *well-drained*

Light: *full sun*

Hawthorns are small, broad trees, often bearing sharp thorns, that produce a lovely spring flower display and an equally attractive show of fall fruit. They are useful as individual specimens, in small groupings, or as large barrier plantings, where their thorns discourage intrusion.

Selected species and varieties: *C. viridis* 'Winter King' (green hawthorn)—to 35 feet tall and wide, dense and wide spreading, with lustrous green leaves in summer that turn purple to red in fall, white flowers in 2-inch clusters in late spring, and red fruit ½ inch in diameter, persisting into winter.

Growing conditions and maintenance: The green hawthorn tolerates a wide range of soils, provided they are well drained. Its dense foliage makes growing grass beneath it difficult. Prune as necessary in winter or early spring.

Daphne
(DAF-nee)
DAPHNE

Daphne odora 'Aureo-marginata'

Hardiness: *Zones 7-9*

Plant type: *shrub*

Height: *3 to 4 feet*

Interest: *flowers*

Soil: *well-drained, alkaline*

Light: *full sun to partial shade*

Winter daphne is a small evergreen shrub whose intensely fragrant flowers appear in late winter. The flowers last for weeks and, if brought indoors, can fill a room with their sweet scent.

Selected species and varieties: *D. odora* (winter daphne)—to 4 feet tall and wide, with a mounded habit, dark green leaves 1½ to 3½ inches long, and extremely fragrant pinkish purple flowers in 1-inch terminal clusters that bloom from late winter to early spring; 'Aureo-marginata' is slightly hardier than the species and has leaves with yellow margins and flowers that are reddish purple toward the outside of the cluster, light pink on the inside; 'Alba' has white flowers.

Growing conditions and maintenance: Winter daphne is probably the least fussy of its genus. It tolerates most soils, though it prefers one that is slightly alkaline to neutral. Prune, if necessary, immediately after flowering. Daphnes often thrive with little or no care, but they sometimes die for no apparent reason.

Deutzia
(DEWT-see-a)
SLENDER DEUTZIA

Deutzia gracilis

Hardiness: *Zones 4-8*

Plant type: *shrub*

Height: *2 to 5 feet*

Interest: *flowers*

Soil: *moist, well-drained*

Light: *full sun to partial shade*

Slender deutzia is a graceful deciduous shrub bearing pure white flowers in midspring. Like forsythia, it has a relatively short season of interest but is easy to grow and adaptable to most sites. Deutzia can be effectively used as a hedge, as a background for perennials, or in a mixed-shrub border.

Selected species and varieties: *D. gracilis*—to 5 feet tall and an equal width, with slender arching stems in a broad mounding habit, serrated leaves 1 to 3 inches long, and white flowers in erect clusters in spring that are effective for 2 weeks; 'Nikko'—compact cultivar 2 feet tall and 5 feet wide, with leaves that turn burgundy in fall.

Growing conditions and maintenance: Planted in spring, deutzia is easy to transplant and grow and is tolerant of most soils. Encourage vigorous growth and abundant flowers by cutting the oldest stems back to the ground after flowering.

Dicentra
(dy-SEN-tra)
BLEEDING HEART

Dicentra formosa 'Luxuriant'

Hardiness: *Zones 3-8*

Plant type: *herbaceous perennial*

Height: *1 to 3 feet*

Interest: *flowers, foliage*

Soil: *moist, well-drained*

Light: *partial shade*

Bleeding heart bears unusual, drooping flowers along arched stems. The leaves are distinctly fernlike, and their soft colors and mounded form add grace to any shady garden.

Selected species and varieties: *D. eximia*—12 to 18 inches tall, with blue-green leaves that form a neat mound and pink to purple, teardrop-shaped flowers that bloom throughout summer; 'Alba' has white flowers. *D.* hybrids—12 inches tall, similar to *D. eximia* in habit and culture; 'Adrian Bloom' has red flowers and blue-green foliage; 'Bountiful', deep pink flowers, blue-green foliage; 'Luxuriant', cherry red flowers, green foliage; 'Zestful', rose-pink flowers, gray-green foliage. *D. spectabilis*—2 to 3 feet tall, with blue-green leaves and large pink-and-white, heart-shaped blossoms in spring; 'Alba' has white flowers.

Growing conditions and maintenance: Although they thrive in partial shade, bleeding hearts will tolerate full shade. Add organic matter to the soil prior to planting. Leaves of *D. spectabilis* die back in midsummer, so place near plants that will minimize the resulting void.

Dictamnus
(dik-TAM-nus)
GAS PLANT, DITTANY

Dictamnus albus 'Purpureus'

Hardiness: *Zones 3-8*

Plant type: *herbaceous perennial*

Height: *2 to 3 feet*

Interest: *flowers, foliage, seed pods*

Soil: *moist, well-drained*

Light: *full sun to light shade*

Gas plant is easy to grow and long-lived, with soft-colored blossoms and shiny, aromatic, dark green leaves. It adds lasting charm to a perennial border. The common name refers to the flammable gas that is secreted by the plant's leaves, stems, and roots.

Selected species and varieties: *D. albus*—produces leathery, lemon-scented leaves, white flowers 1½ to 2 inches across that bloom in early summer on erect stems held a foot above the foliage, and seed pods that are attractive and useful in dried arrangements; *D. a.* 'Purpureus' has pale mauve-purple flowers with darker purple veins.

Growing conditions and maintenance: Select your site for gas plants carefully, because once planted, they do not like to be disturbed. Add organic matter to the soil prior to planting. It often takes a full season or more before plants bloom, but once established, they are reliable garden performers.

Echeveria
(ek-e-VEER-ee-a)
HENS AND CHICKS

Echeveria agavoides

Hardiness: *Zones 9-11*

Plant type: *succulent perennial*

Height: *3 inches to 3 feet*

Interest: *foliage, flowers*

Soil: *well-drained to dry*

Light: *full sun*

Hens and chicks makes an interesting, attractive ground cover or rock-garden plant for warm, dry climates. It is grown primarily for the beauty of its fleshy, succulent, often colorful leaves that form compact rosettes. Bell-shaped nodding flowers develop on slender stems that rise well above the foliage.

Selected species and varieties: *E. agavoides*—6- to 8-inch rosettes of bright green leaves with reddish margins, topped in summer by red-and-yellow flowers. *E. crenulata*—loose rosettes of pale green leaves with wavy margins, growing up to 1 foot long and covered with white powder, and red to orange flowers on stems up to 3 feet tall. *E. imbricata*—4- to 6-inch rosettes of gray-green leaves and loose stems of orange, red, and yellow flowers; develops many offsets around the base.

Growing conditions and maintenance: Hens and chicks thrives in warm locations and is quite tolerant of drought and coastal conditions. It is easily propagated from offsets.

Echinacea
(ek-i-NAY-see-a)
CONEFLOWER

Echinacea purpurea

Hardiness: *Zones 3-9*

Plant type: *herbaceous perennial*

Height: *2 to 4 feet*

Interest: *flowers*

Soil: *well-drained*

Light: *full sun to light shade*

Coneflowers are reliable performers for a sunny border or wildflower garden. They produce durable, long-lasting, daisylike blossoms throughout the summer, followed by stiff brown seed cones that are lovely in dried arrangements.

Selected species and varieties: *E. pallida*—3 to 4 feet tall, with rosy purple or white flowers up to 3½ inches across. *E. purpurea*—2 to 4 feet tall, with pinkish purple or white flowers up to 3 inches across; 'Bright Star' has rosy pink flowers with maroon centers; 'Robert Bloom', carmine-purple flowers with orange centers and a freely branching habit; 'White Lustre', prolific white flowers with bronze cones.

Growing conditions and maintenance: Coneflowers tolerate heat, drought, and wind. Their flowers are borne on sturdy stems that do not require staking. Flower colors are often deeper when plants are grown in partial shade.

Enkianthus
(en-kee-AN-thus)
ENKIANTHUS

Enkianthus campanulatus

Hardiness: *Zones 4-9*

Plant type: *shrub or small tree*

Height: *6 to 30 feet*

Interest: *flowers, foliage*

Soil: *moist, well-drained, acid*

Light: *full sun to partial shade*

Enkianthus produces delicate bell-shaped blossoms that appear in pendulous clusters in spring. Its green leaves turn brilliant shades of yellow, orange, and red in fall. This tall, erect shrub is an ideal companion to azaleas, rhododendrons, and similar acid-loving plants.

Selected species and varieties: *E. campanulatus* (red-veined enkianthus)—6 to 8 feet tall in cooler climates, to 30 feet in warmer zones, with a stiff, upright habit and leaves 1 to 3 inches long, mostly in tufts at the ends of branches; pale yellow or orange individual flowers with red veins open before new leaves emerge in spring and may persist for several weeks.

Growing conditions and maintenance: Incorporate a generous quantity of organic matter into the soil before planting. Mulch to maintain even moisture. Pruning is rarely necessary.

Epimedium
(ep-i-MEE-dee-um)
BARRENWORT

Epimedium grandiflorum 'Rose Queen'

Hardiness: *Zones 5-8*

Plant type: *herbaceous perennial*

Height: *6 to 12 inches*

Interest: *foliage, flowers*

Soil: *moist, well-drained*

Light: *partial to full shade*

The small, heart-shaped leaves of barren-wort are reddish bronze when they first emerge in spring. They soon turn deep green, providing a lush ground cover for shady gardens before turning bronze again in fall. Red, pink, yellow, or white flowers rise above the foliage on delicate, wiry stems in spring.

Selected species and varieties: *E. grandiflorum*—9 to 12 inches tall, forming dense clumps; 'Rose Queen' has deep pink flowers with white-tipped spurs. *E.* x *rubrum*—6 to 12 inches tall, with very showy, bright red flowers flushed with white or yellow. *E.* x *youngianum* 'Niveum'—7 to 8 inches tall, compact, with white flowers.

Growing conditions and maintenance: Barrenwort is a rugged plant that grows in a clump and increases in size without becoming invasive. It can be left undis-turbed indefinitely, or can be easily di-vided to increase the number of plants. Cut it back to the ground in late winter.

Eupatorium
(yew-pa-TO-ree-um)
BONESET

Eupatorium coelestinum

Hardiness: *Zones 5-10*

Plant type: *herbaceous perennial*

Height: *1 to 5 feet*

Interest: *flowers, foliage*

Soil: *moist, well-drained*

Light: *full sun to partial shade*

Boneset flowers late in the season, bear-ing fluffy blue, white, mauve, pink, or purple blooms on erect stems. It is well suited to an informal border or wild-flower garden in sun or shade.

Selected species and varieties: *E. coelestinum*—1 to 2 feet tall, with blue to vi-olet flowers in flat, fuzzy clusters, good for cutting; Zones 6-9. *E. fistulosum* 'Gateway'—erect stems 5 feet tall, topped with huge arcs of purplish flow-ers in summer and fall; Zones 3-9.

Growing conditions and maintenance: Boneset is extremely easy to grow and provides a long season of bloom. Care must be taken in selecting the site, be-cause it can spread rapidly. *E. coe-lestinum* advances by underground run-ners; it is the more invasive species and should be divided frequently to prevent it from taking over the garden. *E. fistulo-sum* 'Gateway' can be cut back nearly to the ground in late spring to produce somewhat stockier plants.

Euphorbia
(yew-FOR-bee-a)
SPURGE

Euphorbia griffithii 'Fireglow'

Hardiness: *Zones 3-10*

Plant type: *herbaceous perennial*

Height: *6 inches to 3 feet*

Interest: *flowers, foliage*

Soil: *light, well-drained*

Light: *full sun to partial shade*

Euphorbia is a large, diverse genus that includes many interesting low-mainte-nance perennials well suited for rock gar-dens, dry herbaceous borders, south-fac-ing slopes, and dry walls. As with another member of this genus, the poinsettia, spurge produces flowers that are actual-ly quite small but are surrounded by showy bracts that create colorful ef-fects both in the garden and in indoor arrangements. Many species produce at-tractive foliage with intense fall color.

Selected species and varieties: *E. corolla-ta* (flowering spurge)—1 to 3 feet tall, with slender green leaves 1 to 2 inches in length that turn red in the fall. In mid to late summer, it bears clusters of flowers surrounded by small white bracts that re-semble baby's-breath and impart an airy, lacy quality to a mixed border or indoor arrangement; hardy in Zones 3-10. *E. ep-ithymoides* (cushion spurge)—forms a neat, very symmetrical mound 12 to 18 inches high, with green leaves that turn dark red in fall. In spring it produces nu-merous small green flowers that are sur-rounded by showy, inch-wide, char-treuse-yellow bracts. Cushion spurge should be planted in partial shade in the South. It performs best in soil that is on the dry side; in moist, fertile soil it may become invasive. A long-lived plant, cushion spurge should be allowed to grow undisturbed, since it may not respond well to transplanting; hardy to Zones 4-8. *E. griffithii* 'Fireglow'—2 to 3 feet tall, with green leaves that turn yellow and red in fall and brick red flower bracts in late spring and early summer; Zones 4-8. *E. myrsinites* (myrtle euphorbia)—6 to 8 inches high, with 12- to 18-inch-long trailing stems and closely set, fleshy, evergreen, blue-green leaves, ½ inch long, that grow in a dense spiral around the stem and remain handsome throughout winter if the plant is sheltered from wind and sun. Small spring-blooming green flowers surrounded by attractive pale yellow bracts measuring 2 to 4 inches across appear in clusters at the ends of the stems. Performing well in the hot, humid summers of the southeastern states, myrtle euphorbia is hardy to Zones 5-9.

Growing conditions and maintenance: Spurges require a sunny, dry location and soil that is not too rich. In moist, fertile locations, growth may become rank, un-

Euphorbia epithymoides

attractive, and invasive. These plants do not like to be transplanted. Use gloves when handling them, as they exude a milky sap that can cause skin irritation. When cutting for indoor arrangements, put a flame to the cut end of the stem.

Forsythia
(for-SITH-ee-a)
FORSYTHIA

Forsythia x intermedia 'Lynwood'

Hardiness: *Zones 5-8*

Plant type: *shrub*

Height: *1 to 10 feet*

Interest: *flowers*

Soil: *loose, well-drained*

Light: *full sun*

The bright yellow flowers of forsythia mark the onset of spring in many areas. Flowers are arranged along the entire length of the arching stems that grow from the base.

Selected species and varieties: *F.* x *intermedia* 'Spectabilis'—8 to 10 feet tall and wide, with leaves 3 to 4 inches long and bright yellow, tapered flowers 1½ inches across; 'Lynwood' has lighter yellow flowers than 'Spectabilis' and grows 6 to 7 feet tall, with a more upright habit, making it useful for mixed-shrub borders, massed on sunny banks, or in small groupings. *F. viridissima* 'Bronxensis'—12 inches tall with a 2- to 3-foot spread, compact and flat-topped; it has bright green stems and yellow flowers that bloom slightly later and are less showy than those of other species.

Growing conditions and maintenance: Forsythias can adapt to partial shade, although flowering will be reduced. Immediately after flowering, prune by removing the oldest stems back to the ground. Do not shear.

Fothergilla
(faw-ther-GIL-a)
FOTHERGILLA

Fothergilla major

Hardiness: *Zones 4-8*

Plant type: *shrub*

Height: *2 to 10 feet*

Interest: *flowers, foliage*

Soil: *moist, well-drained, acid*

Light: *full sun to partial shade*

Fothergilla is a deciduous shrub that provides two seasons of garden interest. In spring, it is covered with small, fragrant, white bottlebrush-type flowers, and in fall the leaves turn shades of yellow, orange, and scarlet; all colors may appear on a single leaf. It is a useful shrub for a mixed border, a mass planting, or a small grouping. It makes an attractive companion to azaleas and rhododendrons.

Selected species and varieties: *F. gardenii*—2 to 3 feet tall with an equal or greater spread, dark blue-green leaves 1 to 2½ inches long, and petalless flowers with a showy stamen growing in 1- to 2-inch-long clusters in spring. *F. major*—6 to 10 feet tall with a slightly smaller spread and leaves 2 to 4 inches long, but otherwise similar to *F. gardenii*.

Growing conditions and maintenance: Fothergilla is easy to grow in soil amended with generous amounts of organic matter.

Gazania
(ga-ZAY-nee-a)
GAZANIA

Gazania x hybrida 'Aztec Red'

Hardiness: *Zones 8-10*

Plant type: *herbaceous perennial*

Height: *6 to 12 inches*

Interest: *flowers*

Soil: *well-drained*

Light: *full sun*

Gazanias are valued for their daisylike blooms in shades of white, yellow, orange, red, lavender, and pink. Their main season of bloom is early spring to early summer, but they often flower year round in mild climates.

Selected species and varieties: Gazanias fall into two distinct types—clumping and trailing. Both types have been extensively hybridized. Clumping gazanias grow 6 to 12 inches high with a 12- to 18-inch spread; *G.* x *hybrida* 'Aztec Red' and 'Fiesta Red' are two outstanding clumping varieties. Trailing gazanias have long, spreading stems and are well suited for growing on banks as a ground cover; varieties include *G.* x *hybrida* 'Sunburst' and 'Sunrise Yellow'.

Growing conditions and maintenance: Although gazanias require good drainage and full sun to look their best, they tolerate drought, coastal conditions, and poor soil. Too much water and fertilizer will weaken them. They spread naturally, and after several years may require thinning.

Geranium
(jer-AY-nee-um)
CRANESBILL

Geranium sanguineum 'Album'

Hardiness: *Zones 4-8*

Plant type: *herbaceous perennial*

Height: *8 to 12 inches*

Interest: *flowers, foliage*

Soil: *moist, well-drained*

Light: *full sun to partial shade*

Cranesbill is valued both for the profusion of flowers that appear in spring and summer, and for the mounds of dense, lush green foliage that turns red or yellow in the fall.

Selected species and varieties: *G. macrorrhizum*—forms a wide-spreading mound 8 to 12 inches high, with aromatic leaves and magenta, pink, or white flowers that emerge in clusters in late spring and early summer; 'Ingwersen's Variety' has lilac-pink flowers; 'Spessart', pink flowers. *G. sanguineum*—bears magenta flowers and forms a deep green mound of foliage 9 to 12 inches tall and 24 inches across that turns red in fall; 'Album' has white flowers. *G. s.* var. *striatum* (also known as *G. s.* var. *lancastriense*)—light pink flowers with dark red veins.

Growing conditions and maintenance: In the warmer zones, cranesbill prefers partial shade. Do not overfertilize, as it will produce rank growth and weakened plants. Divide in spring when clumps show signs of crowding—approximately every 4 years.

Gerbera
(GER-ber-a)
TRANSVAAL DAISY

Gerbera jamesonii

Hardiness: *Zones 8-11*

Plant type: *herbaceous perennial*

Height: *12 to 18 inches*

Interest: *flowers*

Soil: *well-drained*

Light: *full sun to partial shade*

Transvaal daisies produce spectacular 4-inch flowers on sturdy stems, providing a fine display in the garden, in containers, or as cut flowers for indoor arrangements. Although they are hardy only to Zone 8, in cooler areas they can be planted as annuals or dug up in the fall and planted in containers to grow indoors as houseplants.

Selected species and varieties: *G. jamesonii*—has gray-green, deeply lobed leaves 5 to 10 inches long that grow in the form of a basal rosette, erect flower stems 12 to 18 inches tall, and flowers 2 to 4 inches across with strap-shaped petals in yellow, salmon, cream, pink, rose, or red.

Growing conditions and maintenance: Incorporate organic matter into the soil before planting Transvaal daisies, and fertilize regularly. For massing, space plants 2 feet apart. Water deeply, allowing the soil to dry before watering again. Protect plants over the winter in Zone 8 with a loose mulch.

Grevillea
(gre-VIL-ee-a)
GREVILLEA

Grevillea rosmarinifolia

Hamamelis
(ha-ma-MEL-lis)
WITCH HAZEL

Hamamelis x intermedia 'Jelena'

Hedera
(HED-er-a)
IVY

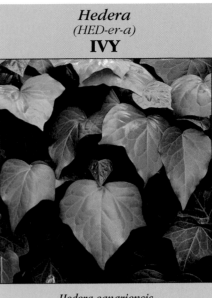

Hedera canariensis

Hardiness: *Zones 10-11*

Plant type: *shrub*

Height: *4 to 6 feet*

Interest: *flowers, foliage*

Soil: *well-drained, acid*

Light: *full sun*

Rosemary grevillea is a tender evergreen shrub with dark, needle-shaped leaves. It produces dense clusters of red-and-cream flowers that cover the entire plant. The flowers attract hummingbirds.

Selected species and varieties: *G. rosmarinifolia*—has a rounded, well-branched form, 1-inch-long narrow leaves that are dark green on top and white below with silky hairs, and flowers 1 inch across.

Growing conditions and maintenance: Rosemary grevillea can withstand heat, drought, and wind. It can be grown in containers and moved indoors in areas where it is not hardy. Water container-grown plants sparingly in winter.

Hardiness: *Zones 5-8*

Plant type: *large shrub or small tree*

Height: *15 to 20 feet*

Interest: *flowers, foliage*

Soil: *moist, well-drained*

Light: *full sun to light shade*

Witch hazel is a deciduous plant with interesting fragrant flowers and vivid fall leaf color. It is a valuable addition to mixed-shrub borders or woodland gardens, and it also performs effectively as a specimen or a screen.

Selected species and varieties: *H. x intermedia*—vigorous plants with an upright, spreading habit, broadly oval leaves 3 to 4 inches long that turn yellow to red in fall, and flowers that emerge on bare twigs in late winter and early spring, with strap-shaped petals ranging in color from yellow to red; 'Jelena' produces copper-colored flowers and orange-red fall foliage; 'Arnold Promise', very fragrant, clear yellow flowers.

Growing conditions and maintenance: Witch hazel thrives in deciduous wooded areas, but performs well in full sun with adequate moisture. Sun-grown plants are usually more dense than those grown in shade. Incorporate organic matter into the soil before planting.

Hardiness: *Zones 4-10*

Plant type: *woody vine or shrub*

Height: *6 inches to 90 feet*

Interest: *foliage*

Soil: *moist, well-drained*

Light: *full sun to full shade*

Ivy produces a dense mat of dark, evergreen leaves that are effective for covering sunny banks, or trailing along the woodland floor in dense shade. Its deep roots help prevent erosion on banks.

Selected species and varieties: *H. helix* (English ivy)—6 to 8 inches high as a trailing ground cover, to 90 feet tall as a climbing vine, Zones 4-9; 'Glacier' and 'Gold Heart' are two of many variegated varieties; 'Needlepoint' has small leaves and a compact form. *H. canariensis* (Algerian ivy)—produces glossy leaves to 8 inches across and tolerates coastal conditions; Zones 9-10. *H. colchica* (Persian ivy)—to 10 inches high, with leaves 5 to 8 inches across; Zones 6-9.

Growing conditions and maintenance: Ivy prefers a rich soil and benefits from a generous helping of organic matter incorporated into the soil. Prune to encourage compact growth and to prevent unwanted spread.

Helianthus
(hee-lee-AN-thus)
SUNFLOWER

Helianthus angustifolius

Hardiness: *Zones 3-9*

Plant type: *herbaceous perennial*

Height: *5 to 12 feet*

Interest: *flowers*

Soil: *moist, well-drained*

Light: *full sun*

Perennial sunflowers are tall, stately plants that put on a dramatic flower show in late summer and fall. They are well suited to the back of a sunny border or the center of an island bed. Their flowers are excellent for indoor arrangements.

Selected species and varieties: *H. angustifolius*—5 to 7 feet tall, 4 feet wide, with yellow petals around dark brown or purple centers forming flowers 2 to 3 inches across in midsummer to late fall; Zones 6-9. *H. maximiliani*—3 to 12 feet tall, with yellow flowers growing in leaf axils along the entire length of the stems, emerging in midsummer in the warmer zones, late summer in the cooler areas, and continuing through fall; Zones 3-9.

Growing conditions and maintenance: Plant sunflowers in soil rich in organic matter. The plants will grow in shade but will develop a more open habit than in sun and will require staking. Cutting back stems by a third in late spring produces bushier plants. *H. maximiliani* tolerates dry conditions.

Helictotrichon
(he-lik-toh-TRY-kon)
BLUE OAT GRASS

Helictotrichon sempervirens

Hardiness: *Zones 4-8*

Plant type: *ornamental grass*

Height: *2 to 3 feet*

Interest: *foliage, flowers*

Soil: *well-drained*

Light: *full sun*

Blue oat grass produces a dense clump of stiff, steel blue foliage and is a valuable addition to a rock garden or a herbaceous border for both color and form. It contrasts well with perennials having green or silvery white foliage. The color is also a lovely complement to the burgundy leaves of shrubs such as barberry 'Crimson Pigmy' or smoke bush 'Royal Purple'. The flowers are buff-colored and appear in graceful sprays above the leaves.

Selected species and varieties: *H. sempervirens*—forms a dense mound 2 to 3 feet high and wide, with light blue-gray leaves and flowers in drooping, one-sided, 4- to 6-inch clusters on slender stems held above the foliage.

Growing conditions and maintenance: Blue oat grass is easy to grow in most soils, including dry, infertile ones. It requires good air circulation to prevent disease. Cut back the foliage in early spring, before new growth begins.

Helleborus
(hell-e-BOR-us)
HELLEBORE

Helleborus orientalis

Hardiness: *Zones 4-9*

Plant type: *herbaceous perennial*

Height: *1 to 2 feet*

Interest: *flowers, foliage*

Soil: *moist, well-drained*

Light: *partial shade*

Hellebores should be placed where their flowers can be viewed at close range. The flowers, which appear very early in the growing season, are also good for indoor arrangements, except for those of the aptly named stinking hellebore.

Selected species and varieties: *H. argutifolius* ssp. *corsicus* (also known as *H. lividus*)—1½ to 2 feet tall, producing glossy, evergreen leaves with toothed margins and long-lasting, saucer-shaped green flowers 2 inches across that appear in early spring; Zones 6-8. *H. foetidus* (stinking hellebore)—18 to 24 inches tall, with dark, leathery, evergreen, compact leaves and light green flowers that bloom in late winter and spring; Zones 6-9. *H. orientalis*—to 18 inches tall, with medium green, toothed, usually evergreen leaves and flowers 2 to 3 inches across that bloom in shades of white, green, purple, and brown from early to late spring; Zones 4-9.

Growing conditions and maintenance: Plant hellebores in spring in soil that is rich in organic matter and retains moisture. Apply a mulch in summer.

Hemerocallis
(hem-er-o-KAL-lis)
DAYLILY

Hemerocallis 'Stella de Oro'

Hardiness: *Zones 3-10*

Plant type: *herbaceous perennial*

Height: *7 inches to 4 feet*

Interest: *flowers, foliage*

Soil: *moist, well-drained*

Light: *full sun to partial shade*

Daylilies offer colorful rewards and require minimal care. Planted in groups, they become a vigorous, soil-stabilizing ground cover that can outgrow most weeds. Their grasslike, arching leaves are attractive throughout the growing season, providing a lush foil for their blossoms. The flowers are borne on stout, branched stems called scapes, and while most blooms last only a day, there are many buds on each scape, so the flowering season continues for weeks. Additionally, breeders have developed a wide range of flowering times, colors, and sizes, so with care in selection, you can have daylilies blooming in your yard from late spring until frost.

Selected species and varieties: The following are just a few of the hundreds of daylily varieties available; they are generally distinguished by their height, flower color, and season: 'Bountiful Valley' grows 28 inches tall and produces prolific, durable, lemon yellow flowers with lime throats that bloom in midseason; 'Catherine Woodbury', 30 inches, pale pink flowers 4 inches across with lavender undertones and yellow throats

blooming in midseason; 'Ed Murray', 30 inches, deep maroon-red flowers of medium size with green throats, midseason; 'Eenie Weenie', a 7-inch-tall dwarf with yellow flowers over an extended season; 'Inca Treasure', 34 inches, large, deep orange, midseason flowers; 'Kindly Light', yellow spider-type flowers 6 inches wide, midseason; 'Mary Todd', 26 inches, early-blooming deep yellow flowers with ruffled edges; 'Oriental Ruby', 34 inches tall, with deep carmine-red flowers in late midseason; 'Peach Fairy', a 26-inch-tall miniature producing 2½-inch-wide melon pink, midseason flowers; 'Ruffled Apricot', 30 inches, very large and showy apricot melon flowers with lavender-pink midribs, blooming in early midseason; 'Singing Sixteen', 20 inches tall with late-season apricot-blend flowers; 'Stella de Oro', the most popular variety of daylily, a 12-inch-tall miniature with fragrant 2- to 3-inch

Hemerocallis 'Cherry Cheeks'

golden yellow flowers emerging mid to late season.

Growing conditions and maintenance: Plant daylilies in spring or fall. In light shade they will produce fewer blooms than in full sun. The flowers of light-colored varieties often show up better when given a little shade. Daylilies compete well with tree roots and tolerate poor soil. They thrive in soil amended with organic matter. Avoid overfertilizing, which causes rank growth and fewer flowers.

Heteromeles
(het-er-oh-MEE-leez)
CALIFORNIA HOLLY

Heteromeles arbutifolia

Hardiness: *Zones 8-10*

Plant type: *shrub or small tree*

Height: *12 to 25 feet*

Interest: *foliage, fruit*

Soil: *well-drained*

Light: *full sun to partial shade*

The California holly has glossy, dark, evergreen leaves. In late summer it produces large clusters of orange-to-red berries that attract birds and other wildlife to the garden. You can cut the prolific berry clusters for indoor arrangements and holiday decorations.

Selected species and varieties: *H. arbutifolia*—to 25 feet tall and equally as wide, with leathery, sharply toothed leaves and inconspicuous white flowers that bloom in spring and are followed by showy clusters of fruit.

Growing conditions and maintenance: Although California holly prefers a fertile, well-drained soil and full sun, it tolerates a wide range of conditions, including drought and partial shade. It can be pruned to reveal its attractive branching habit.

265

Heuchera
(HEW-ker-a)
ALUMROOT

Heuchera micrantha 'Palace Purple'

Hardiness: *Zones 4-10*

Plant type: *herbaceous perennial*

Height: *12 to 24 inches*

Interest: *flowers, foliage*

Soil: *rich, moist, well-drained*

Light: *partial shade to full sun*

Alumroot produces a neat mound of leaves that make an attractive addition to the front of a perennial border. In late spring and summer, a slender stalk of tiny bell-shaped flowers rises well above the leaves. The flowers are very long-lasting.

Selected species and varieties: *H. micrantha* 'Palace Purple'—15 to 18 inches tall, with purple-bronze leaves and white flowers. *H. sanguinea* (coral bells)—12 to 24 inches tall, with dark green, lobed leaves and flowers ¼ to ½ inch long on wiry stems, Zones 4-8; 'Chatterbox' grows 18 inches tall with deep pink flowers; 'June Bride', 15 inches, white flowers; 'Pluie de Feu', 18 inches, red flowers. *H.* x 'Santa Ana Cardinal'—18 to 24 inches tall in clumps 3 to 4 feet across, with rose-red flowers that appear over a 3- to 5-month period; Zones 7-10.

Growing conditions and maintenance: Plant alumroot in spring in soil amended with organic matter. In warm areas, it performs best in partial shade. Remove spent blooms to prolong flowering.

Hibiscus
(by-BIS-kus)
MALLOW

Hibiscus syriacus 'Diana'

Hardiness: *Zones 5-9*

Plant type: *shrub or herbaceous perennial*

Height: *3 to 12 feet*

Interest: *flowers*

Soil: *damp to moist, well-drained*

Light: *full sun to light shade*

The genus *Hibiscus* includes both woody shrubs and herbaceous perennials. All are grown for their large, showy flowers that appear from midsummer until frost. They can be used effectively as a specimen, part of a mixed-shrub or herbaceous border, a hedge, or to dress up a fence or bare wall.

Selected species and varieties: *H. syriacus* 'Diana' (rose of Sharon)—a dense, upright shrub, 6 to 8 feet tall, narrow when young but more wide spreading with age, with medium green, three-lobed leaves that appear late in spring and drop late in fall; pure white, single flowers 6 inches across with red eyes bloom prolifically throughout the summer and make the plant exceptional as a specimen or for a hedge; Zones 5-8. *H. coccineus* (scarlet rose mallow)—a narrow, upright herbaceous perennial, 6 to 8 feet tall, with deeply lobed leaves 5 to 6 inches wide, and funnel-shaped red flowers 5 to 6 inches across, blooming from mid to late summer; Zones 5-9. Two outstanding hybrids are *H.* 'Lady Baltimore', which bears pink flowers with crimson eyes, and *H.* 'Lord Baltimore', with deep

crimson flowers. *H. moscheutos* (swamp mallow)—a herbaceous perennial, 3 to 8 feet tall, with multiple stems from the base, bright green leaves to 8 inches long, and single flowers 6 to 12 inches across from midsummer until frost, Zones 4-9; 'Cotton Candy' has soft pink flowers; 'Satan', deep crimson flowers.

Growing conditions and maintenance: Both rose mallow and rose of Sharon prefer full sun and an evenly moist soil amended with organic matter. They tolerate light shade, but will produce fewer flowers and have a less compact habit than those grown in full sun. 'Diana' rose of Sharon tolerates air pollution and can be grown alongside parking lots. Pruning is not necessary for a natural look and

Hibiscus coccineus

plentiful, medium-size flowers. The natural habitats of swamp mallows are swamps and wetlands, so they are a good choice for damp locations beside a pond or stream. For use as a summer hedge, plant rose or swamp mallows 3 feet apart.

Hosta
(HOS-ta)
PLANTAIN LILY, FUNKIA

Hosta sieboldiana 'Elegans'

Hardiness: *Zones 3-9*

Plant type: *herbaceous perennial*

Height: *8 inches to 3 feet*

Interest: *foliage, flowers*

Soil: *rich, moist, well-drained, acid*

Light: *partial to dense shade*

Although grown primarily for their luxuriant foliage, many hostas produce graceful spires of lilylike flowers during the summer. They are valuable additions to a woodland garden or the front of a shady border.

Selected species and varieties: *H. fortunei* 'Albopicta'—15 inches tall, with leaves having yellow-green centers and dark green margins. *H. plantaginea*—forms a large mound of broad, bright green leaves, with fragrant white flowers on 2½-foot stems. *H.* 'Honeybells'—fragrant lavender flowers with blue stripes on 2-foot stems. *H. sieboldiana* 'Elegans'—large blue-gray leaves and white flowers; 'Frances Williams', large blue-green leaves with broad yellow margins; other fine varieties include 'Gold Standard', 'Blue Cadet', and 'Hyacintha'.

Growing conditions and maintenance: Hostas prefer shade, but will tolerate a sunny location in cooler areas with abundant moisture. Good drainage, especially during the winter, is critical.

Hydrangea
(hy-DRAN-jee-a)
HYDRANGEA

Hydrangea arborescens 'Annabelle'

Hardiness: *Zones 3-9*

Plant type: *shrub, tree, or vine*

Height: *3 to 80 feet*

Interest: *flowers, foliage, bark*

Soil: *moist, well-drained*

Light: *full sun to partial shade*

Hydrangeas are valued for their large clusters of summer flowers. The genus includes deciduous shrubs that go well in mixed borders or mass plantings, small trees that make excellent specimens, and a climbing vine that can grow to 80 feet or more if supported. All have relatively coarse leaves, are easy to grow, and produce long-lasting blossoms that are used in both fresh and dried arrangements.

Selected species and varieties: *H. anomala* ssp. *petiolaris* (climbing hydrangea)—a vine capable of reaching 60 to 80 feet in height but maintainable at a much lower height with pruning; it has very attractive cinnamon brown bark in winter, glossy dark green leaves 2 to 4 inches long, and white flowers in 6- to 10-inch flat-topped clusters emerging early to midsummer; excellent for growing on brick or stone walls, arbors, trellises, or trees; Zones 4-7. *H. arborescens* 'Grandiflora' (hills-of-snow hydrangea)—3 feet tall and equally as wide, with 6- to 8-inch clusters of white flowers in mid to late summer, useful as a foundation planting or an informal hedge, Zones 3-9; 'Annabelle' produces flower clusters up

to 10 inches across that bloom about 2 weeks later than those of 'Grandiflora'. *H. paniculata*—10 to 25 feet tall, 10 to 20 feet wide, an upright, spreading, large shrub or small tree with dark green leaves 3 to 6 inches long and white flowers maturing to dusty pink in grapelike clusters 6 to 8 inches long in midsummer, Zones 3-8; 'Grandiflora' (peegee hydrangea) bears flower clusters up to 18 inches long and makes a spectacular specimen. *H. quercifolia* (oakleaf hydrangea)—4 to 6 feet tall and more than 6 feet wide, with coarse, deeply lobed leaves 3 to 8 inches long that are deep green in summer and turn a brilliant dark reddish bronze in fall and white flowers turning dusty pink,

Hydrangea quercifolia

then brown, in erect clusters up to 12 inches long, Zones 5-9; 'Snowflake' grows flowers in clusters to 15 inches long with layered bracts that give the flowers the appearance of double blooms; 'Snow Queen' has wine red fall leaf color and flowers larger and denser than those of the species.

Growing conditions and maintenance: Hydrangeas thrive in fertile soil; incorporate abundant amounts of organic matter into the soil before planting. *H. arborescens* prefers partial shade; other species adapt well to sun or light shade. Climbing hydrangea requires several years to adjust after transplanting, but once established will grow rapidly.

Iberis
(eye-BEER-is)
CANDYTUFT

Iberis sempervirens 'Snowmantle'

Hardiness: *Zones 4-8*

Plant type: *perennial*

Height: *6 to 12 inches*

Interest: *flowers, foliage*

Soil: *moist, well-drained*

Light: *full sun*

The dark green leaves of candytuft are effective year round at the front of a perennial border, edging a walkway, or cascading over a stone wall. The delicate white flowers that cover the plant in spring are a delightful bonus.

Selected species and varieties: *I. sempervirens*—to 12 inches high and 24 inches wide, with a low, mounded habit, linear evergreen leaves 1 inch long, semiwoody stems, and very showy white flowers in dense clusters 1 inch across; 'Snowflake' grows 10 inches high, with 2- to 3-inch flower clusters; 'Snowmantle', 8 inches high, with a dense, compact habit.

Growing conditions and maintenance: Incorporate organic matter into the soil before planting candytuft. Protect the plant from severe winter weather with a loose mulch in colder zones. Cut it back at least 2 inches after it flowers to maintain vigorous growth.

Ilex
(EYE-leks)
HOLLY

Ilex 'Sparkleberry'

Hardiness: *Zones 3-10*

Plant type: *shrub or tree*

Height: *3 to 70 feet*

Interest: *foliage, fruit*

Soil: *moist, well-drained, acid*

Light: *full sun to partial shade*

Hollies are a diverse group of plants that include both evergreen and deciduous trees and shrubs. Female hollies produce fruit in the fall that is often highly ornamental, but most require male plants within 100 feet for pollination to assure fruit. From low-growing foundation plants to tall, pyramidal specimen trees, there is a holly suitable for nearly every landscape.

Selected species and varieties: *I. aquifolium* (English holly)—to 70 feet, with a pyramidal form, dark, glossy, evergreen leaves with spines, and bright red fruit in fall ¼ inch in diameter; well suited to Pacific Northwest and mid-Atlantic regions; several outstanding cultivars offer leaf variegation or heavy fruit production; Zones 6-9. *I. x attenuata* 'Foster #2'—20 to 25 feet, with a narrow, conical, compact form; bears small, neat, evergreen leaves with spiny margins and deep red fruit that persists through winter; Zones 6-9. *I. cornuta* 'Burfordii' (Burford holly)—to 25 feet, but may be maintained at 8 to 10 feet with pruning, wider than tall; leaves are rectangular, shiny, dark, evergreen with a terminal spine; fruit red,

abundant, no pollination required for fruit set, persists through winter; Zones 6-9. *I. crenata* 'Convexa'—4 to 9 feet, broader than tall, small, oval, convex, evergreen leaves, boxwoodlike appearance, can be sheared, fruit black, Zones 5-8; 'Helleri'—3 feet tall, 5-foot spread, mounded form, Zones 5-8; 'Hetzii'— dwarf form of 'Convexa'. *I. glabra* 'Compacta' (dwarf inkberry)—4 to 6 feet with equal or greater spread, dense, rounded form, leaves evergreen, smooth, to 2 inches long, fruit black, excellent as foundation plant or hedge; Zones 4-9. *I. meserveae* 'Blue Prince'—8 to 12 feet, compact and broadly pyramidal, dark blue-green leaves (evergreen), male clone, Zones 4-9; 'Blue Princess'—12 feet tall by 9 feet wide, leaves evergreen, glossy, blue-green, all female clone, fruit dark red; Zones 4-9. *I. opaca* (American holly)—usually 10 to 15 feet, may reach 40 feet with age, evergreen, pyramidal

Ilex aquifolium cultivar

form, Zones 5-9; 'Cardinal'—compact form of species, small dark green leaves, light red fruit; 'Goldie'—leaves dull green, fruit yellow, prolific; 'Old Heavy Berry'—leaves large, dark green, pea-size red fruit, prolific, vigorous. *I. pedunculosa* (long-stalk holly)—usually 15 feet, may reach 30 feet with age, large, pyramidal shrub or small tree, leaves spineless, 1 to 3 inches, lustrous, dark green turning yellow-green in winter, fruit bright red, ¼ inch in diameter, on 1- to 1½-inch stems, very attractive in fall; Zones 5-8. *I.* 'Sparkleberry'—to 12 feet, upright deciduous shrub, leaves to 3 inches, deep green, fruit bright red, ⅜ inch in diameter, prolific, ripens in late summer, persists into winter; Zones 4-

8. *I. verticillata* 'Winter Red'—8 feet, rounded form, leaves deciduous, dark green, fruit bright red, ⅜-inch diameter, extremely prolific, dramatic after leaves drop in fall; Zones 3-9. *I. vomitoria* (yaupon holly)—15 to 25 feet, upright shrub or small tree, leaves evergreen, dark, fruit translucent, scarlet red, ¼-inch

Ilex cornuta 'Burfordii'

diameter, persists throughout winter, useful as hedge, screen, foundation plant, topiary, takes pruning well.

Growing conditions and maintenance: Hollies perform well in sun or partial shade, though shade-grown plants will produce less fruit. They are tolerant of a wide range of soils as long as drainage is good. They benefit from organic matter added to the soil prior to planting as well as annual late-winter applications of a complete fertilizer. Be sure hollies have plenty of water throughout the growing season. Since male and female flowers are borne on separate plants, it is usually necessary to have both types for berries, even though only the females bear the fruit. (Burford holly is an exception—the all-female plants require no pollen for fruit production.) Not all hollies produce pollen at the same time, so plant a pollinator of the same species. Generally, 1 male plant is sufficient to pollinate 10 to 20 females.

Imperata
(im-per-AY-ta)
JAPANESE BLOOD GRASS

Imperata cylindrica rubra

Hardiness: *Zones 6-9*

Plant type: *ornamental grass*

Height: *12 to 18 inches*

Interest: *foliage*

Soil: *well-drained*

Light: *full sun to partial shade*

Japanese blood grass produces clumps of leaves whose top half turns a rich blood red. It is very effective planted in small groups or large masses at the front of a border. The flowers of this grass are ornamentally insignificant, but its vivid foliage, which provides color from summer through fall, makes it well worth including in a garden.

Selected species and varieties: *I. cylindrica rubra* 'Red Baron'—leaves are 12 to 18 inches long and ¼ inch wide, turning red in early summer; color increases in intensity in fall; outstanding for long-season color contrast.

Growing conditions and maintenance: Japanese blood grass grows in sun or partial shade in nearly any well-drained soil. It is particularly showy when viewed with the sun shining through the colorful leaves. It is completely dormant in the winter, and old leaves should be cut back before new growth emerges in spring. *Note:* If any part of 'Red Baron' reverts to green, it should be removed at once. The green form is highly aggressive and is listed in the United States as a noxious weed.

Iris
(EYE-ris)
IRIS

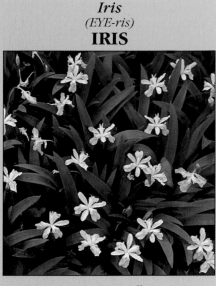

Iris cristata 'Alba'

Hardiness: *Zones 4-9*

Plant type: *herbaceous perennial*

Height: *2 inches to 4 feet*

Interest: *flowers, foliage*

Soil: *well-drained to moist*

Light: *full sun to light shade*

Irises bear unique flowers that present an elegant display in both the garden and cut-flower arrangements. Their blooms are available in a range of colors, and species vary widely in cultural requirements, height, and flower size and type. All iris varieties produce sword-shaped leaves, and all share a distinct flower structure composed of three drooping petallike sepals called falls, three usually erect petals called standards, and three narrow petallike "styles."

Selected species and varieties: *I. cristata* (crested iris)—6 to 9 inches tall, flowers bloom early to midspring and have two yellow or white crested ridges along falls, effective in the front of a border or woodland garden, hardy to Zone 4; 'Alba'—bears white flowers; 'Shenandoah Sky'—offers pale blue flowers; 'Summer Storm'—deep blue flowers. *I. danfordiae* (Danford iris)—4 to 6 inches tall, grown from bulbs, yellow to gold flowers in early spring, hardy to Zone 5. *I. pallida* 'Dalmatica' (orrisroot)—3 feet tall, rigid and erect habit, 24-inch-long gray-green leaves, fragrant bluish purple flowers, blooming late spring or early summer, Zones 4-8; 'Aureo-Variegata'—yellow-striped foliage, dramatic accent to border. *I. reticulata* (netted iris)—3 to 9 inches tall, grown from bulbs, erect habit, purple and yellow fragrant flowers, plants are excellent for rock garden, front of border, or near water, hardy to Zone 5. *I. sibirica* (Siberian iris)—2 to 4 feet tall, foliage grows in dense, erect clumps, attractive throughout growing season, flowers in early summer, good choice for perennial borders, hardy to Zone 4; 'Caesar's Brother'—36 inches tall, blue-black flowers; 'Dewful'—24 inches tall, blue flowers with pale blue styles; 'White Swirl'—40 inches tall, white flowers with touch of yellow.

Growing conditions and maintenance: Iris species vary considerably in their cultural requirements. Crested iris prefers

Iris reticulata

partial shade and a well-drained, not-too-fertile soil. Other species perform better in the sun, though they will tolerate some shade. Siberian iris thrives in a moist, fertile, slightly acid soil, while netted iris prefers a well-drained, alkaline site. Netted irises can be left undisturbed for many years before division is necessary.

Itea
(IT-ee-a)
SWEETSPIRE

Itea virginica

Hardiness:	*Zones 5-9*
Plant type:	*shrub*
Height:	*2 to 5 feet*
Interest:	*flowers, foliage*
Soil:	*fertile, moist*
Light:	*full sun to partial shade*

Sweetspire offers a fine garden display in both summer and fall. Its flowers appear in midsummer, well after most shrubs have finished blooming. In fall its leaves put on a show, turning reddish purple to scarlet and persisting for several weeks.

Selected species and varieties: *I. japonica* 'Beppu'—2 to 5 feet tall with spreading, moundlike habit, plants spread by suckers, leaves are rich green in summer, red in fall, flowers are white and fragrant, useful as a ground cover. *I. virginica* 'Henry's Garnet'—3 to 4 feet tall, 4 to 6 feet wide, green leaves turn purple-red in fall, fragrant white flowers in clusters up to 6 inches long, excellent addition to mixed-shrub border.

Growing conditions and maintenance: Sweetspire is easily transplanted, and new plants can be obtained by dividing an existing specimen. It prefers a rich, moist to wet site. In mild climates it is semievergreen.

Juniperus
(joo-NIP-er-us)
JUNIPER

Juniperus scopulorum 'Skyrocket'

Hardiness:	*Zones 2-9*
Plant type:	*tree or shrub*
Height:	*2 to 60 feet*
Interest:	*foliage*
Soil:	*light, well-drained*
Light:	*full sun*

Junipers vary widely in their height and form, from low-spreading ground covers to tall, columnar trees. All are evergreen, with scale-like leaves that range in color from dark green to silvery blue to yellow.

Selected species and varieties: *J. chinensis* 'Gold Coast'—2 to 3 feet tall, up to 5 feet wide, gracefully mounded habit, foliage soft-textured, golden yellow; Zones 3-9. *J. scopulorum* 'Blue Heaven'—20 to 30 feet, neat pyramidal form, foliage very blue throughout the year, Zones 3-7; 'Skyrocket'—15 to 30 feet tall, 2 to 3 feet wide, form is extremely narrow and columnar, bluish green foliage, dramatic vertical accent; Zones 3-7. *J. virginiana*—40 to 50 feet tall, highly variable spread of 8 to 20 feet, foliage medium green in summer, brownish green in winter; Zones 2-9.

Growing conditions and maintenance: Junipers thrive in open, sunny locations and prefer a sandy soil but tolerate most soils if drainage is good. They tolerate air pollution, and taller types make effective windbreaks.

Kalmia
(KAL-mee-a)
MOUNTAIN LAUREL

Kalmia latifolia 'Ostbo Red'

Hardiness: *Zones 4-9*

Plant type: *shrub*

Height: *7 to 15 feet*

Interest: *flowers, foliage*

Soil: *moist, well-drained, acid*

Light: *full sun to full shade*

In early summer, mountain laurel bears white, pink, or rose-colored blossoms, set off by a background of dark, leathery leaves. It is equally at home as a foundation plant, in a mixed-shrub border, or in a naturalized, woodland garden.

Selected species and varieties: *K. latifolia*—variable height, usually to 15 feet with equal spread, leaves 2 to 5 inches long, evergreen, flower buds are deep pink or red and crimped, flowers are ¾ to 1 inch across in 4- to 6-inch rounded, terminal clusters; 'Nipmuck'—red buds, flowers are creamy white to light pink on inside and dark pink on outside; 'Ostbo Red'—red buds, soft pink flowers; 'Pink Charm'—deep pink buds, pink flowers with red ring on inside near base.

Growing conditions and maintenance: Mountain laurel is easy to grow and virtually maintenance free as long as its cultural conditions are met. While it adapts to sun or shade, it requires a moist, acid soil to which generous amounts of organic matter have been added. Mulch to retain moisture.

Kerria
(KER-ee-a)
JAPANESE KERRIA

Kerria japonica 'Pleniflora'

Hardiness: *Zones 4-9*

Plant type: *shrub*

Height: *3 to 8 feet*

Interest: *flowers, stems*

Soil: *fertile, loamy, well-drained*

Light: *partial to full shade*

Japanese kerria produces masses of bright yellow spring flowers on arched, lime green stems. It is a lively addition to the mixed-shrub border or a woodland garden. Its green stems add color to the winter landscape.

Selected species and varieties: *K. japonica*—3 to 6 feet tall, spreading to 9 feet across, arching green stems zigzag from one node to the next, deciduous, bright green leaves are 1½ to 4 inches long, bright yellow five-petaled flowers, 1½ inches across; 'Picta'—leaves with attractive white margin; 'Pleniflora'—up to 8 feet, habit more erect than species, flowers are double, rounded, golden yellow.

Growing conditions and maintenance: Japanese kerria performs better with some shade; too much sun causes the flowers to fade quickly. Prune to remove dead branches whenever they appear, and remove green shoots that arise among the variegated foliage of 'Picta'. Do not overfertilize, as this causes rank growth and reduces flowering.

Koelreuteria
(kol-roo-TEER-ee-a)
GOLDEN RAIN TREE

Koelreuteria paniculata

Hardiness: *Zones 5-9*

Plant type: *tree*

Height: *30 to 40 feet*

Interest: *flowers, fruit, foliage*

Soil: *well-drained*

Light: *full sun*

The golden rain tree is valued for its summer display of yellow flowers and attractive seed pods in the fall. It is an excellent choice for a lawn tree.

Selected species and varieties: *K. paniculata*—30 to 40 feet tall with equal or greater spread, deciduous, leaves are compound, 9 to 18 inches long, bright green, turning yellow in fall, flowers in midsummer are bright yellow, blooming in loose, showy clusters 12 to 15 inches long, papery seed pods are 2 inches long, changing from green to yellow-tan to brown from summer to fall; 'September'—less hardy than the species, flowers appear several weeks later.

Growing conditions and maintenance: The golden rain tree adapts to a wide range of soils, from light to heavy and from acid to alkaline. It tolerates wind, drought, heat, and air pollution, and adapts well to city conditions. Prune in winter to promote high branching and to remove crowded or crossing branches.

Lagerstroemia
(la-gur-STREE-mee-a)
CRAPE MYRTLE

Lagerstroemia indica 'Natchez'

Hardiness: *Zones 7-9*

Plant type: *large shrub or small tree*

Height: *15 to 25 feet*

Interest: *flowers, bark*

Soil: *moist, well-drained*

Light: *full sun*

Crape myrtles can be grown as large shrubs or small trees. They add interest to the landscape during summer with their vibrantly colored flower clusters and during winter with their smooth, multicolored bark.

Selected species and varieties: While the species is subject to powdery mildew, the following are among the newer varieties that are resistant: *L. indica* 'Choctaw'—dark green leaves turn maroon in fall, long-lasting bright pink flowers in mid to late summer; 'Natchez'—fast-growing, dark green leaves turn orange-red in fall, white flowers; 'Tuskegee'—strong, horizontal growth habit, leaves are glossy, dark green, and leathery, turning orange-red in fall, flowers are dark pink.

Growing conditions and maintenance: Crape myrtles grow best in hot, sunny locations. To expose the ornamental bark, restrict growth to one to four branches from the base, pruning out others that arise. Also prune to remove winter-injured branches, but wait until late spring because they are slow to leaf out.

Lamium
(LAY-mee-um)
DEAD NETTLE

Lamium maculatum 'Beacon Silver'

Hardiness: *Zones 4-8*

Plant type: *herbaceous perennial*

Height: *8 to 12 inches*

Interest: *foliage, flowers*

Soil: *well-drained*

Light: *partial to full shade*

The spreading, trailing habit of dead nettle makes it useful as a ground cover among shrubs or trees, or in the front of a shady border. It helps hide the fading foliage of early-spring bulbs and fills in bare spots, and is also well suited for trailing over a stone wall or cascading from a container.

Selected species and varieties: *L. maculatum* 'Beacon Silver'—effective for brightening a shady part of the garden, silver 1- to 2-inch leaves with narrow green margins, pink flowers in late spring bloom in whorls at the ends of stems; 'Chequers'—green leaves with a wide stripe down the center, pink flowers in late spring through summer.

Growing conditions and maintenance: Dead nettle tolerates a wide range of soils as long as they are well drained. Bare patches may appear if the plant is allowed to dry out too often. It prefers shade but will tolerate sun if sufficient moisture is supplied. To contain its aggressive, spreading habit and to promote compact growth, shear dead nettle in midsummer.

Lavandula
(la-VAN-dew-la)
LAVENDER

Lavandula angustifolia 'Hidcote'

Hardiness: *Zones 5-9*

Plant type: *perennial*

Height: *10 inches to 3 feet*

Interest: *foliage, flowers, fragrance*

Soil: *well-drained*

Light: *full sun*

Lavender is an evergreen perennial with a woody base. Both leaves and flowers are extremely fragrant. Its soft colors and fine texture show up well when combined with more brightly colored perennials.

Selected species and varieties: *L. angustifolia* (English lavender), Zones 5-9; 'Hidcote'—15 to 20 inches, silvery gray foliage, purple flowers; 'Jean Davis'—15 inches, blue-green foliage, pale pink flowers; 'Munstead'—10 to 12 inches, 18 inches in flower, wide-spreading, gray-green foliage, purple flowers, very fragrant. *L. stoechas* (French lavender)—3 feet tall, shrublike, gray-green leaves, purple or white flowers; Zones 8-10.

Growing conditions and maintenance: Lavender prefers a well-drained soil that is not too rich. In areas subject to freezing, French lavender should be grown in a container and brought indoors for the winter. Cut lavender stems back to 8 inches in early spring to encourage compact growth and to remove old woody stems that produce few flowers.

Leptospermum
(lep-toh-SPER-mum)
NEW ZEALAND TEA TREE

Leptospermum scoparium

Hardiness: *Zones 9-10*

Plant type: *shrub*

Height: *6 to 10 feet*

Interest: *flowers, foliage*

Soil: *fertile, moist, well-drained, acid*

Light: *full sun to light shade*

The New Zealand tea tree is a fine-textured evergreen shrub with a dense branching habit and small leaves. Its flowers are borne in winter, spring, or summer, and though blossoms of the species are white, varieties are available with pink or red flowers.

Selected species and varieties: *L. scoparium*—6 to 10 feet, slightly smaller in spread, rounded form, compact, leaves are dark gray-green and aromatic, profuse white flowers are ½ inch across.

Growing conditions and maintenance: The New Zealand tea tree is easy to grow in mild climates in a well-drained acid to neutral soil. It prefers full sun, except in hot, dry areas, where it benefits from partial shade. It thrives under humid coastal conditions. Though it is somewhat drought tolerant, supplemental water should be given, especially where the climate is hot. Prune in early spring.

Leucothoe
(loo-KO-tho-ee)
DROOPING LEUCOTHOE

Leucothoe fontanesiana 'Nana'

Hardiness: *Zones 5-9*

Plant type: *shrub*

Height: *2 to 6 feet*

Interest: *foliage, flowers*

Soil: *moist, well-drained, acid*

Light: *partial to full shade*

Drooping leucothoe is a graceful evergreen shrub whose arching branches support chains of fragrant white flowers in the spring. Branches and leaves extend to the ground, making it a good choice to plant in front of leggy shrubs. It combines well with azaleas and rhododendrons in woodland settings.

Selected species and varieties: *L. fontanesiana*—fountainlike, arching habit, leaves are 2 to 5 inches long, bronze when young, dark green in summer, turning bronze to purple in fall and winter, flowers are white and fragrant, borne in 2- to 3-inch drooping clusters in late spring; 'Nana'—2 feet tall, 6 feet wide; 'Girard's Rainbow'—new leaves emerge variegated white and pink and mature to yellow, copper, and green.

Growing conditions and maintenance: Plant drooping leucothoe in a shady location, adding generous amounts of organic matter to the soil. It will tolerate full sun if abundant moisture is supplied.

Liatris
(ly-AY-tris)
SPIKE GAY-FEATHER

Liatris spicata 'Kobold'

Hardiness: *Zones 3-9*

Plant type: *herbaceous perennial*

Height: *18 inches to 5 feet*

Interest: *flowers*

Soil: *sandy, well-drained*

Light: *full sun to light shade*

The flowers of spike gay-feather are borne on erect stems, and unlike most spike flowers, the top buds open first and proceed downward; the effect is that of a feathery bottlebrush. It provides a striking vertical accent in both the garden and indoor arrangements.

Selected species and varieties: *L. spicata*—usually 2 to 3 feet tall and 2 feet wide but may reach 5 feet tall, leaves are narrow and tapered, up to 5 inches long, on erect, stout stems, flowers are purple or rose, borne closely along the top of the stem in mid to late summer; 'Kobold'—18- to 24-inch dwarf form, bright purple flowers, good for the front or middle of a herbaceous border.

Growing conditions and maintenance: Spike gay-feather prefers a light, well-drained soil and full sun but adapts to light shade and tolerates wet conditions better than other species of *Liatris*. Tall types often need support; however, 'Kobold', with its stout habit, rarely requires staking.

273

Liriope
(li-RYE-o-pee)
LILYTURF

Liriope muscari 'Variegata'

Hardiness: *Zones 4-10*

Plant type: *herbaceous perennial*

Height: *8 to 18 inches*

Interest: *foliage, flowers*

Soil: *fertile, moist to dry*

Light: *full sun to full shade*

Lilyturf produces evergreen grasslike leaves that make an almost impenetrable ground cover. In summer, spikes of blue, violet, or white flowers arise from the clumps of foliage and are followed by dark blue-black, berrylike fruit.

Selected species and varieties: *L. spicata*—8 to 12 inches tall, spreads by underground stems, leaves up to 18 inches long and ¼ inch wide, pale violet to white flowers in loose clusters. *L. muscari*—up to 18 inches tall, leaves 12 to 18 inches long and 1 inch wide, lilac-purple flowers, Zones 6-10; 'Big Blue'—larger leaves and flower spikes than the species; 'Christmas Tree'—lilac flowers on tapered spikes; 'John Burch'—variegated leaves and crested lavender flowers; 'Majestic'—large violet-blue flowers; 'Monroe's White'—large white flowers.

Growing conditions and maintenance: Lilyturf thrives in sun or shade, though plants grown in the sun produce more flowers. It prefers a moist soil but adapts well to drier conditions. Mow or cut back old growth in late winter.

Lonicera
(lon-ISS-er-a)
HONEYSUCKLE

Lonicera heckrottii

Hardiness: *Zones 4-9*

Plant type: *woody vine or shrub*

Height: *2 to 20 feet or more*

Interest: *flowers, foliage*

Soil: *moist, well-drained*

Light: *full sun to partial shade*

Honeysuckles include both vines and shrubs. These species have distinct growth habits and adorn the garden with their abundant flowers in spring without becoming invasive.

Selected species and varieties: *L. flava* (yellow honeysuckle)—vine, leaves are bright green above, bluish green below, yellow-orange flowers in midspring, Zones 6-8; *L. heckrottii* (goldflame honeysuckle)—vine, blue-green leaves, red flower buds open to yellow on the inside and pink outside in spring to early summer, Zones 4-9; *L. pileata*—evergreen or semievergreen shrub, up to 3 feet tall, low, spreading branches with small, lustrous, dark green leaves, Zones 6-9; *L. sempervirens* (trumpet honeysuckle)—dark blue-green leaves, flowers are tubular, orange-red to red, spring-blooming, Zones 4-9.

Growing conditions and maintenance: Plant honeysuckles in moist, well-drained soil amended with organic matter. They thrive in sun or shade, but sun-grown plants flower more heavily. Provide support for twining stems. Prune after flowering to maintain size.

Magnolia
(mag-NO-lee-a)
MAGNOLIA

Magnolia virginiana

Hardiness: *Zones 5-9*

Plant type: *tree or shrub*

Height: *10 to 80 feet*

Interest: *flowers, foliage, fruit*

Soil: *moist, well-drained, loamy, acid*

Light: *full sun to partial shade*

Magnolias include both deciduous and evergreen shrubs and trees. They vary greatly in size and form, but all produce large, lovely flowers in shades from pink and purple to pure white. The fruit of magnolias is a conelike pod, which splits to reveal bright pink or red seeds.

Selected species and varieties: *M. grandiflora* (southern magnolia)—60 to 80 feet tall, 30 to 50 feet wide, low-branching, pyramidal, evergreen or semievergreen to deciduous, leaves are 5 to 10 inches long, tops are dark green and shiny, undersides are light green, brown, or rust-colored, flowers are creamy white and richly textured, 8 to 12 inches across, blooming in late spring and sporadically throughout summer, 3- to 5-inch cone-shaped fruit pods open to reveal scarlet seeds in fall; Zones 6-9. 'Bracken's Brown Beauty'—up to 30 feet, compact habit, small leaves are 6 inches long and dark brown on undersides, flowers are 5 to 6 inches; 'Edith Bogue'—tight pyramidal form, leaves are narrow and deep green, flowers are large and fragrant, probably the hardiest southern magnolia variety; 'Goliath'—large flowers up to 12 inches across; 'Little Gem'—10 to 20 feet tall, shrublike habit, small leaves are 4 inches with bronze undersides, flowers bloom in spring and fall, well suited for small landscapes; 'St. Mary'—20 feet tall with equal spread, compact habit, produces flowers at a young age. *M.* x 'Galaxy' —30- to 40-foot deciduous tree with stout branches, pyramidal habit, medium green leaves, reddish purple flowers up to 10 inches in diameter; Zones 5-9. *M.* x 'Nimbus'—up to 40 feet, single- or multiple-trunk tree, leaves are dark and

Magnolia grandiflora 'Little Gem'

shiny green, flowers are creamy white, very fragrant, blooming in late spring; Zones 5-9. Several hybrids have been developed from crosses of *M. liliiflora* (lily magnolia) and *M. stellata* 'Rosea': They are deciduous with a shrublike habit, 10 to 15 feet tall at maturity, bark is light gray, flower buds are furry and attractive in winter, flowers appear before leaves in spring but later than star magnolia's, so they are less susceptible to damage by late frosts, flowering continues sporadically through summer, Zones 5-9; 'Ann'—10 feet tall with equal or greater spread, blooms earliest among these hybrids, deep purple-red flowers; 'Judy'— 10 to 15 feet tall, erect habit, flowers are deep purple-red on outside, white on inside; 'Randy'—narrow habit to 15 feet, flowers are purple outside, white inside; 'Ricky'—similar to 'Randy', with flowers deep purple on outside and white to purple on inside. *M. virginiana* (sweet bay or swamp magnolia)—size and form vary with growing conditions, 10 to 20 feet tall, large multiple-stemmed deciduous shrub in colder zones, in warmer climates may reach 60 feet as semiever-

green to evergreen pyramidal tree, 3- to 5-inch-long dark green leaves, creamy white flowers, 2 to 3 inches across, blooms late spring and early summer and continues sporadically until fall, 2-inch fruit opens to show bright red seeds; Zones 5-9.

Growing conditions and maintenance: Transplant magnolias in early spring. The southern magnolia often drops many of its leaves when it is transplanted but usually recovers quickly. All require moist, rich, acid soils and grow well in woodland areas with the protection of nearby trees, as long as they are not too close. The southern magnolia prefers a well-drained, sandy soil, while the hybrids and sweet bay magnolias tolerate heavier, poorly drained soils; the sweet bay magnolia thrives even in swampy conditions. The southern magnolia, with its broad evergreen leaves, requires protection from winter winds and sun, espe-

Magnolia 'Ricky'

cially in colder areas; leaves exposed to winter stress look ragged and scorched. Deciduous magnolia flowers can be damaged by late-spring frosts. Give plants a northern exposure to delay flowering, thus reducing possible frost damage.

Mahonia
(ma-HO-nee-a)
MAHONIA

Mahonia bealei

Hardiness:	*Zones 4-9*
Plant type:	*shrub*
Height:	*3 to 12 feet*
Interest:	*foliage, flowers, fruit*
Soil:	*moist, well-drained, acid*
Light:	*partial shade*

Mahonias bear large clusters of yellow flowers in spring, followed by showy blue berries. They are attractive year round as foundation plants and border shrubs, or in a woodland garden.

Selected species and varieties: *M. aquifolium* (Oregon grape)—3 to 6 feet tall, 3 to 5 feet wide, spreads by suckers, compound leaves are evergreen, 6 to 12 inches long, each hollylike leaflet is dark green, turning purplish in winter, flowers are yellow in terminal clusters in early spring, grapelike berries are dark blue in late summer; Zones 4-8. *M. bealei* (leatherleaf mahonia)—6 to 12 feet, upright habit, compound leaves are evergreen and leathery, blue-green leaflets have prominent spines, fragrant yellow flowers in showy clusters in very early spring, steel blue berries appear midsummer; Zones 6-9.

Growing conditions and maintenance: Mahonias prefer partial shade. They perform well under trees but tolerate full sun if adequate moisture is supplied. Protect them from drying winter winds.

Malus
(MAY-lus)
CRAB APPLE

Malus sargentii

Hardiness: *Zones 4-8*

Plant type: *tree or shrub*

Height: *6 to 20 feet*

Interest: *flowers, fruit*

Soil: *moist, well-drained, acid*

Light: *full sun*

Crab apples are small deciduous trees or large shrubs that bear many flowers in spring before the leaves are fully expanded. In summer and fall, the small, brightly colored fruits provide color and interest.

Selected species and varieties: *M.* x 'Donald Wyman'—20 feet tall, 25 feet wide, wide-spreading and rounded tree, lustrous dark green leaves, pink buds open to white, single flowers, fruit is bright red, ⅜ inch in diameter, persists into winter. *M. sargentii*—6 to 8 feet tall, 8 to 16 feet wide, densely branched, mounded shrub form, red flower buds open to white, single flowers, fruit is bright red, ¼ inch in diameter, attracts birds.

Growing conditions and maintenance: Crab apples tolerate a wide range of soil conditions. They are easy to transplant and should be pruned while young to establish the desired shape and to remove suckers. Prune lightly to avoid the development of water sprouts. Pruning should be done immediately after flowering.

Miscanthus
(mis-KAN-thus)
EULALIA

Miscanthus sinensis 'Zebrinus'

Hardiness: *Zones 5-9*

Plant type: *ornamental grass*

Height: *3 to 10 feet*

Interest: *foliage, flowers*

Soil: *well-drained*

Light: *full sun*

The tall flower plumes of eulalia arise in summer and add graceful movement and soft colors to the garden. Both the flowers and the foliage remain attractive throughout the winter. Eulalias are useful as specimens and screens, and add drama to rock gardens and herbaceous borders.

Selected species and varieties: *M. sinensis*—5 to 10 feet tall, narrow leaves 3 to 4 feet long with a prominent white midrib, flowers are feathery, fan-shaped, blooming in late summer to fall; 'Morning Light'—5 feet, variegated leaves with silver midrib and white margins, reddish bronze flowers; 'Purpurascens'—3 to 4 feet, orange-red in fall; 'Variegatus'—5 to 7 feet, leaves have cream-colored stripes; 'Yaku Jima'—3- to 4-foot dwarf; 'Zebrinus'—6 to 7 feet, horizontal yellow stripes on leaves.

Growing conditions and maintenance: Transplant eulalia in spring, selecting a sunny site. It tolerates nearly any well-drained soil. Cut back old foliage in late winter 2 to 6 inches above the ground.

Myrica
(mi-RYE-ka)
BAYBERRY, WAX MYRTLE

Myrica cerifera

Hardiness: *Zones 2-9*

Plant type: *shrub or tree*

Height: *5 to 25 feet*

Interest: *foliage, fruit*

Soil: *adaptable*

Light: *full sun to partial shade*

Bayberries are irregularly shaped shrubs or small trees that serve well as hedges or foundation plants. Their blue-gray fruit, borne on female plants only, is covered with a waxy coating that is used to make bayberry candles.

Selected species and varieties: *M. californica* (California bayberry)—15 to 35 feet tall, 15 feet wide, bronze-colored evergreen leaves, purple fruit in fall and winter; Zones 7-8. *M. cerifera* (southern wax myrtle)—10 to 20 feet tall, equally wide, leaves are semievergreen or evergreen and aromatic, gray fruit clusters along stems of previous season's growth; Zones 7-9. *M. pensylvanica* (northern bayberry)—5 to 12 feet tall with equal spread, suckers help form dense thickets, aromatic deciduous or semievergreen leaves, gray fruit; Zones 2-6.

Growing conditions and maintenance: Bayberries adapt to a wide range of soil conditions. They thrive in sandy, sterile soil and tolerate heavy clay soils. They take pruning well and make attractive, dense hedges.

Nandina
(nan-DEE-na)
HEAVENLY BAMBOO

Nandina domestica 'Gulfstream'

Hardiness: *Zones 6-9*

Plant type: *shrub*

Height: *1 to 8 feet*

Interest: *foliage, flowers, fruit*

Soil: *fertile, moist*

Light: *full sun to partial shade*

Nandina is an upright shrub with extremely ornamental foliage. New leaves emerge bronze or pink in spring, become dark green in summer, and turn deep red in fall. In warmer zones nandina is evergreen; in the northern limits of its range it is deciduous. In late spring, it produces loose, drooping clusters of white flowers, followed by bright red berries.

Selected species and varieties: *N. domestica*—6 to 8 feet tall, upright with multiple stems from the base, compound leaves are 12 to 20 inches long, flowers are white in loose 8- to 15-inch clusters, fruit is bright red, ⅓-inch diameter in grapelike clusters, effective fall into winter; 'Gulfstream'—2 to 3 feet tall, compact, mounded form; 'Harbour Dwarf'—1 to 2 feet tall with a greater spread, mounding habit.

Growing conditions and maintenance: Nandina prefers a moist, fertile soil but adapts to drier conditions. Add organic matter to the soil prior to planting. Prune by removing one-third of the stems (the oldest canes) at ground level in late winter to maintain a dense habit.

Nerium
(NEE-ree-um)
OLEANDER

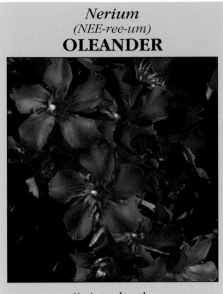

Nerium oleander

Hardiness: *Zones 8-10*

Plant type: *shrub*

Height: *6 to 20 feet*

Interest: *flowers, foliage*

Soil: *moist, well-drained*

Light: *full sun to partial shade*

Oleander is a tough, easy-to-grow evergreen for warm climates. It bears attractive leaves that resemble those of bamboo, as well as clusters of fragrant flowers from spring through fall. All parts of the oleander are poisonous.

Selected species and varieties: *N. oleander*—usually 6 to 12 feet with equal spread, may reach 20 feet, upright stems, bushy, rounded form, leaves are 3 to 5 inches long, leathery, and dark green throughout the year, fragrant flowers form in terminal clusters, are pink, white, or red and very showy, long blooming season; 'Casablanca'—3 to 4 feet, single white flowers; 'Little Red'—red flowers; 'Mrs. Roeddling'—6 feet, smaller leaves result in finer texture, flowers are double and salmon-pink.

Growing conditions and maintenance: Oleanders prefer a moist, well-drained soil but adapt to drier conditions. They tolerate drought, wind, salt spray, and air pollution. Prune in early spring to the desired height and shape and to maintain a dense habit.

Ophiopogon
(o-fi-o-PO-gon)
DWARF MONDO GRASS

Ophiopogon japonicus

Hardiness: *Zones 7-9*

Plant type: *herbaceous perennial*

Height: *6 to 12 inches*

Interest: *foliage, flowers, fruit*

Soil: *moist, well-drained*

Light: *full sun to partial shade*

Dense clumps of grasslike leaves make dwarf mondo grass an excellent ground cover or edging for a bed. It is similar in appearance to liriope but smaller and less hardy. Stems of light blue flowers are produced in the summer, followed by metallic blue berries, though both flowers and fruit are somewhat hidden among the leaves.

Selected species and varieties: *O. japonicus*—6 to 12 inches tall, leaves are dark, evergreen, arching, 8 to 16 inches long, plant spreads by underground runners, tiny individual flowers are lilac-blue and grow in clusters on short stems, steel blue fruit is pea size.

Growing conditions and maintenance: Dwarf mondo grass is adaptable to sun or partial shade, though it prefers some protection from hot afternoon sun. It can be grown under trees and is useful for controlling erosion on slopes. Cut back foliage in early spring before new growth begins. It is easily propagated by division of clumps.

Osmanthus
(oz-MAN-thus)
HOLLY OSMANTHUS

Osmanthus x fortunei

Hardiness: *Zones 7-9*

Plant type: *shrub*

Height: *8 to 20 feet*

Interest: *foliage, flowers, fragrance*

Soil: *moist, well-drained, acid*

Light: *full sun to partial shade*

Holly osmanthus is a large, fragrant, evergreen shrub. Two distinctly different leaves are often present on the same plant: The juvenile leaves are hollylike, with spiny margins, while the adult leaves have smooth margins with a single spine at the tip. In late summer or fall it bears tiny white flowers; although they are largely hidden by the foliage, their presence is unmistakable because they are extremely fragrant. The plant takes shearing well and makes an excellent formal or informal hedge or barrier.

Selected species and varieties: *O. heterophyllus* 'Gulftide'—8 to 10 feet tall, compact, upright habit, leaves are 1 to 2½ inches long, toothed, glossy. *O.* x *fortunei*—15 to 20 feet tall, oval to rounded form, leaves are 2½ to 4 inches long.

Growing conditions and maintenance: Holly osmanthus performs best in a moist, well-drained soil that has been amended with organic matter, but it tolerates drier conditions if grown in partial shade. Plants can be heavily pruned to maintain desired size and shape.

Osteospermum
(os-tee-o-SPER-mum)
AFRICAN DAISY

Osteospermum fruticosum

Hardiness: *Zones 9-10*

Plant type: *herbaceous perennial*

Height: *6 to 12 inches*

Interest: *flowers, foliage*

Soil: *well-drained*

Light: *full sun*

The African daisy is a flowering ground cover for warm zones. It has a trailing habit and spreads rapidly to create a dense mat. Flowers bloom most heavily in late winter and early spring, and intermittently throughout the rest of the year. It makes a lovely show in containers or behind stone walls where it can spill over the edges.

Selected species and varieties: *O. fruticosum*—6 to 12 inches tall with 3-foot spread, stems root where they touch the ground, oval leaves are 1 to 2 inches long, flowers are lavender with purple centers, fading to white, 2 inches across; 'Hybrid White'—more upright habit, white flowers; 'African Queen'—deep purple flowers.

Growing conditions and maintenance: Because the stems root as they grow along the ground, the African daisy is well suited to covering large areas. It thrives in full sun and, once established, tolerates drought. Cut back old plants occasionally to encourage branching and to prevent stems from becoming straggly.

Oxydendrum
(ok-si-DEN-drum)
SORREL TREE

Oxydendrum arboreum

Hardiness: *Zones 5-9*

Plant type: *tree*

Height: *25 to 30 feet*

Interest: *foliage, flowers*

Soil: *moist, well-drained, acid*

Light: *full sun to partial shade*

The sorrel tree provides landscape interest throughout the year. In spring its leaves emerge a lustrous dark green. White, urn-shaped flowers hang in clusters from slender branches in midsummer. The pendulous, light green fruit appears in fall, creating a stunning display against the leaves, which turn a brilliant scarlet. The fruit turns brown and persists into winter.

Selected species and varieties: *O. arboreum*—25 to 30 feet tall and 20 feet wide in cultivation, pyramidal tree with rounded crown and drooping branches, leaves 3 to 8 inches long, fragrant white flowers form in drooping clusters 4 to 10 inches long.

Growing conditions and maintenance: Incorporate generous amounts of organic matter into the soil prior to planting. The trees are slow growing but attractive even when young. Although they thrive in sun or partial shade, plants grown in the sun produce more flowers and better fall color.

Pachysandra
(pak-i-SAN-dra)
PACHYSANDRA

Pachysandra terminalis

Hardiness: *Zones 5-9*

Plant type: *herbaceous perennial*

Height: *6 to 12 inches*

Interest: *foliage, flowers*

Soil: *moist, well-drained, acid*

Light: *partial to full shade*

Pachysandra is a spreading ground cover whose dark green leaves provide a lush carpet beneath trees and shrubs. In early spring, short flower spikes rise from the center of each whorl of leaves.

Selected species and varieties: *P. procumbens* (Allegheny pachysandra, Allegheny spurge)—6 to 12 inches tall, 12 inches wide, leaves are deciduous in cooler zones and semievergreen to evergreen in mild areas, 2 to 4 inches long, prominently toothed, blue-green, often with gray or purple mottling, flowers are white or pink on 2- to 4-inch spikes. *P. terminalis* (Japanese pachysandra)—6 to 8 inches tall, 12 to 18 inches wide, leaves are evergreen, dark, 2 to 4 inches long, flowers are white on 1- to 2-inch spikes.

Growing conditions and maintenance: Pachysandra thrives in the shade; given too much sun, leaves will yellow. It grows well beneath trees. Incorporate organic matter into the soil prior to planting. Space plants 8 to 10 inches apart for a ground cover, and keep new plantings uniformly moist.

Paeonia
(pee-O-nee-a)
PEONY

Paeonia 'Sword Dance'

Hardiness: *Zones 3-8*

Plant type: *herbaceous perennial*

Height: *18 to 36 inches*

Interest: *flowers, foliage*

Soil: *fertile, well-drained*

Light: *full sun to light shade*

Peonies are long-lived plants whose spectacular flowers are set off by mounds of neat foliage. New leaves bear a rosy tint as they emerge in spring, deepening to dark green and remaining attractive throughout the summer until frost. Leaves are compound and form a rounded mound of growth about 3 feet tall and equally as wide. Flowers are large, 3 to 6 inches across, and extremely showy; many are fragrant. Flowers are classified by season (early, mid, late) and form (single, Japanese, anemone, semidouble, and double). The single-flowered form is composed of one row of petals surrounding bright yellow stamens at the center. Japanese and anemone types have a single row of petals surrounding modified stamens that look like finely cut petals. Semidouble peonies have several rows of petals and conspicuous pollen-bearing stamens. Double-flowering forms have a huge, fluffy appearance created by several rows of petals and petallike stamens.

Selected species and varieties: Hundreds of peony varieties offer a selection of height, flower type, season, and color.

'Krinkled White'—27 inches, early-season, single, white; 'Sea Shell'—midseason, single, shell pink; 'Mrs. Franklin D. Roosevelt'—early midseason, double, light pink, fragrant; 'Raspberry Sundae'—27 inches, midseason, double, raspberry pink inner petals, pale pink outer petals, fragrant; 'Therese'—early midseason, double, light pink; 'Gay Paree'—anemone form, midseason, pink with white center; 'Sword Dance'—Japanese form, mid to late season, dark red.

Growing conditions and maintenance: The site for peonies should be well prepared because plants are heavy feeders and prefer to remain undisturbed indefinitely. Incorporate generous amounts of organic matter into the soil, but do not allow manure to come in contact with the fleshy roots. Peonies are best planted in the fall. Place the buds (eyes) 1 to 2 inches below the soil surface; if planted too deep, flowering will be delayed. Full sun will generally produce

Paeonia 'Sea Shell'

the most vigorous growth, but pastel flowers are often seen to best advantage in light shade.

Panicum
(PAN-i-kum)
SWITCH GRASS

Panicum virgatum

Hardiness: *Zones 5-9*

Plant type: *ornamental grass*

Height: *3 to 6 feet*

Interest: *foliage, flowers*

Soil: *moist, well-drained*

Light: *full sun*

Switch grass is excellent for massing as a tall ground cover or screen. Unlike clump-forming grasses, it spreads to cover large areas. In mid to late summer, fine-textured flowers arise from the arching leaves. Both foliage and flowers fade to a soft beige as the weather turns cold, remaining attractive well into winter.

Selected species and varieties: *P. virgatum*—4 to 6 feet tall, leaves are 2 to 3 feet long and ⅝ inch wide, green in summer, turning yellow and red in fall, flowers bloom on large branched stems and are dark red to purple; 'Haense Herms'—3 to 3½ feet, more compact and upright habit, leaves are red from midsummer through frost, seed heads are white-gray; 'Heavy Metal'—3 to 4 feet tall and 2 feet wide, upright, leaves are bluish gray, turning bright yellow in fall, tiny flowers are pinkish tan.

Growing conditions and maintenance: Grow switch grass in full sun. It thrives in moist soil and tolerates much drier conditions, including drought, though it will spread much more slowly. Cut it back to just above the ground in early spring before new growth begins.

Papaver
(pap-AY-ver)
POPPY

Papaver orientale

Hardiness: *Zones 3-8*

Plant type: *herbaceous perennial*

Height: *2 to 4 feet*

Interest: *flowers*

Soil: *well-drained*

Light: *full sun to partial shade*

The silky-textured flowers of Oriental poppies are magnificent though short-lived. They appear in vivid shades of pink, red, salmon, orange, and white in late spring and early summer and last for about 2 weeks.

Selected species and varieties: *P. orientale* (Oriental poppy)—2 to 4 feet, leaves up to 12 inches long, coarse, hairy, toothed, in clumps, flowers on erect stems stand well above the foliage; 'Carousel'—28 inches, compact, petals are white with orange edges; 'China Boy'—flowers are orange and highlighted with white toward inside, maroon center; 'Dubloon'—clear orange double flowers; 'Glowing Rose'—large watermelon pink flowers; 'Helen Elizabeth'—salmon-pink flowers with ruffled edges, early bloomers; 'Snow Queen'—white flowers with black spots.

Growing conditions and maintenance: Plant poppies in well-drained soil; excess winter moisture is often lethal. The foliage dies back after flowering and can leave a void in the garden, so plant among leafy perennials that will fill in the space.

Patrinia
(pat-RIN-ee-a)
PATRINIA

Patrinia scabiosifolia

Hardiness: *Zones 5-9*

Plant type: *herbaceous perennial*

Height: *2 to 6 feet*

Interest: *flowers, seed pods*

Soil: *moist, well-drained*

Light: *full sun to light shade*

Patrinia produces large, airy sprays of flowers late in the summer and fall. These are followed by bright yellow seed pods on orange stems. It is well suited to the middle or rear of a perennial border or a natural garden, where it combines particularly well with ornamental grasses. Patrinia flowers can be cut for long-lasting indoor arrangements.

Selected species and varieties: *P. scabiosifolia*—3 to 6 feet tall, leaves are ruffled, pinnately divided, 6 to 10 inches, and form a large, basal mound, yellow flowers form 2-inch clusters held well above foliage, long-lasting, late summer and fall bloom; 'Nagoya'—2 to 3 feet, compact habit, flowers are almost fluorescent yellow.

Growing conditions and maintenance: Plant patrinias in moist, well-drained soil in sun or light shade. Taller types often require staking. Once established, patrinias are long-lived perennials. They self-sow; to avoid an excess of plants, remove fading flowers before seed is released. They rarely need to be divided.

Pennisetum
(pen-i-SEE-tum)
FOUNTAIN GRASS

Pennisetum alopecuroides

Hardiness: *Zones 5-9*

Plant type: *ornamental grass*

Height: *1 to 5 feet*

Interest: *foliage, flowers*

Soil: *well-drained*

Light: *full sun*

Fountain grass forms large clumps of slender, arching leaves. In mid to late summer, numerous flower stalks arise from the clump, topped with spikes that resemble bottlebrushes. Fountain grass is excellent in small groupings or for massing. It can be used in a herbaceous border, alongside a stream or garden pond, or as an edging along a path.

Selected species and varieties: *P. alopecuroides* (Chinese fountain grass)—3 to 4 feet tall, leaves are 2 to 3 feet long, ¼ inch wide, forming large arching mound, turning a bright almond color in winter, flowers are silvery mauve, 5 to 7 inches long, on erect stems up to 5 feet; 'Hameln'—1 to 2 feet, similar to species with smaller size, finer foliage, and flower heads.

Growing conditions and maintenance: Fountain grass thrives in full sun in nearly any well-drained soil. It tolerates wind and coastal conditions. Cut plants back to 6 inches above the ground before new growth begins in the spring.

Perovskia
(per-OV-skee-a)
RUSSIAN SAGE

Perovskia atriplicifolia

Hardiness: *Zones 5-9*

Plant type: *herbaceous perennial*

Height: *3 to 4 feet*

Interest: *flowers, foliage*

Soil: *well-drained*

Light: *full sun*

Russian sage adds cool colors, pleasing fragrance, and soft texture to any bed in which it is grown. Its leaves are silvery white and aromatic. The flowers are lavender-blue and appear for several weeks in the summer. It is lovely used as a filler among more boldly colored and textured plants in a herbaceous border.

Selected species and varieties: *P. atriplicifolia*—3 to 4 feet tall with equal spread, silver-white leaves and stems have a sagelike aroma when bruised, leaves are 1½ inches long, flowers are pale lavender-blue, two-lipped, growing in branched, spikelike clusters in summer.

Growing conditions and maintenance: Plant Russian sage in full sun; shade causes floppy, sprawling growth. It needs a well-drained soil, and established plants will withstand some drought. Although the lower stems become woody, cut the plant back to within several inches of the ground in early spring to promote bushy growth.

Phlox
(FLOKS)
PHLOX

Phlox divaricata 'Fuller's White'

Hardiness: *Zones 3-9*

Plant type: *herbaceous perennial*

Height: *3 inches to 3 feet*

Interest: *flowers, foliage*

Soil: *dry to moist, sandy to fertile*

Light: *full sun to full shade*

Species of phlox vary widely in their height, habit, uses, and cultural requirements. Some are low-growing spreaders; others are tall, erect border flowers. While some like full sun, others need shade. Some need abundant moisture; others prefer to be dry. Phlox flowers, which are borne singly or in clusters, all have five flat petals and often a conspicuous eye in the center.

Selected species and varieties: *P. divaricata* (wild blue phlox)—9 to 15 inches, spreading, blue flowers, fragrant in spring, Zones 4-9; 'Dirgo Ice'—8 to 12 inches, pale lavender flowers, very fragrant; 'Fuller's White'—8 to 12 inches, white flowers. *P. maculata* (spotted phlox, wild sweet William)—up to 3 feet with cylindrical flower heads in shades of pink to white from midsummer to fall, Zones 3-9; 'Miss Lingard'—6-inch trusses of pure white blossoms. *P. stolonifera* (creeping phlox)—up to 12 inches, spreading, evergreen leaves, dense clusters of flowers in shades of blue, pink, or white, spring bloom, excellent as a ground cover in partial shade, Zones 3-8; 'Blue Ridge'—8 inches, clear blue flowers; 'Bruce's White'—6 inches, white flowers. *P. subulata* (moss phlox, moss pink)—3 to 6 inches tall, spreads 2 feet, evergreen leaves, flowers in wide color range in early to midspring, excellent ground cover for sunny, dry sites, and very effective cascading over stones, Zones 3-9; 'Cushion Blue', 'Emerald Pink', and 'Snowflake' are among the many excellent varieties that offer brilliant spring colors.

Growing conditions and maintenance: Phlox has diverse cultural requirements. With care in selection, an appropriate species can be found for nearly any site. Wild blue phlox thrives in shady, moist, wooded areas, where it naturalizes freely. Spotted phlox prefers a sunny, well-drained site. It is well suited to a sunny border, where it will stand erect without the need for staking. Both creeping phlox and moss phlox form lush mats of evergreen foliage and make wonderful ground covers. Creeping phlox will grow in moist sun or shade; partial shade is ideal. Moss phlox needs a drier site in full sun and is a perfect choice for a dry bank, rock garden, or stone wall. Promote dense growth and reblooming by cutting plants back after flowering.

Pieris
(PYE-er-is)
PIERIS

Pieris japonica 'Deep Pink'

Hardiness: *Zones 5-8*

Plant type: *shrub*

Height: *2 to 12 feet*

Interest: *foliage, flowers, buds*

Soil: *moist, well-drained, acid*

Light: *full sun to partial shade*

Pieris provides beauty all year long. It makes an outstanding specimen, foundation, border, or woodland shrub.

Selected species and varieties: *P. floribunda*—2 to 6 feet tall and wide, bushy, low habit, evergreen leaves 1 to 3 inches long, fragrant white flowers bloom in 2- to 4-inch upright clusters in midspring. *P. japonica* (Japanese andromeda)—9 to 12 feet tall, 6 to 8 feet wide, leaves emerge bronze-pink in spring, become dark green in summer, evergreen, 1½ to 3½ inches long, flowers are white, urn-shaped, in pendulous 3- to 6-inch clusters in early to midspring, flower buds form in late summer in attractive, drooping chains; 'Dorothy Wyckoff'—compact form, red buds open to pale pink flowers; 'Flamingo'—deep rose-red flowers; 'Valley Rose'—tall, open habit, pink flowers; 'White Cascade'—heavy flowering, white flowers, long-lasting.

Growing conditions and maintenance: Grow pieris in well-drained soil supplemented with organic matter. Provide protection from heavy winds.

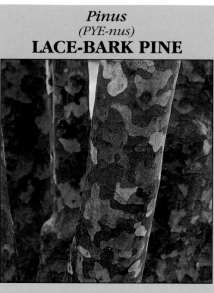

Pinus
(PYE-nus)
LACE-BARK PINE

Pinus bungeana

Hardiness: *Zones 4-8*

Plant type: *tree*

Height: *30 to 75 feet*

Interest: *bark, foliage*

Soil: *well-drained*

Light: *full sun*

The bark of the lace-bark pine exfoliates in irregular plates to reveal attractive tones of brown, creamy white, and green. Though slow growing, it makes an outstanding specimen with year-round garden interest.

Selected species and varieties: *P. bungeana*—usually 30 to 50 feet tall but may reach 75 feet, 20 to 35 feet wide, rounded to pyramidal, picturesque habit, often with multiple trunks, older specimens become broad-spreading, needles are 2 to 4 inches long, stiff, medium to dark green, cones are 2 to 3 inches long, bark exfoliates at very young age, when branches are only 1 inch in diameter.

Growing conditions and maintenance: The lace-bark pine prefers a sunny site with well-drained soil. It is best placed in a spot where the bark can be viewed at close range. It is somewhat weak-wooded, and can be damaged by snow and ice loads. Remove snow before too much weight accumulates.

Pittosporum
(pit-o-SPO-rum)
JAPANESE PITTOSPORUM

Pittosporum tobira

Hardiness: *Zones 8-10*

Plant type: *shrub*

Height: *10 to 12 feet*

Interest: *foliage, flowers*

Soil: *well-drained*

Light: *full sun to full shade*

Japanese pittosporums are handsome evergreens for warm climates. They can be grown unpruned as an informal hedge, or can be sheared for a more formal look. They are attractive as foundation plants, under trees, or in containers. Their flowers, although not very showy, are extremely fragrant in late spring.

Selected species and varieties: *P. to-bira*—10 to 12 feet tall, 15 to 20 feet wide with a dense, impenetrable habit, leaves are 1½ to 4 inches long, leathery, dark green, flowers are creamy white, inconspicuous but fragrant, blooming in the spring.

Growing conditions and maintenance: Japanese pittosporums are durable and easy to transplant. They will adapt to almost any well-drained soil, including sandy, dry locations. They tolerate heat, wind, and salt spray, so are well suited to coastal conditions. Established plants will tolerate drought and withstand heavy pruning. Plants thrive in both full sun and dense shade.

Platycodon
(plat-i-KO-don)
BALLOON FLOWER

Platycodon grandiflorus

Hardiness: *Zones 4-9*

Plant type: *herbaceous perennial*

Height: *10 to 36 inches*

Interest: *flowers, buds*

Soil: *well-drained, acid*

Light: *full sun to partial shade*

Balloon flowers are long-lived perennials that bear blue, white, or pink flowers throughout the summer. The common name derives from the fat, round flower buds that pop open as they mature.

Selected species and varieties: *P. gran-diflorus*—24 to 36 inches, leaves are blue-green, 1 to 3 inches long, in neat clumps, rounded flower buds look inflated and pop when squeezed, flowers are usually blue, saucer-shaped, 2 to 3 inches across, on erect stems; *P. g.* 'Mariesii'—18 inches tall, compact form, bright blue flowers; 'Apoyama'—10 inches tall, violet-blue flowers produced over a long period.

Growing conditions and maintenance: Plant balloon flowers in well-drained, slightly acid soil; they do not tolerate a soggy location. They are late to emerge in the spring, so mark their location in the garden to avoid injury or crowding. These are slow-growing perennials and can remain undisturbed for many years without division.

Plumbago
(plum-BAY-go)
CAPE PLUMBAGO

Plumbago auriculata

Hardiness: *Zones 9-11*

Plant type: *shrub*

Height: *6 to 8 feet*

Interest: *flowers, foliage*

Soil: *well-drained*

Light: *full sun to partial shade*

Cape plumbago is a large evergreen shrub that develops a mounded habit with long vinelike branches. Flowers are azure blue or white, and under ideal conditions they will appear year round.

Selected species and varieties: *P. auriculata*—6 to 8 feet tall, spreading 8 to 12 feet or more, leaves are 1 to 2 inches long, medium to light green, evergreen, flowers are 1 inch across in 3- to 4-inch clusters, blue or white, main blooming season is from early spring through fall.

Growing conditions and maintenance: Cape plumbago is a mounding shrub and can be maintained through pruning as a dense, low hedge or foundation plant. If trained it will climb a trellis or wall, and it is also well suited as a tall ground cover for large, well-drained slopes. Cape plumbago thrives in full sun but tolerates light shade in hot areas; it tolerates coastal conditions as well, but is sensitive to frost. Prune the oldest canes to the ground each year in early spring, and pinch new growth to encourage branching.

Polygonatum
(po-lig-o-NAY-tum)
SOLOMON'S-SEAL

Polygonatum odoratum 'Variegatum'

Hardiness: *Zones 3-9*

Plant type: *herbaceous perennial*

Height: *2 to 3 feet*

Interest: *flowers, foliage*

Soil: *moist, acid loam*

Light: *partial to full shade*

Small, nodding flowers dangle from the graceful, arching stems of Solomon's-seal. Pairs of broad leaves up to 4 inches long line the stems. Solomon's-seal combines well with spring-flowering bulbs or shade-loving shrubs, and the foliage can be used in arrangements.

Selected species and varieties: *P. multiflorum* (European Solomon's-seal)—handsome, bright green leaves up to 6 inches long on stems up to 3 feet long. *P. odoratum thunbergii* 'Variegatum'—white flowers tipped with green and leaves edged in white.

Growing conditions and maintenance: Plant 1 foot apart in cool, moist, shady sites where the soil contains ample organic matter. Propagate from seed or by division in spring.

Potentilla
(po-ten-TILL-a)
BUSH CINQUEFOIL

Potentilla fruticosa

Hardiness: *Zones 2-7*

Plant type: *shrub*

Height: *1 to 4 feet*

Interest: *flowers, foliage*

Soil: *adaptable*

Light: *full sun to partial shade*

Bush cinquefoil is a low-growing shrub with neat foliage and a long flowering season. It has many landscape uses, serving as a low hedge, foundation planting, or edging; it can also be combined with other shrubs or perennials in a mixed border.

Selected species and varieties: *P. fruticosa*—1 to 4 feet tall, 2 to 4 feet wide, compound leaves, new leaves are gray-green, turning dark green, flowers are 1 inch across, bright yellow, from early summer to late fall; 'Abbotswood'—2 feet with white flowers and dark bluish green leaves; 'Coronation Triumph'—3 to 4 feet, gracefully arching habit, lemon yellow cuplike flowers; 'Primrose Beauty'—3 feet, primrose flowers with deeper colored centers; 'Tangerine'—2 to 4 feet, flowers are yellow flushed with orange-copper tones.

Growing conditions and maintenance: The bush cinquefoil thrives in moist, well-drained soil but tolerates poor, dry soil as well. It produces more flowers in full sun but grows well in partial shade. Prune a third of the oldest stems back to the ground in late winter.

Prunus
(PROO-nus)
CHERRY, CHERRY LAUREL

Prunus laurocerasus

Hardiness: *Zones 4-10*

Plant type: *shrub or small tree*

Height: *10 to 50 feet*

Interest: *foliage, flowers, bark*

Soil: *moist, well-drained*

Light: *full sun to moderate shade*

Cherry laurels are large evergreen shrubs with fragrant spring blossoms. They are useful for hedges, screens, and large foundation plantings. Flowering cherries are trees with year-round landscape interest. In spring, flowers cover the branches before the leaves emerge. The summer leaves are a lustrous dark green, and in some varieties they turn red or gold in fall. Winter exposes the shiny reddish bronze bark. The branches gnarl with age.

Selected species and varieties: *P. caroliniana* (Carolina cherry laurel)—20 to 30 feet tall, 15 to 25 feet wide, dense evergreen shrub with irregular outline, often pruned as a formal hedge, leaves are dark green, 2 to 3 inches long, flowers are small, white, fragrant, and appear in early spring; Zones 7-10. *P. laurocerasus* (common cherry laurel)—10 to 30 feet, wide-spreading evergreen shrub, dense, leaves are 2 to 6 inches long, glossy, medium to dark green, flowers are small, white, fragrant, blooming in 2- to 5-inch-long clusters in midspring, Zones 6-8; 'Otto Luyken'—3 to 4 feet tall, 6 to 8 feet wide; 'Schipkaensis'—4 to 5 feet tall, dark green, narrow leaves, hardy to Zone 5; 'Zabeliana'—3 feet tall, up to 12 feet wide, dark green leaves are narrow, willowlike. *P. sargentii* (Sargent cherry)—40 to 50 feet with equal spread, deciduous tree, leaves are 3 to 5 inches, emerging bronze in spring, turning dark green in summer and bronze or red in fall, bark is shiny, reddish brown, with horizontal markings (lenticels), flowers are single, pink, 1½ inches across, opening before leaves emerge in spring, excellent specimen tree; Zones 4-7. *P.* 'Hally Jolivette'—cross between *P. subhirtella* (Higan cherry) and *P. yedoensis* (Japanese flowering cherry), 15 to 20 feet, rounded, shrubby, deciduous tree, pink flower buds open to pale pinkish white, double flowers 1¼ inches across in late spring; Zones 5-7.

Growing conditions and maintenance: Cherry laurels and flowering cherries require a well-drained soil and benefit from the addition of generous amounts of organic matter. Cherry laurels thrive in both sun and shade. Common cherry laurel withstands wind and salt spray, making it useful as a windbreak. Carolina cherry laurel tends to discolor in winter if exposed to sun and heavy winds. Both cherry laurels take pruning well and can be maintained as a formal hedge or left unpruned as a screen. Avoid excess fertilization. The Sargent and 'Hally Jolivette' cherries perform best in full sun. Water during dry periods and provide a year-round mulch. Little pruning is necessary.

Pyracantha
(py-ra-KAN-tha)
SCARLET FIRETHORN

Pyracantha coccinea 'Mojave'

Hardiness: *Zones 6-9*

Plant type: *shrub*

Height: *4 to 16 feet*

Interest: *fruit, flowers, foliage*

Soil: *well-drained*

Light: *full sun*

The scarlet firethorn is a semievergreen shrub with white spring flowers and stunning orange-red berries that ripen in the fall and persist into winter. It can be used effectively as a hedge or barrier; its ½-inch spines along the stems make it impenetrable. It is also a good choice as an espalier specimen, trained against a wall.

Selected species and varieties: *P. coccinea* 'Apache'—4 to 6 feet, compact form, bright red fruit; 'Mojave'—6 to 10 feet, upright, densely branched, orange-red fruit in very heavy clusters; 'Navaho'—up to 6 feet, slightly greater spread, low-growing, mounded habit, orange-red fruit; 'Teton'—up to 16 feet tall, 9 feet wide, upright habit, yellow-orange fruit.

Growing conditions and maintenance: Plant scarlet firethorn in spring, choosing a well-drained site in full sun. Plants will grow in partial shade, but flower and fruit production will be reduced. Prune anytime to maintain desired size and shape.

Pyrus
(PY-rus)
CALLERY PEAR

Pyrus calleryana

Hardiness: *Zones 5-8*

Plant type: *tree*

Height: *40 feet*

Interest: *flowers, foliage*

Soil: *well-drained*

Light: *full sun*

Callery pears are showy, spring-flowering, deciduous trees with glossy green summer leaves that turn deep red to purple in the fall. The small, round, russet-colored fruit provides winter food for birds.

Selected species and varieties: *P. calleryana* 'Capital'—40 feet tall with 12-foot spread, distinctly columnar form with strongly ascending branching pattern, leaves are dark green in summer, red to red-purple in early fall, remaining on tree late, off-white flowers are profuse in early spring, useful as a tall screen or windbreak; 'Whitehouse'—40 feet tall, 18 feet wide, pyramidal form, leaves are long and pointed, glossy green, turning wine red in fall, white flowers in spring, useful where space is limited.

Growing conditions and maintenance: Plant callery pears in late winter or early spring while they are still dormant. They adapt to nearly any well-drained soil and tolerate dryness and pollution. Prune while dormant. 'Capital' may be susceptible to fire blight.

Raphiolepis
(raf-ee-O-le-pis)
INDIAN HAWTHORN

Raphiolepis indica

Hardiness: *Zones 8-10*

Plant type: *shrub*

Height: *3 to 6 feet*

Interest: *foliage, flowers*

Soil: *moist, well-drained*

Light: *full sun*

Indian hawthorn is a medium-size evergreen shrub that produces showy white or pink flowers in early spring. It is useful for massing or growing in containers, and is attractive as an unpruned hedge in southern gardens.

Selected species and varieties: *R. indica*—3 to 6 feet, equally wide, dense, rounded form, leaves are dark, leathery, evergreen, 2 to 3 inches long, flowers are white, pink, or rose-red, blooming in early spring, followed by clusters of purple-black berries that persist through winter; 'Charisma'—3 to 4 feet, light pink double flowers; 'Snow White'—4 feet, white flowers; 'Springtime'—up to 6 feet, deep pink flowers, prolific bloom.

Growing conditions and maintenance: Indian hawthorn thrives in moist, well-drained soils but adapts to drier conditions, and established plants will withstand drought. Plants tolerate the salt spray of coastal conditions. They are well suited to growing in containers and rarely need pruning.

Rhododendron
(roh-doh-DEN-dron)
RHODODENDRON

Rhododendron schlippenbachii

Hardiness: *Zones 3-8*

Plant type: *shrub*

Height: *3 to 10 feet*

Interest: *flowers, foliage*

Soil: *moist, well-drained, acid*

Light: *full sun to partial shade*

The genus *Rhododendron* includes over 900 species of flowering plants that are commonly known as rhododendrons and azaleas. Although the distinguishing features between them are not always clear-cut, most true rhododendrons are evergreen, while most azaleas are deciduous. Also, rhododendron flowers are usually bell-shaped, whereas azaleas are funnel-shaped, and rhododendron leaves are often scaly, while azalea leaves never are. Numerous varieties of the different species afford gardeners choices in size, growth habit, hardiness, flower color, and season. Both azaleas and rhododendrons offer endless landscaping possibilities, from woodland gardens and mixed-shrub borders to specimen or foundation plants. They are effective both in small groupings and in large mass plantings.

Selected species and varieties: *R.* 'Boule de Neige'—5 feet tall, up to 8 feet wide, compact, rounded habit, leaves are dark, evergreen, flowers are white in large trusses; Zones 5-8. *R. calendulaceum* (flame azalea)—4 to 9 feet, with 10- to 15-foot spread, deciduous, upright habit,

leaves are medium green in summer, turning yellow to red in fall, flowers are 2 inches across, scarlet, orange, or yellow, long-lasting, appear in late spring or early summer; Zones 5-7. *R. catawbiense* (Catawba rhododendron)—6 to 18 feet tall with slightly less spread, leaves are evergreen, large, dark, dense all the way to the ground, flowers are lilac-purple with green or yellow markings in 5- to 6-inch trusses, late-spring bloom, hybrids are available with white, pink, red, lavender-blue, and bicolored flowers; Zones 4-8. *R. kaempferi*—up to 10 feet tall, 5 to 6 feet wide, leaves are dark, semievergreen to deciduous, turning reddish in fall, flowers are red, orange, salmon, pink, purple, violet, or white; Zones 5-8. *R. schlippenbachii* (royal azalea)—6 to 10 feet tall, equally wide, upright, rounded habit, leaves are deciduous, dark green in summer, turning red, orange, and yellow in fall, flowers are soft, rose-

Rhododendron 'P.J.M.'

pink, freckled on upper petals, fragrant, blooming in spring; Zones 4-7. *R. vaseyi* (pink-shell azalea)—5 to 10 feet tall with irregular, upright habit, leaves are deciduous, medium green in summer, turning red in fall, rose-pink flowers bloom late spring to early summer, Zones 3-8; 'White Find'—fragrant white flowers with yellow-green blotch. *R. yakusimanum*—3 to 4 feet tall and 3 feet wide with dense, rounded habit, dark leaves, evergreen, flower buds are pink or rose-colored, opening to white flowers in spring, hybrids are available with flowers in shades of pink or red; Zones 5-8. *R. yedoense* var. *poukhanense* (Korean azalea)—3 to 6 feet tall with equal or greater spread, leaves are deciduous in the

North and nearly evergreen in milder zones, dark green in summer, turning orange, purple, or dark red in fall, reddish purple flowers in late spring; Zones 4-8.

Growing conditions and maintenance: Plant rhododendrons and azaleas in moist, well-drained, acid soil amended with generous amounts of organic matter. Do not plant in poorly drained soil, and avoid setting new plants too deep. They grow well in both sun and light shade, though in warmer zones some shade is preferred. Pruning is almost never necessary. Plants do not tolerate alkaline or saline soils, and dry winter winds often cause leaf burn on evergreen types.

Romneya
(RAHM-nee-a)
CALIFORNIA TREE POPPY

Romneya coulteri

Hardiness: *Zones 7-10*

Plant type: *herbaceous perennial*

Height: *4 to 8 feet*

Interest: *flowers, foliage*

Soil: *dry, infertile*

Light: *full sun*

The California tree poppy produces fragrant 3- to 6-inch flowers with silky white petals surrounding a bright golden center. They bloom throughout the summer, and though each flower lasts only a few days, they make a handsome show in both the garden and indoor arrangements.

Selected species and varieties: *R. coulteri*—up to 8 feet tall, 3 feet wide, multiple branched stems, spreading by suckers from roots, leaves are gray-green and deeply cut, fragrant summer flowers are very large with 5 or 6 crinkled white petals that resemble crepe paper surrounding golden stamens, useful for naturalizing on dry banks, may become invasive in a border.

Growing conditions and maintenance: Plant California tree poppies in poor, dry soil in full sun where invasive roots will not cause a problem. They are most successfully grown in Zones 8 to 10 but can survive in Zone 7 with a heavy winter mulch. Cut them back nearly to the ground in late fall.

Rosa
(RO-za)
ROSE

Rosa 'Tuscany'

Hardiness: *Zones 2-10*

Plant type: *shrub*

Height: *4 to 20 feet*

Interest: *flowers, foliage, fruit*

Soil: *well-drained, humus-rich*

Light: *full sun*

The following shrub roses bear lovely, fragrant blossoms, attractive foliage, and showy fruit with very little care.

Selected species and varieties: *R. alba* 'Incarnata' (cottage rose)—4 to 6 feet, double white flowers with pink blush in early summer, scarlet fruit in fall; Zones 4-10. *R. banksiae*—15 to 20 feet, climbing habit requires support, stems are nearly thornless, leaves are evergreen, white or yellow flowers bloom midspring to early summer; Zones 7-8. *R. rugosa* (rugosa rose)—4 to 6 feet tall and wide, leaves are lustrous and deep green in summer, yellow, bronze, or red in fall, flowers are purple to white, fruit is deep red in fall, Zones 2-10; 'Alba'—single white flowers. *R. virginiana* (Virginia rose)—4 to 6 feet tall, dark green summer leaves turn orange, red, and yellow in fall, single flowers are pink, bloom in early summer; Zones 3-8.

Growing conditions and maintenance: Plant roses in well-drained soil amended with organic matter. They require very little pruning. Rugosa and Virginia roses tolerate salt spray and sandy soils.

Rudbeckia
(rood-BEK-ee-a)
CONEFLOWER

Rudbeckia

Hardiness: *Zones 4-9*

Plant type: *herbaceous perennial*

Height: *2 to 7 feet*

Interest: *flowers*

Soil: *well-drained*

Light: *full sun to light shade*

Coneflowers bear prolific yellow flowers with a contrasting center over an exceptionally long season. They are an undemanding perennial and a rewarding addition to nearly any sunny border. They combine particularly well with ornamental grasses in an informal garden.

Selected species and varieties: *R. fulgida* var. *sullivantii* 'Goldsturm'—24 inches tall, compact, dark green leaves set off the flowers perfectly, deep yellow raylike flower petals surround black-brown centers, produced early summer through fall, extremely free-flowering, resistant to powdery mildew. *R. nitida* 'Herbstsonne'—2 to 7 feet tall, bright green leaves, flowers are 3 to 4 inches across and have drooping yellow rays with green centers, bloom from mid to late summer, excellent for the back of borders, often requires staking.

Growing conditions and maintenance: Coneflowers thrive in well-drained soil in full sun and tolerate heat, making them a good choice for southern gardens. They will grow in light shade but produce fewer flowers.

Salvia
(SAL-vee-a)
SAGE

Salvia greggii

Hardiness: *Zones 4-10*

Plant type: *herbaceous perennial*

Height: *2 to 4 feet*

Interest: *flowers, foliage*

Soil: *well-drained*

Light: *full sun*

Sage is a shrubby perennial that offers colorful summer and fall flowers and attractive, often fragrant foliage. It has square stems and small, tubular flowers characteristic of the mint family. Its neat growth habit and long flowering season make it a useful addition to the perennial border.

Selected species and varieties: *S. azurea* ssp. *pitcheri* (Pitcher's sage)—3 to 4 feet tall, 4 feet wide, azure blue flowers from late summer through fall; Zones 5-9. *S. greggii* (autumn sage)—2 to 3 feet tall, fall flowers are red, purple-red, pink, or coral, may become a small shrub in the South; Zones 7-10. *S. x superba* (perennial salvia)—2 to 3 feet tall, 2 feet wide, blue to violet-blue flowers on 4- to 8-inch flower stems throughout summer; Zones 5-8.

Growing conditions and maintenance: Sage thrives in moist, well-drained soil but will adapt to light shade and drier conditions and can withstand drought. Excess moisture in winter usually causes plants to rot. Cut back old stems in late fall or winter.

Santolina
(san-to-LEE-na)
LAVENDER COTTON

Santolina chamaecyparissus

Hardiness: *Zones 6-8*

Plant type: *herbaceous perennial*

Height: *18 to 24 inches*

Interest: *foliage, flowers*

Soil: *well-drained to dry*

Light: *full sun*

Lavender cotton forms a broad, spreading clump of aromatic leaves. It makes an attractive edging for a bed or walkway, or can be used as a low-growing specimen in a rock garden. It can also be sheared to form a tight, low hedge.

Selected species and varieties: *S. chamaecyparissus*—up to 24 inches tall with equal or greater spread, forms a broad, cushionlike, evergreen mound, aromatic leaves are silvery gray-green and ½ to 1½ inches long, yellow flowers are button-shaped in summer and are often removed to maintain a clipped hedge.

Growing conditions and maintenance: Lavender cotton is a tough plant, well suited to adverse conditions such as drought and salt spray. It prefers dry soils of low fertility and becomes unattractive and open in fertile soils. Avoid excess moisture, especially in winter. Prune after flowering to promote dense growth, or shear anytime for a formal, low hedge.

Sedum
(SEE-dum)
STONECROP

Sedum x 'Autumn Joy'

Hardiness: *Zones 3-10*

Plant type: *succulent perennial*

Height: *6 inches to 2 feet*

Interest: *foliage, flowers*

Soil: *well-drained*

Light: *full sun to light shade*

Stonecrops are valued both for their thick succulent leaves and for their dense clusters of star-shaped flowers. They add color and rich texture to a perennial border or rock garden from spring through fall.

Selected species and varieties: *S.* x 'Autumn Joy'—15 to 24 inches tall, attractive all year long, leaves emerge gray-green in spring, flower buds are rosy pink in midsummer, opening to bronze-red flowers in fall, turning golden brown in winter. *S.* x 'Ruby Glow'—8 inches, purple-gray leaves, red flowers in late summer and fall, excellent for front of border. *S.* x 'Vera Jameson'—12 inches, coppery purple leaves, pink flowers in fall. *S. sieboldii*—6 to 9 inches, somewhat trailing habit, blue-gray leaves, pink flowers in fall.

Growing conditions and maintenance: Stonecrops tolerate nearly any well-drained soil, including sterile, dry sites. They spread without becoming invasive and can usually be left undisturbed for many years.

Solidago
(sol-i-DAY-go)
GOLDENROD

Solidago sphacelata 'Golden Fleece'

Hardiness: *Zones 3-9*

Plant type: *herbaceous perennial*

Height: *1 to 3 feet*

Interest: *flowers*

Soil: *well-drained*

Light: *full sun to light shade*

Goldenrod is easy to grow and produces abundant late-season flowers over an extended period. The bold yellow flowers occur in dense, feathery clusters on erect stems. They are a cheerful addition to informal borders, or in fresh or dried indoor arrangements.

Selected species and varieties: A number of excellent hybrids represent improvements to the wild goldenrods; 'Goldenmosa'—30 to 36 inches tall with large dark yellow flowers from late summer through fall; 'Golden Fleece'—12 to 24 inches tall, dwarf, spreading habit, dark green leaves, arching and multiple-branched stems bear bright yellow flowers from late summer to early fall, good choice for ground cover.

Growing conditions and maintenance: Goldenrod thrives in any well-drained soil and looks its best when fertility is low to average; a fertile site leads to rank, invasive growth. Tall varieties often require staking. Contrary to popular belief, goldenrod does not cause hay fever.

Spigelia
(spy-JEE-lee-a)
PINKROOT, INDIAN PINK

Spigelia marilandica

Hardiness: *Zones 5-9*

Plant type: *herbaceous perennial*

Height: *1 to 2 feet*

Interest: *flowers*

Soil: *moist, well-drained, acid*

Light: *partial shade*

Pinkroot bears interesting trumpet-shaped flowers along one side of an arching stem. The 2-inch flowers are red with yellow throats, and all face upward, creating an unusual and pleasing effect. This is a nice selection for the front of a shady border or along a garden path, where its flower display can be viewed at close range.

Selected species and varieties: *S. marilandica*—1 to 2 feet tall, 18 inches wide, erect stems, 3- to 4-inch-long leaves, flowers are pinkish red with yellow throats and trumpet-shaped in elongated clusters at ends of stems, blooming late spring to early summer.

Growing conditions and maintenance: Plant pinkroot in a well-drained, slightly acid soil amended with organic matter. It thrives in partial shade, especially in warmer climates, but tolerates full sun if adequate moisture is supplied. It does not compete well with surface tree roots. Division of the clumps is an easy way to increase plants.

Spiraea
(spy-REE-a)
SPIREA

Spiraea x bumalda 'Anthony Waterer'

Hardiness:	*Zones 3-8*
Plant type:	*shrub*
Height:	*3 to 5 feet*
Interest:	*flowers, foliage*
Soil:	*well-drained*
Light:	*full sun*

Spireas are easy-to-grow deciduous shrubs that produce an abundance of dainty flowers in spring or summer. Spring-blooming spireas bear flowers in clusters along the entire length of the stems; summer-blooming types bear their flower clusters at the ends of stems.

Selected species and varieties: S. x *bumalda* 'Anthony Waterer'—2 to 4 feet tall, 4 to 5 feet wide, leaves emerge bronze in spring and turn blue-green in summer, carmine-pink flowers bloom in 4- to 6-inch clusters in summer. S. x *cinerea* 'Grefsheim'—4 to 5 feet tall and wide, arching stems, soft green leaves are 1 inch long, white flowers bloom along stems in spring. S. *nipponica* 'Snowmound'—3 to 5 feet tall and wide, dark blue-green leaves, white flowers bloom along stems in late spring.

Growing conditions and maintenance: Spireas perform best in full sun; they tolerate partial shade but produce fewer flowers. They adapt to nearly any well-drained soil. Remove faded flowers of 'Anthony Waterer' spirea to encourage a second bloom.

Stachys
(STAY-kis)
LAMB'S EARS

Stachys 'Helene Von Stein'

Hardiness:	*Zones 4-9*
Plant type:	*herbaceous perennial*
Height:	*6 to 18 inches*
Interest:	*foliage*
Soil:	*well-drained*
Light:	*full sun to light shade*

Lamb's ears is a low-growing, spreading perennial that adds soft color and texture to the front of a perennial border, alongside a path, or as a ground cover. Its gray-green leaves are covered with white hairs, giving them the appearance and feel of velvet. Nonflowering varieties eliminate the need for removing flowers that are often considered unattractive.

Selected species and varieties: S. *byzantina* 'Silver Carpet'—12 to 15 inches tall with 18- to 24-inch spread, leaves and stems densely covered with white hairs, leaves up to 4 inches long, no flowers; 'Helene Von Stein'—larger leaves, few flowers, tolerates hot, humid weather.

Growing conditions and maintenance: Plant lamb's ears in well-drained soil that is not too fertile. Excess moisture encourages leaf rot. For use as a ground cover, space plants 12 to 18 inches apart. Remove old leaves before new growth begins in spring.

Stephanandra
(stef-a-NAN-dra)
LACE SHRUB

Stephanandra incisa 'Crispa'

Hardiness:	*Zones 3-8*
Plant type:	*shrub*
Height:	*1½ to 3 feet*
Interest:	*foliage*
Soil:	*moist, well-drained, acid*
Light:	*full sun to light shade*

Lace shrub is a tidy plant with a gracefully mounding habit. It can be grown on banks to prevent erosion or used as a low hedge or tall ground cover. Its dense foliage and low habit make it well suited to growing under low windows or among tall, leggy shrubs in a mixed border.

Selected species and varieties: S. *incisa* 'Crispa'—1½ to 3 feet tall, 4 feet wide, spreads by arching branches rooting readily when they touch the ground, leaves are 1 to 2 inches long, deeply lobed, bright green, turning reddish purple or red-orange in the fall, inconspicuous pale yellow flowers appear in early summer.

Growing conditions and maintenance: Plant lace shrub in moist, acid soil in full sun or light shade. Add generous amounts of organic matter to the soil prior to planting to help retain moisture. Plants require little pruning other than removing winter-damaged tips in early spring.

Syringa
(si-RING-ga)
LILAC

Syringa laciniata

Hardiness: *Zones 3-8*

Plant type: *shrub*

Height: *3 to 6 feet*

Interest: *flowers, foliage*

Soil: *moist, well-drained*

Light: *full sun*

Lilacs are lovely, old-fashioned, deciduous shrubs that produce fragrant, late-spring flowers in dense grapelike clusters. They make attractive landscape specimens and informal hedges, and are well suited to use in a mixed-shrub border.

Selected species and varieties: *S. microphylla* 'Superba'—6 feet tall and 12 feet wide with dense, wide-spreading habit, medium green leaves 1 to 2½ inches long, deep pink flowers, prolific; Zones 4-7. *S. patula* 'Miss Kim'—3 feet tall and wide (but may grow somewhat larger under ideal conditions), dark green leaves 2 to 5 inches long, flowers in 3-inch-long clusters are purple in bud and icy blue when open; Zones 3-8.

Growing conditions and maintenance: Plant lilacs in well-drained soil amended with organic matter. Fertilize every other year. Prune the oldest stems with reduced flower production back to the ground immediately after flowering, and remove faded flowers as well.

Taxus
(TAKS-us)
YEW

Yews are evergreen shrubs with flat, needlelike leaves. The deep green, glossy foliage provides a stunning contrast to brightly colored plants. Yews are effective as foundation plants, hedges, and specimens. Seeds, leaves, and bark are poisonous.

Taxus x media 'Hicksii'

Hardiness: *Zones 4-7*

Plant type: *shrub*

Height: *2 to 20 feet*

Interest: *foliage, fruit*

Soil: *fertile, moist, well-drained*

Light: *full sun to full shade*

Selected species and varieties: *T. baccata* 'Repandens'—2 to 4 feet tall, 12 to 15 feet across, dwarf, wide-spreading habit, extremely dark green leaves, red fruit; Zones 5-7. *T. cuspidata* 'Densa'—3 to 4 feet high, 6 to 8 feet wide, dense habit, dark green leaves, abundant fruit; 'Thayerae'—up to 8 feet tall, 16 feet wide, flat-topped habit. *T. x media* 'Densiformis'—3 to 4 feet tall, 4 to 6 feet wide, dense, bright green leaves; 'Hicksii'—20 feet tall, ascending branches, columnar habit, dark green leaves.

Growing conditions and maintenance: Excellent drainage is essential for growing yews. They perform well in sun or shade and benefit from protection from drying winds. Yews take pruning and shearing well.

Vaccinium
(vak-SIN-ee-um)
BLUEBERRY

Vaccinium corymbosum

Hardiness: *Zones 2-8*

Plant type: *shrub*

Height: *6 inches to 12 feet*

Interest: *foliage, flowers, fruit*

Soil: *moist, well-drained, acid*

Light: *full sun to partial shade*

The blue-green summer leaves of blueberries become a riot of color in fall. Delicate spring flowers and edible, delicious berries add to the landscape value of this native shrub.

Selected species and varieties: *V. corymbosum* (highbush blueberry)—6 to 12 feet tall, 8 to 12 feet wide, multiple-stemmed shrub with rounded, upright habit, leaves are 1 to 3½ inches long, blue-green in summer, turning red, orange, yellow, and bronze in fall, flowers are white, urn-shaped, ½ inch long, fruit is blue-black, ¼ to ½ inch across; Zones 3-8. *V. angustifolium* (lowbush blueberry)—6 inches to 2 feet tall, 2 feet wide, low spreading habit, leaves are ⅓ to ¾ inch long, blue-green in summer, turning red to bronze in fall, flowers are white with red tinge, delicious fruit is blue-black and ¼ to ½ inch across; Zones 2-6.

Growing conditions and maintenance: Plant blueberries in moist, well-drained soil with a pH of 4.5 to 5.5. Add generous amounts of organic matter prior to planting. Mulch to preserve moisture. Prune after fruiting.

Veronica
(ver-ON-i-ka)
SPEEDWELL

Veronica longifolia

Hardiness: *Zones 4-8*

Plant type: *herbaceous perennial*

Height: *10 to 48 inches*

Interest: *flowers*

Soil: *well-drained*

Light: *full sun to partial shade*

The long-lasting flowers of veronica add intense color and a vertical accent to a perennial border.

Selected species and varieties: *V. incana*—white leaves are woolly and form a 6-inch mat, flowers are lilac-blue in early summer on erect, 12- to 18-inch stems. *V. longifolia*—2 to 4 feet, dense lilac-blue flowers bloom for 6 to 8 weeks, midsummer to fall. *V. spicata*—10 to 36 inches tall, blue flowers in late spring to midsummer. *V. teucrium* 'Crater Lake Blue'—12 to 15 inches, flowers are bright blue in loose, terminal clusters, late spring to early summer. Veronica hybrids: 'Blue Charm'—24 inches tall, lavender-blue flowers throughout summer; 'Minuet'—15 inches, pink flowers in late spring and early summer; 'Sunny Border Blue'—18 to 24 inches, leaves are lush, dark green, dark blue flowers bloom summer to fall.

Growing conditions and maintenance: Plant speedwell in well-drained soil. It thrives in full sun and can grow in partial shade but will flower less. Taller types may need support. Deadhead to extend the blooming season.

Viburnum
(vy-BUR-num)
VIBURNUM

Viburnum carlesii

Hardiness: *Zones 4-8*

Plant type: *shrub*

Height: *4 to 10 feet*

Interest: *flowers, foliage, fruit*

Soil: *moist, well-drained*

Light: *full sun to partial shade*

Viburnums are highly ornamental shrubs that provide landscape interest over several seasons. Many produce showy, often fragrant, spring flowers, colorful fall fruit that can persist well into winter, and leaves that are deep green in summer and frequently turn red in the fall.

Selected species and varieties: *V. carlesii* (Koreanspice viburnum)—4 to 8 feet tall and nearly as wide, deciduous, rounded, dense, upright habit, leaves are 1 to 4 inches long, dull, dark green, often turning dark red in fall, flower buds are deep pink, opening to white, extremely fragrant, spring-blooming flowers grouped in 2- to 3-inch clusters, excellent choice for planting near entrance or walkway where fragrance can be appreciated; Zones 4-8. *V. x carlcephalum* (fragrant viburnum)—6 to 10 feet high and wide, deciduous, rounded, open habit, leaves are up to 4 inches long, dark green, turning reddish purple in fall, flower buds are pink, opening to fragrant white flowers in 5-inch clusters in late spring; Zones 5-8. *V. dilatatum* (linden viburnum)—8 to 10 feet tall, 6 to 10 feet wide, upright, deciduous, spreading habit, leaves 2 to 5

inches long, dark green and coarsely toothed, lustrous white flowers in flattened 3- to 5-inch clusters covering entire plant in late spring, fruit is bright red or scarlet, produced in heavy clusters, effective in fall and early winter, best used in groupings such as a screen or shrub border; Zones 5-7. *V. plicatum* var. *tomentosum* (double file viburnum)—8 to 10 feet tall with slightly greater spread, broad, rounded form with horizontal branches, leaves are 2 to 4 inches long, toothed, dark green, turning reddish purple in fall, flowers are white, in 2- to 6-inch flattened clusters, held above the foliage on short stems, accentuating horizontal habit, bright red fruit in late summer is usually eaten quickly by birds, makes a superb specimen, Zones 5-8; 'Shasta'—compact variety, 6 feet tall, 12 feet wide, creamy white flowers. *V.* x 'Eskimo'—4 feet tall, 5 feet wide, compact, uniform habit, leaves are glossy, dark, semievergreen, flower buds are pale pink, opening to creamy white flowers in 3-inch snowball-shaped clusters in spring, dull red fruit turns black in late summer, useful as a specimen or a low hedge; Zones 6-8.

Growing conditions and maintenance: Viburnums transplant easily and thrive in moist, well-drained soil supplemented with organic matter. They adapt to both full sun and partial shade. When necessary, prune viburnums immediately after flowering.

Vinca
(VING-ka)
PERIWINKLE, MYRTLE

Vinca minor

Hardiness: *Zones 3-9*

Plant type: *evergreen ground cover*

Height: *3 to 6 inches*

Interest: *foliage, flowers*

Soil: *moist, well-drained*

Light: *full sun to full shade*

Periwinkle is a wide-spreading evergreen ground cover that provides a dense carpet of leaves in a relatively short time. Its runners extend in all directions along the ground, rooting where they contact the soil. In spring, lilac-blue flowers appear in profusion and continue blooming sporadically into the summer.

Selected species and varieties: *V. minor*—3 to 6 inches tall, spreading indefinitely, fast growing, mat-forming habit, leaves emerge yellow-green and mature to dark, glossy green, ½ to 1½ inches long, flowers are lilac-blue, 1 inch across, blooming mainly in the spring, effective ground cover under trees or in front of shrubs.

Growing conditions and maintenance: Periwinkle spreads quickly in well-drained, moist soil amended with organic matter. In warmer climates, it performs best in light to deep shade. Space plants to be used as ground cover 12 inches apart. Shear once a year after the main flowering season to promote dense growth.

Yucca
(YUK-a)
YUCCA

Yucca filamentosa

Hardiness: *Zones 5-10*

Plant type: *shrub*

Height: *2 to 12 feet*

Interest: *foliage, flowers*

Soil: *light, well-drained*

Light: *full sun*

Yucca develops a rosette of sword-shaped evergreen leaves that provide a striking accent in rock and perennial gardens or among shrubs. In summer, stiff stems arise from the center of the rosette, bearing white, nodding flowers.

Selected species and varieties: *Y. filamentosa* (yucca, Adam's-needle)—2- to 3-foot-tall rosette of leaves, 3- to 12-foot-tall flower scape, leaves are 2½ feet long with sharp terminal spine, threads curl off margins, flowers are creamy white, 1 to 2 inches long, in erect clusters, Zones 5-9; 'Bright Edge'—leaves have gold margins; 'Golden Sword'—variegated leaves with yellow center and green margin. *Y. glauca* (soapweed)—similar habit to *Y. filamentosa* but more delicate, leaves have white margins, flowers are greenish white on 3- to 4½-foot stems, good choice for rock gardens; Zones 4-8.

Growing conditions and maintenance: Yuccas thrive in full sun in soil that is well drained to dry. They are highly tolerant of drought.

Zantedeschia
(zan-tee-DES-kee-a)
CALLA LILY, ARUM LILY

Zantedeschia aethiopica

Hardiness: *Zones 9-10*

Plant type: *herbaceous perennial*

Height: *24 to 36 inches*

Interest: *flowers, foliage*

Soil: *moist, humus-rich*

Light: *full sun to partial shade*

Calla lilies produce bold, arrow-shaped leaves and flowers composed of a gently flaring, white spathe surrounding a central golden spadix. They grow from tender rhizomes and survive winters only in mild climates, unless they are dug up in the fall for indoor storage. They are well suited to growing at the edge of a pond or stream, where the soil is constantly moist. They can also be planted in a moist perennial border or in a container.

Selected species and varieties: *Z. aethiopica* 'Crowborough'—24 to 36 inches tall, 24 inches wide, leaves arise from base and form a dense, erect cluster, white flowers are 6 to 10 inches on leafless stalk, spathe wraps around fragrant yellow spadix, blooming late spring to early summer.

Growing conditions and maintenance: Plant calla lily rhizomes 4 inches deep in soil that is constantly moist. They thrive in bogs and near water. To maintain adequate moisture in garden soil, add generous amounts of organic matter prior to planting.

Encyclopedia of Beneficials, Pests, and Diseases

This encyclopedia will help you recognize the many beneficial insects that inhabit your garden and some of the most common pests and diseases that afflict gardens in the continental United States and southern Canada. Each entry includes a choice of measures designed to prevent problems or to control them if and when they appear in your garden.

The encyclopedia is divided into three sections—Beneficials, Pests, and Diseases. The first section (right) presents 18 kinds of beneficials—beetles, spiders, and other small creatures that feed on pests and serve as natural controls. Each entry describes the creature's life cycle so you can recognize it as a welcome ally at different stages of development. Common pests that each beneficial attacks are included, along with suggestions for attracting the beneficial to your garden.

In the section devoted to pests (pages 301-324), some of the 55 entries cover a single species of pest, while others cover several different pests that are closely related or inflict similar damage. You will find information on the pest's geographical range, the plants it prefers, its life cycle, and descriptions of the damage it inflicts. Recommendations for preventing or eliminating pests include physical controls such as pruning; cultural controls or appropriate gardening techniques; specific beneficials for biological control; and environmentally friendly chemical controls.

The last section (pages 324-339) provides clues for diagnosing 47 infectious and deficiency diseases. You will learn where to look on susceptible plants for typical symptoms and how an infectious disease is transmitted; methods of preventing particular diseases and of controlling them when they appear in your garden; and how to avoid recurrences in the future.

Ambush Bugs

Range: *throughout North America; most prevalent in the West*

Generations per year: *multiple*

Type: *predator*

Ambush bugs are stout bugs that look as if they were wearing armor. They conceal themselves in flowers and wait to attack any unwary insects that come along.

Description and life cycle: Adult ambush bugs have uniquely thickened front legs, equipped for grasping and holding their prey. Most of the several species are small—less than a half-inch long—and are yellowish brown to yellowish green with darker markings. Their coloring provides effective camouflage while they await their prey. The females lay their eggs on plants; nymphs resemble adults but are smaller and wingless.

Beneficial effects: Although small, ambush bugs capture and kill insects considerably bigger than themselves. Both nymphs and adults are predaceous. They prefer to hide in the flowers of goldenrod and boneset. When a bee, wasp, fly, or butterfly visits the flower, the ambush bug uses its strong forelegs to grasp the prey, then sucks out the contents of its body. Ambush bugs do not bite humans.

How to attract: Avoid using pesticides. Grow goldenrod and boneset.

Assassin Bugs

Range: *many species found throughout North America*

Generations per year: *usually 1*

Type: *predator*

There are more than 100 native species of assassin bugs in North America. Some attack humans and other animals and can inflict painful bites, but many are voracious predators of insects and are helpful in reducing populations of a wide array of plant pests.

Description and life cycle: Depending on the species, assassin bugs overwinter as larvae, adults, or eggs. Adults are usually flat, brown or black, and a half-inch long. They have long, narrow heads and curved beaks that are folded back under their bodies; many have a hoodlike structure behind their head. Nymphs resemble the adults but are smaller and wingless; some are brightly colored. Eggs are laid in sheltered locations. Once hatched, the nymphs begin feeding on insects and undergo several molts before becoming adults. Most species complete their life cycle in a single year, but some require several years.

Beneficial effects: Adults and nymphs feed on many plant-eating insects, including beetles, caterpillars, aphids, and leafhoppers. They also feed on mosquitoes, bees, and flies.

How to attract: Assassin bugs occur naturally in most gardens. Avoid the use of pesticides.

Big-Eyed Bugs

Range: *throughout western parts of North America*

Generations per year: *2 or 3*

Type: *predator*

Big-eyed bugs resemble tarnished plant bugs and may be mistaken for that pest. However, this small beneficial insect feeds on many troublesome pests, both as a nymph and as an adult.

Description and life cycle: Adult big-eyed bugs overwinter in plant debris or other protected sites. Adults are ⅛ to ¼ inch long and black or yellow-green, with spots on the head and thorax. They emerge in spring, and females lay eggs on plant stems and the undersides of leaves. Nymphs develop for 4 to 6 weeks, then molt to become adults and repeat the process. The nymphs look like the adults, but are smaller and wingless. Both adults and nymphs move about very rapidly, and both have large, prominent eyes.

Beneficial effects: Big-eyed bugs prey on aphids, leafhoppers, plant bugs, spider mites, and small caterpillars, and feed on the eggs of mites and insects. When pests are scarce, big-eyed bugs feed on flower nectar.

How to attract: Grow goldenrod and tolerate some pigweed, which big-eyed bugs prefer for egg laying. Avoid the use of pesticides.

Braconid Wasps

Range: *widespread throughout North America*

Generations per year: *several*

Type: *parasitoid*

More than 2,000 species of braconid wasps are native to North America. Some are raised and sold commercially.

Description and life cycle: Depending on the species, adult braconid wasps are between ⅒ and ½ inch long. Slender, with a distinctly pinched waist, they may be brown, black, yellow, or red. Adults feed on nectar and pollen. Females inject eggs into a susceptible host. The eggs hatch as white, wormlike larvae that parasitize the host by feeding from within, eventually killing it. Some species feed externally as well. The larvae pupate near, on, or in a host, in white or brown cocoons. The life cycle is short and yields several generations per year. Wasps overwinter as larvae or pupae inside their hosts.

Beneficial effects: Braconid wasp larvae help control a wide range of insect pests, including codling moths, cabbage worms, armyworms, elm bark beetles, hornworms, and aphids.

How to attract: Some species are commercially available, but it is best to encourage native populations. Grow dill, fennel, parsley, and yarrow to sustain adult wasps. Avoid killing caterpillars bearing brown cocoons. Avoid the use of pesticides.

Chalcid Wasps

Range: *widespread throughout North America*

Generations per year: *several*

Type: *parasitoid*

Worldwide, there are more than 100,000 species of chalcid wasps. These include both the trichogramma wasp and *Encarsia formosa,* two highly effective parasitoids of plant pests. Chalcid wasps feed on eggs, larvae, and pupae of their prey; species vary in host preference.

Description and life cycle: Adults are tiny, often only ¹⁄₁₀₀ inch long, and may be black or golden brown. They feed on plant nectar and on honeydew excreted by insect hosts. The females often feed on insect fluids seeping from wounds they make as they lay their eggs. Inserting eggs into a host's body, or under a scale insect's shell-like covering, they often paralyze the host. Larvae develop and feed within the host, eventually killing it; they pupate in or near the host's body. These wasps produce several generations per year; many species overwinter as larvae in hosts.

Beneficial effects: Chalcid wasps are parasitoids of many plant pests, including scale insects, aphids, mealybugs, and tussock moths. One species, *Encarsia formosa,* controls whiteflies.

How to attract: Avoid pesticide use, including sulfur fungicides.

Flower Flies

Range: *many species found throughout North America*

Generations per year: *3 to 7*

Type: *predator*

Flower flies, or syrphid flies, are often called hover flies, for their helicopter-like flying habits. There are more than 800 species native to North America; these differ in both their geographic range and their preferred prey.

Description and life cycle: Adults are ⅓ to ½ inch long and black with yellow or white stripes. They resemble honeybees or hornets in appearance and in their attraction to flowers, but unlike bees, they have only a single pair of wings, large eyes, and no stinger. Flower flies overwinter in the soil as pupae; adults emerge in early spring to feed on flower nectar. Females lay small white, pitted eggs singly among colonies of aphids. The hatching larvae are sluglike, and can be mottled in color, or green, brown, or gray. They feed voraciously on aphids for about 2 weeks, then drop to the soil to pupate. Adults emerge in 2 weeks to repeat the cycle.

Beneficial effects: One larva can consume 400 aphids. Larvae may also feed on mealybugs, mites, scale crawlers, and other small insects.

How to attract: Include daisy-flowered plants that provide abundant nectar and pollen, such as Shasta daisy, cosmos, and coreopsis. Stagger plantings so that there is always something in bloom. Avoid the use of pesticides.

Ichneumon Wasps

Range: *widespread throughout North America*

Generations per year: *1 to 10*

Type: *predator, parasitoid*

Both larval and adult ichneumon wasps (sometimes called ichneumon flies) help control insect pests. Some species have a very narrow host range; others attack a wide variety of insects.

Description and life cycle: Adults vary in size from ¹⁄₁₀ to 1½ inches, and are slender and dark colored. They typically are wide ranging and often feed on nectar or pollen. Females have a long, threadlike ovipositor for inserting eggs into the host eggs or larvae. The larvae generally develop and feed within the host, killing it in the process. Larvae are white grubs, tapered at both ends. In some species, adults kill hosts by stinging them and consuming the body fluids. Most species overwinter as mature larvae in cocoons, or as adult females.

Beneficial effects: Larvae feed within host eggs, larvae, or pupae, providing natural control for a wide range of plant pests. Hosts include sawflies, spruce budworms, tent caterpillars, pine tip moths, European corn borers, and woodborer beetles.

How to attract: Include flowers in the garden to attract and maintain adults. Avoid pesticide use.

Lacewings

Range: *widespread throughout North America*

Generations per year: *3 to 6*

Type: *predator*

Hundreds of species of lacewings are found in North America. Sometimes called aphid lions, and broadly grouped as green or brown lacewings, they are widely distributed and highly beneficial.

Description and life cycle: Lacewings overwinter as adults or pupae. In spring, they emerge as adults, ½ to ¾ inch long with elongated lacy, transparent wings, to feed on pollen and nectar and lay eggs. Green lacewings lay their eggs on the end of a silk thread, while brown lacewings lay eggs directly on leaves. Eggs hatch in less than a week. The larvae are mottled yellow or brown and spindle shaped, with large jaws. They feed for about 3 weeks, pupate for 5 to 7 days, and emerge as adults to repeat the cycle.

Beneficial effects: While lacewing larvae prefer aphids, they also feed on thrips, mealybugs, scales, moth eggs, small caterpillars, other soft-bodied insects, and mites. Adults are rarely predaceous.

How to attract: Grow plants that offer plenty of pollen and nectar, such as dill, fennel, clover, and cosmos. Provide a source of water in dry weather. Buy lacewing eggs from an insectary and distribute them throughout the garden. Avoid use of dormant oil sprays, which may kill overwintering eggs.

Ladybird Beetles

Range: *widespread throughout North America*

Generations per year: *2 to 4*

Type: *predator*

Ladybird beetles, also called lady beetles or ladybugs, are probably the best known of all beneficial insects. Of some 4,000 species worldwide, about 400 are native to North America. Some of the most common and beneficial species include the convergent ladybird beetle, the twice-stabbed ladybird beetle, and the two-spotted ladybird beetle.

Description and life cycle: Adult ladybird beetles are shiny, round, and about ¼ inch long. They may be gray, yellow, or orange-red, with or without black spots; some are solid black, others black with red spots. Larvae are spindle shaped, wrinkled, and up to ⅜ inch long; when young, they are dark and look like tiny alligators. As the larvae mature, they develop conspicuous yellow, red, or white markings. Pupae are reddish black with red markings and are usually attached to the upper leaf surface.

Ladybird beetles overwinter as adults in garden debris. They emerge in spring to feed and lay eggs in clusters among aphids or other potential prey. Once hatched, the larvae feed for about 3 weeks, then pupate, emerging as adults about a week later to repeat the cycle. The convergent ladybird beetle, the most common species in North America, is red-orange with black spots; it is dis-

tinguished by two converging white lines on its thorax. This species migrates, flying hundreds of miles to overwintering sites and returning in spring. The twice-stabbed ladybird beetle is shiny black with two bright red spots, while the two-spotted ladybird beetle is red with two black spots and a black head.

Beneficial effects: Both larvae and adults feed on many soft-bodied insect pests, including aphids, mealybugs, scales, psyllids, whiteflies, and spider mites; they also eat insect eggs. One larva can eat up to 300 aphids before it molts; then, as an adult beetle, it can eat another 300 to 400 aphids.

Food preferences vary with the species. Convergent ladybird beetles feed mainly on aphids; twice-stabbed ladybird beetles prefer scales; and two-spotted ladybird beetles devour both scales and aphids. A related species known as the mealybug destroyer has a strong prefer-

Two-Spotted Ladybird Beetles

ence for mealybugs but also eats aphids and scales. The vedalia ladybird beetle, a red-bodied beetle with black marks, prefers soft scales, while the red-mite destroyer feeds on spider mites. Adults also feed on pollen and nectar.

How to attract: Grow dill and tansy to lure adults with pollen and nectar. If you buy convergent ladybird beetles or mealybug destroyers, note that they tend to fly away when released. In a greenhouse, first close all vents; in a garden, first water well, then free the beetles at night, when they are less active.

Pirate Bugs

Range: *widespread throughout North America*

Generations per year: *2 to 4*

Type: *predator*

Also called minute pirate bugs for their tiny size, pirate bugs are voracious predators, attacking most small insects. Not all of their victims are pests, but their overall effect is beneficial.

Description and life cycle: Pirate bugs overwinter as mated adult females, emerging in spring to insert their eggs into plant stems or leaves. Adults are quick fliers, ¼ inch long, and black with white patches on their wings. Eggs hatch in 3 to 5 days; nymphs are oval, ⅕ inch long, and may be yellow, orange, or brown. Nymphs feed for 2 to 3 weeks on the insects they find on leaves and in flowers, then molt to become adults and repeat the cycle.

Beneficial effects: Both nymphs and adults consume large numbers of small insect pests such as thrips, small caterpillars, leafhopper nymphs, spider mites, and insect eggs. They are especially adept at finding prey in flowers and are therefore particularly good at controlling flower thrips.

How to attract: Grow goldenrod, daisies, and yarrow; adults feed on their pollen. In fall, collect pirate bugs on wild goldenrod and release them in your garden. In a greenhouse, release one pirate bug for every five plants.

Praying Mantises

Range: *various species throughout North America*

Generations per year: *usually 1*

Type: *predator*

Of the 20-odd praying mantis species found in North America, several are imports from Europe and China. All are aggressive predators of other insects.

Description and life cycle: Praying mantises overwinter as clusters of 50 to 400 eggs in an egg case of hardened froth stuck to a plant. In early spring, nymphs emerge and begin to feed, taking ever-larger insect prey as they grow—including other praying mantises. After mating, the female often devours the male before laying eggs. Adults are 2 to 4 inches long and green or brown, with large eyes, long hind legs, and powerful front legs adapted for grasping prey. Nymphs resemble adults but are smaller and wingless.

Beneficial effects: Praying mantises feed on both pests and beneficial insects, including aphids, beetles, bugs, leafhoppers, caterpillars, butterflies, flies, bees, and wasps. Adults feed on larger insects that usually are not pests.

How to attract: Provide shrubs and other permanent plantings as sites for overwintering eggs. Do not release purchased praying mantises, because they may destroy native populations of bees and butterflies. Instead, protect egg cases found in your yard. Avoid pesticide use.

Predatory Mites

Range: *widespread throughout North America*

Generations per year: *multiple*

Type: *predator*

Predatory mites look like plant-feeding mites, but are less hairy and quicker.

Description and life cycle: Adult predatory mites are tiny, about ¹⁄₅₀ inch long. They are usually tan, beige, or red. Nymphs are similar, but even smaller and usually translucent. Females overwinter in soil, crevices in bark, or plant debris. In spring they lay their eggs on leaves near plant-feeding mites. Nymphs hatch in 3 to 4 days and begin to feed. They molt to become adults within 5 to 10 days, and repeat the cycle. There are many overlapping generations each year.

Beneficial effects: Predatory mites have varying preferences in their prey. The phytoseiid mite eats several spider-mite species, and controls that pest well by reproducing twice as fast. Other predator-mite species feed on thrips, other mite pests, and pollen.

How to attract: Grow cattails and dandelions for their pollen. Mist plants to encourage predaceous mites and discourage spider mites. Buy and release commercially available predatory mites. Avoid the use of pesticides.

Robber Flies

Range: *various species throughout North America*

Generations per year: *1- to 2-year life cycle*

Type: *predator*

Robber flies are fast-flying, loud-buzzing insects that snatch their prey in flight. Once a victim is caught, the robber fly inserts its proboscis into the prey and sucks the juices.

Description and life cycle: Adult robber flies resemble wasps or bees but are usually gray, although some species may be yellow or black. Most are ½ to ¾ inch long and hairy, with a long, narrow abdomen. They are equipped with a long, horny proboscis for piercing prey. Females lay their eggs on the ground, and most species overwinter as larvae in the soil. Larvae are white, slightly flattened, distinctly segmented grubs, and feed on a variety of soil-borne insects. Adults prefer sunny sites such as open fields or woodland edges, where they fly about in search of prey. Many species have a 2-year life cycle.

Beneficial effects: Robber flies are fairly indiscriminate predators, but are generally beneficial. Larvae eat a wide variety of white grubs, grasshopper eggs, beetle pupae, and caterpillars. Adults catch and consume many flying insects, including beetles, leafhoppers, butterflies, flies, bugs, and bees.

How to attract: Avoid pesticide use.

Rove Beetles

Range: *widespread throughout North America*

Generations per year: *1*

Type: *predator, parasite, parasitoid*

Of the nearly 30,000 rove beetle species worldwide, about 3,000 occur in North America. They differ in geographic ranges and food preferences. Some are predators of plant pests; some parasitize ants, termites, and fleas; and some feed on decaying organic matter.

Description and life cycle: Rove beetles overwinter as adults, emerging in spring to mate and lay eggs in the soil. Adults are slender, 1⁄10 to 1 inch long, and may be black, brown, or yellow, often with spots. When disturbed, a rove beetle raises the tip of its abdomen in a menacing, combative pose. Most are active at night. The larvae look like wingless adults.

Beneficial effects: Rove beetle species vary in their food preferences. Pests they help control include snails, slugs, aphids, springtails, mites, flies, nematodes, and root maggots. They also help decompose organic matter in the soil.

How to attract: Provide permanent beds to help rove beetle populations develop. Provide daytime shelter with organic mulches and living mulches. Avoid the use of pesticides.

Soldier Beetles

Range: *several species throughout most of the United States*

Generations per year: *1 or 2*

Type: *predator*

Soldier beetles, often called leatherwings, resemble lightning bugs without the light. Both larvae and adults are believed to be predaceous, feeding on a wide variety of insects.

Description and life cycle: Soldier beetles overwinter in a late larval stage, in the soil or under tree bark. Larvae are grub-like, hairy or velvety, and may be brown, purple, or black. In spring they pupate and emerge as adult beetles, usually less than ½ inch long, and dark with orange, yellow, or red markings. Beetles are often found on flowering plants such as goldenrod, milkweed, and hydrangea. Many species include pollen and nectar in their diet. Females lay eggs in masses in the soil or other sheltered sites.

Beneficial effects: The Pennsylvania leatherwing, found east of the Rocky Mountains, feeds on locust eggs, cucumber beetles, corn ear worms, and European corn borers. The downy leatherwing occurs in most of the United States and eats all kinds of aphids. Other species feed on grasshopper eggs and various caterpillars and grubs.

How to attract: Avoid the use of pesticides. Grow goldenrod, hydrangea, and milkweed.

Spiders

Range: *widespread throughout North America*

Generations per year: *1 to many*

Type: *predator*

All of the 35,000 known species of spiders are natural predators of insects. Spiders themselves are not insects but arachnids, in the same family as mites and scorpions; spiders have four pairs of legs and only two body segments. Species most helpful to gardeners include the crab spider and the wolf spider.

Description and life cycle: Spiders lay their eggs in a silk cocoon. The young resemble adults but undergo several molts before becoming adults. Spiders inject captured victims with paralyzing venom and eat them, or wrap them in silk for a later meal.

Spiders are either hunters or trappers. The wolf spider is a hunter that pounces on its prey. Wolf spiders are ground dwellers, ½ to 1⅜ inches long, and active at night. The crab spider is a trapper, spinning a web and waiting for prey to wander in; it often lies in wait near flowers visited by insects.

Beneficial effects: Feeding almost exclusively on the insects they hunt and trap, spiders are highly beneficial in the garden. Most spiders eat a wide variety of insects, but most avoid wasps, hornets, ants, and hard-shelled beetles.

How to attract: Avoid pesticide use. Do not disturb webs.

Spined Soldier Bugs

Range: *widespread throughout North America*

Generations per year: *1 or 2*

Type: *predator*

Spined soldier bugs are common in every part of the United States. The nymphs are voracious predators of some of the most damaging garden and forest pests.

Description and life cycle: Spined soldier bugs overwinter as adults, emerging in spring to lay eggs on plant leaves. One female may lay up to 1,000 eggs. Adults are about ½ inch long and shield shaped. They are pale brown or yellow with black specks and have spined, or pointed, shoulders. Nymphs resemble adults but have no wings. They feed briefly on plant sap, but after their first molt, they eat only insects for 6 to 8 weeks before becoming adults.

Beneficial effects: Nymphs eat a wide variety of caterpillars, including gypsy moths and tent caterpillars. They also feed on the larval stages of fall armyworms, sawflies, Colorado potato beetles, and Mexican bean beetles.

How to attract: Maintain permanent perennial beds to provide shelter for native populations of spined soldier bugs. Avoid pesticide use. If you buy spined soldier bugs commercially, release them at the rate of two to five nymphs per square yard of garden. Pheromone lures are also available.

Tachinid Flies

Range: *widespread throughout North America*

Generations per year: *1 to 3*

Type: *parasitoid*

There are more than 1,200 native species of tachinid flies. The adult flies live on nectar and honeydew, but the larvae parasitize many serious plant pests.

Description and life cycle: Tachinid fly larvae overwinter inside a host insect. These tiny white maggots feed on the host from the inside out, eventually killing it. The larvae pupate in or near the host's carcass; adult flies emerge and mate. Adults are ⅓ to ½ inch long, gray, brown, or black in color, and look like big, bristly houseflies but have only two wings. Females lay eggs on young host larvae or on leaves where potential hosts are feeding. Eggs or nymphs may be eaten by the host insect, or the nymphs may bore into the host, then feed and develop there.

Beneficial effects: Tachinid fly larvae kill the larvae of many harmful species, including armyworms, cutworms, tent caterpillars, cabbage loopers, ear worms, gypsy moths, hornworms, and codling moths. Some species also infest sawflies, squash bugs, and grasshoppers.

How to attract: Grow dill, parsley, and sweet clover; their flowers attract adult tachinid flies. Avoid killing caterpillars with white eggs on their backs. Avoid pesticide use.

Aphids

Range: *most of the United States and southern Canada*

Generations per year: *20 or more*

Host(s): *most ornamentals and vegetables*

More than 4,000 species of aphids are known; most plants are susceptible to at least one.

Description and life cycle: Aphids overwinter as eggs. During the growing season, they feed on soft plant tissues and produce several generations each year. Adult aphids are pear shaped, less than ⅛ inch long, and may be green, yellow, black, brownish, or gray. The nymphs are smaller versions of the adult.

Damage and detection: Feeding in large groups, aphids suck plant sap, leaving leaves wilted and yellow and flowers deformed. They secrete a sticky substance called honeydew, which drops onto plants. Honeydew serves as a growing medium for sooty mold, an unsightly black fungus that further damages plants by blocking light. Aphids also spread certain viral diseases.

Control: PHYSICAL—Knock aphids off affected plants with a jet of water; use reflective mulch and sticky traps; cut off heavily infested leaves. BIOLOGICAL—Convergent ladybird beetle; green lacewing; syrphid fly; aphid midge. CHEMICAL—Horticultural oil; insecticidal soap; pyrethrins; rotenone.

Armyworms

Range: *east of the Rocky Mountains; Arizona, New Mexico, California*

Generations per year: *2 to 6*

Host(s): *turf grasses and vegetables*

The armyworm is a serious pest of grasses and vegetable crops. Its favorite hosts include corn and grasses.

Description and life cycle: Larvae are 1 to 2 inches long and pale green to greenish brown, with yellow or white stripes; they overwinter in plant debris or in soil. Adults are grayish brown moths, with a wingspan of 1 to 2 inches, and are active only at night. Moths lay eggs on the lower leaves of plants and produce as many as six generations per year, depending on the species and the climate.

Damage and detection: Larvae hide during the day in protected areas and feed at night on leaves, stems, and buds. Large numbers can defoliate plants overnight.

Control: PHYSICAL—Handpick worms. CULTURAL—Keep weed growth down; till soil to expose pupae to predators. BIOLOGICAL—Beneficial nematodes; birds; Bt; ground beetles; toads; trichogramma wasps. CHEMICAL—Horticultural oil in July to control second generation; neem.

Bagworms

Range: *east of the Rocky Mountains*

Generations per year: *1*

Host(s): *trees and shrubs*

The bagworm feeds on the leaves of many deciduous and evergreen trees and shrubs, especially juniper and arborvitae.

Description and life cycle: Bagworms overwinter as eggs inside small bags, hatching in late spring or early summer. Each dark brown larva spins a silken bag some 2 inches long around itself and covers it with bits of plant debris. In late summer, the larva attaches its bag to a twig and pupates. In a few days, adult males emerge from their bags as black, clear-winged moths and fly off in search of adult females, which remain inside their bags. Females lay 500 to 1,000 eggs after mating, and then both sexes die.

Damage and detection: Larvae feed on a host's leaves, often stripping twigs bare and giving the plant a ragged look. Heavy infestations may defoliate entire trees. The bags are very easy to spot.

Control: PHYSICAL—Handpick and destroy bags in winter or early spring, before eggs hatch; set pheromone traps. BIOLOGICAL—Bt when larvae begin to feed; parasitic wasps. CHEMICAL—Rotenone applied when bags are small, usually in June.

Bark Beetles

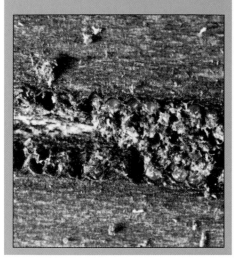

Range: *most of the United States and southern Canada*

Generations per year: *1 to 3*

Host(s): *deciduous and coniferous trees*

Bark beetles include many species of minute or small beetles that are typically stout and cylindrical in shape; the scientific name of the family to which all the species belong means "cut short" in Greek. These pests tunnel into tree bark to lay their eggs. They attack various hosts, but most evergreen and many deciduous trees are susceptible to one or more species. Some of the most destructive bark beetles include the ambrosia beetle *(Corthylus punctatissimus),* the elm bark beetles *(Scolytus multistriatus* and *Hylurgopinus rufipes),* the pine engraver *(Ips pini),* the shothole borer *(Scolytus rugulosus),* and the Southern pine beetle *(Dendroctonus frontalis).*

Description and life cycle: Adults are commonly black or brown and less than ¼ inch long; they have short snouts and are covered with fine hairs or bristles. The adult beetle—in some species the male and in others the female—bores into the bark of a living or rotting tree to make a tunnel in which the female deposits her eggs. When the eggs hatch, the larvae begin to feed on the wood, creating tunnels, or galleries, beneath the bark, usually at right angles to the original tunnel bored by the male. The adult male ambrosia beetle carries fruiting bodies of a fungus into the tunnels to serve as food for the larvae. At the ends of the galleries, the larvae pupate, then emerge as adults to mate and repeat the process for a total of two or three generations a year, depending on the species and location. Beetles overwinter in a dormant state in the galleries.

Damage and detection: Evidence of bark beetle infestation includes holes in the bark that frequently ooze sap. Sawdust from the hole may be found at the base of the tree. Shothole borer holes are numerous and small, giving the tree the appearance of having been hit with buckshot. Tunneling by feeding larvae destroys tissue in the cambium—the layer that produces new growth—and can eventually kill the infested tree. Those not killed by beetle damage are susceptible to invasion by pathogens. In the case of the elm bark beetle, it spreads the fungus responsible for Dutch elm disease. The adult elm bark beetle tunnels and lays eggs in weakened or diseased elm wood, which is often infected with Dutch elm disease. When the new generation of adults emerges, they fly to healthy leaves of nearby elms and spread the disease as they feed.

Control: PHYSICAL—Remove and destroy infested trees; prune and destroy infested branches; set pheromone traps. CULTURAL—Plant species that are resistant to Dutch elm disease. BIOLOGICAL—Beneficial nematodes; braconid wasps.

Billbugs

Range: *United States and southern Canada in grassland regions and lawns*

Generations per year: *1*

Host(s): *grasses*

Billbugs are named for the adult's peculiar bill-like, elongated snout. The larvae do most of the damage to lawns.

Description and life cycle: Billbugs overwinter as adults in the soil. They are ¼ to ½ inch long and may be gray, brown, or black. They emerge in spring to feed and lay their eggs on the leaf sheaths of grass. The hatching larvae—white, legless, and very small—begin feeding on stems, then move into the soil to feed on grass roots.

Damage and detection: Symptoms of billbug damage include brown or yellow patches in the lawn, showing up first during periods of drought, especially near driveways or sidewalks, where soil tends to be driest. Sawdustlike material around grass stems may also indicate billbug feeding. Infested areas of turf are easy to pull up because the roots have been eaten.

Control: CULTURAL—Plant grass varieties that are resistant to billbugs. PHYSICAL—Dethatch lawn if thatch layer is more than ¾ inch thick. BIOLOGICAL—Beneficial nematodes. CHEMICAL—Neem.

Blister Beetles

Range: *most of the United States and southern Canada*

Generations per year: *1*

Host(s): *many ornamentals and vegetables*

Most common east of the Rocky Mountains, blister beetles feed on the flowers and foliage of many ornamentals, vegetables, and fruits; members of the tomato family are favorite hosts. When crushed, these beetles emit a liquid that causes blisters on the skin; hence their common name.

Description and life cycle: Larvae of the blister beetle overwinter in the soil. They pupate and emerge as adults in midsummer. The adults have an elongated body, less than ¾ inch long, and may be black, brown, gray, blue, or striped. Females lay their eggs in grasshopper burrows, and when the larvae hatch, they feed on grasshopper egg masses.

Damage and detection: Large numbers of beetles can defoliate plants very rapidly. Only the adult is damaging; the larva is considered beneficial because it serves to control grasshoppers.

Control: PHYSICAL—Handpick beetles, wearing gloves to protect skin; cover valuable plants with cheesecloth. BIOLOGICAL—Beneficial nematodes. CHEMICAL—Pyrethrins; rotenone.

Borers/Clearwing Moths

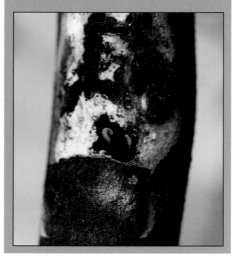

Range: *throughout the United States and southern Canada*

Generations per year: *1*

Host(s): *many ornamentals and vegetables*

There are many species of clearwing moths. The larvae, or caterpillars, cause serious injury to a wide variety of woody and herbaceous plants by boring into stems, twigs, or trunks and feeding on interior plant tissues. Some of the most destructive are the dogwood borer, greater peach tree borer, lilac borer, and rhododendron borer.

Description and life cycle: Most clearwing moths overwinter as larvae in host tissue. They are ⅛ to 1 inch long and yellow or white with dark heads. In spring the larvae pupate and emerge as adult moths, swift fliers that resemble wasps. The wings are at least somewhat transparent, and the bodies are often striped with yellow, brown, or orange bands. Females lay eggs on bark or stems of susceptible host plants, especially near wounds.

After hatching, the larvae enter their host through wounds, scars, or twig crotches. The dogwood borer (known in the South as the pecan borer) infests many hardwood trees, including cherry, apple, hickory, willow, birch, and oak. It afflicts cultivated dogwoods more often than those growing in the wild. The greater peach tree borer infests stone fruits, birch trees, and several species of ornamental shrubs. It enters plants near the base of the trunk and some-

times invades surface roots. The lilac borer attacks not only lilacs but also privet and ash trees. It generally enters a host within 3 feet of the soil line. The rhododendron borer, the smallest of the clearwing moths, is most serious in the mid-Atlantic region. It attacks mountain laurel as well as both azaleas and rhododendrons.

Damage and detection: Symptoms of borer infestation include wilted leaves; loose, sloughing, or cracking bark; and dieback of branches. Any evident holes are usually the exit holes, since entry holes are so tiny they go undetected. The borer feeds on and destroys the cambium—a layer of tissue that produces girth-increasing growth—and often girdles the plant. Branches above the site of infection usually die. If the borers

Lilac Borer

invade the host near the soil line, the entire plant dies.

Control: PHYSICAL—Remove infested branches and badly infested plants; encircle peach trees with a 4- to 6-inch ring of tobacco dust in spring; set pheromone traps. CULTURAL—Keep trees and shrubs healthy and vigorous, and avoid mechanical injuries, since borers generally enter through wounds or scars. BIOLOGICAL—Bt; parasitic wasps. CHEMICAL—Horticultural oil.

Cabbage Loopers

Range: *throughout the United States and southern Canada*

Generations per year: *2 to 7*

Host(s): *many ornamentals and vegetables*

Cabbage loopers feed on members of the cabbage family and other vegetables, as well as many herbaceous ornamentals including carnations, chrysanthemums, nasturtiums, and geraniums. Cabbage loopers closely resemble the imported cabbage worm in appearance and in the damage they cause.

Description and life cycle: Cabbage loopers overwinter as pupae on plant leaves or stems. Adults emerge in spring as brown moths with a silver spot on each forewing, and a wingspan of 1½ to 2 inches. Eggs are laid on host plants, where they hatch in about a week. The caterpillars are green, with white stripes down their back. They feed for 2 to 4 weeks before pupating.

Damage and detection: The larvae chew large, irregular holes in leaves. While their color provides an effective camouflage, their damage is easily spotted.

Control: PHYSICAL—Handpick larvae and destroy greenish white eggs; use row covers. BIOLOGICAL—Apply Bt at 2-week intervals; lacewings; trichogramma wasps; birds. CHEMICAL—Pyrethrins; rotenone; sabadilla.

Cankerworms

Range: *Maine to North Carolina, west to Missouri; Colorado, Utah, California*

Generations per year: *1*

Host(s): *deciduous trees and shrubs*

Cankerworms are often referred to as inchworms or measuring worms because of the way they arch their backs as they move. They feed on the leaves and buds of many deciduous plants; beech, cherry, elm, maple, and oak are favorite hosts.

Description and life cycle: Fall cankerworms overwinter as eggs, hatching in spring when trees and shrubs are putting out new leaves. The slender caterpillars may be green, brown, or black, with white stripes; they grow to 1 inch in length. They feed for 3 to 4 weeks, then crawl into the soil to pupate. Adults emerge in late fall to lay their eggs on the bark of trees. Spring cankerworms are similar but overwinter as moths that emerge in spring.

Damage and detection: The leaves are chewed to the midrib. Heavily infested plants are defoliated.

Control: PHYSICAL—Wrap sticky bands around trunks of susceptible trees before egg laying occurs; destroy egg masses. CULTURAL—Till the soil to expose pupae. BIOLOGICAL—Bt; spined soldier bugs; trichogramma wasps. CHEMICAL—Horticultural oil; neem.

Chinch Bugs

Range: *throughout the United States, southern Canada, and Mexico*

Generations per year: *2 or 3*

Host(s): *grasses*

Chinch bugs are found throughout North America but are most prevalent in the Mississippi, Ohio, and Missouri river valleys, as well as Texas and Oklahoma.

Description and life cycle: Chinch bugs overwinter under plant debris as adults, which are about ⅕ inch long and have a black body and white wings. In spring the females lay eggs over a period of 3 weeks. Young nymphs are bright red with a white band across the back; older nymphs are black with white spots.

Damage and detection: The nymphs are the most damaging stage. They feed on both the roots and stems of grasses, sucking juices and secreting toxic salivary fluids. Infested turf turns yellow and often dies in patches. Injury resembles that of Japanese beetle grubs and is most serious during hot, dry periods.

Control: PHYSICAL—Dethatch heavily thatched lawn. CULTURAL—Plant resistant varieties; reduce nitrogen fertilizer. BIOLOGICAL—Big-eyed bugs; lacewings; ladybird beetles; pirate bugs. CHEMICAL—Flood an infested area with soapy water and cover with a light-colored flannel sheet; the bugs will crawl onto the underside of the sheet to escape the soap. Kill them by dipping the sheet in a large container filled with hot soapy water; neem; pyrethrins; sabadilla; soap sprays.

Cicadas

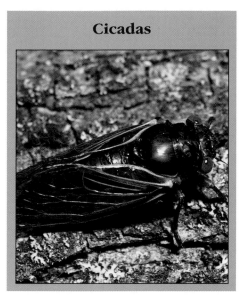

Colorado Potato Beetles

Conifer Sawflies

Range: *eastern United States, west to Texas and Oklahoma*

Generations per year: *variable*

Host(s): *deciduous trees and shrubs*

Periodical cicadas live either 13 or 17 years, but because generations overlap, almost every year brings at least a few periodical cicadas. The dog-day cicada is also known as the annual cicada—erroneously, since it has a 2- to 4-year cycle. Its generations also overlap, with some of the pests appearing every year.

Description and life cycle: Cicadas spend most of their lives as nymphs underground, feeding on plant roots. They emerge and climb into trees for their last molt. The adults are 1 to 2 inches long. Within weeks they mate, lay eggs, and die. Eggs hatch in about 2 months; the new nymphs burrow into the soil.

Damage and detection: Although adult cicadas suck sap from young twigs, they do their greatest harm laying eggs. The female cuts into the bark of twigs and splinters the sapwood as she deposits her eggs. One female may make 20 separate egg pockets, each of which can cause twig dieback and make the host vulnerable to infection.

Control: PHYSICAL—Apply sticky bands to tree trunks; remove injured twigs before eggs hatch; cover shrubs with netting. CULTURAL—Avoid planting young trees when major outbreaks are expected. BIOLOGICAL—Beneficial nematodes.

Range: *throughout the United States except the South and the Pacific Northwest*

Generations per year: *1 to 3*

Host(s): *many solanum family members*

The Colorado potato beetle is a serious garden pest in most parts of the country. In addition to potato plants, eggplants, peppers, tomatoes, and petunias are often attacked.

Description and life cycle: The Colorado potato beetle overwinters as an adult. It is oval, ⅓ inch long, with yellow-and-black-striped wing covers. Beetles emerge in spring, feed, and lay eggs that hatch in about a week. The plump larvae are orange-red with black spots. They feed, reenter the soil to pupate, and emerge as adults in 1 to 2 weeks.

Damage and detection: Adults and larvae alike decimate the foliage and stems of potatoes, tomatoes, and related plants, reducing yields in both quantity and quality. Heavy infestations can be fatal, especially to young plants. While feeding, beetles leave highly visible black excrement on leaves and stems.

Control: PHYSICAL—Use a thick organic mulch to inhibit migrating larvae; handpick beetles, larvae, and eggs. CULTURAL—Rotate crops; plant resistant varieties. BIOLOGICAL—Bt San Diego strain; ladybird beetles; spined soldier bugs. CHEMICAL—Neem; pyrethrins; rotenone.

Range: *eastern United States to the Mississippi River, southeastern Canada*

Generations per year: *1 to 5*

Host(s): *coniferous trees and shrubs*

Conifer sawflies are among the most damaging insect pests of pine, spruce, and hemlock. There are several species, each with its own range of host plants.

Description and life cycle: With sawlike egg-laying organs, females slit needles and deposit eggs in the slits. Depending on the species, sawflies overwinter as eggs or as cocooned pupae in soil or on lower tree bark. Larvae are as much as 1 inch long and gray, green, yellow, or tan, with dark brown or red heads and black dots along their bodies. Adults are less than ½ inch long and stout, with translucent wings.

Damage and detection: Hundreds of larvae feed together on the current season's needles, devouring an entire shoot before moving on to the next. Their color blends with the foliage, so they often do serious damage before they are detected. Left untreated, they can defoliate and even kill the host.

Control: PHYSICAL—Spread flannel dropcloths under trees, shake limbs to dislodge larvae, and destroy them in a soap solution. CULTURAL—Keep trees healthy and vigorous. BIOLOGICAL—Parasitic wasps; predaceous beetles; shrews; tachinid flies. CHEMICAL—Horticultural oil; soap sprays.

Corn Ear Worms

Range: *throughout the United States, especially southern and central states*

Generations per year: *2 to 7*

Host(s): *corn and tomato*

The corn ear worm is also known as the tomato fruit worm, depending on the host it infests. It may also attack potatoes, beans, peas, peppers, and squash.

Description and life cycle: Corn ear worms overwinter as pupae in the soil. In spring the gray-green or brown moths emerge and lay eggs on corn silk or the undersides of leaves; the eggs hatch in a few days. The larvae, ½ inch long, are green, yellow, or white caterpillars with black longitudinal stripes. They feed for 3 to 4 weeks, then return to the soil to pupate. In the North, they usually produce two generations each year; in the South, as many as seven.

Damage and detection: Larvae feed on corn silk, leaves, and fruit, inhibiting pollination, disfiguring ears, and opening them to invasion by other insects or pathogens. Similar damage occurs with other hosts.

Control: CULTURAL—Till vegetable garden in fall to expose pupae. PHYSICAL—Handpick worms. BIOLOGICAL—Larvae are cannibalistic and help control their own numbers; Bt; tachinid flies; trichogramma wasps. CHEMICAL—Neem; ryania.

Crickets and Grasshoppers

Range: *widespread throughout North America*

Generations per year: *1 to 3*

Host(s): *most ornamentals and vegetables*

Crickets and grasshoppers are common pests that attack almost all cultivated plants. Although they usually cause only minor damage to crops, populations may build up, and migrating swarms devour nearly all vegetation in their path. Such attacks are infrequent in North America, but the common name of one species, the Mormon cricket, is a reminder of the swarm that attacked the crops of Mormon settlers in Utah in 1848. This pest, which is actually a grasshopper and not a true cricket, ranges from California to Minnesota and Kansas. Including the Mormon cricket, there are only five North American grasshopper species that become numerous enough to damage crops significantly. Weather conditions play an important role in determining the size of grasshopper populations in a given year. They are smaller in years with a cool, wet spring and summer, but a long, hot, dry season can cause the populations to rise dramatically. True crickets are less destructive than grasshoppers. They damage seedlings and are also household pests, feeding on clothing, paper, and foods such as fruit and potatoes.

Description and life cycle: The many species of grasshoppers differ in appearance, range, and preferred host. Most species produce one generation per year, although in the South, a few produce two. Like other grasshoppers, the Mormon cricket overwinters in soil as eggs that hatch the following spring. The nymphs go through seven molts before taking on their final adult form, some 2 to 3 months after hatching. The nymphs feed on any available plant material, ex-

Mormon Cricket

hausting one food source completely before moving on to another. In late summer adult females, which are about 1 inch in length, deposit tiny sacs or packets—holding up to 100 or so eggs—in soil. Female and male adults continue to feed until they are killed by cold weather.

Crickets produce one to three generations per year, overwintering in the South as nymphs or adults and in cooler climates as eggs. After hatching, nymphs go through 8 to 12 molts before emerging as full-size adults that are ¾ to 1 inch long and dark brown or black, with wiry antennae. They often have large hind legs and flat, folded wings, although some species are wingless. Males of species common to the United States make a loud, chirping noise by rubbing together parts of their forewings. Most crickets are nocturnal and seek shelter during the day, some in vegetation and others in the ground. Females lay their eggs in soil or in plant stems in late summer or early fall. In winter, adult crickets frequently seek shelter indoors.

Damage and detection: Among the most damaging of grasshopper species is the migratory grasshopper, which causes significant crop losses in the western United States and southwestern Canada. It feeds in swarms, stripping away the leaves and stems of nearly all vegetation in areas of up to several square miles. Migratory grasshoppers prefer grasses but in their absence will feed on virtually any other kind of plants. The swarm then migrates to another feeding ground. Other species feed in a similar manner but may have a narrower range of hosts.

Crickets, like grasshoppers, are not a serious problem until they are present in large numbers. Masses of field crickets damage plantings of tomatoes, peas, beans, cucumbers, and squash by consuming seeds or seedlings. Further damage occurs when adults and nymphs chew on the foliage and flowers of vegetable crops. Tree crickets injure stems of trees or shrubs by inserting their eggs into the plant tissue.

Control: CULTURAL—Cultivate soil in fall to expose overwintering eggs. PHYSICAL—Use row covers; trap in jars buried to the brim and containing a mixture of 1 part molasses to 9 parts water. BIOLOGICAL—The pathogen *Nosema locustae* is effective for long-term control over large areas; beneficial nematodes; blister beetle larvae; praying mantises; predatory flies. CHEMICAL—Insecticidal soap.

Cucumber Beetles

Range: *United States and Canada, east of the Rocky Mountains*

Generations per year: *1 to 4*

Host(s): *many vegetables and ornamentals*

Widespread east of the Rockies, cucumber beetles are most damaging in the South, where they often produce four generations a year. They attack cucumbers, melons, squash, and other members of the cucumber family. Ornamentals commonly infested include chrysanthemums, cosmos, dahlias, roses, zinnias, and grasses.

Description and life cycle: Adults are ¼ inch long and yellowish green with black spots or stripes. They overwinter in garden debris, emerging in spring to lay eggs at the base of host plants. The eggs hatch in about 10 days, and slender, white larvae, which reach ½ inch in length, burrow into the soil to feed on plant roots and pupate. Emerging as adults, they feed on leaves, flowers, and fruit, and repeat the cycle.

Damage and detection: Larvae feeding on roots stunt and may kill plants. Adults chew holes in leaves and flowers; some species also eat fruit. Adults and larvae can carry cucumber mosaic virus and cucumber wilt, diseases that can kill plants.

Control: PHYSICAL—Handpick beetles; use row covers. CULTURAL—Plant varieties resistant to the diseases carried by cucumber beetles. BIOLOGICAL—Beneficial nematodes; braconid wasps; tachinid flies. CHEMICAL—Rotenone; sabadilla.

Cutworms

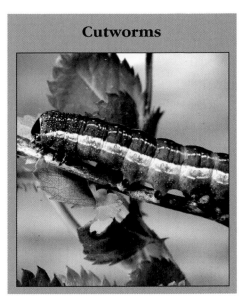

Range: *various species throughout North America*

Generations per year: *1 to 5*

Host(s): *most herbaceous plants*

The roughly 3,000 species of cutworms in North America can be grouped according to their feeding habits as tunnelers, climbers, and subterraneans.

Description and life cycle: Most cutworms overwinter as larvae or pupae. The soft, gray-brown larvae, 1 to 2 inches long, feed at night, burrow into the soil during the day, and curl into a C-shape when disturbed. They pupate in the soil and emerge as night-flying adult moths, brown or gray, with a 1½-inch wingspan. Females lay their eggs on leaves and stems; eggs hatch in 2 to 10 days.

Damage and detection: Tunneling cutworms chew on seedlings near the soil surface, making them topple and die. Climbing cutworms feed on leaves and flowers of vegetables and herbaceous ornamental plants. Subterranean cutworms feed on roots and underground stems, causing wilting and stunting.

Control: PHYSICAL—Use plant collars around seedlings. CULTURAL—Till soil in fall to expose the larvae or pupae; till again in early spring and wait 2 weeks before planting. BIOLOGICAL—Beneficial nematodes; braconid wasps; Bt; tachinid flies; trichogramma wasps.

Elm Leaf Beetles

Range: *throughout North America wherever elms grow*

Generations per year: *1 to 4*

Host(s): *elm, zelkova*

Both adults and larvae of the elm leaf beetle cause serious damage to elms, especially in California, where there are three or four generations each year.

Description and life cycle: Adult elm leaf beetles overwinter in protected places such as the crevices in tree bark, garages, or sheds. The beetle is yellow or dull green and ¼ inch long. In spring, as tree leaves unfurl, beetles fly to elms to feed and mate. Females lay eggs in clusters on the leaves. Larvae are up to ½ inch long and yellow-green with black stripes and head. They feed on the undersides of leaves for several weeks, then move down the tree to pupate on the trunk or on the ground. In about 2 weeks adults emerge to repeat the cycle.

Damage and detection: Adults chew roughly round holes in leaves; larvae skeletonize foliage, leaving only veins. Leaves turn brown and drop prematurely, often to be replaced by a new flush of foliage just in time for the next generation of beetles. Repeated defoliations can weaken a tree, making it vulnerable to Dutch elm disease, borne by elm bark beetles *(pages 302 and 339)*.

Control: PHYSICAL—Handpick adults; apply sticky bands. BIOLOGICAL—Bt San Diego strain; chalcid wasps; tachinid flies.

European Corn Borers

Range: *north and central United States and southern Canada*

Generations per year: *1 to 3*

Host(s): *many herbaceous plants*

Although the European corn borer, as its name suggests, is primarily a pest of corn, it also attacks many other plants, including tomato, celosia, sunflowers, cosmos, hollyhocks, chrysanthemums, asters, and dahlias.

Description and life cycle: The European corn borer overwinters as larvae in plant debris and pupates in early spring. Adult moths are pale brown, with dark markings on their wings and a 1-inch wingspan. Females lay masses of eggs on the undersides of leaves. Eggs hatch in about a week and the larvae begin to feed. Larvae are 1 inch long when fully grown, and beige with brown spots and dark heads. They feed for 3 to 4 weeks, pupate, and repeat the cycle.

Damage and detection: Larvae bore into corn ears at either end to feed on kernels. They also feed on tassels and leaves. On other plants, the larvae tunnel into stems and fruits.

Control: PHYSICAL—Remove and destroy plant debris. CULTURAL—Plant varieties resistant to borers; time plantings to avoid peak periods of borer infestation. BIOLOGICAL—Bt, applied before larvae enter stems or ears; braconid wasps; ladybird beetles; tachinid flies. CHEMICAL—Pyrethrins; ryania; sabadilla.

Flea Beetles

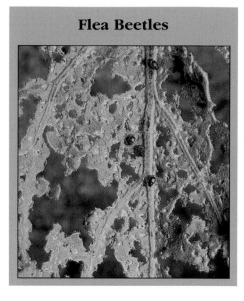

Range: *several species throughout North America*

Generations per year: *2 to 4*

Host(s): *most herbaceous plants*

Flea beetles, common garden pests, attack most herbaceous ornamentals and vegetables. They are especially troublesome on members of the cabbage family and the solanum family, which includes eggplant, peppers, potatoes, and tomatoes. The beetles get their name from the way they jump when disturbed.

Description and life cycle: Flea beetles overwinter as adults near the soil surface, emerging in spring to feed and mate. Beetles are small—¹⁄₁₀ inch long—and black, brown, or bronze; they lay eggs in the soil near hosts. The larvae, ¾-inch, legless white grubs with brown heads, eat plant roots, pupate, and emerge as adults to repeat the cycle.

Damage and detection: Adults chew tiny round holes in leaves, making the plant look as if it's been peppered with shot. Seedlings are seriously weakened or may be killed by a heavy infestation. Larvae weaken plants with their root feeding. Flea beetles carry several viral diseases.

Control: PHYSICAL—Use row covers; spray with jets of water; ring plants with diatomaceous earth or wood ashes. CULTURAL—Cultivate soil often to expose eggs and larvae. BIOLOGICAL—Beneficial nematodes; braconid wasps; tachinid flies. CHEMICAL—Pyrethrins; rotenone; sabadilla.

Gall Mites

Range: *various species throughout North America*

Generations per year: *many*

Host(s): *many trees and shrubs*

Mites are not insects; they belong to the arachnid class, which includes spiders. There are many species of mites, each with its own range of host plants. Some of the most common mites are the maple bladder gall mite, the maple spindle gall mite, and the hickory bladder gall mite. Other mite species cause galls on beech, cherry, elm, linden, and poplar.

Description and life cycle: Most mites are too small for the unaided eye to see, and their life cycles are poorly understood. Maple gall mites overwinter as adults in maple bark. In early spring, individual mites enter leaves, injecting a toxin that stimulates the leaf to develop an enlarged growth called a gall. Each mite feeds inside its gall, and the females lay eggs in their galls; when the eggs hatch, the resident adults move to new leaves. Mites often produce a new generation every 2 to 3 weeks.

Damage and detection: The maple bladder gall mite causes wartlike growths on the upper sides of maple leaves; these galls gradually turn from green to brilliant red. The maple spindle gall mite causes narrow, spindlelike projections; another mite causes colorful, feltlike patches. A large number of galls may distort leaves, but the damage is rarely serious.

Control: BIOLOGICAL—Predatory mites.

Gall Wasps

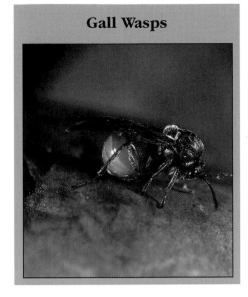

Range: *various species throughout the United States and Canada*

Generations per year: *2*

Host(s): *oak, rose, and thistle families*

Gall wasps stimulate host plants to form enlarged growths called galls on leaves, twigs, or stems. There are hundreds of species of gall wasps, which have specific host ranges and produce characteristic galls. Most of these galls, while unsightly, do little harm to the host.

Description and life cycle: Adult gall wasps overwinter in the gall and emerge in spring. Females lay eggs on the host; after hatching, the larvae begin to feed. Where each one feeds, it stimulates the host to form a new gall, then uses this mass of plant tissue as food and as shelter during pupation. Adults emerge in summer to produce a second brood; this generation overwinters as adults in new galls.

Damage and detection: Galls may form on leaves or stems of host plants. They are often high in tannins and have been used in the past to make ink. While the galls may be somewhat unsightly, they rarely injure or even weaken a plant.

Control: PHYSICAL—Prune and destroy overwintering galls to reduce the gall wasp population.

Gypsy Moths

Range: *eastern and central United States; sometimes the Pacific Northwest*

Generations per year: *1*

Host(s): *many trees and shrubs*

The gypsy moth was introduced to Massachusetts from Europe in 1869 in an effort to improve American silk production. Accidentally released, it spread rapidly throughout New England, feeding on a wide variety of deciduous and evergreen trees and shrubs. Among its preferred hosts are oak, apple, alder, hawthorn, poplar, and willow. Its spread has continued throughout the eastern and central United States and southeastern Canada. In the West, there are occasional outbreaks in Washington, Oregon, and California. A closely related Asian species has appeared on the West Coast, where it is attacking an even wider range of plants than the gypsy moth.

Description and life cycle: Gypsy moths overwinter as eggs, which hatch in April or early May. The larvae are gray caterpillars that grow up to 2 inches in length and have tufts of brown hairs on the sides of their bodies. They are easy to identify because of the distinctive markings on their backs—five pairs of blue tubercles or dots, followed by six pairs of red dots. At first, larvae feed at night on leaves of trees and shrubs, and take shelter under fallen leaves, in woodpiles, or in other dark or shady places during the day. As the larvae grow larger, they begin to feed during the day as well as at night.

When a tree suffers an unusually heavy infestation, the larvae are so numerous that their excrement rustles like a gentle, constant rain as it falls through the leaves, accumulating in a visible layer of tiny tan pellets on the ground. After approximately 7 weeks of feeding, each caterpillar finds a protected spot, such as a crevice in the bark or the crotch of a branch, in which to pupate. Adult moths emerge from mid to late summer.

The moths are an inch long, with a 2-inch wingspan. Wings are gray-brown in the male, off-white in the female, with dark wavy markings in both. The males fly freely, but the females do not fly until after mating. The females lay their eggs in fuzzy, chamois-colored masses of 100 to 1,000 on any hard surface. Gypsy moth

Gypsy Moth Caterpillar

egg masses are often found attached to vehicles or camping gear and may be inadvertently transported over many miles by such means. Checking infested trees and nearby buildings for these egg masses and eliminating them when found is one way to reduce future infestations.

Damage and detection: Gypsy moths defoliate plants, leaving only the midrib of each leaf. Infested plants are left weakened and susceptible to disease. Deciduous trees often die if defoliated two or three consecutive seasons, and evergreens may die after a single defoliation.

Control: PHYSICAL—Handpick egg masses; paint egg cases with creosote; apply tree bands and sticky bands around trees; set pheromone traps. CULTURAL—Plant resistant varieties. BIOLOGICAL—Bt; chalcid wasps; ground beetles; tachinid flies; trichogramma wasps. CHEMICAL—Neem; pyrethrins; ryania.

Hemlock Woolly Adelgids

Range: *eastern United States from North Carolina to Connecticut*

Generations per year: *2 or 3*

Host(s): *eastern hemlock, spruce*

The hemlock woolly adelgid is an extremely destructive pest of eastern hemlock *(Tsuga canadensis)*. It also occurs in the Pacific Northwest but is not as serious a problem there because western hemlocks are somewhat resistant.

Description and life cycle: The hemlock woolly adelgid overwinters as a tiny adult covered with a protective white, cottony sac about ¼ inch long. From February to June, the female lays 50 to 300 eggs inside her sac. Chocolate-colored, oval nymphs hatch in spring and early summer, then crawl away from the egg sac and settle into their own feeding sites. Some of the nymphs mature into wingless females and stay on the same hemlock, where they produce another generation. Other nymphs mature into winged adults that spend part of their life cycle on spruce trees.

Damage and detection: The woolly egg sacs are easy to see at the base of needles. Needles turn yellow, then brown, and drop off. The adelgids suck sap and weaken trees. If left untreated, an infested tree generally dies in 4 years. In cases of severe infestation, it may die within as little as 1 year.

Control: CHEMICAL—Horticultural oil or insecticidal soap, applied as soon as infestation is detected.

Hornworms

Range: *widespread throughout North America*

Generations per year: *1 to 4*

Host(s): *tomato, pepper, eggplant*

The hornworm, which is the larva of the sphinx moth, is large and eats voraciously; even a single hornworm feeding on a plant can cause significant damage.

Description and life cycle: Hornworms overwinter in the soil as brown, 2-inch pupae. These emerge in summer as mottled gray moths with yellow-spotted abdomens and a 4- to 5-inch wingspan, and lay eggs on the undersides of leaves. When the eggs hatch, the emerging larvae are bright green caterpillars 3 to 4 inches long, with diagonal white side bars and a black, green, or red horn at the tail end. The caterpillars eat leaves for 3 to 4 weeks before entering the soil to pupate.

Damage and detection: Hornworms eat large holes in leaves and fruit. Their color camouflages them well in foliage, but the sudden appearance of leafless stems gives away their presence, as do greenish black droppings on the leaves.

Control: CULTURAL—Cultivate soil in fall. PHYSICAL—Handpick caterpillars, unless their backs bear the white cocoons of braconid wasps, a natural predator. BIOLOGICAL—Braconid wasps; lacewings; ladybird beetles; trichogramma wasps. CHEMICAL—Bt; pyrethrins; rotenone.

Imported Cabbage Worms

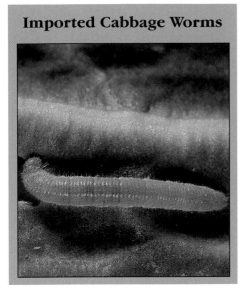

Range: *widespread throughout North America*

Generations per year: *3 to 6*

Host(s): *members of the cabbage family*

Brought from Europe in the late 19th century, the cabbage worm is now a common pest in gardens throughout the United States. The larva of the cabbage butterfly, it attacks ornamental kale along with its edible relatives.

Description and life cycle: Cabbage worms overwinter as pupae in garden debris. Adults emerge in early spring as day-flying, white or pale yellow butterflies, with dark gray or black wing tips and a 1½-inch wingspan. Eggs are laid on the underside of hosts' leaves, and hatch in 4 to 8 days. Each larva—1¼ inches long, velvety green, with one yellow stripe along its back—feeds for 2 to 3 weeks, then pupates on or near its host. A new generation of adults emerges in 2 to 3 weeks. Generations overlap, so infestations may appear continuous.

Damage and detection: Larvae chew large, ragged holes in leaves; tunnel into heads of cabbage, kale, and cauliflower; and eat broccoli florets. They leave large amounts of green-black droppings.

Control: PHYSICAL—Handpick larvae; use row covers. BIOLOGICAL—Bt at 1- to 2-week intervals; green lacewings; spined soldier bugs; trichogramma wasps. CHEMICAL—Neem; rotenone; sabadilla.

Iris Borers

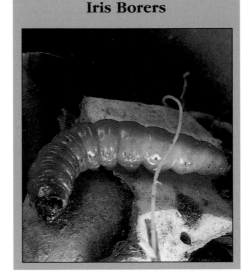

Range: *eastern North America, west to Iowa, north to Ontario, and south to Georgia*

Generations per year: *1*

Host(s): *iris*

In its geographic range, this larva is the most serious insect pest of the iris. The night-flying miller moth is the adult stage.

Description and life cycle: Iris borers overwinter as eggs on old leaves. They hatch in midspring as green larvae that mature to dusky pink with brown heads; the backs bear a light stripe and rows of black dots. Fat and up to 2 inches long, the larvae tunnel into iris foliage to feed for several weeks, then pupate in the soil near the iris rhizomes. The adult miller moths emerge in late summer; they have brown forewings, yellow hind wings, and a 2-inch wingspan. They lay eggs on leaves and flower stalks.

Damage and detection: Larvae tunnel through leaves and crowns and into rhizomes as they feed; infested leaves develop ragged edges and areas that appear water soaked. Infested rhizomes are extremely vulnerable to bacterial soft rots.

Control: PHYSICAL—Remove and destroy leaves and stems in late fall to eliminate eggs; dig up infested rhizomes and either discard them or poke a wire into visible borer holes to kill pests; dust with sulfur before planting.

Japanese Beetles

Range: *eastern United States, southeastern Canada, occasionally California*

Generations per year: *1*

Host(s): *more than 275 species of plants*

Native to the Far East, Japanese beetles were introduced to the United States around 1916. They first appeared in New Jersey but have gradually spread north to Nova Scotia and Ontario, west to the Mississippi River, and south to the Gulf of Mexico, and are occasionally found in California. They cause serious damage to a wide variety of plants in both the larval (grub) stage and the adult (beetle) stage. Among their preferred hosts are rose, grape, willow, hibiscus, apple, hydrangea, linden, raspberry, and grasses. They are particularly destructive in nurseries and orchards, and on golf courses.

Description and life cycle: Japanese beetles overwinter as partially grown grubs in the soil below the frostline. Grayish white with dark heads, grubs are fat and up to ¾ inch long; they are usually found curled in a C-shape. They feed on the roots of grasses before pupating in late spring or early summer, and emerge as adults in May, June, and July.

Beetles are ½ inch long, with shiny, metallic blue or green bodies and copper-colored wings. Their bodies are covered with grayish hairs, with tufts of white hairs on the abdomen. Beetles fly only during the day and prefer feeding in sunny locations. When they find a suitable host plant, they release feeding and sex pheromones that attract many other Japanese beetles. They feed for 30 to 45 days, then the females lay as many as 60 eggs each, in clusters of one to four, several inches deep in the soil. Females prefer to lay eggs in loose, acid soils in sunny sites; the heaviest infestations usually occur in soils with a pH of 5.3 or lower. Grubs hatch in about 2 weeks and feed on grass roots until cold weather forces them to burrow below the frostline. In spring, grubs migrate back to the soil surface and resume feeding on roots.

Damage and detection: Grub damage begins as patches of turf that grows poorly and starts to turn yellow. These patches get larger and gradually turn brown. To check such a patch for Japanese beetle grubs, peel back the turf and examine the root zone; severely damaged turf has lost most of its roots and can be rolled up like carpet to reveal the grubs. Unnoticed and untreated, an infestation of grubs can do irreversible damage, even kill an entire lawn. Adult beetles ignore grasses, preferring to attack woody and herbaceous ornamentals as well as vegetables and fruits. Feeding in groups in daytime, they chew away leaf tissue between the veins, skeletonizing foliage; they may cause defoliation. They also feed on buds and flowers, causing disfiguration.

Control for adults: PHYSICAL—Handpick beetles in the early morning while they are sluggish; knock beetles off foliage onto a sheet spread under infested plants; collect beetles with hand-held vacuum, then immerse them in soapy water. CHEMICAL—Neem as a repellent; pyrethrins; rotenone.

Control for grubs: CULTURAL—Check lawn for grubs in early spring or fall by selecting four or five different areas, marking off a square foot, and peeling back the sod. Control is warranted if you find more than 10 grubs per square foot. BIOLOGICAL—Beneficial nematodes, milky spore; parasitic wasps; tachinid flies. CHEMICAL—Neem.

Lace Bugs

Range: *various species throughout North America*

Generations per year: *2 to 5*

Host(s): *many woody and herbaceous plants*

Lace bugs are sucking insects that feed primarily on woody ornamentals such as rhododendron, hawthorn, pyracantha, and azalea. One species infests chrysanthemums and asters. Species vary in both geographic range and host preference.

Description and life cycle: Lace bugs overwinter as eggs or adults in garden debris. Nymphs undergo five molts in as little as 2 to 3 weeks to become adults. They are tiny and dark; many are covered with spines. Adults are ⅛ inch long, with lacy wings that are nearly transparent. Adults lay black eggs on the undersides of leaves, along the midrib, usually near the tops of plants.

Damage and detection: Both nymphs and adults feed in clusters and suck the plant's juices, leaving the upper sides of leaves stippled or blanched. Plants lose color, become unsightly, and bloom poorly. Nymphs feeding on the undersides of leaves excrete distinctive brown, sticky droppings. Repeated infestations can weaken and kill plants.

Control: PHYSICAL—Spray with water. CULTURAL—Maintain vigor and health of plants. CHEMICAL—Horticultural oil; insecticidal soap; neem; pyrethrins; rotenone; sabadilla.

Leafhoppers

Range: *widespread throughout North America*

Generations per year: *2 to 5*

Hosts(s): *most ornamentals and vegetables*

North America has more than 2,700 leafhopper species. They especially favor calendula, marigold, and other members of the composite family, but also attack other herbaceous and woody ornamentals, vegetables, and fruits.

Description and life cycle: Adult leafhoppers overwinter on host plants. In spring the females insert eggs into leaf or stem tissue. Adults are wedge shaped, ¹⁄₁₀ to ½ inch long; most are green, brown, or yellow, with colorful spots or bands. Nymphs are smaller, often wingless versions of adults. Each generation lives only a few weeks.

Damage and detection: Nymphs and adults feed on the undersides of leaves, sucking sap and injecting their toxic saliva into the plant. Heavy infestations can stunt, bleach, or mottle leaves; leaves may brown at the margins and drop prematurely. Leafhoppers also carry serious plant diseases such as aster yellows and curly top virus.

Control: PHYSICAL—Use row covers; strong streams of water. CULTURAL—Till soil in fall. BIOLOGICAL—Big-eyed bugs; lacewing larvae. CHEMICAL—Horticultural oil; insecticidal soap; rotenone; sabadilla; systemic pesticide.

Leaf Miners

Range: *throughout North America*

Generations per year: *variable*

Host(s): *many ornamentals and vegetables*

Leaf miners are the larvae of different species of beetles, flies, sawflies, and moths, and feed between the upper and lower surfaces of leaves. Among the plants often disfigured by leaf miners are azalea, birch, boxwood, chrysanthemum, columbine, holly, and delphinium.

Description and life cycle: Birch leaf miners, which also infest elms, overwinter as larvae in cocoons in the soil and pupate in spring. The adults, which are black with transparent wings, emerge in spring, mate, and lay eggs in leaves. The hatching larvae feed inside the leaves, then pupate. This species has up to four generations a year. The boxwood miner has only one generation per year. Eggs are laid in leaves in midspring; the larvae overwinter in leaves and pupate the following year. Adults are very small, gnatlike flies. They emerge in midspring and mate, lay eggs, and die in a few days.

Damage and detection: Larvae feeding inside leaves make blotches, blisters, or winding tunnels. These mines weaken plants and are very unsightly.

Control: PHYSICAL—Use row covers; destroy damaged leaves; remove such weed hosts as lamb's-quarters and dock. CULTURAL—Rotate crops. BIOLOGICAL—Lacewings; birds. CHEMICAL—Horticultural oil; neem.

Locust Leaf Miner Beetles

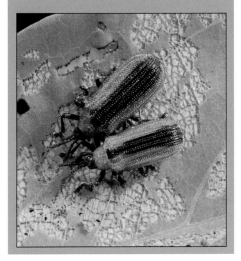

Range: *eastern United States, west to the Mississippi River*

Generations per year: *1 or 2*

Host(s): *primarily black locust*

The locust leaf miner beetle feeds on black locust trees, making them extremely unsightly. It also feeds on a number of other hosts in the legume family, such as sophora and American yellowwood, but rarely does much damage.

Description and life cycle: The adult beetle overwinters in a sheltered site, then emerges in spring to feed on the margins of growing leaves of black locust. The ¼-inch adult is orange-yellow, with a wide black stripe along the back. Females lay eggs in clusters of three to five on the undersides of leaves. Larvae are flattened and yellow-white with dark heads; on hatching, they tunnel into leaves, feed for a month, and pupate. There is often a second generation.

Damage and detection: Feeding at the margins of leaves, adults cause little damage, but larvae tunnel into leaves to form mines that create irregular blotches, spreading back from the leaf tip. Leaves turn brown and drop prematurely. Sometimes trees produce a second set of leaves, which are often infested with the second generation of leaf miner beetles. Repeated infestations can weaken trees.

Control: BIOLOGICAL—Wheel bugs; trichogramma wasps.

May/June Beetles

Range: *throughout the United States; most troublesome in the South and Midwest*

Generations per year: *1- to 4-year life cycles*

Host(s): *many ornamentals; lawn grasses*

The adult stage of this pest is known as the May beetle, June beetle, or daw bug; the larva is often called a white grub. Both the adults and the larvae cause plant damage.

Description and life cycle: May beetles overwinter as larvae in the soil, feeding on roots, especially those of lawn grasses. The grubs are ½ to 1½ inches long and white with dark heads. Depending on the species, they stay in the larval stage 1 to 3 years. Then they pupate, emerging in late spring as 1-inch black, brown, or green beetles. Active at night, the beetles feed on the foliage of a wide range of trees and shrubs, vegetables, and flowers. By day, they hide in debris or foliage. Eggs are laid in the soil and hatch in about 3 weeks.

Damage and detection: Grubs eat roots of grasses and other plants such as potato and strawberry, giving them a wilted, stunted look. Where grubs dig out dime-size holes in turf, grass turns brown. Adults chew ragged holes in leaves.

Control: PHYSICAL—Handpick beetles. CULTURAL—Cultivate soil in fall to kill larvae. BIOLOGICAL—Beneficial nematodes; milky spore; vertebrate predators of grubs, including birds, skunks, and moles. CHEMICAL—Neem; pyrethrins.

Mites

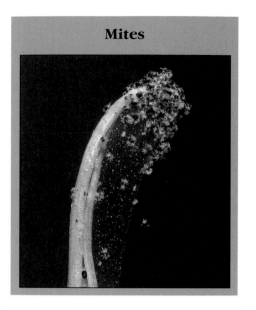

Range: *widespread throughout North America*

Generations per year: *many*

Host(s): *many ornamentals and vegetables*

Mites are not insects but belong to the class of animals called arachnids, which includes ticks and spiders. Of the hundreds of mite species, most benefit gardeners by feeding on pests. Other species, however, are parasites of plants or animals. Among the most damaging to plants are the two-spotted spider mites, cyclamen mites, and rust mites.

Description and life cycle: Mites have short life cycles; in warm climates, homes, and greenhouses, reproduction is continuous. Uncontrolled populations of mites can build rapidly, resulting in serious plant infestations and losses.

Outdoors, most plant-feeding mites overwinter as adults or eggs, in garden debris or on the bark of trees or shrubs. Mites are barely visible to the naked eye; a spider mite is about the size of a grain of salt, less than 1/20 inch long. Magnification through a hand lens shows that the adult spider mites have 8 legs and hairy, oval-shaped bodies. They may be brown, green, red, or yellow; their color varies, to a large degree, according to their diet. Nymphs are similar to adults but smaller, and early stages have only 6 legs.

Cyclamen or rust mites, about one-fourth the size of adult spider mites, are hardly visible without a hand lens that magnifies at least 15x. Adult cyclamen mites are pinkish orange; nymphs are translucent. Rust mites have only 4 legs, are wedge shaped, and are usually pinkish white or yellow.

Mites emerge in spring to feed and mate. Eggs are laid on the host plant and usually hatch in less than a week. The new generation reaches maturity in 5 to 10 days. New broods are produced continuously until cold weather sets in.

Damage and detection: In both nymph and adult forms, mites feed on plants by sucking the cell sap, generally feeding in large colonies. Because of their minute size, however, their damage tends to go unnoticed until long after they have become established in a planting.

Spider mites cause leaves to become stippled, bleached, yellow, or brown. Leaves often drop prematurely, weakening plants and stunting fruit. A heavy spider mite infestation may cover affected plant parts with a fine webbing, spun by the mites as they feed. Spider mite damage is most severe in the hot, dry, and dusty conditions that accelerate their reproduction rate.

Cyclamen mites generally infest new, unfolding leaves. As the leaves continue to develop, they appear crinkled and deformed; stems may fail to elongate normally. Cyclamen mites also attack young flowers, causing growth distortions. On strawberries, they feed on the fruit, stunting its development and making it look dry and shriveled. Rust mites damage the surfaces of the leaves on which they feed, disrupting the chlorophyll and turning leaves brown or rust colored.

Control: PHYSICAL—Remove and destroy heavily infested leaves, branches, or entire plants; spray with water. BIOLOGICAL—Lacewings; ladybird beetles; predatory mites. CHEMICAL—Use insecticides only as a last resort, as they may harm predators and result in a greater mite problem; horticultural oil, insecticidal soap; neem; pyrethrins.

Pine Tip Moths

Range: *various species throughout North America*

Generations per year: *1 to 5*

Host(s): *pine trees*

Seven species of pine tip or pine shoot moths occur in different parts of the United States. Although they have different hosts among the many species of pine, the damage they do is similar.

Description and life cycle: Pine tip moths hibernate as larvae or pupae in the tips of shoots or in buds. Adults are night-flying moths, reddish brown to gray, with a wingspan up to ¾ inch. Females lay their eggs at the tips of host branches. Larvae are about ½ inch long, and may be brown, reddish brown, or yellow; they tunnel into the bases of needles and buds to feed. They pupate in these hollows or near the base of the tree. Most species produce one generation each year. The Nantucket pine tip moth, however, may produce as many as five.

Damage and detection: Larvae kill the host's shoot tips, leaving them brown and dry. Pine resin and insect excrement accumulate near the feeding site. Buds are blasted, and growth is stunted or produces a tuft of thin, weak twigs. Heavy infestations can kill young trees.

Control: PHYSICAL—Prune and destroy infested branches in early spring to remove overwintering larvae or pupae. BIOLOGICAL—Braconid wasps; predatory spiders. CHEMICAL—Systemic pesticide.

Plant Bugs

Range: *widespread throughout North America*

Generations per year: *1 to 5*

Host(s): *many ornamentals and vegetables*

The plant bugs are a large family of insects that includes predaceous and beneficial species as well as several serious pests. Among the most common pests are the four-lined plant bug and the tarnished plant bug, or lygus bug. The four-lined plant bug feeds on more than 250 plant species. Its geographic range is east of the Rocky Mountains. Most of its hosts are herbaceous ornamentals, such as aster, chrysanthemum, dahlia, phlox, and zinnia. It also infests such ornamental trees and shrubs as azalea, dogwood, forsythia, rose, and viburnum.

The more common tarnished plant bug, found throughout North America, is probably the most damaging member of this family. It attacks over 385 plant species, including most vegetables and fruits as well as numerous woody and herbaceous ornamentals.

Description and life cycle: Four-lined plant bugs overwinter as eggs in young plant shoots. The egg clusters, protruding from slits made across the stem, are easy to see in fall after the leaves have dropped. They hatch in spring, and the nymphs feed for about a month before their final molt to become adults. Nymphs are bright red, yellow, or orange with black spots. Adults are ¼ to ⅓ inch long and greenish yellow, with 4 black stripes and yellow or bright green forewings. There is one generation per year.

Tarnished plant bugs overwinter as adults under bark or in garden debris, emerging in early spring to attack opening buds. Females lay eggs in the stems and flowers of herbaceous host plants. Adults are ¼ inch long, oval, and mottled brown and tan; each forewing has a black-tipped yellow triangle. Eggs hatch in about 10 days. The yellow-green nymphs resemble the adults but are wingless. They feed for 3 to 4 weeks, then molt to become adults, and repeat the cycle. There are as many as five generations per year.

Damage and detection: Plant bugs injure their host by sucking plant sap in both nymph and adult stages. Four-lined plant bugs feed on leaves, removing the chlorophyll and causing spots that lose color or turn brown or black. The injured

Tarnished Plant Bug

area may fall out, or the entire leaf may fall prematurely. The tarnished plant bug feeds on leaves, stems, buds, fruit, and flowers. Adults feeding on buds in spring often kill the growing tip of a twig. As a consequence, lateral shoots develop, giving the plant a bushy, often stunted appearance. Besides sucking sap, the tarnished plant bug injects a toxin that disrupts plant growth.

Control: PHYSICAL—Use row covers; remove plant debris where eggs or adults may be overwintering; set white sticky traps. BIOLOGICAL—Big-eyed bugs; braconid wasps; chalcid wasps; damsel bugs; pirate bugs. CHEMICAL—Insecticidal soap; rotenone; sabadilla; apply sprays in the early morning, when bugs are sluggish.

Planthoppers

Range: *throughout the United States and southern Canada*

Generations per year: *1*

Host(s): *ornamentals, vegetables, and fruits*

Planthoppers infest a broad range of trees, shrubs, and woody vines, and a few herbaceous ornamentals, as well as vegetables and fruits. Some of the more common plants attacked include boxwood, viburnum, magnolia, maple, oak, and many fruit trees. Although various species are found throughout the United States, planthoppers are most troublesome in the South.

Description and life cycle: Planthoppers overwinter as eggs in the twigs of host plants. Hatching in late spring, the nymphs are white or yellow-green. They cover themselves with a white, cottony material and suck plant sap from leaves or shoots. In about 9 weeks, nymphs molt to become adults up to ⅓ inch long that are brown, gray, green, white, or yellow. Females slit the bark of twigs and lay eggs in the slits.

Damage and detection: The white cottony covering of planthoppers detracts from the appearance of ornamentals. Egg laying may cause some dieback in twigs, but planthoppers seldom do other harm. In fruit trees, however, the loss of sap injures fruit and foliage.

Control: PHYSICAL—Spray with water. CHEMICAL—Pyrethrins.

Psyllids

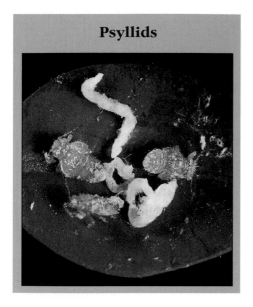

Range: *widespread throughout North America*

Generations per year: *1 to 5*

Host(s): *many ornamentals and vegetables*

Each of the many psyllid species has its own preferred host. The boxwood psyllid and the pear psyllid are two of the most damaging species.

Description and life cycle: Boxwood psyllids overwinter as eggs that hatch in spring. The nymphs feed on new leaves, secreting a waxy material for their own protection. After several weeks, the nymphs become gray-green adults, with transparent wings ⅛ inch across. Females insert eggs in the base of buds; there is one generation per year. Pear psyllids hibernate in bark crevices or plant debris as tiny brown adults with transparent wings. In early spring they fly to pear trees, mate, and lay eggs; nymphs suck sap from leaves. There are three to five generations per year.

Damage and detection: Nymphs harm plants by sucking sap. Some cause gall formation; others spread serious plant diseases. Boxwood psyllids distort new leaves and stunt twig growth. Pear psyllid nymphs turn leaves yellow, carry the pear-decline virus, and secrete honeydew, which supports sooty mold fungus.

Control: PHYSICAL—To discourage feeding, remove any water sprouts that appear. BIOLOGICAL—Chalcid wasps; lacewings; pirate bugs. CHEMICAL—Horticultural oil; rotenone.

Rose Chafers

Range: *widespread throughout North America*

Generations per year: *1*

Host(s): *many*

Because the rose chafer prefers a light, sandy soil, its range is somewhat limited. Where it is found, it feeds on bramble fruit, grape, peony, hollyhock, rose, strawberry, and many other fruit, vegetable, and ornamental plants.

Description and life cycle: Larvae, or grubs, overwinter in the soil, pupating and emerging as adults in spring. They often appear suddenly in swarms to feed on leaves, flowers, and fruit. Adults are ½-inch, reddish brown beetles with spiny legs. They feed for 4 to 6 weeks, then females lay eggs in clusters in the soil. Eggs hatch in about 2 weeks. The larvae are ¾-inch white grubs with brown heads; they feed on the roots of grasses.

Damage and detection: Adults eat flowers and fruit, skeletonize leaves, and soil other plant parts with black excrement. The larvae do minor root damage. Rose chafers are poisonous to many birds.

Control: PHYSICAL—Handpick beetles, use row covers; set white sticky traps. CULTURAL—Cultivate soil to destroy larvae and pupae. BIOLOGICAL—Beneficial nematodes for grubs. CHEMICAL—Pyrethrins; rotenone.

Sawflies

Range: *various species throughout North America*

Generations per year: *1 to 6*

Host(s): *many trees and shrubs*

Although the hundreds of species of sawflies look similar and cause similar damage, each has particular host preferences. Sawflies are common pests of azaleas, birches, dogwoods, roses, and many other deciduous and evergreen trees and shrubs.

Description and life cycle: Most sawflies hibernate as larvae or pupae in cocoons in the soil. Some species may remain in this state for two or more seasons. Emerging in spring and summer, adults resemble clearwing wasps, which belong to the same family. Instead of a stinger, however, females have a sawlike organ for inserting eggs into leaves or needles. Newly hatched larvae are wormlike and are usually green, yellow, or brown. They feed in colonies until mature, then drop to the ground to pupate.

Damage and detection: Larvae eat their host's leaves, beginning with the outermost portions. They feed in masses, completely defoliating one branch before moving on to the next, and sometimes stripping an entire tree. Some sawfly species mine leaves, bore into fruit, or stimulate galls.

Control: CULTURAL—Remove garden debris. PHYSICAL—Spray plants with water. BIOLOGICAL—Parasitic wasps. CHEMICAL—Horticultural oil; ryania.

Scale Insects

Range: *widespread throughout North America*

Generations per year: *1 to 6*

Host(s): *many*

The roughly 200 species of these piercing-sucking insects can be divided into two major groups: armored scales and soft scales. The armored scales bear a hard, scalelike shell that entirely covers the insect's body and can be separated from it. The soft scales have a waxy covering that does not quite enclose the body and cannot be separated from it. Scales attack many trees and shrubs and can be troublesome indoors on houseplants and in greenhouses, where their reproduction is continuous. Scale species differ in both geographic ranges and hosts.

Description and life cycle: Scales may overwinter as eggs, nymphs, or adults. In many species, female adults look significantly different from males; they may lay eggs or give birth to live nymphs. Called crawlers, young nymphs are soft bodied and about 1/10 to 1/16 inch long. They crawl out of the shell to feed, sucking plant sap. They may remain on the same plant or be carried by wind to infest a new plant. The crawler stage may last for a few hours or a few days. The female nymph then settles onto one spot and secretes her protective shell. She pupates within the shell, matures, and lays her eggs there. Male crawlers pupate to become winged adults.

Common armored species include:

- euonymus scale, which attacks many species of bittersweet, citrus, euonymus, lilac, and pachysandra. Mature females overwinter on branches under their protective brown, shell-like scales; males overwinter under narrow, white scales. The pale yellow crawlers begin to appear in late spring. There are one to three generations per year.
- juniper scale, which infests arborvitae, cypress, incense cedar, and juniper. The insects overwinter as fertilized females under round white scales with yellow centers. Crawlers appear in early summer. Males have slender white bodies. There is one generation per year.
- obscure scale, most troublesome in the South. It infests shade trees and is a serious pest of pecan. The insects overwinter as fertilized females, and

Wax Scale

crawlers are present throughout the summer. The shell is gray and roughly circular. One generation is produced each year.

- oystershell scale, which is very widespread in its geographic range but most common in the northern parts of the United States. This pest can occur in such large numbers that the shells cover all of the bark of a host plant. While oystershell scale attacks many deciduous trees and shrubs, it is most troublesome on apple, ash, lilac, pear, poplar, and willow. The insects overwinter as eggs under the female's grayish brown, oyster-shaped shell. The male shell is smaller and oval. These scales infest only the bark

of their host, and do not feed on leaves. Nymphs appear in late spring and move about as crawlers only a few hours before settling permanently to feed and produce their shells. There are one or two generations per year.

- San Jose scale, which is found throughout the United States and southern Canada. It infests many or-

Oystershell Scale

namental trees and shrubs but is most serious on deciduous fruit trees. Partially grown nymphs overwinter under their scale coverings and resume their feeding and development in late spring. Young scales are light in color but become gray-black and crusty at maturity. Nymphs are yellow. San Jose scale usually occurs in large numbers, making fruit and bark look as if they were covered with ashes. Female scales are round; males are smaller and oval. Generations overlap, and there are as many as five per year.

Common soft species include:

- hemispherical scale, a tropical pest common in southern California and Florida, where it infests a number of ornamental plants and citrus trees. Hemispherical scales are also common pests in greenhouses and of houseplants nearly everywhere, favoring ferns as a host. Young hemispherical scales are oval in shape. The shell of mature females is a nearly perfect hemisphere, shiny and brown. There are one or two generations per year, but they overlap, so all stages may be present at any time.
- wax scale, which is distinguished from other species of scale by its

waxy white covering. Most common in the South, wax scales feed on many hosts, including barberry, boxwood, camellia, euonymus, flowering quince, hemlock, holly, pyracantha, and spiraea. They also attack plants in greenhouses. Most overwintering individuals are adult females, which begin egg laying in midspring. The eggs hatch in late spring or summer, and after a short period of mobility, the crawlers settle to feed and secrete their waxy covering. Some wax scale species settle on leaves, others on stems. There are one or two generations per year.

Damage and detection: Because of their generally dull color and limited mobility,

Euonymus Scale

scales often remain unnoticed until damage to the host has occurred. As piercing-sucking insects that feed on plant sap, many scales settle on stems, others on foliage, often on the undersides of leaves, along the major veins. Leaves of infested plants turn yellow and may drop prematurely; plants lose vigor. Many scales, especially soft scales, secrete honeydew, a sugary, sticky substance that serves as a growing medium for sooty mold. This dark fungus blocks light from the leaf surface, reducing photosynthesis, causing further yellowing, and seriously reducing a plant's ornamental value.

Control: PHYSICAL—Remove scales with a cotton-tipped swab or soft toothbrush dipped in soapy water or a solution of rubbing alcohol and water; prune and destroy infested branches. BIOLOGICAL—Ladybird beetles; parasitic wasps; soldier beetles. CHEMICAL—Horticultural oil.

Slugs and Snails

Range: *widespread throughout North America*
Generations per year: *may live for years*
Host(s): *most ornamentals and vegetables*

Among the hundreds of species of slugs and snails, only a few are significant pests of plants. The difference between a slug and a snail is a shell: A snail has one, a slug does not. Both are mollusks, related to clams and oysters. They need moist conditions and prefer cool, dark places because they dry out easily. For this reason, they are primarily night feeders, although they may come out of their dark hiding places on cloudy or rainy days. Both secrete slimy mucus as they slither along, leaving a narrow, shiny trail in their wake. They are common pests, infesting nearly every garden moist enough to support them.

Description and life cycle: Slugs and snails pass the winter in sheltered locations—often in garden debris, under boards, or in soil. Some species overwinter only as eggs, although most will survive at any stage. In warmer regions and in greenhouses, these pests are active year round.

Each slug and snail is hermaphroditic, having both male and female sex organs. They breed during the warm parts of the year. Adults lay eggs in clusters of 25 or more in moist soil or garden debris. Clear to white and up to ⅛ inch across, eggs hatch in about a month. Slugs can be gray, black, brown, pink, or beige,

and some have spots. Snails are usually brown or gray. Both have eyes at the tips of protruding tentacles; two other tentacles bear smelling organs.

Slugs range from ½ to 8 inches long; a snail's body is rarely larger than 3 inches. Snail shells are spiral shaped and usually between ½ and 1½ inches across. Because of their shells, snails are more protected than slugs, and if conditions become too dry, snails can retreat into their shells and live in dormancy for up to 4 years. Young slugs and snails look like adults but are smaller. Depending on conditions, they take several months or several years to mature.

Damage and detection: Slugs and snails have file-like mouth parts, with which they tear fleshy leaves, especially those near the ground. Because they feed at night, they are rarely seen, but their damage is plain. They make tender

Snail

seedlings disappear overnight. They eat large ragged holes in the middle and along the edges of leaves on mature plants, and defoliate favorite hosts. They also feed on fleshy fruit and vegetables. The slimy trails they leave behind are a telltale sign of a slug or snail infestation.

Control: CULTURAL—Cultivate soil in early spring to expose eggs, juveniles, and adults. PHYSICAL—Handpick at night by flashlight until damage ceases; use copper barriers; set board traps, checking them each morning and destroying pests; bury a shallow pan filled with beer to attract and drown slugs and snails; spread sand or cinders around plants. BIOLOGICAL—Decollate snails. CHEMICAL—Spread diatomaceous earth on the ground around plants.

Sod Webworms

Range: *widespread throughout the United States and southern Canada*

Generations per year: *2 or 3*

Host(s): *turf grasses*

The sod webworm feeds on lawn turf grasses, including bent grass, fescues, Kentucky bluegrass, perennial ryegrass, and zoysia. It also attacks corn.

Description and life cycle: Sod webworms hibernate as larvae in tunnels near the soil surface. The ¾-inch larvae are light brown with dark spots. In spring they feed briefly, pupate, and emerge as adults, which are 1-inch-long, dull gray or brown moths with spotted wings. They fly at night in a zigzag fashion, laying eggs near the base of grass stems. Upon hatching, the larvae feed on grass blades and form tunnels near the soil surface. Pupation occurs in the tunnel. There are usually two or three generations per year, although in warm areas reproduction is continuous.

Damage and detection: Blades are chewed off at the base, creating small brown patches in the lawn. To test for sod webworms, soak damaged lawn areas with a mild detergent solution; if there are more than two webworms per square foot, treatment is recommended.

Control: CULTURAL—Plant turf grass containing endophytic fungi; dethatch in fall. BIOLOGICAL—Beneficial nematodes; birds; Bt; parasitic wasps. CHEMICAL—Insecticidal soap; pyrethrins.

Spittlebugs

Range: *widely distributed throughout North America*

Generations per year: *1 or 2*

Host(s): *many ornamentals and vegetables*

Although spittlebugs have inhabited most of North America for a long time, only in the past two to three decades have their populations increased enough to make them significant plant pests. Sometimes called froghoppers, spittlebugs are related to cicadas and aphids. The several spittlebug species have different hosts and geographic ranges. One of the most destructive species is the Saratoga spittlebug, which infests pines throughout the United States. The most abundant and widely distributed species, the meadow spittlebug, feeds on a broad range of herbaceous plants.

Some spittlebugs complete their entire life cycle on one plant, feeding on the same plant on which the egg was laid. Others feed first on low-growing, herbaceous plants, then migrate to taller, woody plants. Many spittlebugs are most troublesome in high-humidity areas like the Northeast and the Pacific Northwest. Commonly infested hosts include strawberry, legumes, corn, clover, and pines.

Description and life cycle: Spittlebugs overwinter as eggs in grasses or weeds, or on host plants, and hatch in midspring. The nymphs are tiny, wingless, and yellow or green. They produce drops of clear liquid that, when mixed with air, forms a froth around their bodies, protecting them from sun and predators. The nymphs keep hidden under this mass of bubbles, usually in groups of three or four, and feed for 6 to 7 weeks. When adults emerge, they continue to feed, but since they do not create spittle, they can walk, hop, or fly. They move quickly when disturbed and may migrate to other hosts. Adults are usually tan and mottled brown or black, often with stripes or bands on their wings. Bluntly wedge shaped, with sharp spines studding their hind legs, they resemble leafhoppers but are somewhat stouter and ¼ to ⅓ inch long, depending on the species. Females lay rows of white or beige eggs on or near hosts.

Damage and detection: The bubbly froth formed by feeding nymphs is the best evidence of spittlebugs' presence. Both nymph and adult spittlebugs feed on tender stems and leaves, by sucking plant sap. A few spittlebugs on a plant rarely cause significant damage, but when their populations are large, they can cause stunting, loss of vigor, and reduced yields. Heavy infestations of pine and Saratoga spittlebugs can reduce growth of the trees' twigs, and make needles lose color and die. Twigs die back from their tips, diminishing the plant's ornamental value.

Control (only when significant numbers are present): CULTURAL—In fall, remove and destroy plant debris that can harbor overwintering eggs. PHYSICAL—Spray with water; prune and destroy parts of plants where spittle is present; use row covers. CHEMICAL—Insecticidal soap.

Spruce Budworms

Range: *northern half of the United States and most of Canada*

Generations per year: *1*

Host(s): *conifers*

Spruce budworms are the most serious defoliators of coniferous plants in the United States. They prefer to feed on spruce and balsam fir, but they also attack larch, pine, and hemlock.

Description and life cycle: Spruce budworms overwinter as larvae in cocoon-like shelters on twigs of the host tree. In spring they emerge to feed on buds, flowers, and new needles for 3 to 4 weeks. When mature, each of the thick, dark brown, 1-inch larvae ties young shoots together with silk threads, forming a shelter in which to pupate. The adult moths that emerge less than 2 weeks later are capable of migrating long distances. Females lay their eggs on hosts in a series of elongated, overlapping clusters, each of which contains as many as 60 eggs. Larvae hatch in about 10 days and feed until they prepare their winter cocoons.

Damage and detection: Spruce budworms mine needles and buds, and defoliate trees. Heavy infestations often kill hosts in 3 to 5 years. Surviving trees are weakened and susceptible to further insect or disease damage.

Control: BIOLOGICAL—Bt; parasitic wasps.

Tent Caterpillars

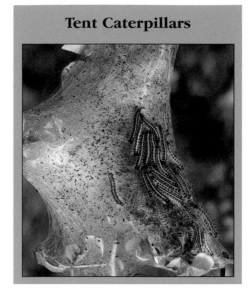

Range: *two species, one in eastern and the other in western North America*

Generations per year: *1*

Host(s): *most deciduous trees and shrubs*

Tent caterpillars spin silk tents in the crotches of trees and shrubs. Plants commonly infested are apple, aspen, crab apple, and wild cherry.

Description and life cycle: Tent caterpillars overwinter as eggs on host twigs. Eggs hatch in early spring, and the larvae move to the nearest crotch and spin a silk tent. They feed at night and return to the protection afforded by the tent by day. The 2- to 2½-inch caterpillars are hairy and black, with white stripes and blue or red side markings. After 5 to 8 weeks, they pupate, emerging about 10 days later as adult moths, tan or brown with striped forewings and a 1- to 1½-inch wingspan. Females lay a black, lumpy ring of eggs around host twigs.

Damage and detection: This pest's large tent is easy to spot. Larvae eat leaves and can cause total defoliation. Trees may produce a second flush of leaves but are weakened and stunted.

Control: PHYSICAL—Handpick pests; prune and destroy infested branches; use sticky bands on trees; remove egg masses in winter. BIOLOGICAL—Bt; parasitic flies; parasitic wasps; spined soldier bugs. CHEMICAL—Insecticidal soap.

Thrips

Range: *widespread throughout North America*

Generations per year: *5 to 15*

Host(s): *most ornamentals and vegetables*

Thrips are tiny insects that feed on a wide range of plants. Some of their favorite hosts are roses, peonies, gladiolus, daylilies, and onions.

Description and life cycle: With a life cycle of about 3 weeks, thrips produce many generations per year, especially in warm climates. They overwinter as adults or eggs. Adults have bristly wings, are yellow, brown, or black, and are only $\frac{1}{50}$ to $\frac{1}{25}$ inch long. Nymphs are even smaller and light green or yellow.

Damage and detection: Thrips usually feed in groups, scraping host tissue with their specialized mouthparts and sucking the released sap. They cause silvery speckling on leaves; infested plants may be deformed or stunted, with buds that turn brown without opening. Some thrips also spread viral diseases.

Control: PHYSICAL—Remove infested buds and flowers; spray with water; use sticky yellow traps. CULTURAL—Remove garden debris to eliminate overwintering adults or eggs; rotate crops. BIOLOGICAL—Green lacewings; ladybird beetles; pirate bugs; predatory mites. CHEMICAL—Horticultural oil; insecticidal soap; rotenone.

Treehoppers

Range: *widespread throughout North America*

Generations per year: *1*

Host(s): *many woody and herbaceous plants*

Treehoppers are unusual-looking insects that infest herbaceous plants as nymphs and trees as adults.

Description and life cycle: Treehoppers overwinter as eggs on bark. In spring the hatching nymphs, green with a humped back, drop to the ground and feed on low-growing herbaceous plants for about 6 weeks. After molting to become adults, they return to trees to continue feeding and to lay eggs.

Damage and detection: In both nymph and adult stages, treehoppers pierce stems and leaves with their mouthparts and suck the sap. The worst damage is done when females slit the bark of twigs and deposit their eggs in the slits. Twigs may dry out and die above the point where the eggs are laid, and they may also be invaded by fungi or bacteria.

Control: CULTURAL—Cultivate soil under fruit trees to eliminate nymph feeding sites. CHEMICAL—Dust plants with diatomaceous earth; horticultural oil.

Webworms

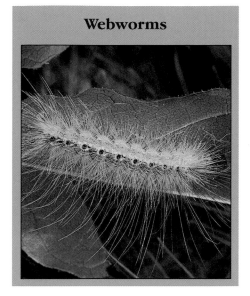

Range: *throughout the United States and southern Canada*

Generations per year: *1 to 4*

Host(s): *many ornamentals and vegetables*

The several species of webworms differ mainly in their preferred hosts. Fall webworms feed on a wide range of deciduous trees and shrubs. Garden webworms feed on many vegetables and strawberries. Juniper webworms attack juniper.

Description and life cycle: Fall webworms overwinter as pupae on tree bark or in plant debris. In spring the adults, 2-inch white moths with brown spots, lay eggs in masses on the undersides of leaves. The hatching larvae spin a web and feed inside it for 4 to 6 weeks. Larvae are about 1 inch long, hairy, and pale green or yellow. When fully grown, they leave the web and pupate on the bark or in plant debris. Garden webworms have a similar life cycle. Larvae are ¾ inch long, hairy, and green to black, often with a stripe. Adults are ¾-inch brown moths with gold and gray wing markings.

Damage and detection: As larvae chew on the leaves, they spin a conspicuous web around the host, sometimes covering the plant entirely. Webworms can completely defoliate hosts.

Control: PHYSICAL—Handpick larvae; prune and destroy branches with webs; rake up and dispose of plant debris in fall. BIOLOGICAL—Bt; trichogramma wasps. CHEMICAL—Pyrethrins; rotenone.

Weevils

Range: *widespread throughout North America*

Generations per year: *1 or 2*

Host(s): *many ornamentals and vegetables*

Weevil species that attack plants in the garden include Asiatic and black vine weevils. These two are particularly damaging to azalea, bramble fruit, camellia, mountain laurel, rhododendron, strawberry, and yew.

Description and life cycle: Most adult weevils have a long, jaw-tipped snout. They are nocturnal and winged but flightless; most are black or brown and are less than ½ inch long. Most weevils overwinter in the soil or in plant debris as pale, legless larvae that feed on roots. In spring they pupate and emerge as adults to feed on a wide range of hosts. Females lay eggs in soil or debris near hosts.

Damage and detection: Larvae feeding on roots cause stunting and wilting, and may kill heavily infested plants. Adults cut large holes or notches along leaf margins or eat leaves to the midrib.

Control: PHYSICAL—Use row covers; handpick adults; CULTURAL—Cultivate soil to expose overwintering larvae; destroy infested plants; remove and dispose of plant debris in fall; rotate garden crops; use sticky traps. BIOLOGICAL—Beneficial nematodes; birds. CHEMICAL—Pyrethrins; rotenone; sabadilla.

321

Whiteflies

Range: *southern United States and West Coast*

Generations per year: *many*

Host(s): *many ornamentals and vegetables*

The 200 or so species of whiteflies are primarily tropical pests. In warm climates they reproduce year round. In cooler regions, they infest greenhouses and feed on houseplants. They may be transported to temperate gardens in the spring on greenhouse-grown stock, but most species will not survive a cold winter. Indoors or out, whiteflies spread fast to nearby plants, and a short life cycle allows them to build up destructive populations in weeks. Whiteflies attack many different plants. Preferred hosts include citrus, gerbera, lantana, poinsettia, and salvia. The ash whitefly is a serious pest in California, where it attacks many ornamental trees and shrubs.

Description and life cycle: Most whiteflies complete their life cycle in about a month; generations overlap and reproduction is continuous. Females lay a circle of black cone-shaped eggs on the undersides of older leaves. Eggs usually hatch in less than a week, and the active, young nymphs move about and begin to feed. Once established in a feeding spot, they undergo their first molt and lose their legs to become immobile. Translucent or light green, tiny and flat, the nymphs are hard to see without a hand lens. They molt into white, mothlike adults, 1/20 to 1/10 inch long. The wings of adult whiteflies are covered with a fine, powdery wax.

Damage and detection: Although whiteflies are small, they are usually easy to detect because they occur in large numbers and feed in groups. When an infested plant is disturbed, they rise in a cloud, then quickly resettle. Both nymphs and adults suck plant sap, usually feeding on the youngest leaves. Nymphs feed from the undersides of leaves, which yellow and drop prematurely. Feeding whiteflies secrete honeydew, a sweet liquid that sticks to plants. Honeydew supports sooty mold, a fungus that blocks light, reduces photosynthesis, and further weakens plants. The ash whitefly's generous secretions of honeydew drip from host

Garden Whitefly

trees onto cars, outdoor furniture, and walkways, creating a sticky mess and attracting ants and wasps. Whiteflies transmit several viral diseases.

Control: PHYSICAL—Rinse plants to remove larvae and adults; wipe off larvae from the undersides of tender leaves with a gloved hand; destroy eggs on the undersides of older leaves; set sticky yellow traps. BIOLOGICAL—Lacewings; parasitic wasps. CHEMICAL—Horticultural oil; insecticidal soap.

White-Fringed Beetles

Range: *eastern United States from New Jersey to Florida, west to Arkansas*

Generations per year: *1 to 4*

Host(s): *most herbaceous plants*

A South American native first seen in Florida in 1936, the white-fringed beetle has spread throughout the southern states and as far north as New Jersey. It feeds on many herbaceous ornamentals, including aster and goldenrod, and on vegetables such as beans, okra, peas, and potatoes.

Description and life cycle: White-fringed beetles overwinter as 1/2-inch, legless white larvae, often 9 to 12 inches deep in the soil. Pupating in late spring and early summer, they emerge as adults that are 1/2 inch long, brownish gray, and hairy, with broad snouts. They have white-banded wings but do not fly. They feed in large numbers and lay eggs for up to 2 months, depositing them on host plants, near the soil. The larvae hatch in about 17 days and enter the soil to feed.

Damage and detection: Adult white-fringed beetles feed on lower stems, often covering them from the roots. The larvae feed on roots and tubers. Infested plants wilt and die.

Control: PHYSICAL—Dig ditches 1 foot deep around the vegetable garden to trap and destroy the flightless beetles. CULTURAL—Spade deeply in early spring to expose larvae.

White-Marked Tussock Moths

Range: *eastern United States and Canada, west to Colorado and British Columbia*

Generations per year: *1 to 3*

Host(s): *deciduous trees and shrubs*

Tussock moths are feeders of ornamental deciduous trees and shrubs and may seriously weaken them.

Description and life cycle: Tussock moths overwinter as eggs, which hatch in spring. The larvae are caterpillars, 1¼ inches long, with distinctive tufts of long black and shorter white hairs. Caterpillars feed for several weeks, then pupate. In 2 to 4 weeks, adults emerge. Males are gray with dark wing markings; females are lighter and nearly wingless. Females lay eggs in masses covered with a white, frothy material that hardens as it dries. The number of generations per year varies with the climate.

Damage and detection: Tussock moths are leaf feeders. They skeletonize leaves and defoliate plants.

Control: PHYSICAL—Remove egg masses or paint them with creosote. BIOLOGICAL—Bt; trichogramma wasps. CHEMICAL—Horticultural oil.

Wireworms

Range: *widespread throughout North America*

Generations per year: *1- to 6-year life cycle*

Host(s): *many*

Wireworms are tough-skinned larvae of the various species of click beetles. These larvae live in the soil, where they feed on the underground parts of a wide range of plants, including herbaceous ornamentals and vegetables.

Description and life cycle: Some wireworm species complete their life cycle in 1 year; others take as long as 6 years. Adult click beetles overwinter in the soil, coming to the surface in spring. They are about ½ inch long, narrow, and black or brown. Females lay their eggs 1 to 6 inches below the surface. Larvae hatch within a few weeks and begin to feed, continuing for up to 6 years. Gray, creamy, or dark brown, they are ½ to 1½ inches long, jointed, and have shiny, tough skin. Pupation occurs in late summer.

Damage and detection: Wireworms feed on seeds and bore into corms, roots, and other underground plant parts, opening the plants to decay-causing bacteria and fungi.

Control: PHYSICAL—Bury pieces of potato or carrot to trap wireworms, then dig and destroy the pests. CULTURAL—Cultivate soil often to expose larvae. BIOLOGICAL—Beneficial nematodes.

Woodborer Beetles

Range: *various species throughout the United States and southern Canada*

Generations per year: *1- to 3-year life cycle*

Host(s): *many deciduous trees*

The many species of woodborer beetles differ in their geographic ranges and preferred hosts. They are broadly classified as flatheaded or roundheaded borers, according to the shape of the larva's head. Among the many destructive species are the bronze birch borer, the lurid flatheaded borer, the flatheaded apple tree borer, and the two-lined chestnut borer.

The bronze birch borer attacks birch, cottonwood, poplar, and willow. It is found throughout the northern parts of the United States, south to Virginia and in Arizona, New Mexico, and southern Canada. The lurid flatheaded borer infests hickory and alder trees throughout the eastern part of North America. The flatheaded apple tree borer attacks most deciduous shade and fruit trees and is found throughout the United States and southern Canada. The two-lined chestnut borer occurs east of the Rocky Mountains and sometimes in California; its preferred hosts include beech, chestnut, and oak.

Description and life cycle: Most borers spend the greater part of their lives as larvae, and it is during this stage that they inflict the most serious damage. Borers overwinter as larvae in their host. In spring they feed and pupate, then emerge in the summer as beetles. Females lay their eggs in bark crevices, especially near wounds. Soon the larvae hatch and bore into the tree, where they feed on the bark, the sapwood (the layer of young tissue that includes the plant's food- and water-conducting layer), or the older heartwood. Larvae stay in the tree for 1 to 2 years.

The adult stage of the bronze birch borer is a beetle resembling the lightning bug, ¼ to ½ inch long, with a green-black body and a bronze head. The larvae are creamy white, slender, and flattened and are ½ inch long when fully grown. Adult lurid flatheaded borers are shiny, dark brown beetles about ¾ inch long. The flatheaded apple tree borer adults are flat, dark brown, and ½ inch long; larvae are white with flat, brown heads, and reach 1¼ inches in length. The two-lined chestnut borer adult is dark green or bluish black with yellow or bronze stripes, and is about ¼ inch long; the larva is cream colored and grows to about ½ inch in length. This species usually requires 2 years to complete its life cycle.

Damage and detection: The adults feed to some extent on the host's foliage, but their damage is insignificant compared to the often lethal mining done by the larvae. By the time this internal borer damage is noticed, it is usually too late to save the tree. The larvae tunnel through the young sapwood, cutting off the flow of water and nutrients up and down the tree. Leaves turn yellow and branches die back. As the upper branches die, the tree sends up many shoots from the crown. Most trees that do survive borer infestations display swollen areas on their trunks where new tissue has grown and healed around the damage. Borers are most often attracted to trees that have been damaged by other insects or that have sustained mechanical injuries.

Control: PHYSICAL—Remove damaged limbs. CULTURAL—Avoid mechanical injuries to trees; feed and water trees to minimize stress and keep them healthy and vigorous; plant resistant species, such as black birch and river birch. BIOLOGICAL—Parasitic wasps; woodpeckers.

Anthracnose of Sycamore

Type of disease: *fungal*

Host(s): *sycamore*

Anthracnose of sycamore trees is a conspicuous cosmetic disease but is seldom fatal. Caused by one species of fungus, it develops in cool, damp spring weather. A number of closely related fungi cause anthracnose in other kinds of trees, including ash, elm, oak, walnut, hickory, and maple.

Symptoms: There are three distinct phases of sycamore anthracnose, each affecting different portions of the plant. In the shoot-blight phase, new leaves and shoots turn brown and die rapidly; they look as if they have been killed by frost. In the leaf-blight phase, large irregular brown areas develop along the veins. Trees look tattered and may defoliate completely; repeated defoliations weaken the tree. In the third phase, twig cankers develop and girdle and kill branches. However, when the weather warms up, the fungus recedes and a new set of leaves restores the tree's vigor.

Transmission: The fungus overwinters in twig cankers and on fallen leaves. Its growth is favored by cool, damp conditions. It is spread by wind and rain.

Control: PHYSICAL—Gather and destroy all fallen leaves and twigs in fall; fertilize trees to maintain their vigor; prune branches with cankers. CULTURAL—Replace sycamores with London plane trees, which are similar in appearance but resistant to anthracnose.

Colletotrichum Anthracnose

Type of disease: *fungal*

Host(s): *many herbaceous plants*

The term *anthracnose* is derived from the Greek word for ulcer and refers to the ulcerlike lesions that appear on leaves, stems, and fruit. There are many species of *Colletotrichum,* and each has a specific group of hosts. Herbaceous plants are more susceptible, although some woody plants are also attacked. Commonly infected ornamental plants include orchids, hollyhocks, pansies, foxgloves, and turf grasses.

Symptoms: Infected fruit, stems, or leaves develop small sunken spots with a water-soaked appearance. Spots often enlarge and may coalesce into irregular dark areas. Sometimes leaf spots turn black; the blackened tissue then falls out to leave ragged holes. In damp weather, pinkish spore masses ooze from the center of the lesions. Infected fruit darkens and rots.

Transmission: The fungus overwinters in seeds and in garden debris. Spores are spread by splashing water, insects, and garden tools.

Control: PHYSICAL—Prune infected stems; remove and destroy severely infected plants and fallen leaves. CULTURAL—Plant resistant varieties; use certified, disease-free seed; rotate crops; avoid handling plants when wet.

Discula Anthracnose of Dogwood

Type of disease: *fungal*

Host(s): *flowering dogwood, Pacific dogwood*

Discula anthracnose of dogwood, which is caused by the *Discula destructiva* fungus, was first discovered in the early 1970s. In the eastern part of the United States, the disease affects the native flowering dogwood *(Cornus florida);* on the West Coast, it attacks another native, the Pacific dogwood.

Symptoms: In late spring, tan spots with purple margins appear on leaves. Blighted leaves remain attached to the trees. Small, uniformly spaced brown dots—spore-producing structures—appear on spotted leaves and twigs. As the infection progresses, branches die. Trees may produce numerous water sprouts. Cankers form on the trunk. When the cankers girdle the trunk, the entire tree dies.

Transmission: This fungus thrives in cool, moist conditions, and spores are spread by rain and dew. Landscape trees are less susceptible if planted in a sunny location with good air circulation.

Control: PHYSICAL—Prune water sprouts in summer. CULTURAL—Plant resistant species and varieties; plant trees in open areas with at least a half-day of sun; keep them mulched and water them deeply during dry spells but avoid wetting leaves. CHEMICAL—Spray infected trees with a fungicide containing propiconazole or chlorothalonil every 2 weeks from the time new leaves emerge until daytime temperatures are above 80°F.

Aster Yellows

Type of disease: *bacterial*

Host(s): *many herbaceous plants*

The bacteria that cause aster yellows infect more than 40 different families of plants. Ornamentals often attacked include asters, gladiolus, calendulas, cosmos, delphiniums, flax, hydrangeas, phlox, strawflowers, and zinnias.

Symptoms: Symptoms of aster yellows vary somewhat depending on the host, but infected plants generally develop spindly stems and clear veins. The internodes of stems are short and sometimes curled, giving the plant a dwarfed, bushy appearance. Flowers and leaves are frequently deformed. On asters, leaves turn yellow and flowers are green and dwarfed, if they appear at all. Gladiolus and zinnias are dramatically dwarfed.

Transmission: Aster yellows is transmitted from infected to healthy plants by leafhoppers, which pick up bacteria while feeding. The pathogens overwinter in infected perennials, including common weeds such as thistle, wild chicory, dandelion, wild carrot, and wide-leaf plantain.

Control: PHYSICAL—Eradicate potential weed hosts; remove and destroy infected plants; use row covers to protect vegetables from leafhoppers.

Black Knot of Prunus

Type of disease: *fungal*

Host(s): *many Prunus species*

Black knot is a serious disease of more than 20 species of *Prunus,* including cherry, plum, flowering almond, apricot, peach, and chokecherry. It occurs throughout moist, humid regions of the United States and Canada, wherever susceptible plants are grown.

Symptoms: Rough, black, spindle-shaped swellings or knots develop on small branches over a 2-year period. The first sign of infection emerges in spring, when the bark ruptures and an olive green fungal mass appears. It can grow to 12 inches in length and may be two to four times as thick as the branch. This growth eventually hardens and turns black and knotty. As the infection progresses, branches become girdled and die. Trees are stunted and unattractive, and varieties planted for fruit are unproductive.

Transmission: Spores of this fungus are spread by wind in early spring.

Control: PHYSICAL—Prune any infected branches at least 4 inches behind any visible damage in winter or early spring, disinfecting pruners after each cut in a 10-percent bleach solution; eradicate or prune wild cherries and plums in the vicinity as a preventive measure.

Black Spot

Type of disease: *fungal*

Host(s): *roses*

While black spot of rose occurs wherever roses are grown, it is severe only in humid climates. It is especially troublesome east of the Mississippi River and on the West Coast. Rose varieties differ in their susceptibility. Those with yellow or gold flowers are generally more susceptible than varieties with red or pink flowers.

Symptoms: Round black spots with fringed margins appear on the upper surfaces of leaves and on young canes in spring. At the center of the spots are tiny blisterlike, spore-producing structures that are visible with a hand lens.

Transmission: The black spot fungus survives the winter in a dormant state on infected canes and fallen leaves. In greenhouses, it is active year round. It is spread by splashing water and by the gardener's hands, tools, and clothing.

Control: PHYSICAL—Prune to increase air circulation; remove and destroy infected leaves and canes. CULTURAL—Grow resistant varieties; avoid wetting foliage when watering. CHEMICAL—Spray dormant plants with lime-sulfur; during the growing season, spray with a fungicidal soap or a fungicide that contains triforine, mancozeb, or chlorothalonil.

Botrytis Blight

Type of disease: *fungal*

Host(s): *many*

Various *Botrytis* species cause blighting on a wide range of herbaceous and woody ornamentals, soft fruits, and vegetables. Certain species such as *B. cinerea,* which causes gray mold blight, have a broad host range. Common hosts include poinsettia, chrysanthemum, and rhododendron. Others such as *B. tulipae,* which causes a blight on tulips, and *B. paeoniae,* which causes blight on peonies, are very host specific. All species produce similar symptoms and are favored by cool, moist conditions.

Symptoms: Leaves and flowers of infected plants develop irregularly shaped, water-soaked spots that dry and turn tan or brown. Similar spots on stems form cankers that girdle stems, causing dieback. Seedlings are often killed. Infected fruit turns soft and mushy. In humid conditions, a fuzzy gray mold develops on the surface of infected tissue.

Transmission: Botrytis is spread by splashing rain and wind. The fungus persists in infected tissue and in soil.

Control: PHYSICAL—Remove and destroy fading blossoms and infected plants or plant parts. CULTURAL—Space plants to promote air circulation; avoid wetting foliage; use healthy plants and bulbs for propagation. CHEMICAL—Spray with a fungicide containing chlorothalonil or mancozeb.

Cercospora Leaf Blight

Type of disease: *fungal*

Host(s): *many*

There are hundreds of *Cercospora* species, which attack leaves and shoots of trees, shrubs, vegetables, and herbaceous ornamentals. Most species attack one plant or a few closely related plants. Often infected are arborvitae, azalea, cryptomeria, cypress, dahlia, geranium, mountain laurel, and red cedar.

Symptoms: Leaves or needles of infected plants develop spots that often enlarge and coalesce. On carrot, celery, geranium, and many other hosts, the spots are yellowish at first, then turn ash gray and become paper-thin as they enlarge. Entire leaves die, and in severe cases all of the foliage dies. A fine gray mold develops on infected tissue. Leaf spots may be bordered by a dark purple margin. On cypress and arborvitae, needles and branchlets turn brown or purplish and drop off, especially on the lower portion of the plant.

Transmission: Leaf-blight fungus overwinters in or on seed or on infected leaves or needles. Warm, humid weather favors its spread and development. Spores are spread by wind and rain.

Control: PHYSICAL—Prune out infected stems or branches, and rake up and destroy infected leaves or needles. CULTURAL—Plant disease-free seed. CHEMICAL—Spray plants with Bordeaux mixture or a fungicide containing chlorothalonil.

Diplodia Tip Blight

Type of disease: *fungal*

Host(s): *2- and 3-needle pines*

Diplodia tip blight infects older pines, especially those under stress. Most often attacked are Scotch, Austrian, mugo, ponderosa, red, scrub, and Japanese black pines.

Symptoms: The first symptom usually noted is the browning of new needles, particularly on branches near the base of the tree. The dead needles remain attached to the tree; infected branches ooze resin. Close observation reveals small black spore-producing structures embedded under the needle sheath and in dead needles, on old cones, and in bark. After several seasons of repeated infection, branches take on a clubbed appearance and eventually die.

Transmission: Spores are produced from early spring to late fall, especially during periods of wet weather. They are spread by splashing rain, insects, birds, and pruning tools. The fungus invades the tree through young needles, buds, and shoots or through wounds. It persists over winter on infected trees and on the ground nearby.

Control: PHYSICAL—Prune and destroy dead branches in fall; collect and destroy infected needles and twigs on the ground. CHEMICAL—Spray with a fixed-copper fungicide, thiophanate-methyl, or Bordeaux mixture when new needles begin to emerge from the candles and again 10 days later.

Fire Blight

Type of disease: *bacterial*

Host(s): *members of the rose family*

Fire blight occurs only in plants belonging to the rose family. Landscape plants often damaged include crab apple, cotoneaster, flowering quince, hawthorn, mountain ash, pear, and pyracantha.

Symptoms: In early spring, bees and other pollinators carry bacteria into flowers, which turn brown and shrivel. The bacteria then invade twigs, producing cankers. Bacteria oozing from cankers can be blown or splashed onto young shoots and leaves. The shoots turn dark brown or black, and the leaves turn black and remain on the tree, which looks as if it has been scorched by fire. In highly susceptible plants, cankers form on the trunk and large branches.

Transmission: The bacteria overwinter in branch and trunk cankers. In humid weather, bacteria-laden ooze is produced along the edges of cankers. Insects feeding on the ooze carry the bacteria to flowers. Throughout the growing season, bacteria may be spread from blighted shoots, and cankers may be spread by wind. Fire blight is most severe in regions of warm, humid weather.

Control: PHYSICAL—During winter or dry weather, prune out all visible cankers; avoid wounding plants. CULTURAL—Plant resistant cultivars; avoid excessive nitrogen fertilizer because it produces very succulent growth that is more susceptible to fire blight.

Southern Blight

Type of disease: *fungal*

Host(s): *many*

Southern blight occurs in the eastern United States from New York south but is most serious in the Southeast, because it is a disease of hot, humid weather. It infects hundreds of herbaceous and woody plants and is particularly hard on ajuga, artemisia, chrysanthemum, lamb's ears, lavender, santolina, sage, thyme, and tomato and legume family members.

Symptoms: The southern blight fungus can be recognized by the sclerotia—small tan lumps about the size of a mustard seed—that appear on the blighted plant and the surrounding soil or mulch. Infection starts from these "mustard seed" sclerotia in soil or mulch. Plants rapidly yellow, wilt, and die. Infected bulbs and fleshy roots rot. Look for a white cottony growth on stems and surrounding soil. Small, round fruiting bodies about 1/16 inch in diameter may be present near the soil surface in warm, humid conditions.

Transmission: The fungus survives in the soil for many years as sclerotia. Its growth is favored by hot, wet weather and acidic soils. It is spread by running water and infested tools, soil, mulch, or compost.

Control: PHYSICAL—Remove and destroy diseased plants and the white, cottony fungal growth around them. CULTURAL—Solarize the soil of a new bed; thin perennials to improve air circulation; mulch plants with a thin layer of solarized or sterile sharp sand.

Bacterial Canker of Stone Fruit

Type of disease: *bacterial*

Host(s): *fruits, shrubs, and vegetables*

Different forms of the bacterium *Pseudomonas syringae* are responsible for canker of stone fruit, infecting many unrelated hosts and causing a variety of symptoms. Ornamentals affected include flowering stock, lilac, oleander, rose, and sweet pea.

Symptoms: All parts of peach, plum, apricot, and other stone fruit trees are subject to infection, but the most destructive symptoms are the gummy cankers on the branches and trunk, which exude a foul-smelling secretion. Flower buds may be killed while they are still dormant or after they have emerged; leaves may wilt or die. On lilacs, leaves and shoots display brown, water-soaked spots, and flower buds turn black. Infected oleanders develop oozing, bacteria-laden galls on branches, leaves, and flowers.

Transmission: The bacteria responsible for these diseases are spread by water. Mild, wet weather favors their growth and development.

Control: PHYSICAL—Prune and destroy infected branches, disinfecting pruners after each cut. CULTURAL—Thin plants to encourage good air circulation; avoid the use of high-nitrogen fertilizers.

Canker and Dieback

Type of disease: *fungal*

Host(s): *many woody plants*

Botryosphaeria dothidea infects over 50 species of woody plants, including apple, azalea, eucalyptus, fig, forsythia, pecan, pyracantha, quince, rhododendron, rose, sequoia, sweet gum, and willow. This fungus is also responsible for the most destructive canker disease of redbud.

Symptoms: On redbud, cankers begin as small, sunken, oval spots that enlarge and girdle branches, causing wilting and dieback above the canker. The canker turns black at the center and cracks at the margins. Similar symptoms occur on forsythia. On roses, leaves turn brown and die but remain on the plant. On rhododendron, watery spots occur on leaves and twigs, followed by twig dieback. Cankers on the trunks of willows are generally fatal in a few years. Apple trees develop watery lesions on the bark, and vigor gradually declines. When an infected branch or stem is cut crosswise, there is usually a pie-shaped section of discolored tissue.

Transmission: Canker and dieback fungi are spread by wind, rain, insects, and pruning tools.

Control: PHYSICAL—Cut infected branches to wood that is not discolored and destroy, disinfecting pruners with a 10-percent bleach solution after each cut. CULTURAL—Keep plants vigorous and water them during periods of drought.

Cytospora Canker

Type of disease: *fungal*

Host(s): *many trees and shrubs*

Many species of fungi cause cankers on trees and shrubs; most have a narrow host range. Cytospora canker is especially troublesome on Norway spruce, Colorado blue spruce, and *Prunus* species. It also attacks maple, cottonwood, black cherry, willow, and poplar.

Symptoms: On spruce, the cankers most often form on branches near the ground and enlarge to girdle the branches. Needles dry up and the branches die back. Infected areas ooze an amber-colored sap that turns white as it dries. On poplar, cankers form on the trunk and the larger branches, discoloring the bark and causing dieback. Weakened trees often die.

Transmission: These fungi survive the winter on infected plant parts. They are spread by splashing rain, insects, and pruning tools. Trees that have suffered injuries or have been weakened by conditions such as drought, hail, or a late-spring freeze are more likely to be infected than healthy, intact trees. Wounds and leaf scars provide entry points for fungi.

Control: PHYSICAL—Remove and destroy infected branches when the weather is dry, making pruning cuts at least 6 inches below the canker and disinfecting pruners with a 10-percent bleach solution after each cut. CULTURAL—Keep plants vigorous; avoid wounding and excessive use of nitrogen fertilizer; do only essential pruning on susceptible species.

Nectria Canker

Type of disease: *fungal*

Host(s): *many trees and shrubs*

Coral spot nectria canker, tubercularia canker, and perennial nectria canker are common in landscape plants, including apple, beech, boxwood, elm, honey locust, magnolia, maple, and zelkova.

Symptoms: Coral spot and tubercularia cankers are usually noticed in late spring, when shoots or entire branches wilt and die. At the base of the diseased branch are peach-colored to orange-red fruiting bodies emerging through openings or wounds in the bark. If the plant is in good health, it can usually resist attacks.

Perennial nectria cankers, which persist for years, begin as small sunken areas, often surrounding a twig stub or a wound. As they grow they develop a series of concentric ridges of bark around the original spot; in time the ridges can become quite large. Bright red-orange fruiting bodies are produced on the bark ridges and on exposed wood in the canker's center from fall through spring.

Transmission: Nectria fungi produce spores that are spread by wind, rain, insects, and animals.

Control: PHYSICAL—Prune out infected branches in late spring through summer; do not prune in fall and winter. CULTURAL—Avoid wounding plants; select species that are well adapted to your climate, to avoid damage from environmental stress; fertilize properly and water during drought to maintain plant vigor.

Damping-Off

Type of disease: *fungal*

Host(s): *most seedlings*

Damping-off is a disease of seedlings caused by a variety of different fungi, including species of *Pythium* and *Rhizoctonia.* These fungi may also attack seeds or older plants.

Symptoms: When these fungi attack seeds, the disease is known as preemergent damping-off; seeds rot without germinating. Called postemergent damping-off when seedlings are infected, the disease usually occurs at or just below the soil line. The stem turns soft and brown, and the seedling topples over and dies. When the fungi attack older plants, brown lesions form on the stem or roots. When abundant, these lesions cause stunting, wilting, and sometimes death.

Transmission: The fungi responsible for damping-off are found in soil and water throughout the world. They survive on dead organic matter when they have no living host.

Control: CULTURAL—Use a soilless growing medium for seedling propagation; promote rapid growth with optimum light and temperature levels, and provide good drainage and air circulation; rotate crops in the vegetable garden. CHEMICAL—Buy pretreated seeds or treat seeds with captan.

Decline

Type of disease: *infectious/environmental*

Host(s): *trees and shrubs*

Decline is a general loss of health that is not attributable to a single pathogen or pest. Rather, it is the result of stress that can arise from a variety of factors, usually over a period of years. Both infectious agents and environmental conditions may be involved. They may act on the plant at the same time or in sequence.

Symptoms: Symptoms of decline vary among plant species. Generally, yellowing and wilting of leaves, dieback of branches, and stunted or distorted growth are seen. Declining trees show reduced twig growth, and in advanced decline, dead branches, or stag heads, protrude from the healthy canopy. Eventually the plant may die, although this may take years. Some of the factors often associated with decline are repeated insect infestations, infectious disease, soil compaction, root damage, injury to the trunk, an inappropriate site, girdling roots, a chronic water deficit, and poorly drained soil. Plants weakened by adverse cultural conditions may be especially vulnerable to pathogens and are very attractive to woodboring insects.

Control: Once decline has become obvious, it is often too late to save the plant. However, it is important to identify the source or sources of stress so you can take measures to prevent decline in new plants installed in the same area.

Blossom-End Rot

Type of disease: *environmental*

Host(s): *tomatoes and other vegetables*

Blossom-end rot is a disease caused by a deficiency of calcium at the blossom end of susceptible fruit. Plants frequently affected include tomato, pepper, watermelon, and squash. While there may be a substantial supply of calcium in the soil, it may not reach rapidly growing fruit when the weather is hot and dry and irrigation is irregular or inadequate. Another common factor is overzealous nitrogen fertilization.

Symptoms: Blossom-end rot first appears as a brown discoloration at the blossom end of a tomato or other susceptible fruit. The spot enlarges and darkens, eventually becoming sunken and leathery. This tissue may cover the bottom third to one-half of the fruit and is subject to invasion by pathogens.

Control: CULTURAL—Apply limestone or gypsum to provide adequate calcium (a soil test can determine how much to apply); mulch to keep soil evenly moist; provide additional water during drought; avoid excessive nitrogen fertilization.

Iron Deficiency

Type of disease: *nutritional*

Host(s): *all plants*

While iron is rarely deficient in soils, it may be unavailable to plants because it exists in an insoluble form. This is a common problem for acid-loving plants growing in neutral or alkaline soils, which have a pH of 7 or higher. Iron may also become chemically bound and unavailable to plants when large amounts of phosphate fertilizers have been added to the soil. Plants growing in sandy soils in cold, wet conditions are more likely to experience iron deficiency.

Symptoms: Iron is essential for chlorophyll synthesis, and when it is deficient, young leaves are yellow with green veins, a symptom called interveinal chlorosis. Leaves are smaller than normal, and their margins often turn brown. If the deficiency is severe, leaves turn reddish brown and drop prematurely. Overall growth of the plant is stunted.

Control: CULTURAL—Avoid liming turf near acid-loving trees and shrubs; apply iron sulfate to soil to supply iron and acidify soil; replace acid-loving species and varieties with plants that tolerate a higher soil pH.

Magnesium Deficiency

Type of disease: *nutritional*

Host(s): *all plants*

Magnesium is required for healthy plant growth and development because it is a constituent part of the chlorophyll molecule. This element is also essential for various processes controlled by enzymes. It may be naturally deficient in soils, as is common on the Atlantic and Gulf coasts, or it may have been removed by heavy cropping or constant leaching by rain. This deficiency is common in very acid soils and in gardens to which excessive amounts of potassium fertilizers have been applied.

Symptoms: Deficiency symptoms show up first on older growth. The tip and margins of an affected leaf typically turn yellow, then brown, though in some plants the discoloration is reddish. The abnormal color spreads between the veins to the center and base of the leaves, which often drop prematurely. On some plants the leaves become puckered. In the case of conifers, needles that are 2 years old or older turn yellow. Continued magnesium deficiency causes stunting.

Control: CULTURAL—Apply Epsom salts, which contain magnesium; till in dolomitic limestone, which contains magnesium and also raises the pH; use balanced fertilizers that contain magnesium; do not fertilize with wood ashes because of their high potassium content.

Nitrogen Deficiency

Type of disease: *nutritional*

Host(s): *all plants*

Nitrogen is an essential element for healthy vegetative growth, protein synthesis, and other critical plant functions. A lack of available nitrogen in the soil, which is more common in unusually cold, wet conditions, results in poor growth and weakened plants.

Symptoms: A plant's oldest leaves are the first to show signs of nitrogen deficiency: They turn yellow, then brown, and drop off. New leaves are smaller than normal and lighter in color because of the decreased synthesis of plant proteins. Leaf margins may turn brown. The plant grows slowly, and its stems are slender and weak. Fruit and vegetable yields are reduced.

Control: CULTURAL—Apply nitrogen-rich fertilizers such as blood meal, soybean meal, fish emulsion, or urea to the soil; incorporate well-rotted manure or compost into the soil every year; do not apply fresh organic matter such as uncomposted woodchips, leaves, or sawdust, because soil microbes will tie up available nitrogen as they attack the cellulose in these materials.

Potassium Deficiency

Type of disease: *nutritional*

Host(s): *all plants*

Potassium is essential to such processes as nitrogen metabolism and water uptake and movement. It acts as a catalyst for numerous other reactions, especially in growing points—buds, shoot tips, and root tips.

Symptoms: Potassium moves easily within a plant. Because it tends to move to the youngest growth, older plant parts are the first to show signs of deficiency. Leaf margins turn yellow or brown, and the discoloration then moves into the leaf between the veins. Some leaves turn reddish purple rather than brown. Dead areas along leaf margins may drop out, giving leaves a ragged edge. Growth slows, and leaves may drop prematurely. Flowering and fruiting are reduced. Plants are more subject to damage by freezing and a variety of pathogens.

Control: CULTURAL—Apply a potassium-rich fertilizer such as kelp meal; apply wood ashes in small quantities; if the soil is very sandy, allowing potassium to leach out quickly, incorporate organic matter to increase the soil's water-holding capacity; incorporate vermiculite, a good source of slow-release potassium, into the soil.

Dodder

Type of disease: *parasitic*

Host(s): *many plants*

Dodders are stringy, leafless plants that lack roots and chlorophyll and parasitize a wide range of plants to obtain water and nutrients. They are particularly troublesome in areas where clover and alfalfa, two favorite hosts, are grown.

Symptoms: Dodder seed germinates and produces a slender stem that curls around the nearest plant. The stem develops "feeding pegs," which invade the host and absorb juices. As it continues to grow, the tangled mass of yellow to orange spaghetti-like stems increases while the host plant loses color and vigor and may die. Other common names for dodder include devil's hair, gold thread, strangle weed, pull down, and hell-bind.

Transmission: Dodder is transmitted as seed in mulch, humus, compost, and soil, where it can survive for up to 5 years. Dodder seed may also contaminate commercial seed lots.

Control: PHYSICAL—Thoroughly clean tools and other equipment after use in a dodder-infested area; remove and burn all dodder and its host plants before the dodder produces seed. CULTURAL—Use dodder-free seed and nursery plants. CHEMICAL—Treat the infested area with a preemergent herbicide; kill germinating dodder seeds.

Downy Mildew

Type of disease: *fungal*

Host(s): *many*

There are seven genera of fungi that cause downy mildew. Most of these fungi have a narrow host range. Among the most common ornamental plants attacked are Boston ivy, grape, pansy, redbud, rose, snapdragon, sunflower, and viburnum.

Symptoms: The first visible symptom of downy mildew infection is the development of angular yellow spots on the upper leaf surface. These areas gradually turn brown, while corresponding spots on the underside of the leaf develop a white, tan, gray, or purple downy growth that can be seen in early morning during humid weather. Fruit and young stems may also be covered with the downy fungal growth. Plants may be stunted, and grapes and other susceptible crops are often completely ruined. Most downy mildews are favored by cool weather, and all require moist conditions.

Transmission: The spores of downy mildew fungi are spread by wind, rain, insects, and infected seed.

Control: PHYSICAL—Remove and destroy plant debris and infected plants; space plants widely to provide good air circulation. CULTURAL—Use resistant varieties; rotate crops. CHEMICAL—Spray with a copper fungicide, sulfur, Bordeaux mixture, mancozeb, or chlorothalonil.

Azalea Leaf Gall

Type of disease: *fungal*

Host(s): *many plants of the heath family*

Though seldom a serious threat, azalea leaf gall is unattractive. It is a fairly common problem on azaleas, especially in the South. Other susceptible plants include Japanese andromeda, blueberry, mountain laurel, and rhododendron.

Symptoms: Symptoms vary somewhat depending on the host. On azalea, bladder-shaped galls form on all or part of a leaf or flower. The galls are soft when they are young, eventually hardening and darkening with age. As a gall develops, a white velvety layer that produces spores appears on its surface.

Transmission: This fungus overwinters in infected tissue and rapidly spreads during periods of warm, wet weather, particularly in shade. Galls do not appear until the following spring.

Control: PHYSICAL—Handpick and destroy galls, preferably before the white spore-producing layer appears. CULTURAL—Make sure susceptible plants have good air circulation; avoid watering with a sprinkler in spring, when mature galls produce spores—wet foliage increases the chance of spreading the infection.

Crown Gall

Type of disease: *bacterial*

Host(s): *many plants*

Crown gall is caused by a bacterium that lives in the soil. It has one of the broadest host ranges of any bacterial plant pathogen. Common ornamental hosts include aster, chrysanthemum, euonymus, flowering quince, forsythia, honeysuckle, and willow.

Symptoms: Rounded corky galls develop on roots, on stems near the soil line or, in the case of grafted plants, near the graft union. At first the gall is soft and either white or flesh colored. It darkens and its surface becomes rough as it grows, sometimes to several inches in diameter. Infected plants may be stunted and weakened and more susceptible to environmental stress.

Transmission: The bacterium responsible for crown gall can persist in the soil for several years. It spreads from one region to another in shipments of infected nursery stock. The bacterium enters plants through wounds.

Control: PHYSICAL—Remove and destroy infected plants. CULTURAL—Plant disease-free stock; avoid wounding plants, especially near the soil line.

Leaf Blister and Leaf Curl

Type of disease: *fungal*

Host(s): *fruit and ornamental trees*

Several species of *Taphrina* are responsible for leaf blister and leaf curl. Ornamental trees commonly infected include birch, elm, flowering cherry, maple, oak, ornamental plum, and poplar.

Symptoms: Symptoms of leaf blister and leaf curl vary somewhat depending on the plant. In the case of cherry leaf curl, which infects both ornamental and edible cherry, peach, and plum trees, portions of the leaves pucker, thicken, and turn yellow or reddish brown. Leaves drop prematurely. Twigs develop knobby swellings from which a cluster of new shoots, called a witch's broom, arises. These twigs often die over winter. Oak leaf blister often begins as raised, cup-shaped areas that range from a quarter inch to several inches in diameter and are silver-gray on the lower leaf surface and yellow above. As with cherries, the leaves drop prematurely. Similar symptoms occur on maple, poplar, elm, and birch.

Transmission: The fungus overwinters on the bark, twigs, and buds of infected trees. Spores are spread by rain and infect young tissues only.

Control: CULTURAL—Plant resistant varieties; prune to promote good air circulation. CHEMICAL—Apply lime-sulfur to susceptible plants while they are dormant.

Bacterial Leaf Scorch

Type of disease: *bacterial*

Host(s): *black oak, elm, maple, sycamore*

The bacterium *Xylella fastidiosa* causes leaf scorch on a variety of landscape trees. It is common on American elm, species in the black oak group, mulberry, sycamore, and some maples. Unlike leaf scorch that is caused by drought, drying winds, or root damage, bacterial leaf scorch is unevenly distributed in the tree canopy and on individual leaves.

Symptoms: Bacterial leaf scorch appears in midsummer as irregular brown or reddish brown areas along the leaf margin. These areas are typically bordered by a yellow halo. As the scorch progresses toward the midrib, the leaves curl and drop prematurely. Infections recur from year to year, slowing growth and causing dieback of branches. On sycamore, mulberry, and red maple, the leaves develop patterns of light brown and reddish brown that are bordered by a yellow halo. Plants may be infected with the leaf-scorch bacterium yet display few symptoms.

Transmission: Leafhoppers and spittlebugs carry the leaf-scorch bacterium from plant to plant.

Control: PHYSICAL—If only a few branches show leaf scorch, cut the infected branches back to a point well below leaves showing symptoms. CULTURAL—Remove diseased, failing trees and replace them with less susceptible varieties.

Alternaria Leaf Spot

Type of disease: *fungal*

Host(s): *many woody and herbaceous plants*

A number of *Alternaria* species cause leaf spot on a wide variety of plants, including fruits, vegetables, herbaceous perennials, and woody ornamentals, among them carnation, catalpa, chrysanthemum, flowering tobacco, geranium, hibiscus, magnolia, marigold, Shasta daisy, stock, and zinnia.

Symptoms: Leaves develop small dark brown to black spots. Often numerous, the spots first appear on the plant's lowest leaves and progress upward. As spots enlarge, they develop concentric rings like a bull's-eye target. Stems may have sunken lesions that girdle and kill them, and fruit and tubers may be spotted. In moist weather the spots on fruit are sometimes covered with fuzzy black structures that produce spores.

Transmission: Alternaria fungi overwinter in infected plant debris or on seeds. Spores are spread by wind, rain, and tools.

Control: PHYSICAL—Remove and destroy infected plant debris. CULTURAL—Plant resistant varieties; use disease-free or treated seed; rotate crops. CHEMICAL—Treat infected plants with chlorothalonil.

Bacterial Leaf Spot

Type of disease: *bacterial*

Host(s): *many*

Species of two different genera of bacteria, *Pseudomonas* and *Xanthomonas,* are responsible for leaf spots on an extremely wide range of plants. Ornamental plants susceptible to bacterial leaf spot include begonia, California laurel, English ivy, geranium, and gladiolus.

Symptoms: The spots are usually brown and are often surrounded by a yellow halo; they may appear on stems and fruit as well as on leaves. Some of the spots are round, while others are elongated streaks bounded by leaf veins running parallel to one another. A branching or fish-bone vein pattern gives spots a triangular outline. As a spot enlarges, the damaged tissue may drop out, making "shot holes" in the leaf. Spots can also coalesce and cover the entire leaf. Leaves often drop prematurely; bacterial spot of English ivy, for instance, can temporarily defoliate a planting.

Transmission: The bacteria are transmitted by water, tools, and infested soil. They overwinter in infected plant parts, on seeds, and in the soil.

Control: PHYSICAL—Remove and destroy infected plants and debris. CULTURAL—Plant resistant varieties; use pathogen-free seed; rotate crops. CHEMICAL—Treat infected plants with a fungicide that contains copper.

Septoria Leaf Spot

Type of disease: *fungal*

Host(s): *many*

There are many species of *Septoria* responsible for leaf-spot and blight diseases on a wide range of plants. Common ornamental hosts include azalea, aster, chrysanthemum, dogwood, poplar, and tomato.

Symptoms: Like alternaria leaf spot, the symptoms of septoria leaf spot arise first on lower leaves and progress upward on the plant. The typical spot is angular, small, and initially yellow, later turning brown, with black spore-producing bodies scattered over the surface. On some plants the spots have purple margins. Diseased leaves often turn yellow and drop prematurely. When a tomato plant loses a substantial portion of its foliage, the fruit exposed to the sun may be ruined by sunscald.

Transmission: The spores of septoria are spread by rain, irrigation water, tools, and animals. The fungi overwinter in or on seeds and in plant debris.

Control: PHYSICAL—Remove and destroy debris. CULTURAL—Plant resistant varieties; use disease-free or treated seed; rotate crops. CHEMICAL—Spray with a fungicide such as Bordeaux mixture or chlorothalonil.

Mosaic

Type of disease: *viral*

Host(s): *many*

There are several viruses that cause mosaic disease, some with a narrow host range and others capable of infecting many different hosts. The tobacco mosaic virus is common in gardens and greenhouses, attacking such ornamental hosts as ash, episcia, flowering tobacco, gloxinia, petunia, and streptocarpus. Other mosaics occur on such hosts as birch, canna, carnation, coleus, horse chestnut, rose, and ranunculus.

Symptoms: A mottling of leaves is the most obvious symptom of a mosaic infection. The irregular patches or streaks of abnormal color range from light to dark green and yellow. The leaves are often distorted, and growth is almost always stunted.

Transmission: Some mosaic viruses are transmitted by insects such as aphids. Many are spread from an infected plant to healthy ones on a tool or on the gardener's hands, as is the case with the tobacco mosaic virus. It can persist for years in dried tobacco.

Control: PHYSICAL—Remove and destroy infected plants; smokers should wash hands before handling plants. CULTURAL—Plant resistant varieties. BIOLOGICAL—Use beneficial predators to control insects that carry the viruses. CHEMICAL—Use organic pesticides on insects that spread the viruses.

Needle Cast

Type of disease: *fungal*

Host(s): *conifers*

A variety of different species of fungi are responsible for needle cast, a name shared by several diseases in which a conifer sheds a large portion of its needles prematurely. Some species are common only in the Northwest, while others are largely limited to the Southeast and the Gulf Coast region. There are also a number of species that occur throughout the United States. Many of the needle-cast fungi attack a single species or just a few closely related species. Common hosts include Douglas fir *(Pseudotsuga),* fir *(Abies),* pine, and spruce.

Symptoms: Mottled yellow spots on needles are the earliest sign of disease, appearing from spring through fall. Separate at first, they tend to form bands around the needles as the disease progresses. The needles turn brown and are often shed 6 months to a year after the first spots appear. Young trees are particularly susceptible and may be killed by repeated defoliation.

Transmission: Needle-cast spores are spread locally by rain and over great distances by wind. There must be an extended period of damp or wet weather for needles to become infected.

Control: PHYSICAL—Clean up and destroy fallen needles. CULTURAL—Plant resistant species; allow enough space around plants for good air circulation.

Foliar Nematodes

Type of disease: *parasitic*

Host(s): *many herbaceous ornamentals*

Foliar nematodes infect the leaves and buds of a variety of herbaceous plants, including African violet, anemone, begonia, chrysanthemum, cyclamen, ferns, hosta, iris, lily, primrose, and orchids. They are most destructive in areas with humid summers; the nematodes move through the film of water on a wet plant from one leaf to another. These tiny roundworms enter leaves through their pores.

Symptoms: New shoots may be stunted, twisted, and misshapen. Abnormally colored areas of pale green, yellow, or red-purple appear on the leaves. These spots are bounded by the veins and are roughly triangular in plants with branching veins; in plants with parallel veins, such as hosta and lily, they are elongated stripes. The leaves turn brown or black and die.

Transmission: Foliar nematodes can survive for 3 or more years in soil, compost, and plant debris. They are common in woodland plants and are usually introduced into the garden by infected but healthy-looking plants. They are spread from plant to plant by these materials or by splashing water.

Control: PHYSICAL—Remove and destroy seriously infected plants; pick and destroy all leaves showing symptoms as well as the leaves immediately surrounding them. CULTURAL—Inspect plants for signs of infection before buying; do not plant susceptible plants in infested soil.

Pinewood Nematodes

Type of disease: *parasitic*

Host(s): *pines*

Pinewood nematodes are indigenous to the United States. Native pine species are resistant to infection but become vulnerable when subjected to drought, poor soil, or other environmental stresses. Exotic species such as Austrian, Japanese black, and Scotch pines are highly susceptible.

Symptoms: Needles turn yellow, then turn brown and wilt but remain on the tree. An infestation may kill individual branches or the entire tree.

Transmission: Pinewood nematodes are spread by the flying long-horned or cerambycid beetle, which feeds on growing branch tips. As the insect feeds, it releases nematodes that enter the plant through wounds. Inside, they multiply rapidly and spread through the trunk and branches. One beetle may carry as many as 20,000 nematodes.

Control: PHYSICAL—Remove and destroy infected trees promptly.

Root Knot Nematodes

Type of disease: *parasitic*

Host(s): *many woody and herbaceous plants*

Root knot nematodes are the most common plant parasitic nematode, infecting over 2,000 plant species. There are more than 50 species, which vary in their geographic ranges and attack different kinds of plants, among them banana, boxwood, geranium, gladiolus, grape hyacinth, morning glory, pachysandra, peony, privet, rose, and hibiscus.

Symptoms: Root knot nematodes are the easiest nematodes to identify because of the galls that form on the roots of infected plants. These galls are part of the root and cannot easily be rubbed off. Symptoms in aboveground portions of the plant include stunting, yellowing, wilting during hot weather, and death. Infected plants are more susceptible to fungal and bacterial wilts, root rots, and crown gall.

Transmission: The nematodes overwinter in infected roots or soil and are spread by soil, transplants, and tools. They invade root tissue to feed and reproduce. A generation takes about 21 days. Each female nematode produces 200 to 500 eggs in a mass that protrudes from the galls. After the eggs hatch, the larvae move through the soil and invade the roots of other plants.

Control: CULTURAL—Plant resistant varieties; add organic matter to the soil; do not plant susceptible plants in infested soil; solarize soil to kill nematodes; rotate susceptible and nonsusceptible plants.

Powdery Mildew

Type of disease: *fungal*

Host(s): *many*

Powdery mildews are caused by more than 100 species of fungi. They occur worldwide, attacking over 7,000 kinds of plants. Ornamental hosts include begonia, chrysanthemum, euonymus, gardenia, hawthorn, hydrangea, lilac, phlox, rose, sycamore, turf grasses, and zinnia.

Symptoms: The white, powdery growth that appears on leaves and buds and occasionally on shoots makes powdery mildew easy to identify. Most species of powdery mildew fungi spread rapidly when the weather is dry and days are warm and nights cool. The fungi are also favored by poor air circulation. Infected leaves turn yellow and may drop, and growth is stunted and often distorted. Plants are weakened, and some annuals may be killed. In fall, fruiting bodies form on the mildew, starting out as tan-yellow specks before turning dark brown-black.

Transmission: Spores are spread by wind. They thrive in shade and survive over winter on infected plants.

Control: PHYSICAL—Spray plants daily with water, which kills spores; remove and destroy badly infected plant parts or entire plants. CULTURAL—Plant resistant varieties; allow adequate room between plants and thin overcrowded growth. CHEMICAL—Apply a summer oil or a fungicide containing propiconazole, triadimefon, or triforine.

Brown Rot of Stone Fruit

Type of disease: *fungal*

Host(s): *stone fruit and some ornamentals*

Brown rot occurs worldwide, wherever peaches, plums, cherries, and other stone fruits are grown, and is particularly troublesome in warm, humid regions. It also attacks a number of landscape ornamentals, including flowering quince, chokeberry, western sand cherry, and flowering almond.

Symptoms: The first symptom to appear is brown spots on blossoms. The spots spread rapidly to cover the entire flower and stem. During humid weather, a brown fuzz covers infected parts. As the disease progresses, cankers develop on twigs near the flower stem and sometimes cause girdling and dieback. Next, ripe fruit develops water-soaked, brown spots that enlarge and expand rapidly. Rotted flowers and fruit shrivel and may remain on the plant for a long time. Fuzzy gray mold forms on the bark.

Transmission: Spores are spread by wind, rain, and insects. The fungus overwinters in the dry, shriveled fruit, called mummies, and on twig cankers.

Control: PHYSICAL—Dispose of all fruit mummies and prune out twigs with cankers. CHEMICAL—Protect fruit with a fungicide spray such as propiconazole or triadimefon.

Mushroom Root Rot

Type of disease: *fungal*

Host(s): *many*

Mushroom root rot, also known as armillaria root rot, oak-root fungus, and shoestring root rot, occurs throughout the United States. It infects a wide range of trees and shrubs; herbaceous plants are occasionally infected. Particularly susceptible are azalea, boxwood, oak, pine, rhododendron, rose, spruce, and sycamore.

Symptoms: Plants may suffer a mild infection for years with no symptoms. Then, when they are subjected to stress from drought, defoliation by insects, or another disease, the symptoms of mushroom root rot begin to appear. Among these are yellowing; wilting; premature dropping of leaves; dark, spongy bark; dieback of branches; tough, fan-shaped growths under the bark; and, in fall and winter, clusters of honey brown mushrooms at the base of the plant.

Transmission: The fungus spreads underground from infected to healthy plants by the black or brown cordlike structures, or shoestrings, it produces. In addition, airborne spores from the mushrooms can enter plants through wounds to start new colonies.

Control: PHYSICAL—Remove and destroy infected plants, including stumps and roots; remove soil from around rotted stumps, since the fungus persists in soil. CULTURAL—Plant resistant species; wait several years before replanting an infected site with susceptible varieties.

Phytophthora Root Rot

Type of disease: *fungal*

Host(s): *many*

Several *Phytophthora* species with different geographical ranges and different hosts cause root rots in a wide range of trees, shrubs, and herbaceous plants. Ornamentals often infected include azalea, calla lily, camellia, eucalyptus, Fraser fir, oak, periwinkle, pine, rhododendron, rose, snapdragon, and yew. Wet soils and cool temperatures favor the fungus.

Symptoms: Small feeder roots die back, and brown lesions appear on larger roots. Because of this damage, roots cannot take up adequate amounts of water and nutrients. The symptoms produced vary in different hosts. Wilting is common, growth is frequently stunted, and twigs may suffer dieback. Foliage may be sparse, yellowed, abnormally small, or misshapen. Infected plants are especially vulnerable to environmental stresses and to other diseases. Established plants may survive for a number of years, while seedlings may succumb within days of infection.

Transmission: Phytophthora root rot fungi overwinter in infected roots or soil. Spores are spread by infested soil and water, and in some cases, seed.

Control: PHYSICAL—Remove and destroy seriously infected plants. CULTURAL—Plant resistant species or varieties; incorporate composted tree bark into the soil to suppress fungus growth; improve soil drainage.

Rust

Type of disease: *fungal*

Host(s): *many*

Some 4,000 species of rust fungi are known to cause diseases on plants. Many of these fungi require two different kinds of plants in order to complete their life cycle, while a smaller number infect only one kind of plant. Commonly infected ornamentals include carnation, crab apple, hollyhock, red cedar, rose, snapdragon, spruce, and white pine.

Symptoms: Crusty rust-colored, orange, dark brown, or purplish spots dot the undersides of leaves and stems. The upper surfaces of infected leaves become mottled with yellow. On a severely infected plant, leaves shrivel but remain attached. Plants are weakened, and their growth is often stunted.

Transmission: Rust fungi overwinter on infected hosts and in plant debris. Spores are spread by wind and splashing water and by infected nursery plants or cuttings.

Control: PHYSICAL—Remove and destroy infected plant parts in fall and again in spring. CULTURAL—Plant resistant varieties. CHEMICAL—Spray with sulfur, lime-sulfur, Bordeaux mixture, propiconazole, triadimefon, or triforine during the growing season.

Cedar-Apple Rust

Type of disease: *fungal*

Host(s): *red cedar, apple, and crab apple*

The cedar-apple rust fungus requires both an apple and a cedar host to complete its life cycle. Spores produced on red cedars (*Juniperus virginiana*) infect apple trees and ornamental crab apples, and spores produced on apples infect red cedars. This disease is common from the Mississippi Valley eastward.

Symptoms: In early spring, orange gelatinous tendrils emerge from spherical leaf galls 1 to 2 inches in diameter on red cedar; the galls reach this stage 18 months after the tree is infected. In early to midsummer, bright yellow spots with orange-red margins appear on apple and crab apple leaves. The spots are ⅛ to ½ inch in diameter. Spotted leaves may turn yellow and fall prematurely. Fruit may have sunken brown spots and be lumpy and deformed.

Transmission: The cedar-apple rust fungus overwinters on the cedar host as immature galls. Spores are spread by wind to the alternate host.

Control: CULTURAL—Plant resistant apple or crab apple cultivars; do not plant red cedars within 500 yards of apples.

Apple Scab

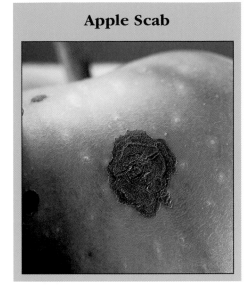

Type of disease: *fungal*

Host(s): *apple and crab apple*

Apple scab is the most important disease of apples and ornamental crab apples and can cause severe injury from defoliation. This disease is most troublesome in areas with frequent rainfall, high humidity, and mild temperatures in spring and summer.

Symptoms: Dull olive green spots ¼ inch or more in diameter with a velvety surface appear in spring on leaves, flowers, shoots, and young fruit. The spots are slightly raised on fruit and become dark, scabby, and cracked. Leaves and fruit are deformed, and if the plant is highly susceptible, they fall prematurely.

Transmission: The apple-scab fungus overwinters on fallen leaves. In early spring it develops fruiting bodies that release spores spread by wind. During the growing season, spores are washed down by rain from leaf and fruit spots to infect other leaves and fruits.

Control: PHYSICAL—Rake and destroy fallen leaves and fruit. CULTURAL—Plant resistant varieties.

Sooty Mold

Type of disease: *fungal*

Host(s): *many*

Several genera of fungi are responsible for the disorder known as sooty mold. These fungi do not attack plants directly. Instead, they feed on the sugary secretions, or honeydew, produced by sucking insects such as aphids, leafhoppers, mealybugs, psyllids, scales, and whiteflies. Besides being unsightly, a heavy growth of sooty mold can slow plant growth by shading the leaf surface and reducing photosynthesis.

Symptoms: A black growth appears on leaves and twigs that may be fine and sootlike or lumpy or crusty with spiky protuberances. The mold can be scraped off the plant surface.

Transmission: Cool, moist conditions favor the growth of sooty mold. Its spores are spread by rain and wind.

Control: PHYSICAL—If the plant is small, wipe off the mold with a damp cloth. BIOLOGICAL OR CHEMICAL—Identify the insect pest responsible for producing the honeydew, and choose an appropriate control measure. If you cannot find honeydew-producing insects on a plant with sooty mold, the honeydew may be dripping down from an infested overhanging plant.

Dutch Elm Disease

Type of disease: *fungal*

Host(s): *elms*

Dutch elm disease (DED) has caused a devastating loss of elms since its introduction to the United States around 1930. Although DED affects many species of elm, the American elm is especially susceptible and nearly always dies.

Symptoms: The fungus grows in the vascular system, producing toxins and clogging the flow of water and nutrients. Symptoms usually begin with the sudden, severe wilting of leaves on a single branch. Leaves curl, turn yellow and then brown, and may fall or stay attached to the branch. The infection can spread rapidly, causing death within a year. In some cases the disease advances slowly, and the tree dies over several years' time.

Transmission: The fungus overwinters in the bark of dead or diseased elm trees and is carried by elm bark beetles, which introduce it into healthy trees as they feed. The fungus is also transmitted through natural root grafts occurring between an infected and a healthy tree.

Control: PHYSICAL—Remove dead elms; prune wilting branches 12 inches below wood showing symptoms, disinfecting pruners between cuts. BIOLOGICAL—Control elm bark beetles with beneficial nematodes or braconid wasps. CULTURAL—Plant DED-resistant elms. This is the most effective measure against the disease. CHEMICAL—Treatment with a fungicide should be done by professionals only.

Fusarium Wilt

Type of disease: *fungal*

Host(s): *many*

Many strains and species of *Fusarium* cause wilt diseases on herbaceous ornamentals and vegetables. Most strains are highly host specific. Common ornamental hosts include China aster, carnation, cattleya orchid, chrysanthemum, cyclamen, and gladiolus.

Symptoms: Leaves of infected plants turn yellow and droop. Brown patches appear on leaves, often spreading to cover the entire leaf. Lower leaves are usually affected first, and symptoms may initially occur on only one side of the plant. Plants may be permanently stunted or may wither and die. This is one of the most serious diseases of China asters, causing plants to wilt and die at any stage of growth; leaves turn straw yellow and curl. Leaves and flower spikes of infected gladiolus are stunted, and flowers are small and faded. The stems may split, revealing brown streaks in the conductive tissues.

Transmission: Fusarium is a soil-borne pathogen that is spread in infested soil and by infected seeds and plants. Resistant varieties may become susceptible if they are injured by insects or nematodes.

Control: CULTURAL—Plant resistant varieties; purchase disease-free plants; solarize infested soil.

Verticillium Wilt

Type of disease: *fungal*

Host(s): *many*

Widely occurring verticillium wilt is most troublesome in the temperate zones, attacking over 200 species of plants. Some strains are highly host specific; others attack a broad range of plants. Susceptible ornamentals include aster, azalea, barberry, catalpa, chrysanthemum, dahlia, daphne, magnolia, maple, nandina, peony, photinia, privet, and snapdragon.

Symptoms: Symptoms usually appear first on the infected plant's lower or outer leaves. Leaves develop a yellowish tinge and droop, then turn brown and die. On herbaceous plants, the leaves shrivel and remain attached to the stem for some time. Individual stems or the entire plant dies, and vascular tissue in the stems is streaked with brown. On woody plants, symptoms include elongated cankers, wilting, premature defoliation, and dieback. Symptoms may be acute, spreading over the entire plant within a few weeks, or chronic, gradually progressing over several seasons.

Transmission: Verticillium fungus is a soil-borne pathogen that enters a plant through its feeder roots or wounds. It can survive in soil for as long as 20 years.

Control: CULTURAL—Plant resistant species such as conifers and ginkgos; purchase disease-free plants; solarize infested soil; keep plants vigorous and protect them from drought stress, especially in the first 3 years after transplanting.

Picture Credits

The sources for the illustrations that appear in this book are listed below. Credits from left to right are separated by semicolons; credits from top to bottom are separated by dashes.

Cover: © Walter Chandoha, 1998. Back cover insets: © Michael S. Thompson—art by Stephen R. Wagner—© Jane Grushow/Grant Heilman Photography, Lititz, Pa. End papers: © Charles Mann, courtesy Filoli Center, Woodside, Ca. 1: R. Todd Davis. 2: Bernard Fallon/Sandy Kennedy/Kennedy Landscape Design Associates, Woodland Hills, Ca.; © Roger Foley/designed by Oehme, van Sweden and Associates, Inc.; © Walter Chandoha 1998; Cynthia Woodyard. 3: © Roger Foley/designed by Oehme, van Sweden and Associates, Inc.; Leonard G. Phillips; © Dwight R. Kuhn; Virginia R. Weiler/designed by Kim Hawks, Niche Gardens, Chapel Hill, N.C. 4, 5: Rosalind Creasy/designed by Rosalind Creasy, Landscape Designer. 6, 7: © Michael S. Thompson/designed by James R. Ely; Catherine Davis/designed by Yunghi C. Epstein, Landscape Architect. 8, 9: Roger Foley/designed by Joanna Reed, Longview Farm; Roger Foley/designed by Sheela Lampietti, Landscape Designer. 10, 11: Robert Walch/designed by David E. Benner, Horticulturist. 12, 13: Dency Kane/designed by Marla Gagnum, East Hampton, N.Y.; Dency Kane/Landscape by Atlantic Nursuries, Dix Hills, N.Y. 14, 15: Charles Mann. 16, 17: © Roger Foley/designed by Osamu Shimizu; Roger Foley. 18, 19: Jerry Pavia/designed by Fay B. Ireland. 20, 21: Bernard Fallon/Sandy Kennedy/Kennedy Landscape Design Associates, Woodland Hills, Ca. 22, 23: © David McDonald/Photo Garden/designed by Steven Antonow; Roger Foley/designed by Joanna Reed, Longview Farm. 24, 25: © David McDonald/Photo Garden/designed by Northwest Perennial Alliance; Leonard G. Phillips/designed by Mr. and Mrs. John C. Seidler. 26, 27: Mike Shoup.

28: Rosalind Creasy/designed by Rosalind Creasy, Landscape Designer (2). 29: © Michael S. Thompson/designed by James R. Ely (2)—Catherine Davis/designed by Yunghi C. Epstein, Landscape Architect (2). 30: Roger Foley/designed by Joanna Reed, Longview Farm (2)—Roger Foley/designed by Sheela Lampietti, Landscape Designer (2). 31: Robert Walch/designed by David E. Benner, Horticulturist (2)—Dency Kane/designed by Marla Gagnum, East Hampton, N.Y. (2). 32: Dency Kane/Landscape by Atlantic Nursuries, Dix Hills, N.Y. (2)—Charles Mann (2). 33: © Roger Foley/designed by Osamu Shimizu (2)—Roger Foley (2). 34: Jerry Pavia/designed by Fay B. Ireland (2)—Bernard Fallon/Sandy Kennedy/ Kennedy Landscape Design Associates, Woodland Hills, Ca. (2). 35: © David McDonald/Photo Garden/designed by Steven Antonow (2)—Roger Foley/designed by Joanna Reed, Longview Farm (2). 36: © David McDonald/Photo Garden/designed by Northwest Perennial Alliance (2)—Leonard G. Phillips/designed by Mr. and Mrs. John C. Seidler (2). 37: Mike Shoup (2). 38, 39: Roger Foley/designed by Oehme, van Sweden and Associates, Inc. 40, 41: © Michael S. Thompson. 42: Leonard G. Phillips/designed by Sally Wheeler and Tom Gilbert, Cismont Manor Farm. 43: Art by Fred Holz. 44: Roger Foley. 45: © Cynthia Woodyard. 46: Rosalind Creasy. 47: Art by Fred Holz. 48: Roger Foley, courtesy William P. Steele III. 49: John Marshall, courtesy Brian Coleman. 50: © Cynthia Woodyard—Roger Foley/designed by Yunghi C. Epstein, Landscape Architect. 51: © Michael S. Thompson. 52, 53: Art by Nicholas Fasciano—John Marshall, courtesy Brian Coleman; Roger Foley. 54: © Roger Foley/designed by Osamu Shimizu. 55-57: Art by Stephen R. Wagner. 58, 59: Jerry Pavia; art by Stephen R. Wagner. 60: Jerry Pavia. 61: Art by Andrew Lewis/ARCOBALENO. 62: ©

Michael S. Thompson. 63: Joanne Pavia. 64: © Jane Grushow/Grant Heilman Photography, Lititz, Pa. 65: © R. Todd Davis. 66: © Roger Foley/designed by Oehme, van Sweden and Associates, Inc. 67: Clive Nichols, Reading, Berkshire. 68: Andrew Lawson, Charlbury, Oxfordshire. 69, 70: © Michael S. Thompson. 73: © Allan Mandell. 74: Jerry Pavia. 75: Leonard G. Phillips (2). 76: © Mark Lovejoy–© Charles Mann. 77: Jerry Pavia/designed by Betsy Thomas. 78: Bernard Fallon. 79: © Charles Mann. 80, 81: Andy Wasowski/designed by Robert G. Breunig. 82: Jerry Pavia. 83: Roger Foley. 84, 85: © Karen Bussolini— © Walter Chandoha, 1998; Gay Bumgarner. 86: Jerry Pavia. 87: © 1998 Alan & Linda Detrick. 88: © Michael S. Thompson. 89: Joanne Pavia. 90: © Michael J. Wolf. 91: © Walter Chandoha, 1998. 92: © Charles Mann. 93: R. Todd Davis. 94, 95: © John Marshall; © 1998 Alan & Linda Detrick. 96, 97: © 1998 Alan & Linda Detrick. 98; © judywhite/New Leaf Images. 99: C. Colston Burrell. 100: Dency Kane. 101: © Jane Grushow/Grant Heilman Photography, Lititz, Pa. 102, 103: © Carole Ottesen, except far right © Karen Bussolini. 104, 105: Leonard G. Phillips/designed by Mr. and Mrs. John C. Seidler. 106, 107: Art by Fred Holz. 108, 109: © Jane Grushow/Grant Heilman Photography, Lititz, Pa.—art by Nicholas Fasciano. 110: Art by Nicholas Fasciano. 111: Art by Fred Holz. 112, 113: Cynthia Woodyard (2)—art by Nicholas Fasciano (3); art by Fred Holz. 114: Steven Still. 115: Art by Fred Holz. 116: Art by Fred Holz © Michael S. Thompson. 117: Art by Nicholas Fasciano and Yin Yi. 120: Jerry Pavia. 121: Art by Fred Holz. 122, 123: Jerry Pavia. 124: Map by John Drummond, Time-Life Books. 125: Ken Druse/The Natural Garden. 126, 127: © Roger Foley/designed by Oehme, van Sweden and Associates, Inc. 129: Map by John Drummond, Time-Life Books.

130: Art by Donald Gates. 132: Ken Kay, © 1971 Time-Life Books. 134: © Betts Anderson/Unicorn Stock Photos. 135: John D. Cunningham/Visuals Unlimited—Pam Peirce; background © Dick Keen/Unicorn Stock Photos. 136: © John Colwell/Grant Heilman Photography, Lititz, Pa.—© Jim Strawser/ Grant Heilman Photography, Lititz, Pa. 138: Paul Vincelli, except fairy rings © Stanley Schoenberger/ Grant Heilman Photography, Lititz, Pa. 139: Paul Vincelli (2)—Joe Vargas—Karen Kackley Dutt, PhD; Joe Vargas—Paul Vincelli. 140, 141: Jerry Pavia. 143: Background © Mark E. Gibson. 144: Leonard G. Phillips. 147: Jerry Pavia, courtesy Harry Jacobs/designed by Ron Lutsko/Lutsko Associates, San Francisco, Ca. 148: © Breck P. Kent. 149, 151: Art by Stephen R. Wagner. 152: © William J. Webber/Visuals Unlimited (2); © Larry Lefever/Grant Heilman Photography, Lititz, Pa.—© John D. Cunningham/Visuals Unlimited; Barbara H. Emerson; Science VU/Visuals Unlimited. 153: © Ted Rose/Unicorn Stock Photos; John Gerlach/Visuals Unlimited; © Walt Anderson/Visuals Unlimited—© John Colwell/Grant Heilman Photography, Lititz, Pa.; © Jane Grushow/Grant Heilman Photography, Lititz, Pa.; © Grant Heilman/Grant Heilman Photography, Lititz, Pa. 154: © Jane Grushow/Grant Heilman Photography, Lititz, Pa.; © 1998 Alan & Linda Detrick; John D. Cunningham/Visuals Unlimited—© Jim Strawser/Grant Heilman Photography, Lititz, Pa.; A. Gurmankin/Unicorn Stock Photos; © Liz Ball. 155: © 1998 Alan & Linda Detrick; © Mark E. Gibson; © R. J. Mathews/Unicorn Stock Photos—© William J. Webber/Visuals Unlimited; © Mark E. Gibson; © 1998 Alan & Linda Detrick. 156, 157: David and Steve Maslowski. 158, 159: Robert Walch/designed by George and Carol Miller. 161, 162: Jerry Pavia. 163-166: Art by Sally Bensusen. 167: Art by Robert E. Heynes—art by Sally Bensusen. 168: © Dwight R.

BOOKS

Time-Life Books is a division of **TIME LIFE INC.**

TIME LIFE INC.
PRESIDENT and CEO: George Artandi

TIME-LIFE CUSTOM PUBLISHING

Vice President and Publisher: Terry Newell
Vice President of Sales and Marketing: Neil Levin
Director of Acquisitions: Jennifer Pearce
Director of Special Markets: Liz Ziehl
Editor: Linda Bellamy
Production Manager: Carolyn M. Clark
Quality Assurance Manager: James King

Editorial Staff for
The Big Book of Garden Solutions

Project Manager: Lynn McGowan
Design: Kathleen Mallow
Picture Coordinator: David Cheatham
Special Contributors: Celia Beattie (proofreader),
Lina B. Burton (index), Ruth Goldberg (cover copy)

Editor: Janet Cave
Administrative Editor: Roxie France-Nuriddin
Art Directors: Cindy Morgan-Jaffe, Alan Pitts, Sue Pratt
Picture Editors: Jane Jordan, Jane A. Martin
Text Editors: Sarah Brash, Darcie Conner Johnston, Paul Mathless
Associate Editors/Research and Writing: Megan Barnett, Sharon Kurtz,
Katya Sharpe, Robert Speziale, Karen Sweet, Mary-Sherman Willis

Library of Congress Cataloging-in-Publication Data
The big book of garden solutions : problem-solving
tips and techniques for gardeners / by the editors of
Time-Life Books.
p. cm.
Includes index.
ISBN 0-7370-0041-4
1. Landscape gardening. 2. Gardening.
I. Time-Life Books.
SB473.B489   1999   635.9—DC21   98-46572   CIP